THE PUBLIC SCHOOL IN THE NEW SOCIETY

THE PUBLIC SCHOOL

THE SOCIAL FOUNDATIONS
OF EDUCATION

NEW YORK, EVANSTON, AND LONDON

IN THE NEW SOCIETY

BY GRACE GRAHAM
UNIVERSITY OF OREGON

HARPER & ROW, PUBLISHERS

PICTURE CREDITS

Cover, Robert Simmons. **Title page**, Seattle School District. Chapter opening pages: **1**, Helen Post from Monkmeyer; **2**, Wide World; **3**, Zimbel from Monkmeyer; **4** and **5**, Wide World; **6**, IBM, New York; **7**, Rogers from Monkmeyer; **8**, United Press International; **9** and **10**, Hays from Monkmeyer; **11**, Loredo from Monkmeyer; **12**, Ford Foundation (Arthur Leipzig); **13**, Zimbel from Monkmeyer; **14**, Hays from Monkmeyer; **15**, Strickler from Monkmeyer; **16**, Ford Foundation (William R. Simmons); **17**, Seattle School District.

CONTENTS

22898

PREFACE

Like *The Public School in the American Community,* my earlier work in this field, this book is designed as a basic text for courses commonly called Social Foundations of Education, Social Foundations of Teaching, or Foundations of Education, and sometimes called Educational Sociology. It offers, I believe, a balanced analysis of a somewhat nebulous field of study.

Although the orientation of courses in social foundations is always contemporary, and current research from all the social sciences is grist in an instructor's mill, the text for such a course should provide an integrated overview of the social context of the school. In writing the interpretation of the social scene that follows, I have tried to look backward as well as forward. In other words, I have assumed that an understanding of the school's role in the past is important to understanding its role in the present and the future. Because all social institutions are interrelated, the school is influenced in various ways by other institutions, and the school in turn influences them.

Individuals who work and study in the school also act within a social structure and respond to the expectations of the groups to which they belong. Thus social behavior cannot be explained by a single-cause, determinist theory. An understanding of the school's role in the United States requires that a student examine the values and beliefs of his society as well as its changing institutions, communities, and group relationships. Furthermore, he has to study the patterns of small groups within the school. In this book I have analyzed the most significant of the many social influences upon schools and presented relevant evidence not available for use in my earlier work.

This book not only includes new knowledge from many disciplines but it also clarifies and updates issues presented in the earlier work. The suggestions and reactions of my students and their written criticisms of the text have been carefully considered in this revision. It is in effect a new book in that most of the chapters have been rewritten and new chapters added that focus on contemporary problems of education, such as slum schools and alienated youth. I have tried to present opposing opinions on controversial subjects and to write an unbiased account. Nevertheless students should recognize that research in many social areas is limited, and that my selection of data and interpretation represents my value judgments. With such judgments, they may, of course, disagree.

The assistance of many colleagues who helped me write the earlier work has already been acknowledged. For critical readings of new and revised chapters pertinent to their disciplines, I am deeply indebted to H. Thomas Koplin, economist; James R. Klonoski, political scientist; and Roy H. Rodgers and G. Benton Johnson, sociologists. I am also indebted to associates in the College of Education: Harry F. Wolcott, Chester A. Bowers, and Robert A. Sylwester (formerly of Concordia Teachers College) for critical readings of various chapters. I am grateful to Chester A. Bowers for writing the chapter on "Special-Interest Groups and the Schools," and to John C. Connelly of San Francisco State College for supplying the material on which the chapter on "Elementary School Culture" is based. With one exception, the line drawings in the text were suggested by Robert A. Sylwester. Roy Paul Nelson, School of Journalism at the University of Oregon, suggested the line drawing called "Faith and Knowledge." I appreciate these contributions.

I am especially appreciative of the encouragement, editorial assistance, and critical reading of the entire text by Constance Bordwell, Department of English. I also thank Mrs. Barbara Frederick and Mrs. Reba Charles for proofreading galleys, and Miss Viola Volkens, Secretary in the College of Education, for many favors that made my task easier.

GRACE GRAHAM

August 1968

THE PUBLIC SCHOOL
IN THE NEW SOCIETY

1. INTRODUCTION: UNDERSTANDING THE SCHOOL IN ITS SOCIETAL SETTING

Traveling in Wonderland with the naïveté that characterizes us all, Alice asked:

"Would you tell me, please, which way I ought to go from here?"

"That depends a good deal," said the Cat [with irrefutable logic], "on where you want to get to."[1]

—LEWIS CARROLL

The purpose of this book is to help students understand the school as a social institution within the American society that it serves. The kind of formal schooling that the people of any society accept for their children is an expression of what the influential members of that society prize and what they believe young people need to learn. Thus to a considerable degree what students are taught in schools depends

[1] Lewis Carroll, *Alice's Adventures in Wonderland,* The Heritage Illustrated Bookshelf, 1941, p. 85.

upon what people in a particular society accept, at a particular time in their history, as proper schooling for the young.

Practices in school, then, reflect the changing values and beliefs to which people in a society subscribe. In the sense in which the terms will be used in this book, *values* are ideals, expectations, and goals that people accept. *Beliefs* are their ideas, explanations, and convictions about reality, not based on objective evidence. Practices in schools not only reflect social changes in values and beliefs, but also reflect other changes that occur for various reasons in other social institutions. But the school institutes social change as well as reacting to it. Nevertheless, the processes of adjusting to societal changes, and to those that the school itself initiates, do not assure that desired changes will occur immediately or at the same rate of speed.

Educational reformers and critics often forget that education is part and parcel of the society it serves. Like Thales of Miletus, who fell into a well while gazing at the stars, they stumble over social obstructions while making idealistic plans for schools. To revise our educational system so that it meets the changing needs of students and of society, the reformer must first understand our society and our schools. As a navigator plotting his course must know where he is, how he got there, and what lies ahead, those who would improve schools must first know how and why current practices came to be and what changes in the larger society make changes in schools necessary and desirable. They must also understand how changes instituted within the school will influence the larger society.

Perhaps students reading this text may say, "But I am not yet either an educational reformer or a critic. I am interested in anything that will make me a better counselor, administrator, or teacher." The next section explains how a study of the social foundations of education will help persons become effective educators.

REASONS FOR UNDERSTANDING THE SCHOOL IN ITS SOCIETAL SETTING

A teacher has been called the "vicar of society," for like the clergyman who is considered to be God's deputy, the teacher is, in a sense, society's representative. In this capacity he epitomizes the knowledge, beliefs, and values of the social order and transmits his understanding of its heritage to young people. In a simple culture where people cling to the same points of view about most matters of importance, the teacher's path is relatively smooth. He is judged in terms of how well he teaches, not what he teaches. In a culture as complex as that of the United States, where people hold many different opinions, the teacher in a vicar role may find himself in a quandary as to what content, what values, and what beliefs most people in the society want taught.

The study of American society yields no ready answer to this predicament, but an understanding of what different factions believe and why they believe what they do helps a teacher to become objective. A teacher may insist that his job is to disseminate knowledge, not values and beliefs that lie outside the scope of scientific investigation. Then these questions arise: Can the teacher operate in a value vacuum? Does not the teacher transmit values willy-nilly even when he has no such intention? Perhaps the person who denies that he teaches anything but accumulated knowledge is also unconsciously teaching his own goals, ideals, and convictions that may not be acceptable to his pupils. Then his effectiveness in motivating learning is limited by his own ethnocentrism and microscopic view of the mainsprings of human behavior.

A common-sense interpretation of the vicar role might be that the teacher hired by the local community should teach what its residents want taught. Following this course, however, the teacher ignores the rights of the larger society to representation. Smith, Stanley, and Shores propose that teachers use the democratic tradition as a touchstone.[2] For example, suppose that a biology teacher finds himself in a community in which most people relegate Indian residents to an inferior status and teach their children that Indians are biologically inferior. Should he teach the scientific facts about differences among the races of man? The local community might say no; the democratic tradition of the larger society, which assumes freedom of inquiry, would say yes. By the same token, the teacher has no right to teach his own idiosyncratic beliefs that fail to square with the same tradition of free inquiry.

Another reason for studying the societal setting of schools is that we may understand why we teach what we do and how to make needed revisions in school curriculums. A question that pupils often ask is: Why do we have to study English grammar or history or some other subject in the school's program? Often teachers react negatively to such questions and offer superficial explanations. Probably no other single question is more important. Why, indeed, do we teach what we teach? Did some pressure group slip this subject into the course of study? Whose interests are served by this study? If we cannot justify

---

[2] B. Othanel Smith, William O. Stanley, and J. Harlan Shores, *Fundamentals of Curriculum Development*, World Book, 1950, pp. 147–152.

what we teach in terms of agreed-upon cultural needs and the best educational practice, a revision of the curriculum is needed.

Though able to justify their own courses, some teachers are less aware of reasons for curriculums in other areas or at other levels. When the high school teacher scathingly criticizes the work of the elementary teacher, is he cognizant of the purposes and rationale of modern elementary school programs within the cultural context? When a teacher cannot view the educational scene in its totality and in its societal setting, he does not fully comprehend the contribution of the part to the whole nor see his own work in proper perspective. He may not realize that present-day curriculums may not be in harmony with societal needs. Indeed, the assumption is that a study of the social environment of the school usually fails to vindicate the status quo, for the curriculum should change as the needs of the society change. Therefore, a continuous study of the changing culture is basic to intelligent curriculum development.

Closely related to understanding the cultural bases for curriculum is the contribution that a study of society makes to a teacher's understanding of criticisms of education. How should criticism be evaluated? Is a teacher confused by every critic? Can he rationally accept criticism, recognizing that conflict is inevitable in a heterogeneous, changing social order made up of many special-interest groups? Or does he revise his educational philosophy and teaching practices with every hint of adverse criticism? The story of the man with a donkey tells how everyone the man met suggested a change in his behavior. The man first rode the heavily laden beast of burden, then led him, carried the donkey's pack, and in the end carried both the donkey and the pack to satisfy different critics, and thus satisfied none. Lest we be as foolish, we must be able to evaluate criticisms of education in terms of a philosophy based upon the best knowledge we have, the highest ideals of our society, and an adequate insight into the patterns of culture that shape our social order.

Among the practical outcomes that may follow from a study of society is a better insight into the roles of other persons. Such understanding is one of the cornerstones of sound human relationships. When teachers see their own roles and those of administrators, members of boards of education, parents, pupils, and representatives of organized groups as adjustments to social pressures, they are better equipped to act constructively. By knowing reasons for behavior and understanding underlying motivations, they can anticipate and prevent conflicts as well as guide cooperative action. An awareness of the roles of others also deepens one's appreciation for their contributions and forces one to recognize the interdependence of mankind.

The study of the school in society makes the teacher a more competent member of his profession in its struggle for leadership in school affairs. In an era when almost everyone has become an authority on public education, those who have devoted their lives to schools must win public support by offering unassailable evidence of their qualifications for leadership. Smith contends that "the teaching profession can assume leadership in helping the public make wise choices about necessary changes in schools only as members of the profession have developed an adequate understanding of the social foundations of their institution, the school."[3]

The study of the school in its social context gives a teacher insight into many complex school problems. He should become a better teacher if he has analyzed his own values and those of his culture. He knows why the school teaches what it does and what trends in our society suggest further changes in curriculums. He meets criticisms with mature judgment, better understands the behavior of others, and offers constructive leadership for the improvement of education.

THE RATIONALE OF THIS BOOK

One may study the social foundations of education from such vantage points as social influences upon school organization, course content, and teacher-pupil relationships. Or one may choose a particular discipline, such as anthropology or sociology, and draw implications for education. This book presents an overview of the school in its societal setting, and draws from findings in various social sciences.

Part I explores current beliefs and realities in schools. It examines possible influences upon school practices of the beliefs, including the values these beliefs sustain, held by businessmen and others who subscribe to the businessman's creed, persons of different social classes, and democratic theorists. In a sense, members of each of these groups hold an ideology. Often they do, in fact, hold three overlapping ideologies—one centering in economic matters, another in social class, and another in democracy.

What then are ideologies, and to what extent do they, in fact, influence school practices? As defined by McClosky, ideologies are:

systems of belief that are elaborate, integrated, and coherent, that justify the exercise of power, explain and judge historical events,

[3] William O. Stanley, B. Othanel Smith, Kenneth D. Benne, and Archibald W. Anderson, *Social Foundations of Education*, Dryden, 1956, p. 4.

identify political [and social] right and wrong, set forth the intercon-
nections (causal and moral) between politics [and social movements]
and other spheres of activity, and furnish guides for action.[4]

In studying a social group, anthropologists analyze both the "real
world" of actual behavior—what people really do—and the ideal
world of normative behavior—what people think they ought to do.
Both worlds are, in fact, "real," because a person's behavior is influenced as much by what he and others believe he ought to do as by
what he and others expect that he may do in a specific situation.
Although the ideologies that people hold do indeed influence their
behavior, the question of whether they should influence school practices is unanswered. Part I tells how some ideologies influence school
practices.

In a pluralistic society such as ours, composed of diverse special-
interest groups, agreement as to what values are dominant is not easily
reached. Many scholars, philosophers, and social scientists have tried
to list, define, and describe what Americans hold dear. Their statements differ because values can only be inferred from consistencies in
the talk, writing, and behavior of a people. No instrument exists that
can delve into the minds and hearts of men to measure their value
system. The complexity of the United States—its polyglot peoples,
heterogeneous religious and other free-standing groups, social-class
differences, rapidity of cultural change, and mental mobility fostered
by migrations and mass media—defies analysis and the search for
similarities. Nevertheless, many writers isolate a core of values in
somewhat the same terms.

Robert C. Angell describes the American ideal of the good life as
consisting of four clusters of values that center around (1) patriotic
loyalty to the national state, involving a feeling of community; (2) the
dignity of the individual—acceptance of the moral worth of the
common man, of freedom for the individual, and of the personal responsibility that such freedom entails; (3) democracy as a social
organization influencing social as well as political behavior; and (4)
technological efficiency as the means to furthering man's control of
nature.[5] In *An American Dilemma*, Gunnar Myrdal speaks of the
commonly accepted, idealistic "American creed of liberty, equality,
justice, and fair opportunity for everybody" as a compartmentalized

[4] Herbert McClosky, "Consensus and Ideology in American Politics," *American Political Science Review*, 58 (June, 1964), 362.
[5] Robert C. Angell, *The Integration of American Society, A Study of Groups and Institutions*, McGraw-Hill, 1941, pp. 206–209.

valuation conflicting with less idealistic value orientations derived from group prejudices, concern for social status, economic gain, and similar interests.[6] Saxon Graham finds that belief in freedom, individualism, equality, progress, social mobility, material wealth, and humanitarianism are among the major values in our society. He states that "Americans interpret both freedom and equality largely in a materialistic sense" and that "American beliefs appear to be more materialistically oriented than those of many other societies."[7]

In a comparative study of the value systems of the United States and Germany based on responses of middle-class boys to a variety of test instruments, David C. McClelland concludes that Americans are much more concerned with achievement and self-development and much more likely to participate in group activities than are Germans. Americans prize "free choice according to one's desires or wishes," "action," "achievement," and "humanitarianism," yet they "prefer not to deviate too far from the group norm." Their respect for majority opinion and their "other-directedness" keep their unbridled individualism in line. Carried to excess, however, other-directedness can lead to overconformity, and individualism can lead to license.[8] In more general terms, McClelland is reporting such values as freedom, democracy, achievement, and humanitarianism.

McClosky and other political scientists have found that Americans approve almost unanimously such words as "freedom," "democracy," and "free enterprise," although they disagree with specific statements designed to test the application of these concepts.[9]

Robin Williams' extended list of values includes the *"formal-universalistic values of Western tradition:* rationalism, impersonal justice and universalistic ethics, achievement, democracy, equality, freedom, certain religious values, worth of individual personality"; the *"gratifications,"* such as "material comfort"; the *"instrumental interests* or means-values, for example, wealth, power, work, efficiency"; and the *"particularistic, segmental or localistic values* that are best exemplified in racist-ethnic superiority doctrines."[10]

If these are indeed the primary value-orientations in American culture, one would expect to find the major values emphasized within

[6] Gunnar Myrdal, *An American Dilemma,* Harper & Row, 1944, pp. xlvii–xlix.

[7] Saxon Graham, *American Culture,* Harper & Row, 1957, p. 138.

[8] David C. McClelland, *The Roots of Consciousness,* Van Nostrand, 1964, chap. 4.

[9] McClosky, *op. cit.,* pp. 362–368.

[10] Robin M. Williams, Jr., *American Society: A Sociological Interpretation,* Knopf, 1960, pp. 468–469.

the schools. Williams believes that certain cultural themes, no one of which is "clearly dominant" or unchecked by counter-themes, do, in fact, pervade public school education:

1. Emphasis is put upon the practical usefulness of formal education. Contemplative or speculative thought, art, and highly abstract theoretical work are relatively little valued.

2. Emphasis is put upon competitive success.

3. Continuous and widespread stress is put upon conformity to group standards, largely those of broadly middle-class strata.

4. Great attention is paid to the creed of democratic values, and teacher-student relations are supposed to be "democratic."

5. In practice, public schools attempt to develop national solidarity —that is, patriotic values and beliefs.[11]

The businessman's creed, middle-class ideology, and democratic ideals seem to be the chief sources of the themes Williams cites as common to American schools. Part I, therefore, is devoted to these three sources of values.

In Part II, changes in social institutions that affect the school are discussed. The emphasis is upon changes occurring in government, the family system (especially in child-rearing practices), and the scientific establishment (especially in its effects upon knowledge and technology). Also noted in terms of effects upon schools is the change of the United States from a sparsely populated, primarily rural society characterized by face-to-face relationships into what may be called a mass society characterized by a large population, a high level of technology, impersonal relationships, and ubiquitous mass media. Finally, the influences upon schools of a powerful central government and of well-organized special-interest groups are discussed. Significant changes in other social institutions have induced significant changes in schools.

Changes in social institutions have occurred in all societies in all periods of history. Although in ancient times change was sometimes so slow as to be almost imperceptible, its inevitability has long been accepted. What is significant about change in a highly industrialized society like the United States is its speed.

The most spectacular changes in terms of the rapidity of change, and certainly the easiest to measure, are those that are the direct results of mechanization. It is easy to document the rapidity of change in the industrial and agricultural productivity of labor per man-hour, the expanding Gross National Product, the rising per-capita income, the number of new products, and the increased speed of communica-

11 *Ibid.*, p. 296.

tion and transportation. The increase in speed of transportation is an excellent illustration. See Table 1.

TABLE 1. **Increasing Speed of Transportation**

Mode	Approximate Date of Innovation	Top Speed —Miles per Hour[a]
Foot runner	Until 15,000 B.C.	10
Domesticated horse	15,000 B.C.	30
Train and steamboat	1825	125
Airplane	1908	350
Jet airplane	1944	4,000
Manned space ship	1961	200,000 to 2 million (?)

[a] Top speed generally not reached at time of innovation.

The advances in transportation, with its marked acceleration beginning around the turn of the century when the airplane was invented, have been matched in other technological areas. The result is well known. In less than a century scientific advances and economic activity have made the United States the land of mass production.

Less easily recognized than technological changes are the changes that have taken place in our social institutions. Social changes, including ways of thinking about and solving problems, are as important, if not more important, than changes in technology. In Chapters 5 through 9, changes in social arrangements and social inventions are considered in greater detail than are those in technology.

Changes affecting schools brought about by urban growth appear in Part III, "The Local Community and Its Schools." Such placement is obviously arbitrary in that the process of urbanization has influenced all of the institutions discussed in Part II. The reason for discussing urban problems as local problems in this text derives from the influence of local communities on school problems. How then shall we define community and school community, and why is it important to a teacher to study his school's community?

Sociologists agree that they disagree on a definition of community. Blaine Mercer's definition of a community includes the elements commonly stressed by social scientists: "A human community is a functionally related aggregate of people who live in a particular geographic locality at a particular time, share a common culture, are arranged in a social structure, and exhibit an awareness of their uniqueness and separate identity as a group."[12] Other writers point out that the boundaries of a community are not precise and may differ from a political border or a trade area, and that an individual or a family may belong to more than one community. They conclude that area, people, and psychological identification are necessary components of community, but that the essence of the community is the *relationships among the people* living there.[13] The major emphasis of the discussions in Part III is upon the community as a superstructure embracing institutions, organizations, groups, and individuals. The people are bound together in formal and informal associations by hierarchical systems of status and pervasive patterns of beliefs, values, traditions, and ways of thinking and reacting that make community behavior understandable and to some extent predictable. To anticipate reactions in a local setting, it is necessary then to probe community structure (the web of relationships), value-systems, and functions.

The community that a school serves is often conterminous with the "real" community, but it may be only a segment of a community, or it may include parts of two or more communities. That is, the school community is not always a community in a technical sense. Sometimes it is a neighborhood; at other times, when the school draws pupils from more than one community, its community is a complex of two or more entities. Since modern American communities, even in rural areas, are characterized by change and complexity, the expectation that school personnel know the forces operating in the school community may seem to be unreasonable. The difficulty is compounded because no two communities are identical, and studying types of communities leads to only limited understanding of any given community. Moreover the school as a social institution within the social system of the community is somewhat isolated from other social institutions, notably the economic and political units. The obstacles to learning about any particular school community are formidable, but for compelling reasons teachers and school officials need as much information as possible.

The American community administers its schools through local school boards. It therefore determines major policies for the school partly through its financial contribution, which in most communities is more than half of the school's budget. Thus, to a considerable extent, what teachers are paid; the quantity and quality of school facilities,

---

[12] Blaine E. Mercer, *The American Community*, Random House, 1956, p. 27.
[13] Lowry Nelson, Charles E. Ramsey, and Coolie Verner, *Community Structure and Change*, Macmillan, 1960, pp. 10–27.

equipment, and special services; the curriculum and the student activity programs; and the kind of discipline that prevails in schools are determined locally.

Social factors within the community also influence the personality development of pupils. A teacher cannot understand Johnny's behavior, motivations, values, attitudes, prejudices, manners and morals, speech patterns, or even his sense of humor without being aware of the cultural milieu of his home and community. Since the classroom is not insulated from other learning situations, the effective school gears its program to the educational needs of its pupils. The claim of American education that schools provide for individual differences is an empty boast if the pupils' community backgrounds are ignored.

The teacher should also recognize that the work of the school is facilitated by an intelligent utilization of community resources. By cooperating with other community institutions—the home, church, press, juvenile agencies—and with numerous community organizations, service clubs, youth groups, and parent associations, the welfare of children is advanced. The community itself is useful as a laboratory for learning. Classroom work is made concrete, challenging, and vital by a wise use of community materials, field trips, and resource persons. Someone said that if scientists were fish, the last thing they would discover is water. So it is with many teachers—the last thing they use as a teaching aid is often the most readily available.

Because the community provides the physical and social environment of the school, learning about the community in which a teacher works helps him to understand why his school is the kind of school it is, enables him to make constructive suggestions for its improvement, and aids him in becoming a more effective teacher. If educators do not understand the educational goals held by people in the community, do not analyze the needs of students in terms of their environment, and do not know who makes community decisions, they cannot successfully initiate improvements in schools. Teachers and school officials, who improve their schools and adjust curriculums to local needs, supply community leaders with information pertinent to local problems and work cooperatively with members of the community to achieve goals.

The chapters of Part III present data to help teachers understand why communities, especially school communities drawing heavily from members of a minority group, differ. One chapter is devoted to the changing job of the school in a community. This chapter assumes that national as well as local influences help determine the role of the school in its community.

In Part IV, aspects of school culture are discussed. In using the term "culture," which appears in a number of different contexts throughout the book, we use a concept that cannot be defined except in the sense that a particular writer uses it. In other words, he defines it stipulatively. The definition of "culture" is for anthropologists what the definition of education is for educationists and what sin is for clergymen. Alfred Louis Kroeber and Clyde Kluckhohn, two famous anthropologists, found more than a hundred definitions of "culture" written by anthropologists. In this text, the term "culture" will be used in the sense of the learned and patterned ways of life, including patterns of human interaction, of a group of people. Culture then includes mental aspects—the customs, morals (standards of right and wrong), rules, beliefs, values, and ways of behaving—as well as material aspects (artifacts), which in their totality constitute the ways of life of a group. In this sense, the school has a culture, or if you prefer a subculture.

Within the subculture of the school, students become socialized. Through the process of socialization each person learns to satisfy his needs as an individual within a range of behavior considered suitable in a particular society or group. Thus the process of socialization includes restrictions placed on antisocial impulses that would destroy society and opportunities for individual development. Clearly the school is not the only place in which the young learn what is considered "normal" behavior, for they also learn the values and kind of behavior that their families, friends, and others in their society expect. Learning behavior that is appropriate to all situations is, of course, very difficult in a highly complex, densely populated, industrialized society such as ours because of the many heterogeneous groups who expect different kinds of behavior of their young people. In many instances, the expectations of such groups are at variance with the school's expectations.

In the school, as we shall see in the descriptions of three elementary school classes, not all teachers expect the same kinds of behavior in their classes. The discussion of adolescent peer groups' expectations adds another insight into the process of socialization. Children are socialized within the culture of the school; teachers, also, are expected to satisfy their needs within a range of "approved" behavior patterns. The final chapter in this book describes an ideal school culture which does not now exist in many schools.

This text, then, is concerned with ideologies held by various Americans that influence the roles they play and their relationships with school officials. It is concerned with changes in American institutions and with factors in local communities that affect schools. It is concerned with life styles within the school itself. Since many matters cannot be covered in detail, students should supplement their reading of the text with readings in depth of specific points of interest. Although it is not designed to give definitive answers to school problems, the book provides an overview of current social influences upon education and encourages students to think in terms of the role of the school in a free society.

IMPORTANT CONCEPTS

Belief. See p. 2.

Businessman's creed. See pp. 18–21.

Community. See pp. 9–10.

Culture. See pp. 12 and 305 ff.

Ethnocentrism. The belief that one's own group, race, or society is superior to other groups, races, or societies; contempt for the outsider and his ways.

Gross National Product. The total monetary value of all final goods and services produced in a country during one year.

Hierarchical structure. See p. 130.

Humanitarianism. Acceptance of humanitarian principles and practices; i.e., having concern for and helping to improve the welfare of mankind.

Ideology. See pp. 5–6.

Individualism. A social theory that emphasizes the importance of the individual and his right to independent action. See p. 342.

Institution. An organization of a public or semipublic character, designed to serve some socially recognized and authorized end. Examples are the school, church, and hospital.

Mass society. See pp. 141–144.

Milieu. Environment; surroundings.

Normative behavior. See pp. 6, 263.

"Other-directedness." Concern for the opinions of others.

Pluralistic society. A society that encompasses a diversity of ethnic groups and a multiplicity of social attitudes and practices. See p. 6.

Prejudice. A judgment or opinion formed before carefully examining all relevant facts and issues. See p. 255.

Rationalism. The principle or habit of accepting reason as the supreme authority in matters of opinion, belief, or conduct.

Resource persons. Individuals other than the classroom teacher who supplement classroom instruction in their fields of specialization.

Role. The behavior associated with a particular status. See pp. 336 and 4–5.

Social class. See p. 45 ff.

Social mobility. The movement of persons from social group to social group. Such movement may result in a change in social-class status.

Socialization. See p. 12.

Special-interest group. A group that aggressively pursues an interest of deep concern to members of that group. See pp. 158–159.

Status. One's position in a group. See p. 336.

Structure. The established pattern of internal organization of any social group.

Value. See p. 2.

I. BELIEFS AND REALITIES IN SCHOOLS

2. THE BUSINESSMAN'S CIVILIZATION AND THE SCHOOLS

What is honored in a country will be cultivated there.

—PLATO

The United States is said to be a businessman's civilization, a description that may be more disparaging than precise. The term suggests that the dominant groups in this country have been businessmen and industrialists—not scholars, noblemen, military or political elites, or ecclesiastical leaders, who are credited with developing the ethos of various other peoples of the world. Calling the United States a businessman's civilization further suggests that the economic institution is a superstructure strongly influencing other institutions in the society.

This chapter is concerned with the influence upon schools of the businessman's ideology and of his corporate interests in schools.

THE BUSINESSMAN'S CREED
AND THE SCHOOL

In this country people in all walks of life tend to share the value orientation of the business community. What accounts for the widespread acceptance of the business ideology? Early in our national history it was not foisted on a gullible public by a sinister combine of business leaders; rather it was warmly supported by ministers in their pulpits and embraced by a people who accepted its tenets as compatible with the "American way of life."

General acceptance of the "businessman's creed"—materialism, hard work, activity, competition, and practical realism—with minor variations, has been continuous throughout our national history. In the beginning years of the Republic, Jefferson espoused a version of the creed as congruent with the interests of farmers at a time when manufacturers and businessmen welcomed government subsidies, fiscal controls, and tariffs. Not until after the Civil War did many businessmen join farmers in extolling the virtues of limited government and individual initiative. Perhaps the philosophy of Herbert Spencer and others who promoted the doctrine of social evolution trickled down to the rank and file and reinforced the creed. Nevertheless, nineteenth-century shopkeepers, tradesmen, manufacturers, and other organizers of businesses in rural America had little reason to systematize and express in writing what they believed. The economic system, by and large, seemed to work. Each employer felt he had the right to run his business as he saw fit with a minimum of interference from government or labor. Such beliefs of businessmen, who had become the nation's heroes and models for young people, were rarely questioned.

Since the 1880s the economic system has, however, undergone radical change that has nearly eliminated the small, independent businessman. Yet his value-orientation, more appropriate in earlier years than today, has persisted, especially among businessmen who are conservative in the sense of opposing change. In recent years the small businessman's ideology crystallized into a formal creed has, in fact, been deliberately perpetuated by spokesmen for big business. These advocates began to warn of dangers if this creed were not accepted.

When representatives of an institution try to "hard-sell" its creed, they seek to preserve a value-system in a rapidly changing environment. The laissez-faire ideology, which they advocate, undoubtedly lost adherents during the Great Depression of 1929–1933. As small businesses were supplanted by giant corporations, many salaried employees and junior executives developed somewhat different values from those of businessmen of the old school. Meanwhile, intellectuals, humanitarians, labor leaders, and others who subscribe to the ideologies of the New Deal, the New Frontier, and the War on Poverty have been challenging the business creed. For these reasons conservative businessmen have publicized a creed and sought to convince others of its merit.

The Publicized Business Creed

While spokesmen for big business have verbalized a creed, researchers have attempted to analyze its underlying values. Sutton and his collaborators, for example, studied advertisements, articles, speeches, editorials, pamphlets, books, and statements in Congressional hearings by businessmen and representatives of industrial organizations in an effort to determine the ideology of modern business. Their research revealed that the dominant theme is praise for the achievements of American capitalism, particularly in its output and its effect upon the standard of living. These achievements are explained by pointing to the "unique American system" of "free enterprise" (a euphemism for capitalism) and limited government. The economy is, in fact, the core of the American system, according to the creed, and all freedoms—religious, educational, political, and personal—are dependent upon the system of "free enterprise." The validity of the system, its supporters claim, lies in its accord with the laws of human nature because, they say, competition and freedom are fundamental to human nature. They also maintain that free enterprise is the moral choice of Americans.

These researchers point out that the business creed claims that the typical American business enterprise is small, that even the large establishments that grew from humble beginnings are decentralized, and that big businesses are owned by thousands of Americans from every walk of life. A commercial firm operates as a "family" or "team" to promote the general welfare. At this point advocates of the creed split into two slightly divergent factions: spokesmen for the managerial group stress that management consciously directs economic forces for the common good; spokesmen for the "classical" capitalists claim that the common weal is a natural outcome of free competition.[1]

The main value extolled by the business community, researchers

---

[1] Francis Xavier Sutton et al., *The American Business Creed,* Harvard University Press, 1956, pp. 19–66 *passim.*

state, is individualism, which includes moral responsibility for one's own actions and freedom to make choices in terms of self-interest. Conversely, the creed scorns the welfare state that curtails individual freedom by taxes and laws designed to aid and protect the weak. Materialism is frankly praised, and hard work, activity, competition, and practical realism are considered prime virtues. The impractical dreamer, religious ascetic, contemplative scholar, or romantic idealist is accorded little sympathy or reward. The greatness of a society is measured in terms of its material wealth and industrial output, yet the great society can never be satisfied. It must continue to progress through the ingenuity and boldness of its commercial leaders. And all men have an equal chance, business executives say, to become leaders in the business world if they learn to compete successfully.[2]

Justifications of the Business Creed

Widespread approval of a philosophy that rationalizes self-interest in terms of the good of the whole, praises the survival of the strong, and equates virtue with riches can best be understood in historical context. The reader will recall that at the Constitutional Convention, Americans rejected monarchy and aristocracy, a strong centralized government, established churches, and other systems of ascribed status. In 1865 the defeat by Yankee traders and industrialists of southern planters, who had founded an aristocracy of sorts resting on slavery, laid to rest the last challenge to the preeminence of merchant princes and industrial magnates.

A dominant value system, as well as the absence of a competing elite, assured the acceptance of the businessman's ideology. Early Americans embraced the Protestant Ethic, not only in New England but also wherever the Scotch-Irish and Huguenots settled. The Protestant Ethic, Max Weber maintained, produced an unintended by-product—the spirit of capitalism. Followers of Calvin, Luther, and other Protestant leaders regarded work as a means of glorifying God and self-indulgence as one of the deadly sins. They also subscribed to a rational view of life. In other words, they believed that man by calculated effort could change the course of events. Calvinistic, Lutheran, and Puritan traditions exalted occupations to "callings" and made prime virtues of individualism, austerity, thrift, and hard work. The man who worked in single-minded devotion to his business was rewarded with success as an early manifestation of God's favor, and he did not spend his gains in riotous living. Whether or not a person

[2] *Ibid.*, pp. 251–263 *passim.*

accepts Weber's thesis that the rise of capitalism is associated with the Protestant Reformation, he can hardly deny that Protestant ministers reinforced many of the values that American businessmen prized.

Americans were influenced also by the European Enlightenment, by American literature that emphasized individualism, and by the pioneer experience that added a distinctive American ingredient to the concept of individualism. Persons with substantial savings and entrepreneurs (enterprisers willing to assume risks) were essential components in the development of industrial capitalism. Although the American business ideology that gathered strength from these cultural heritages was more egalitarian in theory than in practice, it promised prestige and social status based on merit. Thus early in our national history, the average American found a moral justification for capitalism.

The twentieth-century American is likely, however, to react ambivalently to the creed. Most Americans, including businessmen, accept the need for governmental regulations of free enterprise to protect public interests, yet at the same time they view extensions of governmental power with alarm. They are increasingly aware that all men do not have an equal chance to succeed in the market place, yet they harbor doubts about the character and energy of those who fail.

Selling the Business Creed to Schools

The business creed is being disseminated in free pamphlets to American school children largely through the efforts of the National Association of Manufacturers (NAM). In addition to pamphlets the Association supplies schools with free speakers, films, and HOBSO (How Our Business System Operates) kits.

The Chamber of Commerce of the United States encourages its chapters to sponsor several projects for pupils and teachers. Among these projects are Career Conferences for Teenagers, Teacher Recognition Days, and Business-Education Days, all of which are held in many communities in every state. The national organization sells "How-to-do-it" booklets and other pamphlets at nominal rates. One of these booklets, *How to Plan Economic Understanding Projects,* describes activities such as student attitude surveys, tours of business and industry, economic workshops, economic teaching units and aids, essay contests, speakers bureaus, and junior achievement programs.

The purposes of Chamber activities are to disseminate vocational information, to stress the value of schooling, and to explain the economic system to pupils and teachers. The brochure describing how to plan B-E Day features "techniques perfected to explain the American economic system to educators: What it is. How and Why it provides the world's highest standard of living." In 1967 the education manager of the national organization estimated that from 75,000 to 100,000 teachers attend a B-E Day program each year.

In the usual pattern of B-E Days, small groups of teachers visit a plant or business establishment for a half-day, confer with executives in the afternoon, and have dinner with the management. The teachers are given free pamphlets or charts for use in their classes so they can tell pupils about their tour. In some communities, businessmen later visit the schools and have lunch with the teachers.

Teachers are usually enthusiastic about these outings, which are generally scheduled on school time. They learn something of local business enterprises and industries about which they ought to be informed, but whether they learn "the true facts about free enterprise," as a bulletin of the U. S. Chamber of Commerce claims, may be doubtful.

Labor leaders have frequently disapproved of B-E Days, presumably because they feel teachers are being exposed to management's, but not labor's, point of view. The American Federation of Teachers, an affiliate of the AFL–CIO, has taken a strong stand against these Days on the grounds that schools should not be closed at taxpayers' expense to permit an activity of a special-interest group.

Evaluating the Business Creed

It is difficult to separate the creed from the vocational and economic information contained in businessmen's contributions to schools. The pamphlets that the NAM distributes are cleverly written presentations of a point of view; NAM speakers are high-powered orators, likely to captivate high school audiences with their eloquence. Both pamphlets and speakers are guilty of oversimplification, omissions, and distortion rather than of untruths. The men who participate in local Chamber of Commerce projects are, of course, less expert as propagandists and probably do not see themselves in this role. Nevertheless, they often articulate the business creed in various ways.

What are some of the common oversimplifications, omissions, and distortions in the creed?

THE EXAGGERATED CLAIMS OF THE BENEFITS OF FREE ENTERPRISE. In boasting that the high standard of living enjoyed by Americans is a triumph for the system of free enterprise, businessmen tend to ignore other factors of equal importance, such as the abundance of natural resources, popular acceptance of material change, competence of the labor force, national unity, and governmental support. They fail to concede that in a capitalistic system the rich have been accused of "stealing from the poor" and that the welfare state and communism emerged out of injustices of laissez-faire capitalism.

THE BUSINESS CREED DESCRIBES BIG GOVERNMENT, ITS VILLAIN, AS WASTE-FUL OF TAXPAYERS' MONEY, INCOMPETENT, AND BUREAUCRATIC. A large part of the modern business community is, however, fully aware of the need for, and desirability of, government regulation of the national economy.

THE CONFUSION OF WELFARE PROGRAMS AND SOCIALISM WITH SOVIET IMPERIALISTIC COMMUNISM. The business creed scorns the poor as incompetent people unwilling to work. Government programs to help the poor are therefore branded as "socialistic-communistic." Unanalyzed name-calling not only retards social progress at home but also limits efforts to understand competing economic systems.

THE ASSUMPTION THAT CAPITALISM, EITHER AUTOMATICALLY OR DELIB-ERATELY, PROVIDES FOR THE COMMON GOOD. Are the prices charged for drugs exorbitant? Are these prices an example of the drug industry's concern for the general welfare?

THE CLAIM THAT PRICES ARE KEPT LOW THROUGH COMPETITION. The market situation today is called an *oligopoly*, that is, a market shared by a few sellers. Often one very large firm in an industry serves as a "price leader," and is readily followed by others in the field. For instance, U. S. Steel, price leader in the steel industry, sets its prices high enough to earn a small profit even if its plants operate only two days a week. Heilbroner concludes that such "target pricing" has virtually eliminated price cutting. "Competition among oligopolists today," he writes, "means winning business away from another by advertising, customer service, or product design—not by 'chiseling' on price."[3]

THE BELIEF THAT COMPETITION IS FUNDAMENTAL TO HUMAN NATURE. Much evidence from history, including that of Europe in the Middle Ages, and from anthropology refutes this tenet.

THE PREMISE THAT SINCE MEN HAVE AN EQUAL CHANCE TO COMPETE IN A FREE MARKET, SCHOOLS SHOULD TEACH YOUNG PEOPLE HOW TO COM-PETE. Researchers find that the Horatio Alger hero was never more than a myth. The average business leader of the late nineteenth century was

[3] Robert L. Heilbroner, *The Making of Economic Society*, Prentice-Hall, 1962, p. 134.

the son of a well-heeled father, not a poor immigrant. Even if business competition does provide equal chances for all, does every pupil have an equal chance to compete for grades in school?

THE ALLEGED DEPENDENCE OF ALL OUR LIBERTIES UPON FREEDOM IN THE MARKET PLACE. Social scientists, though recognizing the interdependence of institutions in a society, find it easy to attack such a cause-and-effect argument. Scandinavians who proudly boast of their "welfare state" are no less free than Americans. Nevertheless, American social scientists, like other Americans, usually recognize "free enterprise" as one of our freedoms.

THE BOAST THAT A SOCIETY THAT IS WEALTHY IS GREAT. Many young people challenge this belief. Hippies go so far as to claim that a steady job "makes ants of men." Many youth leaders believe a search for community among men to be more significant to human potentialities than accumulating material possessions. Isn't it possible, as Kimball and McClellan suggest, that the moral justification for our great material wealth lies in the ideal of self-fulfillment?[4] Shouldn't the businessman of the future learn to view this wealth as the means whereby man is freed from the pressures of work and to regard his job as one, but only one, of the possible means of self-fulfillment?

Although NAM pamphlets and speakers and Chamber of Commerce sponsored visits to industry on B-E Day do little to raise the level of economic literacy of teachers, the activities of the Joint Council on Economic Education represent a useful educational effort. The Council's program brings high-school teachers together with leaders in business, agriculture, government, labor relations, industry, and finance for several weeks to study the American economy. Undoubtedly a better understanding of economic theory is sorely needed in this country. An effective way to achieve this is to engage teachers and prospective teachers in the serious study of economics.

Recent Changes in the Business Creed

Whereas the statements of the business creed promoted in the NAM pamphlets and in some places in B-E Day programs express the ideology of conservative business interests, a new ideology and a new set of values are emerging that more nearly represent the point of view of middle-level employees of large corporations. In *The Organization Man,* a popular description of this new group's ideology, William H.

---

[4] Solon T. Kimball and James E. McClellan, Jr., *Education and the New America,* Random House, Vintage Edition, 1966, pp. 237–238.

Whyte, Jr. claims that an ethic he calls the Social Ethic is replacing the Protestant Ethic in the business value system.

Whyte dates the decline of the Protestant Ethic from the founding of American business corporations and the subsequent development of a business bureaucracy. He points out that the "organization man" does not need to be thrifty; his company makes deductions to pay for his hospital insurance, pension, and bonds; he cannot survive as a "rugged individualist"—he must learn to work successfully with others; he works hard but he feels guilty about it. The "organization man" accepts the Social Ethic: He believes that creativeness emerges from the group process and that the primary need of the individual is "belongingness"; he thinks that the science of human relationships can in time pave the way for smooth interpersonal relations and bring about belongingness.[5]

Analyses by other writers point to changes in man's behavior in this century. Eric Fromm, for example, contrasts the capitalistic society of the nineteenth century and that of the twentieth century in this way:

> Summing up then, we may say that the social character of the nineteenth century was essentially competitive, hoarding, exploitative, authoritarian, aggressive, individualistic. . . . We may . . . emphasize . . . the great difference between nineteenth- and twentieth-century Capitalism. Instead of the exploitative and hoarding orientation we find the receptive and marketing orientation. Instead of competitiveness we find an increasing tendency toward "teamwork"; instead of striving for ever-increasing profit, a wish for a steady and secure income; instead of exploitation, a tendency to share and spread wealth, and to manipulate others—and oneself; instead of rational and irrational but *overt* authority, we find *anonymous* authority—the authority of public opinion and the market; instead of individual conscience, the need to adjust and be approved of; instead of pride and mastery, an ever-increasing though mainly unconscious sense of powerlessness.[6]

David Riesman in *The Lonely Crowd* suggests a similar change in character structure in modern society. He maintains that persons in the United States today tend to be "other-directed," dependent upon the expectations of others, instead of "inner-directed," dependent upon stable goals.[7]

Whyte, Fromm, and Riesman are describing changes in the American value system that are not articulated by business spokesmen;

[5] William H. Whyte, Jr., *The Organization Man*, Simon and Schuster, 1956, pp. 6–18.
[6] Erich Fromm, *The Sane Society*, Holt, Rinehart and Winston, 1955, p. 99.
[7] David Riesman, *et al.*, *The Lonely Crowd*, Yale University Press, 1950, chaps. 1, 5, 6, and 7.

nevertheless the new point of view has permeated American business. So it is that businessmen who differ in beliefs are exemplifying by actions, if not by words, two clusters of values to American youth: first, work hard, be practical, be competitive, stay busy, and you will succeed; and second, learn to get along with others, adjust, manage others, know the right people, be sociable, and you will succeed. The current emphasis on learning to work successfully with others is not completely a denial, however, of the businessman's creed of individualism and freedom to promote one's self-interest; it is perhaps merely an extension of this line of thought. The successful business executive today does not ride roughshod over others; he manipulates people, persuades them, "handles" them so that his own interests seem to be synonymous with their welfare.

BUSINESS VALUES IN THE SCHOOLS

American young people who are bombarded with propaganda exalting the successful businessman, the possessor of earthly treasures, the man of action, have poor models for becoming anything else. Their model and ideal has been the practical man of good "common sense" who derides the theorist and belittles the scholar. American boys know that the humanities do not tell them how to make money and that their teachers, who may be among the best-educated adults in their community, often earn less than laborers. In spite of this knowledge, adolescents usually believe that they "will have a better chance" if they stay in school. They have probably been exposed to that frequently used—and not completely honest—motivational device: the dollar valuation ascribed to each additional year of schooling attained. Furthermore, their parents and teachers stress the economic value of an education. These pressures lead young people to place high values on vocational education and on the "polish" of the college man that may be of benefit in the business world. High school and college students, even girls whose real goal is matrimony, feel obliged to choose an occupational goal toward which to direct their studies. Many in college avoid majoring in studies of little pecuniary value. The students' interest in an occupational slant to whatever they study encourages a vocational emphasis in courses that may rightfully fall under the heading of general education. For example, colleges may offer "Speech for Teachers" or "English for Engineers."

Despite the promise of leadership to those of merit, American boys know that the business community does not measure merit primarily in terms of excellence in scholastic achievement. They have heard that "who you know is more important than what you know." The ideal

Horatio Alger hero who conquered adversity and rose from "rags to riches" is being displaced by the affable junior executive, an expert in smooth interpersonal relations. Therefore students want to learn social skills, impress others favorably, and meet the "right" people, especially in college. They are as concerned with a good record of participation in cocurricular activities as they are with a respectable academic record because they know that college admission authorities often consider such participation in entrance selections and that personnel officers who hire young people look for "well-rounded" applicants.

Not all students, of course, aspire to become successful businessmen. A sizable group of adolescents who see little value in school offerings want to quit school to work for money, the symbol of status and freedom. These young people are usually the children of parents who have lost the competitive race for worldly goods. Trapped in school by compulsory education laws, they become reluctant learners and trouble-makers. Others from privileged homes also react negatively to school offerings, saying they are "irrelevant" to modern life.

Other young people, often encouraged by ambitious parents, become excessively competitive in their fight for high academic marks. Just as in the larger society where the amassing of dollars may overshadow the satisfactions of the work done, in the school the attainment of a high scholastic record may be of greater significance for some students than the learning that the grades are supposed to symbolize. Another group of students, strongly motivated toward a professional goal such as medicine, law, or engineering, are serious students, particularly in their fields of interest. And finally, a few students, often disdainful of material rewards, are genuinely eager to become scholars to satisfy their desire to know.

Business Values and School Practices

In general, teachers seemingly stress many of the values that businessmen praise highly. For example, teachers struggle to inculcate respect for hard work, punctuality, neatness, a sense of duty, and acceptance of the sanctity of private property. Less often than in earlier decades do today's teachers hold out unattainable goals to pupils, promising success as the result of hard work, irrespective of scholastic aptitude. Most teachers, however, still have great optimism in regard to a pupil's chances of academic success if he *works hard enough*. Sometimes, even though a pupil drives himself toward an objective he cannot possibly achieve, some teachers still brand the poor scholar as lazy. Usually teachers grade their pupils to some extent on the basis of how hard they try: The weak student who plods doggedly often receives a grade higher than his academic achievement warrants, whereas the bright youngster who does not work is likely to get less than he deserves. Therein is the maxim of hard work demonstrated. Many teachers refuse to accept work that is late, punish the tardy pupil, and reward neatness more than content.

Teachers are also likely to assume that the strongly motivated, acquisitive, competitive, and self-interested individual exemplifies human nature at its best. Many admire material success and point with pride to former pupils and fortunate relatives who have accumulated wealth. The argument they use to persuade potential dropouts to stay in school is that schooling pays off in dollars and cents. This emphasis by educators on the economic rather than on the intellectual and aesthetic contributions of education to a full life indicates the extent to which teachers themselves accept the businessman's creed. Teachers, who feel themselves underpaid, rate the status of teaching lower than does the general public, which suggests that teachers regard material compensation as the chief criterion of status. Few Americans quarrel with the teachers' acceptance of the value of hard work, punctuality, neatness, responsibility and respect for property, but liberal thinkers and humanitarians often object to the rigidity and single-minded devotion with which these values are imposed upon children.

The organization of American schools is analogous in many respects to a business organization. The school board is analogous to a board of directors; the superintendent of schools holds a position similar to that of the manager of a big business, and to a considerable extent his effectiveness is judged in terms of his success in financial administration. Supervisors, department heads, principals, and assistant principals hold line positions; specialists in public relations, health, guidance, psychological services, and remedial work are considered staff personnel, as are their counterparts in industry. The status of a teacher is roughly that of the skilled or white-collar worker. The business practice of paying substantially higher salaries to administrators than to experts, technicians, and other workers is also followed in schools. Recent agitation for merit pay for teachers is inspired to a large extent by businessmen, who fail to see differences between the job of a teacher and that of a salesman, office worker, or technician. Units of study in modern jargon have become "packaged programs."

The ledger of the business world has its counterpart in schools in the teacher's grade book. Daily grades are ultimately translated into numerical "grade-point averages." An intricate bookkeeping system preserves records of pupil achievements. Listings on honor rolls, membership in honorary societies, awarding of scholarships, and granting of other privileges are based in part upon the accumulation of "points."

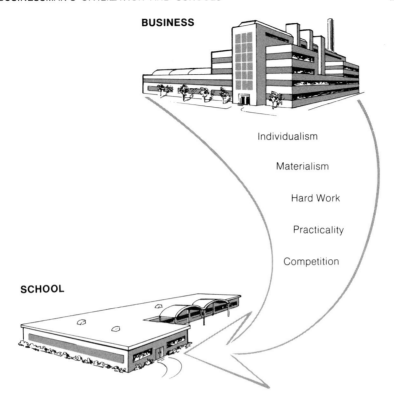

BUSINESS

Individualism

Materialism

Hard Work

Practicality

Competition

SCHOOL

Until recently no other peoples in the world believed so strongly as those in the United States that the acquisition of knowledge can be quantified and recorded numerically. In the last few years, educators in several new nations, after studying in this country, have, perhaps unwisely, introduced similar practices in their own countries.

The proliferation of courses in business education at both the high school and college level is mute testimony to the influence of business interests. The American school's strong leaning toward a practical, vocational orientation is to a considerable degree a reflection of a similar stress in the larger society. The importance adults attach to smooth interpersonal relationships is also reflected in school programs. Group techniques are justified because they contribute to amicable personal interactions and group cohesion. The cocurricular program is founded in part on the assumption that it is important "to learn to get along with others." Counselors, teachers, and parents urge youngsters to take part in these activities in order to become "well adjusted." The guidance program is predicated upon the supposition that "adjustment," often interpreted as conformity to standards of the group and acceptance by one's peers, is essential to learning, success, and happiness.

If the "athletic tail wags the academic dog," those most responsible for this situation are likely to be local businessmen. Attempts of school leaders to play down competitiveness in school activities, especially in the athletic programs, have met with little success. Coaches soon learn that "moral victories," good sportsmanship, and splendid teamwork rarely bring the accolades given to winning teams. Businessmen, convinced that sports promote the competitiveness needed for success in life, are active supporters of athletic programs.

Adults outside the school also like the competitive report card. They equate competition for grades in school with competition in the business world, and assume that each individual has an equal opportunity to succeed in school or in business. Many educators, convinced that neither pupils with above-average chances of success nor those with little chance are benefited by highly competitive classes, have tried to eliminate grades. But parents are unhappy with reports that do not give them an interpretation of how their child's performance compares with that of others. Principals report that mothers of elementary school children, once they are persuaded to accept the importance of cooperativeness in their child's development, may then desire to be assured that their youngster is the *most* cooperative.

When parallels between business and educational practices are pointed out to teachers, they often comment that they had never before thought of the similarities. It is, of course, common for individuals to accept the traditional and to agree with influential groups, but creative approaches to education are not initiated by those who never question the reasons for current situations. We cannot approve existing practices until we ask searching questions such as these: Is the supervisory function in a bureaucratic school system necessary? Are the substantially larger salaries paid to administrators in a school justified? Does this practice often entice a superior teacher to become a mediocre supervisor? Are all subjects of equal importance as suggested by our unit system of credits? Is a student's adjustment to his peers of greater value than the development of his individuality when the latter includes stating unpopular truths, fighting for moral principles, and pursuing intellectual interests? Which is more important, training a child to compete successfully or educating a human being who is concerned with the well-being of others?

The answers to such questions require study, research, and value judgments. Upon analysis, some school policies and practices may be praised, some may be condoned, and some may be condemned. When

practices cannot be justified from the point of view of the best education for young people, the school is responsible for providing leadership to effect changes. That undesirable practices—for example, undue
emphasis upon interscholastic athletics—have become established in
certain schools attests to the ineffectuality of educational leaders rather
than to the effectiveness of American businessmen.

School Leaders Accept
the Businessman's Social Philosophy

A recent study of top leaders in the United States concludes that of
the one hundred most influential men in this country roughly one-
fourth are industrialists. Only two of the group are professors, one is a
scientist, none is a public school leader.[8] At the community level the
policy-makers "most often represent the largest local industries, banks,
law firms, commercial houses, and newspapers." Educators along with
clergymen and politicians are described as a "fringe group" who may
be consulted upon occasion.[9] The inability of educational leaders
to influence the making of decisions pertinent to the general welfare is
nothing new.

Merle Curti's historical account of the social philosophy of American
educators discloses that, with very few exceptions, school leaders have
consistently supported conservative, wealthy interests in their efforts to
resist social change except in the field of education itself. Between
1820 and the Civil War, educational spokesmen, carefully avoiding
issues such as slavery and the evils of industrial capitalism, wooed the
assistance of powerful interests with claims that financial support of
schools would prevent crime, poverty, revolution, and other social ills,
and that it would secure property holdings and increase wealth by
supplying literate workers. From the Civil War until World War I,
educators, excepting John Dewey and a few others, promoted social
ideas thoroughly consistent with those of profit-oriented industrialists.
They attributed the farmers' grievances of the 1880s and 1890s to
inadequate agricultural education in rural schools; strikes and violence
among workers to their lack of a high school education wherein they
would have learned the advantages of cooperation over conflict; and
child labor to parental attitudes rather than to the need for higher
farm prices and higher wages for workers. During the Wilson reform
educators showed a brief flurry of interest in social liberalism, but the
results were little more than Americanization programs for immigrants

[8] Floyd Hunter, *Top Leadership, U.S.A.*, University of North Carolina Press,
1959, p. 199.
[9] *Ibid.*, pp. 5–6.

and teaching patriotism. Then, except for a few outspoken critics of the social order, American educators complacently settled for "normalcy" until the Great Depression.

In thus describing educational leaders, Curti does not deny the idealistic motives of those who sought to improve the lot of the working class through education for better jobs and for social mobility. In fact, the mere extension of schooling to the masses is itself a change in the status quo. Nevertheless, American educational leadership has been conservative, not crusading. Only during the depression of the 1930s, when business support was withdrawn, teachers were unpaid, and schools were closed, did many school leaders bitterly attack the National Association of Manufacturers, the U. S. Chamber of Commerce, bankers, and other business groups. Curti's account ends with a description of the state of affairs in 1935.[10] His 1959 revision discusses briefly the conservatism of present-day educators.[11]

What we may say about the social philosophy of school leaders in recent years can be no more than a subjective interpretation. It is clear, however, that school leaders no longer engage in the virulent criticisms of big business that were common in the 1930s. In postwar America educationists write about such social issues as education for democratic behavior, for gifted children, for better intergroup relations, for international understanding, and in the 1960s, for disadvantaged children. As in earlier years, not many leading educators are militantly crusading for social reforms in the larger society. The official position of the NEA on integration of schools, belatedly stated in 1959, is more cautious than that of the American Association of University Women. Only very recently are a few educators found in the front ranks of the battles for slum clearance, extension of social security laws, or civil-rights legislation. It would be interesting to know to what extent educational leadership is influenced by top policy-makers in the United States who were said to be not deeply concerned about the problems of minority and underprivileged groups[12] until riots occurred in major cities.

American teachers and principals are even more conservative than their spokesmen. Despite the more heterogeneous social-class and ethnic origin of teachers today, the general value orientation of most teachers is still in line with that of the middle-class white-collar and managerial group. Although teachers, like other Americans, have re-

---

[10] Merle Curti, *Social Ideas of American Educators,* Scribner's, 1935, pp. 194–200, 203–260, 542–591 *passim.*

[11] Merle Curti, *Social Ideas of American Educators,* rev. ed., Littlefield, Adams, 1959, pp. xxv–xliv.

[12] Hunter, *op. cit.,* p. 212.

jected to some extent the version of the business creed espoused by the National Association of Manufacturers and other conservative groups, they accept without question much of the business ideology.

As Curti states in his revision of *Social Ideas of American Educators,* "The school structure itself, in origin and in growth, has been much less the expression of humanitarianism and democracy and much more the result of, and dependent upon, dominant economic interests than is commonly supposed." He adds that educational leaders "are deeply influenced by a point of view which they have unconsciously absorbed from their social environment, by a frame of reference which constantly limits their thought." They cannot, he believes, contribute to the building of a better social order unless they analyze their values and rise above the "more or less obsolete ideas and emotional attitudes related to their class and personal backgrounds."[13]

BUSINESS CORPORATIONS AND SCHOOLS

The corporate organization has been the social form that has made the United States a businessman's civilization. It has made possible, according to Adolph Berle, "the highest concentration of economic power in recorded history. . . . Some of these corporations are units which can be thought of only in somewhat the way we have heretofore thought of nations."[14] In 1965, for example, General Motors had a gross corporate product exceeding that of Sweden. Approximately 200 giant corporations own one-half of all the assets of the manufacturing, mining, public utilities, and transportation sectors of the American economy.[15]

The Corporation as "Private Government"

A corporation is defined as an association of individuals, created by law or under authority of law, having a continuous existence irrespective of that of its members. Early corporations were the nation-state and the Church. These organizations spawned countless other corporations—charitable associations, educational institutions, hospitals, orphanages, foundations, municipalities, labor unions, and the most powerful of all, the business corporation. The corporate form flourished because of its immortality (survival after death of individuals), limited liability, and its ability to act legally as a person.

[13] Curti, 1959, *op. cit.,* pp. 590–591.
[14] Adolph A. Berle, Jr., *Economic Power and the Free Society,* The Fund for the Republic, 1957, pp. 14–15.
[15] Heilbroner, *op. cit.,* p. 126.

The business and industrial corporation and, less frequently, its counteraction, the labor union, and, still less frequently, the charitable or educational corporation have sometimes been described as "private governments." At this point our concern is only with the power of the business corporation.

The corporations' decisions relate to many economic areas of significance to individual Americans. They influence prices, investments, employment, purchasing power, and the size and distribution of national production; "in effect they levy taxes on the consumer and make alliances with foreign corporations in cartel agreements."[16] The top-level managers do these things without a vote of confidence from the American people and usually without the explicit approval of the owners (stockholders). The corporations also have power to affect a great many lives, those of consumers as well as employees. Not only have they modified the traditional value system, as mentioned earlier in this chapter, but also they have developed a "corporate citizenship."

A group of Americans, typified as the "organization men," the "other-directed men," and the "new middle class," are the white-collar, middle-level management employees of big corporations. These men and their families, often upper-lower class in social origin, are rootless in the suburban communities in which they live from time to time, citizens only in a national sense, and dependent upon the corporation for a sense of belonging and economic security. Individuals of the New Middle Class differ politically from those of the Old Middle Class, traditionally the backbone of democratic citizenry, in that they have sacrificed the freedom that comes from being one's own boss as a farmer or independent businessman for the security of life-long careers as company men. They have become "corporate citizens," who avoid political party activity because "the company" may disapprove and because they have no primary interests at stake in politics. They may become active, however, in civic welfare work at the community level, and they usually vote in presidential elections. It should be readily apparent that problems of education, especially education for citizenship, are intensified in suburban schools in which the children of these apolitical migrants are enrolled.

Although corporate life may be weakening the very foundations of democracy by eliminating a literate group from political activity at local and state levels, the new concept of the corporation as a "corporate citizen" is said to include concern with all social problems. According to this theory, the giant corporation as a private sector of power in a pluralistic society is more than a mere business; it is a social institu-

[16] Max Lerner, *America as a Civilization: Life and Thought in the United States Today,* Simon and Schuster, 1957, p. 284.

tion created to collectivize capital, but it is a socially conscious institution because its survival depends upon its acting as a socially responsible "corporate citizen."

Corporate Giving

The newly developing "corporate conscience" is expanding earlier concepts of philanthropy. No longer is philanthropy solely an individual concern, for business managers now make donations on behalf of stockholders. In the first half of this century many persons doubted that charitable gifts taken from stockholders' profits were legal; they contended that the purpose of business was to make money, not to give it away. The legality of such gifts has, however, been established in most states, but the motive of such philanthropy is much less explicit. Companies usually begin their charities at home with gifts to local drives and neighborhood colleges. When they expand and diversify their contributions, the only guiding principle seems to be that the gifts shall benefit both the company and the society.

Many possible reasons have been given for corporations' giving away money. One such reason a cynic suggests is, "High taxes and smart tax lawyers." The Internal Revenue Act of 1935 does indeed exempt from taxation a business' charitable donations up to 5 percent of net income. James Cook, president of Illinois Bell Telephone Company, is quoted as saying, "To state it quite flatly, when we help in the improvement of a community, we enhance the chance of business success there."[17] He knows that citizens in communities of high socioeconomic and educational levels purchase more goods and facilities than do those in impoverished communities. Many business managers also believe that they can operate public services more efficiently and economically than can governmental bureaucracies. A more important reason for giving, however, may be that a company wants to improve its "image." Sometimes corporate gifts evoke caustic remarks from outsiders, such as, "Now they're giving back some of what they stole from us."

Many businesses and industries now funnel their gifts through a foundation. A philanthropic foundation is a tax-exempt, nonprofit corporation organized for the specific purpose of distributing funds to worthy causes. The oldest general-welfare foundations, such as the Peabody Fund, Rockefeller's General Education Board, the Rosenwald Fund, and the Carnegie Foundation, were established and financed by wealthy individuals and families. These foundations and others were

[17] "Business Sets Up Its Own Great Society," U. S. News and World Report, 62 (April 3, 1967), 73–75.

active after the Civil War and well into the twentieth century in furthering secondary education, teacher education, and Negro education in the South, but the bulk of the funds went to colleges and universities.

Since 1950 several changes have occurred in corporate giving. First, the amount of money donated has increased and the number of foundations has multiplied. Companies are expected to increase their donations from 30 million dollars in 1936 to a billion dollars by 1970. Second, schools and colleges are now getting, especially from foundations, a larger share of the total donations for welfare. Third, whereas before 1951 practically all corporate money went into scholarships and fellowships, since that date much more of this money has been donated to schools for general education. Finally, gifts for raising faculty salaries and for experimenting in elementary and secondary schools, a small part of the total contributions, have been larger in recent than in earlier years.

Corporate Funds and
Higher Education

Meanwhile, business firms contribute to the funding of schools in another way by hiring universities and colleges to do research pertinent to their enterprises. They probably spend as much on these contracts as they donate. Many companies encourage their employees to contribute toward scholarships to colleges by matching their donations with company awards. Businessmen on boards of trustees, especially of private schools, often concoct plans that take advantage of the tax-exempt status of a school to increase its profits from rentals, leases, gifts, and other business ventures. When these profits and the funds derived from contracts are added to corporate gifts, the total represents a considerable sum.

How does the increased reliance upon business financing of colleges and universities affect the quality of education? The advantages are obvious. Schools at all levels need the money, particularly "venture money" for experimentation and research that otherwise cannot be financed. Some of the disadvantages are also readily apparent. Most of the funds go to a few of the largest and wealthiest universities in the United States; much of it is tagged for specified scientific research of immediate benefit to sponsors; not enough is available for theoretical scientific research and the rest of the curriculum; some of the money goes for researches of limited value without regard for the more urgent needs of general education.

When grants are made for specific academic purposes, whether by the federal government or by any other agent, educational activity is likely to be distorted. For example, recently social scientists have been encouraged by business contacts to concentrate upon applied science to the neglect of theoretical research. Kornhauser believes that rewards from applied research have lured social scientists away from "the basic job of developing a body of abstract generalized knowledge on man and society." He also deplores the "remarkable coincidence of social science findings with sponsors' convictions," and he comments critically:

> Social scientists are pulled away from disinterested scientific endeavors to become useful technicians and sometimes special pleaders. . . . They too often come to deserve the question: Whose social scientists are you?[18]

Another important consideration, mentioned by Kornhauser, is that an "administratively oriented social science . . . aimed at knowledge and techniques for leaders and influencers" is more interested in "how to use so-called democratic discussions and group-decisions to gain acceptance of ideas" than in "how people can protect themselves against manipulative practices." He thinks that the "partisan influence" of business groups would not matter so much if "interest groups and organizations of all kinds were equally able and willing to sponsor research."[19]

Recent Interest of Foundations in Elementary and Secondary Schools

The agitation about the need for improving public schools has caused some foundation money to be diverted into the lower schools. The Ford Foundation, mainly through its Fund for the Advancement of Education, has made numerous grants. Ford has sponsored research and experiments in team teaching, teacher aide programs, variations in class size and scheduling, independent study, programs for gifted pupils, school plant construction and management, and visual and sound devices including educational TV. It has given fellowships to secondary teachers for advanced study in liberal arts, and has paid liberal arts college graduates to combine a year's internship with professional study designed to qualify them for teaching in the elementary school. The foundation has financed university research in

---

[18] Arthur Kornhauser, ed., *Problems of Power in American Democracy,* Wayne University Press, 1959, p. 200.
[19] *Ibid.,* pp. 192–202 *passim.*

several social areas of concern to public schools, notably delinquency, international understanding, and urban growth. The W. K. Kellogg Foundation has sponsored research designed to improve the professional education of public school administrators, special education for the handicapped, and school-community relationships. Carnegie funds paid for the Conant studies in identifying and utilizing talent in high schools.

Stephen M. Corey was one of the first to point out the possibly deleterious influence of foundations upon public education. He lamented the simple answers proposed by foundations to complex problems, for example the fifth year of professional training and internship as the best preparation for teaching, Dr. Conant's 21 specific recommendations as just what the high schools need, and teacher aides as the solution for the teacher shortage. He said he thought that foundations were too hungry for publicity, too eager to *anticipate* solutions as the outcomes of the research they sponsor, and too willing to generalize the findings even when the experimental design was weak. He pointed to the need for foundations' differentiating sharply between "supporting research and experimentation, on the one hand, and promoting a favored solution to an educational problem, on the other."[20]

The criticisms aimed at university research in the social sciences are also pertinent to research in public education. Experimenters in teaching by television and teaching machines too often become "special pleaders" for these methods. Studies in administrative behavior for school executives, like those in business leadership, sometimes smack loudly of learning how to manipulate others.

Many of these criticisms are valid, but the fault does not lie solely with bias on the part of foundations. Educational leaders should make proposals worthy of the support of foundations. Often they fail to develop experimental designs of high quality or to offer proposals. If researchers receiving foundation grants write reports that lack objectivity, the researchers and not the foundations are culpable.

One of the reasons, however, for the failure of many school systems to volunteer for experimentation is teacher apathy and resistance to change. A conservative core of teachers, like any other group with a vested interest, may block creative proposals that would win foundation grants. Such teachers not only defeat the very purpose of foundations, which is to provide "risk money" for educational ventures, but

---

[20] Stephen M. Corey, "Foundations and School Experimentation," *Educational Leadership, 17* (December, 1959), 135–136, 175.

also make criticisms of experiments financed by foundations sound querulous and petty. If teachers do not want others' ideas imposed upon them, they should come up with their own proposals.

Big Business and the War on Poverty

In the last few years, large corporations and businessmen in some cities have "set up their own Great Society," claims the *U. S. News and World Report.* Representatives of Philco, Westinghouse, Xerox, Burroughs, RCA, and IBM are managing training in Job Corps centers. Equitable Life Assurance Society is hiring school dropouts in the New York office. Businessmen in St. Louis, Philadelphia, and cities in Indiana have helped find jobs for the unemployed. Other large corporations have renovated tenements, sought to solve problems of air and water pollution, and established information and counseling centers for disadvantaged people, especially disadvantaged Negroes. In 1967 the insurance industry pledged one billion dollars to help fight the war on poverty. George Champion, chairman of Chase Manhattan Bank, said, "I can think of nothing that would put the brakes on big government faster than for business to identify critical problems and take the initiative in dealing with them before Washington felt the need to act."[21]

Clearly the "corporate conscience" ought to be concerned with social welfare in that unemployment as well as air and water pollution are largely undesirable byproducts of industrial capitalism. Absentee landlords of the business community are also to some extent responsible for the deterioration of tenement housing in the slums. Conscience aside, businessmen stand to gain financially from high employment and well-trained workers. They are, in fact, doubly rewarded when the government pays handsomely for industry-sponsored training programs, such as the Job Corps.

Businessmen have, however, no mandate from the people to "identify cultural problems and take the initiative in dealing with them." The business of businessmen is business. They do not constitute a public body designed to promote the general welfare. The people have no voice when businessmen collect taxes in the form of high prices nor when businessmen decide what causes, educational or charitable, will be helped with stockholders' money. Voters cannot "turn the rascals out." Despite the common criticisms of government, it is a safer mechanism for evaluating and implementing social objectives than is a corporation.

[21] *U.S. News and World Report, 62* (April 3, 1967), 74.

Big Business in the Education Market

Businessmen's influence in educational matters is, however, likely to expand much more rapidly though sales to schools than through foundation grants, research contracts, industrial training, and programs for dropouts. Since the passage by Congress of the Elementary and Secondary Act of 1965, giant corporations—among them IBM, Raytheon, Xerox, General Electric, and others in the Who's Who of Industry—have discovered the education market. As Francis Keppel indicates, "A billion dollars looking for a good, new way to be spent does not ordinarily turn the American businessman into a shrinking violet."[22]

Businessmen's eagerness to help school administrators and teachers spend the new Federal money will also help assure that additional funds for education will be voted by legislators. Myron Lieberman points out, "After all, the businessman wants to be sure that his potential customers can afford to buy what he is selling."[23]

It is primarily the uses of large-scale electronic data processing systems in schools that excites the interest of industry. "Industry is strongly committed," says Edward L. Katzenbach, vice president and general manager, Education Division, Raytheon Company, "to utilize its broad technological knowledge; its administrative, engineering, and systems analysis talent; its research and development and manufacturing resources; and its energy in helping to improve education."[24]

Possible changes in education that may result from increased use of computers and other "hardware" in education will be discussed in Chapter 6. In this section, only businessmen's interest in sales to schools, already a multibillion dollar account, is being considered. The real impetus for the technological revolution in education is coming from industry. If school leaders and teachers do not seize the initiative, they may find in 10 or 15 years that business leaders are influencing the content of education through computer education even more than publishers of textbooks have influenced its content in the past.

SUMMARY

Clearly American schools have been influenced by the ethos of our businessman's civilization. The results are evident in the curriculum,

[22] Francis Keppel, "The Business Interest in Education," *Phi Delta Kappan,* 48 (January, 1967), 188.

[23] Myron Lieberman, "Big Business, Technology, and Education," *Phi Delta Kappan, 48* (January, 1967), 185.

[24] Edward L. Katzenbach, "Industry Can Serve," *Phi Delta Kappan, 48* (January, 1967), 193–194.

school organization, and school practices, and in the value system subscribed to by many teachers and pupils. In recent decades research sponsored by corporate firms and foundations and corporate gifts to schools have directly influenced the course of American education. Businessmen's interest in potential educational markets for electronic data processing equipment suggests the possibility that the content of the curriculum is more likely than in the past to be influenced by big business. Such influences should be evaluated by teachers and school leaders in relation to educational goals.

The relationship between businessmen and consumers is to some extent reciprocal. Educators are not obliged to serve as agents for propaganda nor for research useful only to businessmen's interests. On the one hand, school leaders do not have to accept grants incompatible with educational philosophy. On the other, they can, in fact, cooperate with businessmen in their production of programmed and other materials of great value in the education of children.

IMPORTANT CONCEPTS

Ascribed status. One's position or standing derived from the position of one's family or other unearned basis.

Businessman's creed. See pp. 18–21.

Egalitarian. Equalitarian; the belief that all persons should have equal political and social rights.

Entrepreneur. A person who organizes and manages any enterprise, especially a business, usually with considerable initiative and risk. See p. 21.

Ethos. The sum of the characteristic culture traits of a group.

Laissez faire. A theory of noninterference ("hands-off") in the affairs of others, which is especially acceptable to those who advocate limited governmental action in economic affairs.

Moral. Right or wrong, good or evil, appraised in terms of a group's standard of values.

"Practical realism." A tendency to face facts and be matter-of-fact rather than visionary or imaginative.

Protestant ethic. See pp. 20–21.

Social ethic. See p. 25.

Social evolution. A doctrine which assumes that processes of social development are more or less analogous to those of biological evolution; i.e., variation, struggle for existence, selection, and adaptation.

Welfare state. A state in which the welfare of its citizens is promoted largely by the organized efforts of the government rather than of private institutions.

3. INFLUENCES OF SOCIAL CLASSES IN SCHOOLS

Every man is in certain respects:
a) like all other men; b) like some
other men; c) like no other man.
—CLYDE KLUCKHOHN AND
HENRY A. MURRAY[1]

Social distinctions among groups of persons are not new in America. In
early colonial days a farmer or an artisan of humble standing in the
community was called "goodman," and the title of "mister" was re-
served for gentlemen. The deference accorded a plantation owner, a
wealthy merchant, or a minister in the Massachusetts theocracy was
quite different from the treatment given indentured servants, slaves,
and free men of limited means. Long before sociological studies of
social class were made, everybody knew that some people had a
"higher standing" or a "lower standing" than others. Nevertheless, the

[1] Clyde Kluckhohn and Henry A. Murray, *Personality in Nature, Society and Culture,* Knopf, 1949, p. 35.

earliest studies of class in this country, particularly those of the Warner School in the 1930s and 1940s, created great interest among sociologists and educationists. A popularized discussion of the theme, *The Status Seekers* by Vance Packard, published in 1961, and other descriptions of social class appearing in popular magazines at about the same time have been widely read in this country and abroad.

The initial reaction to studies of social classes by many Americans was resistance to the findings because they outraged the basic American belief in equalitarianism. Even though everybody knew that there were and always had been social distinctions in this country, Americans did not like to admit their existence. Social-class differences negate claims that every man has an equal chance to rise if he works hard enough and that "I am as good as the next man." Despite resistance to studies of social classes, the concept of differing classes has been gradually accepted and by the 1960s references to "upper class," "middle class," and "lower class" in the mass media and everyday conversation were commonplace.

Many studies of the influences of social classes upon pupils in schools have been made. Such studies resulted in labeling schools and teachers as "lower-middle class" and in charging schools with not meeting the educational needs of "lower-class" children. In an attempt to clarify such charges, the first section of this chapter deals with the concept of social classes, the second section, with the beliefs and practices commonly attributed to the major social classes, and the final section, with implications of such distinctions for school practices.

THE CONCEPT OF SOCIAL CLASSES

Many social scientists have been disturbed by glib presentations of social class that distort the concept into a rigid deterministic mold. As Max Lerner says, "To draw a profile of American social strata is more elusive than almost anything else in American life."[2] Social scientists do not even agree on the meaning of the term "social classes," the number of such classes, or how to measure the differences among such classes as may exist. They do, however, ascribe to complex, industrialized societies a web of dynamic relationships that involve and influence individuals and institutions. These relationships, they say, tend to be shaped by hierarchical positions of groups in a society. In other words, they see a society as stratified (arranged in layers), with individuals and groups holding higher or lower or equivalent positions in relation to one another.

Finding the bases of such stratification is not simple. Obviously American society has never been class-conscious in the Marxian sense, which pits those who work for others against owners and managers, i.e., proletariat vs. bourgeoisie. Milton M. Gordon suggests that three factors or variables, all intertwined, account for stratification in the United States. First, economic power that is determined by income, credit rating, steadiness of employment, employment control over others, and similar elements. Second, political power defined in terms of control, direct or indirect, of formal governmental structure and of opinion-forming agencies, such as the mass media, churches, schools, and civic organizations. Third, social status that may arise from a specific position, occupational or avocational, that a person holds, the respect or esteem that he gains from the success with which he carries out the role associated with this status, and his general reputation that he earns because of his individual qualities. Of the three factors, Gordon believes that social status, which he tends to equate with social class, is the most significant factor producing social divisions. In addition to economic power, political power, and social status that stratify all Americans, he says that a further differentiation is made on

[2] Max Lerner, *America as a Civilization: Life and Thought in the United States Today,* Simon and Schuster, 1957, p. 473.

the basis of ethnic origin, national backgrounds, and religious differences. The latter variables crisscross the other factors in stratification, giving a different position in the social structure to individuals and families who are not "typically American," irrespective of their occupations, wealth, and political influence.

One can explain differences in the social structure of subcommunities, Gordon theorizes, by variations in four dimensions: (1) social class, determined largely by economic power and associated with political power; (2) ethnic, religious, and national backgrounds; (3) rural-urban location; and (4) regional area.[3]

Definitions of Social Class

The average American probably sees differences among social classes largely in terms of material accumulations. He believes that some individuals and some positions deserve higher financial rewards than others. Assuming that a man's gains have been won honestly, his neighbors are as likely to admire and applaud his achievements as they are to begrudge him the fruits of his success. Until recently almost all Americans accepted this view and regarded class differences as moral and proper because they believed they had equality of opportunity, even if it existed in fantasy to a greater extent than in fact. Recent charges of middle-class exploitation of the lower classes have, however, largely discredited this assumption of equalitarianism particularly among lower-class Negroes and idealistic college youths.

Although many scholars use the term "social class," few of them specify precisely what they mean by it. Do the terms "social class" or "socioeconomic level" as used by some scholars merely refer to a statistical aggregate of people in the same income bracket or at the same occupational level? Are there, in fact, well-defined classes in the United States into which people can be categorized? Is "social stratification" actually only another way of referring to a continuum of prestige ratings? If classes exist, why do many people not know to what class they belong? Why are so many people deviants from the norms of their social class? These are the kinds of questions that many sociologists are asking. They are also questioning the methodology of much of the research.

The term *social class*, as used herein, refers to a large number of the population who hold similar positions in respect to prestige within their society, who hold many beliefs and values in common, and who are willing to accept others within the same aggregate as equals or

[3] Milton M. Gordon, *Social Class in American Sociology*, Duke University Press, 1958, chap. 8.

intimates. Obviously such a stipulative definition does not make sorting persons into classes any less difficult.

Researchers in towns and smaller cities have used numerous techniques to establish class categories, such as informants' ratings, interviews, observations, and studies of participation, organizational memberships, and genealogies. Warner developed a short-cut method called the Index of Status Characteristics, which correlates highly with the more costly and time-consuming methods that require extensive interviewing. By the I.S.C. method a person is given weighted scores for occupation, source of income, house type, and dwelling area.[4] Hollingshead's Index of Social Position, another simplified method of determining social class, uses ecological area of residence, occupation, and education as factors.[5] Still another method, developed by Ellis, asks a person to identify his father's or his own occupation in specific detail.[6] Other investigators get a rough measure of social classes from demographic studies of occupational and income levels.

The stress placed on income and occupations as indices of social strata in the United States seems to be justified. Numerous studies have demonstrated that income and occupational groups consistently differ in their activities, values, and attitudes and that from study to study occupations are given similar prestige ratings. Nevertheless, social-class position is not directly comparable to either wealth or occupational stratum. It may be true, as Baltzell's study in *Philadelphia Gentlemen* suggests, that wealth held by families over a span of generations does assure upper-class placement, but new money does not earn such status for its possessor. The rating of occupations is not directly related to income earned in that many skilled workers earn more than some white-collar employees, yet the latter are likely to be rated higher in social class. Nor do persons within an occupational group actually hold the same social rating. Notwithstanding these limitations to using income and occupation as determinants of social class, it is agreed that social class in this country has an economic foundation and that occupation is the best single clue to social class.

Number and Size of Social Classes

The number of social classes identified by a researcher and the size of each depends upon several factors such as the method used in

[4] For a complete explanation of I.S.C. method, see W. Lloyd Warner *et al.*, *Social Class in America*, Science Research Associates, 1949.

[5] August B. Hollingshead and Fredrick C. Redlich, *Social Class and Mental Illness*, Wiley, 1958, appendix 2, pp. 387–397.

[6] Robert A. Ellis, W. Clayton Lane, and Virginia Olesen, "The Index of Class Position: An Improved Intercommunity Measure of Stratification," *American Sociological Review*, 28 (April, 1963), 271–277.

determining social class, location of the community studied, and the principal occupations of people who live there. In 1941 Warner and Lunt's study of "Yankee City" in New England revealed this distribution: upper-upper class, 1.4 percent; lower-upper class, 1.6 percent; upper-middle class, 10 percent; lower-middle class, 28 percent; upper-lower (working) class, 33 percent; and lower-lower class, 25 percent.[7] Other researchers in the east and midwest using the Warner technique have arrived at similar distributions except for, in some instances, the distinction between upper- and lower-upper class. A disadvantage of studies of the Yankee City type is that the methods of research depend in part upon persons knowing one another and therefore are best adapted for small cities and towns. Warner's shortened I.S.C. Method, although usable in large cities, cannot be validated without a sample study of informants' judgments. His criteria, "house type" and "dwelling area" are also not very meaningful in mass-produced housing tracts.

Other researchers using different techniques sometimes encounter other problems. For example, Gross found in a Minneapolis survey that when persons were simply asked to what class they belonged, 14 percent said "no class," 20 percent said "don't know," 5 percent gave no response, and 15 percent gave responses other than upper, middle, lower, or working class.[8] In other words, over half of the respondents seemed to have not seen themselves as members of a social class.

In 1960 Havighurst estimated the following distribution of five social classes in the United States:[9]

Class	Percent
Upper	2
Upper-middle	8
Lower-middle	30
Upper-lower	40
Lower-lower	20

[7] W. Lloyd Warner and Paul S. Lunt, *The Social Life of a Modern Community,* Yale University Press, 1941, p. 88.

[8] Neal Gross, "Social Class Identification in the Urban Community," *American Sociological Review, 18* (August, 1953), 402.

[9] Robert J. Havighurst, "Social-Class Influences on American Education," in National Society for the Study of Education, Sixtieth Yearbook, part 2, *social Forces Influencing American Education,* University of Chicago Press, 1961, p. 121.

Havighurst's classifications and estimates are probably as good as any that can be made, but like the studies on which his estimates are based, his figures suggest clearcut lines between the various social classes. Actually even in small towns, informants were unable to agree on a category for a number of persons and families. In such cases, researchers admittedly classified such persons arbitrarily. Researchers stress the conclusion that lines drawn between social classes are not real and that individuals and families are often inconsistent in their adherence to the behavior patterns and other characteristics associated with the class to which they are assigned.

The dangers of generalizing the findings of studies made in towns and small cities to metropolitan areas should be evident, and not many studies have been made of big cities or of communities in the Far West. There may be many more than five or six recognizable classes in large urban centers. (Some informants thought there were eight to eleven or more even in smaller places.) It should be readily apparent, too, that no one community can nor does represent all the ramifications of the social-class system of the total population of the United States. Demographic studies show a larger percentage of lower socioeconomic groups in manufacturing and transportation centers; a larger percentage of white-collar workers in retail trade, public administrative, entertainment and recreation centers, and in college communities.[10] Many smaller cities have no upper class in a national sense. Common-sense observation reveals that lumbering towns and textile-mill villages have more people of lower-class status and fewer of middle-class than do trade centers in prosperous agricultural areas. Furthermore, American social structure is still in a state of flux. New occupations requiring special skill and knowledge are constantly emerging to attract workers from less skilled pursuits. To quote Lerner, "It may well be many years before one can formulate a coherent theory of power and class in America."[11] In the meantime let us not think of social class distinctions as real when they are only conceptual tools useful in analysis.

Let us not forget, too, that social class is not the sole determinant of one's status. The esteem that comes from a job well done, irrespective of what the job may be, and the respect that one earns as a father or mother, as a citizen, and as an honorable person of good repute are important factors in determining one's standing in his community. With these reservations in mind, we now move to a discussion of behavior patterns, values, attitudes, and motivations said to be associated with different social classes or life styles.

[10] Otis D. Duncan and Albert J. Reiss, Jr., *Social Characteristics of Urban and Rural Communities, 1950*, Wiley, 1956, pp. 272–273, 297, 338–342.
[11] Lerner, *op. cit.*, p. 473.

CHARACTERISTICS ATTRIBUTED
TO VARIOUS SOCIAL CLASSES

Despite justifiable doubts about crystallized class formations in the United States, the Lynds, Warner and associates, and other researchers have performed a valuable service in describing differing life styles within the American society.[12] Although specific cultural traits may and do vary over the years, understanding the patterns of thought and behavior found within the social class of a child's family and neighborhood is significant to a teacher. Obviously discrepancies exist between what specific individuals and families do, believe, and value and what may be commonly accepted activities and thoughtways within a given social class. There are many deviants from social-class norms. Factors such as schooling, individual differences, and influences of the mass media make the process of socialization within any group something less than thorough. Many families are characterized by what sociologists call status inconsistencies, that is, they occupy marginal positions between classes and, as a consequence, may inculcate in their children selected cultural traits assigned to more than one social class. The adherence to class characteristics is found to be closer in a homogeneous than in a heterogeneous neighborhood where ethnic origin, religion, and the like, in addition to class differentials, complicate social relationships. It should also be remembered that the line between classes adjacent in rank is blurred if it exists at all, and that the differences may be relatively small. Thus the intent of the following discussion of class characteristics is not to stereotype individuals; rather its purpose is to provide insight into climates of opinion common among certain subcommunity groups.

The Upper Class

Not very much is known about the characteristics and values of the upper class. What researchers mean by the term *upper class* is ambiguous. Persons labeled upper class in small cities and towns are usually in no sense upper class on the national scene. They may be, however, very influential, socially and economically, within a limited sphere. Researchers in small towns and cities in New England and in

[12] The studies by Robert S. Lynd and Helen Merrell Lynd, *Middletown*, Harcourt, Brace, 1929; and *Middletown in Transition*, Harcourt, Brace, 1937, were the first intensive studies of an American community. They describe the occupational, familial, educational, leisure-time, and community activities of a "business class" and a "working class."

the Deep South usually found that the local "aristocracy," who constituted only about 3 percent of the population, were divided into upper-upper and lower-upper classes on the basis of how long their pre-eminence as a family had lasted. Members of the upper classes of small cities, particularly along the eastern seaboard, are described as exceedingly proud of their lineage, eager for their offspring to marry within their own class and not disgrace the family name by being caught in illicit activities, conservative in taste, and not very active in community affairs except in behind-the-scene positions and philanthropic roles.

Members of the upper class are often cavalier in their attitudes toward matters of decorum and morality—the generally accepted customs of conduct and right living that prevail in this country. For this reason they are sometimes described as being more like the lower than the middle class. Their "moral" standards, notably in respect to extramarital relationships, are less rigid than those of the middle class. Friedenberg calls the "slum kid" the "last aristocrat" because he is arrogant, free and easy, expressive of his sexuality, and nonconforming. He believes that a talented boy from a slum would adjust more readily in an upper-class, private school than in a public school.[13] Perhaps the positions of those at the top and those at the bottom of the social structure are similar in respect to nonconformity: Neither group is striving to be accepted, the elite does not have to; the disadvantaged person does not feel he would be accepted if he did try.

Probably the elite of small cities are more conforming, however, than the elite of metropolitan areas, who comprise most of the upper class when judged in terms of national influence. Baltzell described members of Philadelphia's old upper class. He said they belong to a metropolitan elite that includes fashionable old families from San Francisco to Boston, Philadelphia, or Baltimore.[14] They are a business aristocracy composed mostly of bankers and lawyers, and their families were educated at private schools and ivy league colleges. They live in the same wealthy metropolitan suburbs, belong to the same clubs and the same churches (Episcopal in Philadelphia), patronize the arts, and isolate themselves from contact with the lower class. Some of these Philadelphians are now for the first time in decades becoming interested in politics.[15] In his study of men of power behind the scenes in

---

[13] Edgar Z. Friedenberg, "The Schools: An Unpopular View," *American Child*, 45 (May, 1963), 5–10.

[14] E. Digby Baltzell, *Philadelphia Gentlemen, The Making of a National Upper Class*, Free Press, 1958, p. 5.

[15] *Ibid.*, pp. 385–395.

national government and economic life, Floyd Hunter found a small number of men in metropolitan centers throughout the United States who knew each other, exchanged ideas, and decided upon policies that they then tried to put into effect.[16] Presumably some of these men may be classified as upper class. There are other elite groups—leaders in politics, military affairs, corporations, labor unions, churches, the opinion industry, artistic pursuits, and education, some of whom are expense-account wealthy "exurbanites." These individuals are men of power and prestige on the national scene but they are not members of the upper class, as usually defined, unless they have been born to that status. They may marry into the upper class and, if exceptionally talented, they may move into the upper class.

Upper-class values are of little direct concern to public schools because few children from the upper class attend public schools, but indirectly the sociopolitical views of this group are very important to public education because of the relative power and influence of many upper-class people. In general, the high-income group (the upper 10 percent), some of whom are upper class, tend to be conservative, to disapprove of strong labor unions, to resist extensions of governmental influence, and to support special-interest groups that promote their interests.

The Middle Class

Studies made in small towns usually find an upper- and a lower-middle class. The demarcation between the two tends to follow differences in income and occupation (professionals and more successful businessmen being placed in the top category and sales persons, office workers, a few skilled and semiskilled workers, and less successful businessmen in the bottom classification). Their values and life styles differ in degree rather than in kind. Since the lower-middle class more or less imitates the upper-middle class, a broad classification of middle class would perhaps reflect characteristics more typical of the upper-middle than of the lower-middle class. Among the activities and values commonly attributed to middle-class status are aspirations to respectability and conventionality in family life, moral outlook, and sex behavior. They are the "joiners," the workers for community welfare, the pillars of well-established religious groups. They see wealth and education as the means to mobility and they seek to acquire both. Because they are especially eager to maintain their status above the

[16] Floyd Hunter, *Top Leadership, U.S.A.*, University of North Carolina Press, 1959, chap. 8.

lower class, they discourage their children from cultivating friends among those less advantaged than themselves. Parents are devoted to their children and ambitious for them. In fact, they often compete through their children and are therefore excessively concerned with school affairs and cultural activities that are thought to be good for the children. They insist upon high standards of cleanliness, neatness, punctuality, dependability, and responsibility. In the home they also emphasize correct English, good grooming, etiquette and manners, and the social amenities. They teach their children to settle their differences without fighting. They encourage their children to defer present pleasures for future rewards, to value education, and to respect authority and the law. Family relationships, particularly toward the upper end of the class, tend to be equalitarian.

Membership in the middle class has undergone marked change during the last two or three decades. Historically the old middle class was composed of farmers who owned land, small businessmen, professionals, shopkeepers, and other tradesmen. The new middle classes are composed of clerical workers, technicians, managers, new professional groups, government bureaucrats, distributors, advertisers, and other relatively new white-collar vocational groups. Members of the old middle class have diminished in relative importance in respect to determining the middle-class life style. Many of the newcomers, upwardly mobile from the lower class, are said to value security and a good salary much more than did the independent, self-employed entrepreneurs of the old middle class. Numerous writers have painted a dim picture of middle-class life today. United by no bond other than the desire to maintain status, subscribing to different economic and political beliefs, living different life styles, losing relative positions on the income scale to union-organized workers, members of the new middle classes are described as anxious conformists. They are said to be excessively concerned about their personalities because they sell only their skills to the companies for which they work. They are the "yes-men" who mask their real feelings and thoughts in order to curry favor. This description is oversimplified, of course, because in fact, the middle class is the "pivot class" setting the tone of consumption and dominating the culture. People in this class are not the sources of power politically nor economically, but from among them have sprung some of the most creative talents in America. They share in varying degrees what has been called a *corporate morality*—the idea that humanitarianism is more important than property. Thus they serve as a cushion between the wealthy and the poor, siding with management more often than with labor, but sometimes lending support to the less privileged. In recent years the alleged conservatism of persons in the middle class, especially of well-educated members of middle-middle and upper-middle class groups, is open to question.

There is much vagueness about membership of the middle class because in large urban centers there are so many middle-class groups of differing life styles. Social class status in the metropolis cannot rest upon intimate associations. Although city dwellers defy the easy classifications, they fall into many subclasses that manifest in varying degrees some of the characteristics ascribed to the middle class.

The Working Class

The group of people called the working class in this discussion is usually called the upper-lower class, a term that conveys to most people and to them a stigma. Steadily employed blue-collar workmen in the United States do not identify with the lower class, or a proletariat, but rather with the middle class. The very small success of Communists in recruiting members among American workingmen is clear proof of their identification. In some respects characteristics of the working class and the lower-middle class are much alike. Many working-class people cherish respectability, conventional morality and sex behavior, family life, and such virtues as punctuality and acceptance of responsibility as much as do lower-middle class people. They are likely to be as ambitious for their children as those above them in social class. These similarities, which seem to be increasing, have led some writers to group the two classes together as Common Man Americans.

Despite these similarities, members of the working class and the lower-middle class are sufficiently different in other ways to justify separating them into two classes. Whereas the lower-middle class is composed of persons holding ill-paid, white-collar jobs, members of the working class have jobs in the manual trades in which they may earn more money than do those in petty white-collar jobs. Often they spend their earnings for different purposes than would persons in the lower-middle class.

Other differences also clearly set members of the working class apart from the middle class. They are almost always less well educated than those in higher classes. They tend to have a pragmatic orientation to education—they want to learn what they regard to be useful and practical. The value of education to them is that education helps one learn how to deal with "red tape," to get and hold desirable jobs, and to avoid problems related to signing contracts and the like. They are not usually interested in literature, the arts, and the social sciences, but they have great respect for modern science.[17]

Working-class parents do not approve of progressive education because its methods of child training conflict with those to which they subscribe. Their homes tend to be patriarchal with the father serving as disciplinarian. Although many of the differences between the middle-class and the working-class methods of child care seem to have disappeared in recent years, the stress upon child obedience remains in the working-class home. Physical punishment of the young is common in these homes. Children are also encouraged to resort to physical force in settling arguments rather than to exercise self-restraint and settle differences rationally. Children may have less continuous supervision and may roam the streets more at will than those in the middle class, but they are expected to obey their parents at home and their teachers at school.

Many working-class parents are ambitious for their children and want them to have a better education than they had, but these parents often lack the knowledge they need in order to guide young people socially and vocationally. Poorly educated themselves, they do not know how to provide cultural advantages for their children nor how to motivate their interests in academic areas. Until recent years, most families in the working class have usually lived close to a subsistence level. They have, therefore, not been accustomed to saving and making long-range plans for the education of their children. But there are exceptions among working-class families, and the number of students in college from this class is increasing steadily. Many teachers in public schools have their origin in the working class. The mobility of many working-class people into the middle classes is, in fact, one of the reasons for the lack of a feeling of class consciousness in this country.

Nevertheless, ambitious working-class children who aspire to middle-class status have to overcome a number of handicaps because many of the attitudes and social customs learned in working-class homes are inappropriate in middle-class groups. Their parents are antagonistic to "big shots" and usually not favorably disposed toward intellectuals. The relationships of their father and mother are less equalitarian than that of parents of middle-class children. People in the working class tend to be more hedonistic than those in the middle class; they spend freely when they have money. Their social interests are limited and few of them take an active role in community affairs except possibly in a church. Their leisure interests are likely to be confined to do-it-yourself projects, spectator and group sports, bowling, viewing television,

[17] Frank Riessman, *The Culturally Deprived Child*, Harper & Row, 1962, pp. 12–14.

church socials, and visits within their extended families. Males attend occasional stag parties in taverns, homes, and fraternal organizations.

Not all children from this class expect or want to move into the middle class. In some cases they may see their parents' life style as that which they prefer. In a number of ways it is indeed a comfortable way of life. It is noncompetitive, relaxed, equalitarian, and secure in its affectional relations within the extended family. The worries of working-class people are real (money to pay debts, illnesses, desertions, divorces), not the vague fears and pressures that haunt many in the middle class. Another significant characteristic in the life style of members of the working class is the so-called *ethic of reciprocity*—they give cheerfully of their time, money, and skills to one another without expecting repayment other than that some day others may do something for them.

The primary handicap that children who wish to remain in the working class may suffer is that they may fail to stay in school as long as they should. Many of them will not be able to find jobs with as little or little more education than their fathers had. Since automation is eliminating many skilled as well as semiskilled jobs, working-class youths need to attain considerable competence in technical skills to attain the financial security that their fathers now have. Moreover, automation is likely to reduce the hours in the work week. In this event, working-class pupils need to acquire skills and appreciations that help provide meaning in leisure pursuits. To become good citizens, they need also to develop greater concern than many of their fathers show for those less fortunate than themselves and for political and civic activities.

The Lower Class

Persons classified as lower-lower class are sometimes described as "not respectable," "poor white trash," "scum," or something else to indicate their lowly position. Lately, in an attempt to avoid the pejorative connotation, they have been called the "culturally deprived," the "underprivileged," or the "socially disadvantaged." They are indeed the unskilled, the unemployables, the poorly educated, the vagrants, the outcasts, and the unfortunates. If they must be labeled descriptively, the less offensive term is *socially disadvantaged* because it is neither disparaging in connotation nor inaccurate in denotation.[18] The War on Poverty is designed to improve the life style of the poor, most of whom are lower-lower class.

It is a mistake, however, to assume that all very poor people share

[18] The term *culturally deprived* is inaccurate because no one who lives in a human group is deprived of culture.

the beliefs and patterns of living prevailing among those of the lower-lower class. As already stated, occupation and income are not sole criteria for determining social class. Some persons who by definition are poverty-stricken are much like working-class or even middle-class people. The differences between values and practices of those in the working class and those in the lower-lower class are, in fact, differences in degree more often than differences in kind.

Like working-class people, lower-lower class people value the ethic of reciprocity, the security of a large extended family, and punishment as a means of controlling children. They also resent snobbery and believe that one should fight with his fists for his rights. Parents, too, especially if they are Negro, may value education for their children, but they usually do not know how to motivate their children's interests in school nor can they financially afford to provide books, trips, and other educative experiences for them.

In the lowest social group, homes are crowded not only with children but also with relatives. Family life is likely to be disorganized by frequent divorces, desertions, and common-law marriages. Promiscuity and prostitution are not uncommon; obscenity and profanity punctuate conversations. Children are treated like little adults. Children are frequently responsible for the care of brothers and sisters only a few years younger. Under such circumstances children are informed early in life in respect to marital relations, the exigencies of life, and economic realities. They often learn, "You'll work hard enough, but you won't get anywhere." They share with their parents a fatalistic outlook that causes them to attribute whatever happens to good or bad luck. Like their parents, they usually acquire a low self-image not only because they realize their parents are not respected but also because they themselves suffer personal indignities at the hands of others.

In such situations children escape the unhappiness and discord in their homes by joining their peers on the street. Acceptance by age-mates becomes of great importance to these young people because they find among them warmth, status, and gaiety that they cannot find at home or at school, as will be later elaborated.

Some lower-class boys join with other emotionally disturbed youth of the lower and working classes in illegal activities. Albert K. Cohen's hypothesis, in which he seeks to explain the subculture of the delinquent gang, is that the gang simply reverses middle-class values. The youths know what these values are from television, movies, schools, and other sources. They are so frustrated, Cohen believes, by their inability to meet middle-class standards that they react by slashing out at society. The psychologists call this defense mechanism *reaction formation;* that is, one does exactly the opposite of what one really wants to do. The delinquent regains his self-respect by proving that he does not want to be middle-class. The gang commits vandalism because the middle-class ethic respects private property; it fights because the dominant ethic says it shouldn't fight; it is irrational and hedonistic because the middle class values long-term planning, fore-thought, and thrift; it is nonutilitarian, stealing "for the hell of it," because the middle class disapproves of purposeless activity and makes theft a crime.[19] There are, of course, other theories of the causes for delinquency. Cohen's theory is of interest at this point because it implies that middle-class values not only produce respecta-ble young people but delinquent gangs as well.

Differences in motivations, values, social environments, and charac-teristic patterns of behavior of children from different social classes have significant implications to teachers. Although not many studies give clues as to why some children are deviants from the norms of their class, analyses of social-class influences upon children increase our insight into the complexities of human behavior in the classroom.

Notwithstanding the usefulness of such studies, social status is by no means the only variable that influences behavior. Whether the family lives in a rural or urban neighborhood is another factor; its religion is another; and the degree of discrimination to which a person is exposed still another. Persons of color—Indian, Mexican American, Puerto Rican, and Negro—are found in disproportionate numbers to whites in the lower-lower class. The attitudes and values of minority groups are also shaped by family systems that deviate from the norms assumed to be prevalent in the social classes. The lower-class Negro family, for example, differs considerably from the lower-class white family or the Mexican American family.

SOCIAL-CLASS DIFFERENCES
AND SCHOOLS

The fluidity of the open-class system in the United States is pre-sumably maintained largely through the ready access of all to educa-tional opportunity. The chief avenues to social mobility lie in possess-ing outstanding talent, appearance, or superior education. Since many persons are neither physically attractive nor talented to a conspicuous degree, they must turn to education as the means by which they may rise in status. Since education is so important to mobility, many people are indignant when they hear that members of the lower classes do not, in fact, find equality of opportunity in American schools.

[19] Albert K. Cohen, *Delinquent Boys,* Free Press, 1955, pp. 121–137.

Schools in this country are described as middle-class institutions since the value system of the school culture is that of the middle class. Public school teachers are usually middle-class in orientation even if their class of origin was not middle class. The stress given to middle-class values is reasonable because these are the dominant values in American society and because many parents from the lower classes expect the schools to prepare their children for mobility. Despite such justification of common school practices, the lower-class child is disadvantaged in competing within a school culture that upholds values and patterns of behavior that conflict with those he has learned at home. He is handicapped by the cultural limitations of his home environment, economic hardships, and the low social position of his parents.

Socioeconomic Differences and Educational Statistics

The relationship of socioeconomic level, determined by occupation and income, and certain statistics in education is well established. Alfred Binet, the father of mental tests, recognized differences related to social backgrounds in the test scores made by children. In 1916 Terman wrote that children of the "superior social class" scored 14 points higher on the average than did those of the "inferior social class."[20] Allison Davis pointed out that tests of mental ability do not accurately measure the Intelligence Quotients of children from lower-class homes because the tests are culture-laden in a way favoring middle-class children.[21] Although overlaps of individual scores exist among socioeconomic levels, the averages of the upper classes are higher than the average of the lower classes. There is still controversy about why these differences exist and just what the tests actually measure. It is generally agreed, however, that although the tests measure achievement as well as aptitude, they do not measure innate ability, and that they are useful, taken in conjunction with other evidence, in predicting scholastic success. In line with such predictions and perhaps partly because of them, children from the lower classes tend to make lower grades and earn lower scores on tests of achievement than do those from the upper classes.

The number of pupils who drop out of school before they graduate from high school is related to their socioeconomic level. Pupils whose

[20] Lewis M. Terman, *The Measurement of Intelligence*, Houghton Mifflin, 1916, chap. 5.

[21] Allison Davis, *Social Class Influences Upon Learning*, Harvard University Press, 1948, pp. 46–88.

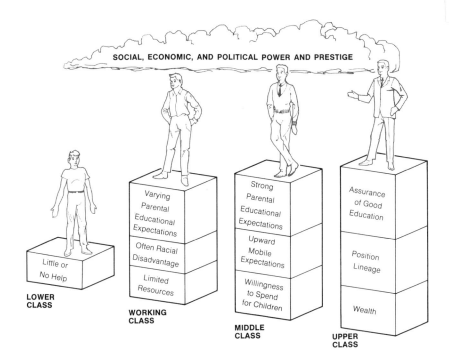

SOCIAL, ECONOMIC, AND POLITICAL POWER AND PRESTIGE

Little or No Help

LOWER CLASS

Varying Parental Educational Expectations

Often Racial Disadvantage

Limited Resources

WORKING CLASS

Strong Parental Educational Expectations

Upward Mobile Expectations

Willingness to Spend for Children

MIDDLE CLASS

Assurance of Good Education

Position Lineage

Wealth

UPPER CLASS

parents are wage earners or unemployed are more likely to drop out of school than are children whose parents earn larger and more stable incomes. Children from less-privileged homes are more frequently absent from school, more often sick, and less active in cocurricular activities than are middle-class children. The educational and occupational aspirations of children from the lower classes are also generally low.

It is significant, however, that the number of school dropouts has been reduced in recent years, that the median grade level of American adults is rising, and that the number of young people from the lower classes in college is increasing. Havighurst estimates that between 1940 and 1960 the percentage of college entrants from the lower-lower class increased from 0 to 10 percent, of those from the upper-lower class increased from 5 to 25 percent, of those from the lower-middle class increased from 20 to 55 percent, and of those from the upper and upper-middle class from 80 to 85 percent.[22]

This trend is likely to continue because a technological society cannot meet its occupational need without a greater number of highly trained people than were formerly needed. Until this century, schools

[22] Havighurst, *op. cit.*, p. 123.

tended to perpetuate social-class lines by educating few from the lower classes beyond a minimal level. But, as Burton Clark points out, the role of the school and of the college in promoting social mobility grows when education becomes available to all and when technical competence is in great demand.[23] The poor, able working-class boy with access to government loans and scholarships can and does succeed via the community college and the state university. Nevertheless, his chances of doing so are less than those of a middle-class child.

Comparative Educational Advantages

In the following discussion, the contrasts are more nearly descriptive of children of the upper-middle and those of the lower class than they are of children of "common man" groups. We are talking, therefore, chiefly of pupils in schools like those in wealthy suburbia and in the slums, or of the coteries of upper-middle class and lower-class pupils in comprehensive schools. Pupils of the lower-middle and working classes lie between these extremes.

When children from lower-class homes enter the first grade, their troubles in school begin. Unless they have lived in communities that have had Head Start programs, they are not likely to have had pre-school experiences. Because they have not been read to, talked to, nor had experiences in their homes that help develop concepts, they are usually not ready to learn to read. They may be unable to distinguish between sounds, particularly "b" and "p." They are likely to demonstrate what Bereiter and Engleman call the "giant word syndrome"— rather than learning individual words, they catch the main sounds of common phrases.[24] As a result, they cannot break phrases into words and use them in new sentences.

Children from disadvantaged homes are handicapped in their school work by their lack of the kinds of experiences middle-class children commonly have with ideas and language presented in picture books, stories, and trips to interesting places. A third-grade teacher after showing her class a picture of a lion in a jungle asked her pupils to tell a story about the picture.

Charlie said, "The lion lives in the jungle. She is laying a egg."

Bertha said, "The lion is crawling on the tree. The lion's name is Penny. He is a mother lion."

As they grow older, differences between disadvantaged children and

[23] Burton R. Clark, *Educating the Expert Society*, Chandler, 1962, pp. 75–79.
[24] Carl Bereiter and Siegfried Engleman, *Teaching Disadvantaged Children in the Pre-School*, Prentice-Hall, 1966, p. 34.

the more privileged groups increase. They have learned to communicate in the "public language" of their home and neighborhood rather than in the formal language of the school. They cannot understand a teacher, Bernstein says, who uses a different language. The disadvantaged child understands "Shut up!" but not "I'd rather you made less noise." According to Bernstein, his language is a form of condensed and abbreviated speech that "encourages an immediacy of interaction, a preference for the descriptive rather than the analytic, a linguistic form such that what is *not* said is equally and more important than what is said." His curiosity has been curbed by parents who refuse to answer "why" questions, and his capacity for rational thinking delayed by categorical statements ("Because I tell you") of his parents.[25]

Retarded linguistic development is perhaps the most serious handicap for a disadvantaged child in school, although he has others. He has not learned to concentrate; he has, in fact, learned in his noisy, crowded home to shut out sounds. Hence he has difficulty listening to a teacher, especially when she talks too much. Also, he has no place to study at home. Faced with a choice between studying and watching television in the same room with his family, he usually chooses TV. Deutsch found that the tasks that the disadvantaged child performed at home tended to be motoric, concrete, and of short duration.[26] Thus he is not prepared at home for verbal, abstract learning that extends over a relatively long period of time. He is likely to be a slow learner. If a very bright child can overcome all these handicaps, he still may not want to do well in school. Loyalty to his peers, who may regard the good student as a traitor, may preclude his attempting to excel in school work.

The seeming inability to postpone present pleasures for future rewards is another serious handicap of disadvantaged children, and of many working-class children. Although researchers have found somewhat conflicting evidence, the weight of such evidence shows a social-class relationship between deferred gratifications of needs (such as affiliation, sex, independence, material possession, aggression) and the need to achieve.[27] Perucci suggests that upper-strata youths who do not have a great need to achieve may nevertheless achieve because

[25] Basil Bernstein, "Social Class and Linguistic Development: A Theory of Social Learning," in A. H. Halsey *et al.*, *Education, Economy, and Society*, Free Press, 1961, pp. 293, 300.

[26] Martin Deutsch, *Minority Group and Class Status as Related to Social and Personality Factors in Scholastic Achievement*, Monograph No. 2, Society for Applied Anthropology, 1960, p. 28.

[27] See summary of research in Robert Perucci, "Education, Stratification, and Mobility," in Donald A. Hansen and Joel E. Gerstl, *On Education—Sociological Perspectives*, Wiley, 1967.

their "general way of life" makes decisions for them concerning high school graduation and entering college.[28] Kahl points out that their trust of people smooths their way socially and their faith in their future encourages them to plan.[29] To succeed in school the lower-class youth, however, has to make independent decisions and develop social relationships and habits of planning foreign to his subculture.

Why do some children develop the need to achieve whereas others do not? McClelland found a high relationship between the need to achieve and "parents' high standards of achievement, warmth and encouragement, and a father who is not domineering and authoritarian."[30] These conditions are fairly common in middle-class homes. None of them is common in lower-lower class homes. Yet an increasing number of young people from disadvantaged as well as working-class homes do demonstrate the need to achieve and are graduating from high school and attending college.

Joseph A. Kahl tried to find the answer to why some intelligent "common man" boys are more ambitious educationally and occupationally than others. By interviewing the boys and their fathers, he decided that a core value in the homes of the ambitious boys was "getting ahead," whereas a core value in the homes of the boys who were not ambitious was "getting by." The fathers of ambitious sons usually were not satisfied with their own progress and blamed their inadequate educations for their lack of success. The fathers of less ambitious boys seemed resigned to their lot. The boys who planned to go to college but who came from homes that had not encouraged them to go had been influenced by friends. Kahl states that at the time an intelligent boy reaches the seventh grade he makes his initial choice as to whether or not he will do well academically.[31] (A survey by the College Entrance Examination Board also found the seventh grade to be the year when most pupils decide to go to college.)

A more recent study of California high school boys found that the ethos of the school is important to the aspirations of members of the student body. More middle-class boys go to college if they have attended predominantly middle-class schools than they do if they have attended predominantly working-class schools. Working-class boys tend to have higher aspirations when the ethos of their school is

[28] *Ibid.*, p. 132.
[29] Joseph A. Kahl, "Some Measurements of Achievement Orientation," *American Journal of Sociology*, 70 (May, 1965), 677.
[30] David C. McClelland, *The Roots of Consciousness*, Van Nostrand, 1964, p. 39.
[31] Joseph A. Kahl, "Educational and Occupational Aspirations of 'Common Man' Boys," *Harvard Educational Review*, 23 (Summer, 1953), 186–203.

middle-class than when it is working-class.[32] They are more likely to plan for college if they have college-oriented friends and are active in school activities than otherwise.[33]

Other researchers have found that upwardly mobile young people are likely to have mothers who are better educated than their fathers.[34] Since most women in the lower class, however, are likely to have attended school longer than their husbands, some other factor such as dissatisfaction with her mate's job or her own white-collar job must be operative in such cases. Still other researchers have found that adults outside the family, particularly high school teachers, were very influential in raising the level of aspirations of lower-class pupils.[35]

Low self-concept is a final serious handicap to academic success of disadvantaged children. Brookover and Gottlieb cite research that shows a relationship between pupils' generalized self-concepts and their achievement in school. The studies also revealed that the self-concepts of individuals varied by subject matter areas. In other words, a pupil is likely to get a better grade if he thinks he can. Whether he thinks he can is dependent, in part, upon what he thinks "significant others"—mother, father, teacher, and peers—think of his ability.[36] The self-concept of the disadvantaged lower-class child in respect to his academic aptitude is likely to be low. In addition to his frequent failures, the attitudes toward him of his teachers, not to mention his parents, confirm his low assessment of his talents. His peers are unlikely to encourage him to see himself as capable of good school work.

The obstacles to learning that the disadvantaged child brings to school with him are compounded by further obstacles that he meets in the school environment. On the other hand, the middle-class pupil, who experiences few obstacles to learning in his social environment usually finds it relatively easy to adjust to the school's subculture. He

---

[32] Alan B. Wilson, "Residential Segregation of Social Classes and Aspirations of High School Boys," *American Sociological Review*, 24 (December, 1959), 836–845.

[33] Robert A. Ellis and W. Clayton Lane, "Structural Supports for Upward Mobility," *American Sociological Review*, 28 (October, 1963), 754–755.

[34] Seymour Martin Lipset and Reinhard Bendix, *Social Mobility in Industrial Society*, University of California Press, 1960, pp. 238, 249–250; Fred L. Stodtbeck, "Family Interaction, Values, and Achievement," in David C. McClelland, ed., *Talent and Society*, Van Nostrand, 1958, pp. 181–184, 189–191; W. Lloyd Warner and James C. Abegglen, *Big Business Leaders in America*, Atheneum, 1955, pp. 77–78.

[35] Ellis and Lane, *op. cit.*, pp. 750–751, 754.

[36] For summary of research see Wilbur B. Brookover and David Gottlieb, *A Sociology of Education*, 2nd ed., American Book, 1964, pp. 468–480; and Ruth C. Wylie, *The Self Concept: A Critical Survey of Pertinent Research Literature*, University of Nebraska Press, 1961.

may, of course, have psychological problems, limited academic aptitude, and difficulties in learning and in winning social acceptance, but his problems seldom arise out of a conflict between social-class values and practices in home and school.

Differential Opportunities in Schools

The comprehensive public school is praised by advocates on the grounds that it provides curriculums designed to meet the needs of all pupils and reduces differences among social classes because rich and poor "rub elbows" in the same academic classes in school. In many comprehensive schools such claims cannot be substantiated. The University of Pittsburgh's Project Talent survey revealed that in 1960, 54 percent of the high schools had homogeneous grouping. The practice is also common in elementary schools. Grouping pupils homogeneously according to academic ability confers high status to those in the "bright" and "gifted" sections. In 1960, 49 percent of the high schools, according to findings of Project Talent, used a system of tracking. Assigning pupils to college-preparatory, general, and commercial courses tends to relegate those who are not taking courses designed for college entrance to inferior status. Tracking and homogeneous grouping have the effect, in general, of separating children from middle-class homes and those from lower-class homes. The best grades usually go to children from middle-class homes. Leadership positions in the cocurriculum tend to be held by the same children. Hence children from lower-class homes feel that the school brands them as "inferior."

In many ways teachers seem to tell children that all work is honorable but that some types of work are more honorable than others. The public school curriculum is geared largely to white-collar jobs. Individuals invited to visit schools as resource persons are usually professionals and businessmen, not blue-collar workers. A study of "community helpers" at a conceptual level appropriate to primary grades is common, but upper elementary children and high school pupils seldom learn about the work of mechanics, technicians, service workers, or semiprofessionals. Elementary school reading texts portray white-collar workers and their homes. As a consequence, children inadvertently learn that blue-collar jobs in which their parents work are not very desirable and that the school is not really interested in helping pupils prepare for such jobs. The general curriculum, a hodgepodge of classes, to which many youths of the lower classes are assigned, seems to them to offer little of value vocationally.

Many young people from the lower classes feel that they are not learning anything worth learning. They may also feel left out of the social life of the school. Early researchers, such as Hollingshead in Elmtown, found that middle-class boys and girls dominated the cocurricular activities and that the chief reason young people from the lower classes dropped out of school was that they felt they did not belong. This situation still exists in most comprehensive schools, but in some schools what sociologists call "status upsets" have occurred. A recent study of ten Illinois high schools found that the social structure at Elmtown, one of the schools studied, had changed. The researcher learned that the leading cliques among the junior and senior girls were predominantly working-class girls and that the leading boys' cliques in high schools were even less influenced by social class than were the girls' cliques.[37]

The preeminence of the middle class in the school's social life may change for several reasons. In smaller schools weak leadership in the middle class may be superseded by strong leadership in the working class. Continued prosperity that enables working-class parents to buy good clothes and other symbols of adolescent status may induce changes in the school status system. The school faculty may influence status upsets through its use of rewards, but the marked increase in the number of children from working-class and lower-class homes going to high school and college probably has the most effect.

Early researchers found that children in eastern and midwestern schools chose their friends largely from among children in their own social class.[38] In California researchers arrived at different conclusions. They found that social-class membership had very little influence upon children's choices of friends.[39] Another study of adolescents in Ohio confirmed the California findings.[40] A reasonable conclusion is that the influence of family background in determining the social acceptability of children in comprehensive schools may vary from place to place.

Comprehensive schools, however, are more likely to be found in towns, small cities, and rural areas than in large cities. In cities, elementary schools and, to a lesser extent, high schools are likely to draw pupils from a limited range of social classes. In such schools, Coleman concluded, the importance of family background in the

[37] James S. Coleman, *The Adolescent Society,* Free Press, 1961, pp. 200–205.

[38] Bernice L. Neugarten, "The Democracy of Childhood," in W. Lloyd Warner *et al., Democracy in Jonesville,* Harper & Row, 1949, chap. 5; and August B. Hollingshead, *Elmtown's Youth,* Wiley, 1949, p. 212.

[39] S. Stansfelt Sargent, "Class and Class Consciousness in a California Town," *Social Problems, 1* (June, 1953), 22–27.

[40] Harold R. Phelps and John E. Horrocks, "Factors Influencing Informal Groups of Adolescents," *Child Development,* 29 (March, 1958), 69–86.

school's status system is related to the number of upper-middle class children in the school.

In metropolitan schools, differences in educational opportunity are likely to be greater between schools enrolling children of the middle class and those enrolling children of the lower classes than are differences within a particular school. These inequalities will be discussed in detail in Chapter 11. At this point only the most commonly mentioned differences in opportunity will be noted. Schools in middle-class neighborhoods are more likely to offer curriculums in line with pupil needs, to have adequate facilities, counselors, and experienced teachers, and to spend more for education than are schools in lower-class neighborhoods. Teachers in middle-class schools are more likely to understand the behavior of their pupils and to achieve friendly and cooperative relationships with them than are their counterparts in slum schools.

Hopefully someday such differences will be erased. Since the mid-sixties, funds from the federal government have been disbursed to help the poor, to encourage research in learning problems of disadvantaged children and in methods of teaching, and to provide financial support for programs designed to upgrade education, particularly of disadvantaged children. It is still too early to assess results of these efforts.

SUMMARY

Several tentative conclusions about the influence of family background upon the social system within a school may be drawn. First, middle-class children have an initial advantage in acquiring status with their peers and teachers because they usually can succeed academically with less difficulty, have better clothes, and have more opportunity to develop their personalities. Second the social advantages to children of family status varies with locality. Social class is more important in schools located in New England and the South than it is in the Far West, in older small cities and towns than in newly established places, and in schools with large upper-middle class enrollments than in schools where the student body is largely working-class in origin. Third, status upsets are more common than they once were. And fourth, although the social system in the comprehensive school usually tends to follow socioeconomic lines, deviations can and do occur. The extent to which undesirable social distinctions exist in a school depends upon the school culture, the community and regional cultures, and upon the quality of faculty leadership.

In large city schools where pupils are segregated largely by the socioeconomic differences among their parents, the influence of social class may be more pernicious than it is in the comprehensive schools.

Such segregation is dangerous because it tends to reduce social mobility of the lower classes and to encourage a rigid system of stratification. To a considerable extent, segregation of the disadvantaged has deprived them of equal opportunity because their schools have been found to be inferior in many ways.

An awareness of such inequities has motivated many persons to castigate teachers, school board members, or parents. Finding a scapegoat is not, however, a very enlightened approach to improving conditions. Nor is the reaction of college students who see evil in the whole system of stratification. In truth, a social system is dysfunctional if it permits some of its members, especially children, to suffer. Notwithstanding the frequent perpetuation of intellectual and social deadwood at the top, social stratification in a society as complex as that of the United States is not only inevitable but also desirable from the point of view of encouraging talent. Even if the abolition of social classes were desirable, it is not in the school's power to make such changes. All that school administrators and teachers can do is provide equality of opportunity at school for all children. Recognizing that the school has failed to do so is the first step toward mitigating the inequalities that exist.

IMPORTANT CONCEPTS

Cocurriculum. School-sponsored student activities, or extracurricular activities, that are distinct from, but supportive of, the academic curriculum.

Ethic of reciprocity. See p. 55.

Ethnic origin. Of a particular racial or cultural group such as Afro-American or Italian.

Hedonistic. Characterized by the attitude that the pursuit of pleasure is the chief aim of life.

Homogeneous grouping. A grouping of students who display seemingly similar characteristics such as academic ability. See p. 64.

Social class. See p. 45 ff. for a full definition of this hard-to-define term.

Status inconsistencies. A concept suggesting that the behavior of most people, especially those in marginal positions, often differs from that of other members of the class to which they have been assigned. See p. 65 for discussion.

Status upset. A group or an individual supplants another group or another individual in high position.

Stratification. As used in social science, the horizontal division of society into fairly definite and identifiable layers, such as class. See pp. 44–45.

Tracking. The assignment of students to a course of study, such as academic or vocational, which is presumably appropriate to the students' needs, interests, and aptitudes.

4. THE DEMOCRATIC SOCIETY AND THE SCHOOLS

Tell it like it is, man!

Throughout our history as a nation, teachers have tried to strengthen national unity and an acceptance of democratic traditions by Americanizing the children of immigrants and transmitting to the young a common heritage. They have attempted to inculcate a respect for law and authority, a concern for the well-being of others, and a feeling of personal responsibility for political decisions. Until this century, however, the methods used included reading didactic stories of American patriots, memorizing patriotic maxims ("Give me liberty or give me death"), using rituals (the flag salute), and studying the structure of American governments. Many teachers still use such methods.

In recent decades, however, the school's task of educating children to live in a democratic society is being interpreted differently. John

Dewey and his followers have urged that schools should provide *experiences* in democratic living. They say that schools must offer direct participation in democratic activities since such participation is no longer available to most pupils outside of school. Such demands prompt such questions as "What is democracy? Do democratic people hold certain values or have certain characteristics that differ from those of nondemocratic people? What is democratic behavior? What kinds of school experiences help pupils learn to behave democratically?

In the first part of this chapter, democracy and democratic ideals are discussed; in the second part, the role of the school in a democratic society is considered; and in the third part, the effectiveness of the school in teaching pupils how to live in a democratic society is explored.

CHARACTERISTICS OF A DEMOCRATIC SOCIETY

Becker says, "Democracy is a word that connotes different things to different people, a kind of conceptual Gladstone bag which, with a little manipulation, can be made to accommodate almost any collection

of social facts we may wish to carry in it."[1] Democracy then is a
"slippery and abstract" term often used by Communists to describe the
governments of nations that by American standards are undemocratic.

Just what then is an American definition of democracy? Robert A.
Dahl, a political scientist, says, "But at a minimum, it seems to me,
democratic theory is concerned with processes by which ordinary
citizens exert a relatively high degree of control over leaders; this is a
minimal definition that can be easily translated into a variety of more
or less equivalent statements, should the reader not care for the
particular language I choose to use."[2] He thinks that the essential
differences between democracy and dictatorship are that, unlike dicta-
tors, democratic leaders are subject to election or defeat by voters and
that political parties and their leaders must compete continuously for
popular support.[3]

In the United States democracy works, Dahl says, because "our
society is essentially democratic." What does this statement mean?
Anyone reading this statement out of context is likely to interpret it
according to his own political philosophy. If he accepts a normative
theory of democracy, he may assume that Dahl means Americans
accept democratic values. If he accepts an empirical theory of democracy, he may assume that Dahl means that the political elite who
influence the course of government tend to behave democratically. If
he is a cynical Negro, he may simply say, "Not so." The next two
sections will attempt to clarify these points of view.

The Normative Theory of Democracy

A normative theory is an expression of the ideals, expectations, and
standards that a group is said to hold. Weldon says of the writers of
our Constitution, "They needed a democratic Constitution because
they were democratically minded men; they did not become democratically minded because they adopted that kind of Constitution."[4]
Until recently political philosophers assumed that citizens of a democratic society shared certain political standards of right and wrong.

The assumption that citizens in a democratic society tend to hold
certain basic values in common can be traced in American writings
from Jefferson's words in the Declaration of Independence ("We hold
these truths to be self-evident . . .") to recent books by Hallowell,

[1] Carl Becker, *Modern Democracy*, Yale University Press, 1941, p. 4.
[2] Robert A. Dahl, *A Preface to Democratic Theory*, University of Chicago Press,
1956, p. 3.
[3] *Ibid.*, pp. 131–132.
[4] Thomas Dewar Weldon, *States and Morals*, McGraw-Hill, 1947, p. 188.

Walter Lippmann, Schumpeter, and others[5] who believe the "bulk" or at least the leaders of such a society must value liberty and equality highly if democracy survives. Our early statesmen's beliefs are reflected in the language of the Declaration of Independence and in the Constitution. Tyranny, they believed, severely deprived a citizen of his "natural rights." They did not, however, agree precisely on which "rights" were "natural rights." Nevertheless, historically the case for political equality and popular sovereignty has usually been deduced from beliefs in "natural rights."

In addition to the centuries-old faith in "natural rights," American democratic ideals are rooted in our heritage: the Greeks' reliance on reason; the Judeo-Christian ethic of concern for others, the Protestant congregation's acceptance of discussion as the means, with God's help, whereby truth may be found; the Enlightenment's concern for individualism and rational thinking, its doctrine of the dignity and perfectibility of man, and its optimistic belief in progress.

The concept of "natural rights," which endows the individual with "inalienable rights," provided the moral justification for freedom. It is an old idea. The Stoic philosophers, Cicero, and the medieval Christian philosophers maintained that the state must limit its power in accord with certain eternal principles of right and justice. The seventeenth- and eighteenth-century philosophers believed that the universe operated under fixed laws of nature, laws that man could fathom through the use of reason.[6] The English, after centuries of struggle, translated their concept of the natural rights of man into the first really effective constitutional government. Thomas Jefferson used the same concept in justifying the American Revolution.

Most early democratic theorists, European and American, emphasized the search for the natural law or moral law, i.e., God's Will, in man's deliberations, but they did not exclude worldly knowledge and experience. On the contrary, in the tradition of the Greeks, they put great stress upon the use of reason in finding the "higher law." In the United States today the moral law is still appealed to by States' Righters, Black leaders in their fight for equality, Supreme Court justices, and any citizen who feels free to ignore a law that he believes to be unjust. It is thus apparent that a presupposition of classic democratic theory is that man is a moral being with a conscience.

Americans "naturalized" the concepts they borrowed from the mainstream of Western thought and added their own interpretations.

[5] See John H. Hallowell, *The Moral Foundation of Democracy*, University of Chicago Press, 1954; Walter Lippmann, *Essays in Public Philosophy*, Little, Brown, 1955, p. 100; and Joseph A. Schumpeter, *Capitalism, Socialism, and Democracy*, Harper & Row, 1950, p. 296.

[6] See Becker, *op. cit.*, pp. 19–27 for a discussion of the Enlightenment world view.

During the pioneer period individualism evolved into something different from that cherished by men of the Enlightenment. American individualism came to allow for more experimentation. Americans believed that man's lot could be improved; the future was bright. Lacking a feudal past with established privileged orders and an autocratic government or church, they exercised a freedom that encouraged the exaltation of popular democracy. They contended not only that government should be limited in its powers but also that people should have a say in how the government is run.[7] Like Colonel Rainboro, one of Cromwell's officers who supported manhood suffrage by saying, "Really I think the poorest he that is in England hath a life to live as the richest he," most Americans believe that a man, whatever his limitations, has the right to direct his own life.

In 1958 Clyde Kluckhohn, an anthropologist, concluded that democratic ideals have been "remarkably stable" since the eighteenth century and despite some changes have remained "highly influential in the life of the United States."[8] In 1964 Herbert McClosky, a political scientist, said the tenets of liberal democracy form "an integrated body of ideas which has become part of the American inheritance." Liberal democracy, he pointed out, includes agreement on

> such concepts as consent, accountability, limited or constitutional government, representation, majority rule, minority rights, the principle of political opposition, freedom of thought, speech, press, and assembly, equality of opportunity, religious toleration, equality before the law, the rights of juridical defense, and individual self-determination over a broad range of personal affairs.[9]

Without a doubt Americans accept the legitimacy of government in the United States and, as several polls indicate, they value as principles the concepts of freedom and equality.

Empirical Theory of Democracy

Despite such apparent consensus, political scientists have become increasingly skeptical of the universality of democratic beliefs among

[7] See Henry Steele Commager, *The American Mind,* Yale University Press, 1952, pp. 26–30 for a discussion of how Americans "naturalized" foreign philosophies.

[8] Clyde Kluckhohn, "Have There Been Discernible Shifts in American Values During the Past Generation," in Elting Elmore Morison, ed., *The American Style: Essays in Value and Performance,* Harper & Row, 1958, pp. 145–217.

[9] Herbert McClosky, "Consensus and Ideology in American Politics," *American Political Science Review,* 58 (June, 1964), 362–363.

Americans. They think a man reflects his real beliefs better when he says what he thinks ought to be done in a specific instance than when he says he believes in "democracy," "freedom," and "equality." In other words, deeds not words are the best indicators of what people really believe. Prothro and Grigg, attempting to measure consensus with respect to democratic beliefs, decided that the most essential principles in a democracy are majority rule and minority rights. At the abstract level, they found that 94.7 to 98.0 percent of the voters in two communities endorsed the general ideas of democracy, majority rule and minority rights. But their responses to over half of the specific statements designed to embody democratic principles (for example, "If a person wanted to make a speech in this city against churches and religion, he should be allowed to speak.") came closer to disagreement than to consensus. The more highly educated the respondent, the more likely he was to choose responses in line with democratic ideals. Prothro and Grigg concluded that Carl J. Friedrich "appears to have been correct in asserting . . . that democracy depends on habitual patterns of behavior rather than on conscious agreement on 'democratic principles.' "[10] Other political scientists, such as Dahl and V. O. Key, have stated that the stability of democracy may depend more upon the values of the politically active than upon the values of the masses.

McClosky also found that political "influentials" support the "rules of the game" (free speech, free press, equality, political toleration, and procedural rights of the accused) to a greater extent than do the general electorate. In other words, those interested and active in politics are the carriers of the democratic creed. But even among this elite group, disagreements are common. Many members of the influentials are more consistent in their support of the principles of "freedom" than of that of "equality." They not only doubt that men are in fact equal but also they doubt whether men should be regarded as equal. Many influentials seem unable to reconcile their belief in democracy (equalitarianism) and their belief in capitalism (inequalitarianism). No doubt their reactions are further complicated by the several facets of the concept of equality: political (universal suffrage), legal (rights under the law), economic (distribution of property and economic opportunities), and moral (treatment of man as an end and not a means).[11]

[10] James W. Prothro and Charles M. Grigg, "Fundamental Principles of Democracy: Bases for Agreement and Disagreement," *Journal of Politics*, 22 (May, 1960), 282–288, 294.
[11] McClosky, *op. cit.*, pp. 367–368.

Empirical political scientists are examining aspects of democracy other than political beliefs. They are questioning how our government really works. Not by majority rule, Dahl points out, but by rule of a combination of minorities (minorities' rule). In a pluralistic society various special-interest groups that might be called "polyarchies" strike bargains, appease one another, or neutralize one another's influence. Any policy decision made by politicians is likely to have been influenced by some group. To the apathetic masses, rule by "polyarchies" is less frustrating than dictatorship because many points of view are represented, but it is not popular sovereignty in the sense that all points of view are equally represented. Some groups have more control over the decision-making process than do other groups, but all have to be appeased. Nevertheless, Dahl contends "all the active and legitimate groups in the population can make themselves heard at some critical state in the process of decision."[12] Negroes have only recently become a group recognized as legitimate; Communists are still not a legitimate group.

Normative vs. Empirical Theory

Many political scientists accuse teachers of transmitting normative theory, sometimes called "myth," rather than teaching pupils the realities of political life, sometimes called the "real world." In other words, they say that teachers are preparing pupils for a never-never land, which they soon learn does not exist. Their reaction is one of disillusionment and cynicism about so-called democratic processes.

What is the crux of this argument against "classical" democratic theory? According to a common American interpretation, "classical" democratic theory contained the doctrine of popular sovereignty. That is, the people ruled in the manner of a New England town meeting at which policy was decided after lengthy and informed discussions. The power of government officials was limited to give each citizen the widest possible freedom. Critics point out that such an idealized view of democracy is not only unrealistic in modern America but also assumes that man has "natural rights." Such an assumption requires a transcendental, or supernatural view, which is logically indefensible.

Not all political scientists agree that popular democracy is irrational or that the concept lacks meaning in modern society. Thorson, for example, points out that "No one man, no group, whether majority or minority, is ever justified in claiming a right to make decisions for the whole society on the grounds that it knows what the 'right' decisions

[12] Dahl, *op. cit.*, pp. 125–151.

are."[13] One who recognizes human fallibility accepts an ethic of tolerance. If even the wisest men are not always right, then to be democratic a man must tolerate differences of opinion and allow all men to express their opinions. He will also accept change because he knows that a decision made is not necessarily the best decision. Acceptance of majority rule is simply a rational choice, because as Abraham Lincoln said, "Unanimity is impossible; the rule of a minority as a permanent arrangement, is wholly inadmissible; so that, rejecting the majority principle, anarchy or despotism in some form is all that is left."

Robert Dahl also rejects the notion that political equality is a "stupid goal." Accused of subscribing to an elitist theory of democracy because he reported that polyarchies rule in this country, Dahl replied that he was attempting to "explain" not to "prescribe." He also said, "If democracy is one of our goals and if polyarchy is a process for approximating that goal, it follows that we must also value polyarchy as a means," and "I should like to see much higher rates of political activity, particularly among some segments of the population whose participation has been the lowest."[14] Bailey concludes his essay on the role of Congress with the words "to keep us all free."[15] And so he expresses a value judgment about the purpose of the American government.

Political behavioralists are, however, skeptical of what *ought to be*. They repudiate historical research and scorn political philosophers who discuss normative theory. They concentrate their research on *what is*. If they discuss curriculum in public schools, they are likely to decry the unrealities being taught children. A reasonable conclusion is that they are both right and wrong in their judgments.

Such critics are right when they assert that pupils should understand the realities of political life. Without knowledge of political processes, including the bargaining and appeasement of interest groups within polyarchies, they cannot function effectively as citizens in a pluralistic society. Such knowledge need not lead to cynicism. McClosky found, in fact, that those active in politics, those who clearly knew much about the workings of the body politic, were less cynical than were the masses of people.[16]

[13] Thomas Landon Thorson, *The Logic of Democracy,* Holt, Rinehart and Winston, 1962, p. 139.

[14] Robert A. Dahl, "Further Reflections on 'The Elitist Theory of Democracy,'" *American Political Science Review, 60* (June, 1966), 302, 301.

[15] Stephen K. Bailey, "Is Congress the Old Frontier?" in Marian D. Irish, ed., *Continuing Crisis in American Politics,* Prentice-Hall, 1963, p. 85.

[16] McClosky, *op. cit.,* p. 371.

The critics are mistaken, however, when they deny a place in schools for normative theories of democracy. They are saying in effect that a nation needs no ideals, no goals, no yardstick with which to measure the "rightness" of a course of action. Would Negro leaders have won the decision calling for desegregation of schools or the passage of the Civil Rights Act of 1964 and the Voting Act of 1965 if they had not been able to appeal to the ideal of equality of opportunity as well as to rights guaranteed in the Constitution? Let us not forget that until 1954 "separate but equal" schools were declared legal under the Constitution and that the Constitution specifically gives states the right to set requirements for voting.

Even the most cynical of these critics may find some utility in pupils' internalizing normative beliefs, such as the importance of freedom, if for no other reason than that such beliefs enable the United States to maintain a stable government. As Dahl points out,

> But so long as the social prerequisites of democracy are substantially intact in this country, it appears to be a relatively efficient system for reinforcing agreement, encouraging moderation, and maintaining social peace in a restless and immoderate people operating in a gigantic, powerful, diversified, and incredibly complex society.[17]

McClosky comments that the most undemocratic not only are apathetic but also do not seem to realize that they deviate from normative values. "This suggests," he says, "that there may, after all, be some utility in achieving agreement on large, abstract political sentiments.[18]

Teachers should realize, however, that in a crisis, people who imperfectly understand the implications of democratic principles can be dangerous to governmental stability. In their zeal to preserve democracy, they may resort to tactics that would undermine it.

If the case has been made for teachers' exposing pupils to both normative and empirical theory, the next step is to determine what ideals are democratic.

Complexities of
the Democratic Theory

Democratic countries vary in their forms of government. Among the most stable of democracies are seven constitutional monarchies (Great Britain, Denmark, Norway, Sweden, Belgium, Luxembourg, the Netherlands) and three commonwealths associated with Great Brit-

[17] Dahl, A Preface to Democratic Theory, p. 151.
[18] McClosky, op. cit., p. 361.

ain's monarchy (Canada, Australia, and New Zealand). Stable democracies among states with presidents as titular heads—republics (the United States, Switzerland, and Uruguay) are less common. Some democracies, such as Great Britain and Sweden, are partly socialistic in the sense that government owns and operates some of the important means of communication, transportation, and basic industries. Some democratic states operate under a written constitution; others do not. Some republics with written constitutions guaranteeing democratic procedures are not democracies. Some democracies have unicameral (one-house), and others bicameral (two-house) legislatures. Falling into the latter category, the United States carefully differentiates the executive, legislative, and judicial divisions of government, whereas many other democratic governments function successfully without such an elaborate system of checks and balances. It is, then, not its political structure but the prevailing social prerequisites and historical tradition supporting a democracy that spell its success or failure.

Different democratic countries also emphasize different tenets and accept different assumptions about them. The English scoff at the idea that men were created free and equal, saying free and equal creation is neither self-evident nor true. Americans are more likely than Englishmen to view government as an administrative convenience, yet at the same time they are more likely than Englishmen to claim that theirs is a nation under law.

Many other dissimilarities among democratic states could be described, but of greater pertinence to the present discussion are the differences in interpretations of the democratic tenets within the United States. For the person who defines freedom as the absence of governmental restraints, "equality" and "liberty" are opposing goals because when one group of men receives "equal" opportunities, another group's "liberty" is curtailed. Providing educational and social benefits for the poor by taxing the more prosperous is an example. In modern America the two dominant strands of democratic theory have their sources in divergent interpretations of equality and liberty, particularly in the economic area. Those who stress equality, called New Liberals, believe that government should protect the welfare of the common people and assure equality of opportunity through government intervention; those who stress individual liberty, called Classical Liberals, believe that the scope of government should be limited to the maintenance of law and order in a free, competitive society. The former see freedom as the right of an individual to develop his potential abilities because he has equal opportunities to participate socially, economically, and politically. The latter see freedom as the absence of government restraints that may interfere with his individual goals.[19] Finding a balance between extremists who would give government too much power and those who would give it too little power is a continuing problem in American politics. Both equality and liberty are essential to freedom.

The American concept of equality permits socioeconomic differences among men, theoretically on the grounds that superior achievement deserves reward, but rejects hierarchical status in the European sense. Informal person-to-person relationships, especially in the western part of the United States where governors, millionaires, university presidents, and high-ranking business executives are often called by their first names, symbolize the "I'm as good as the next man" attitude, or the lack of deference to persons of high status. But equality is more than superficial familiarity. It includes equal human rights and economic opportunities. Even in the United States these types of equality are not yet won by persons in the lower social strata. Just yesterday "Freedom Now," the Negro slogan, was in reality a demand for equality in the New Liberal sense.

The most treasured aspect of democracy, according to public-opinion polls, is freedom. Traditionally in this country personal freedom has been achieved by protecting individual rights against governmental and other authoritarian controls. An American is free to change jobs, assemble with others, speak his mind, worship as he pleases. Implicit in the granting of such freedoms is the assumption that he is capable of and responsible for directing his own life and that he can make his own decisions. In line with this tradition of individual independence, Americans can also change their minds about what institutional arrangements are most conducive to freedom without imperiling their freedom, as long as they keep a share in the decision-making process. Universal suffrage in a society that claims to be free is essential because freedom means not only that a man is free to do certain things, but also that he has the opportunity in Cicero's words "to participate in power." In these terms, the Negro demand for "Freedom Now" could be interpreted in part as a political battle cry, but it would appeal only to those who associate freedom with justice and with equal rights to life, liberty, and the pursuit of happiness.

In modern America, the concept of freedom includes freedoms other than political. Freedom, as defined by Muller, means "the condition of being able to choose and carry out purposes." He admits that being able to choose and carry out one's own purposes "never assures

[19] See William O. Stanley *et al., Social Foundations of Education,* Dryden, 1956, chaps. 8 and 10, for selected readings to amplify these points of view.

wisdom, virtue, happiness, or any other good."[20] Although such assurance is indeed lacking, freedom, as Adlai Stevenson pointed out, is not a "gift. . . . And if we cannot—by certain discipline, by readiness for reflection and quiet, by determination to do the difficult and aim at lasting good—rediscover the real purpose and direction of our existence, we shall not be free. Our society will not be free."[21]

Freedom then is always allied with social responsibilities. On occasion editors of college newspapers ridicule the "freedom-responsibility kick." Such an attitude shows their failure to understand the complexity of the context in which freedom exists. A man is indeed free if he can pursue his own goals; find his own satisfactions without interference, want, and insecurity; search for and have access to truth; develop and assert his own individuality; express himself; participate in decisions that affect his life; seek and mold his social relationships as he wishes; enjoy privacy; choose his own job; and use his leisure as he likes.[22] But he is not free to abuse the rights of others nor is he free of the restraints judged necessary by legal authorities, employers, school officials, and others responsible for the orderly processes required to reach certain goals in any society. He is, however, free to resist such restraints when they seem to be arbitrary or unnecessary.

The Dynamics of Democracy

Young people are sometimes cynical when they compare ideals of a democracy with practices in a democracy. They point out that the tenets are seldom realized, inequalities exist, and decisions are not always made rationally or cooperatively. In their disillusionment, some of them seem almost willing to reject democracy as a goal. What they fail to see is that democracy is an experimental quest, a growing, creative conception, a dynamic laboratory where men daily seek to realize its ideals. Put another way, democracy is a discipline. It provides guidelines for our thinking in relation to social change. Democracy is a cluster of ideals that we strive to put into practice.

In pointing to inequalities within the United States, students forget that the United States was the first nation to dedicate itself to the ideal of an equalitarian democracy. Athenian democracy embraced slavery,

[20] Herbert J. Muller, *Freedom in the Modern World,* Harper & Row, 1966, pp. ix, xi.
[21] Adlai Stevenson, "Politics and Morality," in Cyril Scott Fletcher, ed., *Education for Public Responsibility,* Norton, 1961, p. 25.
[22] Paraphrased from Raymond H. Muessig, "Youth Education: A Social-Philosophical Perspective," in *Youth Education, Problems/Perspectives/Promises,* Association for Supervision and Curriculum Development, NEA, 1968, pp. 39–40.

the French stressed "liberty" more than "equality" and "fraternity," British democracy during the nineteenth century was safe in the hands of a relatively few property holders and is still dominated largely by the traditional ruling classes. Americans accepted the belief that any American boy, no matter how humble his origin, may become President. They believed that the lot of the common man could be improved, that he had a chance to rise in social status, and that he had the right to share in the making of decisions affecting his own and his country's welfare. The fact that some Americans, especially Negroes, have not yet achieved complete equality does not dim the great American dream. It simply means that we must try harder to make the dream come true. This dream is truly our greatest social invention: it has made the United States the mecca for millions of immigrants, it has given hope to the downtrodden all over the world.

Critics of democracy also say, "But the common man does not solve his problems rationally." It is true that liberal-democratic political theory in the eighteenth century assumed intelligent, educated men united by a harmony of interests, willing to discuss and decide issues rationally, and defensive of the rights of minority opinion. The belief in reason was essentially a belief in "natural aristocrats" who were virtuous, talented, capable of reasoning intelligently and making decisions for the masses. It was to this group that Alexander Hamilton and his collaborators appealed in the Federalist papers for support of the Constitution. Modern democratic societies do not provide the conditions upon which the eighteenth- and nineteenth-century faith in the use of reason was based.

Our contemporary, complex society is characterized by conflicts between powerful special-interest groups. Lacking a well-defined harmony of interests, citizens are likely to adhere emotionally to group loyalties rather than to reason dispassionately. Irrespective of how his decision is reached, no matter how misinformed or irrational he may be, every adult has a vote that counts equally in the political arena. Thus popular politicians, seeking the expedient way to win votes, may avoid intellectual discussions and resort to propaganda techniques and emotional appeals. Although intellectuals heap abuse upon the demagogues for these practices, many psychologists doubt that men can ever, even when listening to rational arguments, completely eliminate the influence of emotional reactions from his decision-making process. Even if we disagree with those who say man will not or cannot think rationally, we cannot deny that sometimes he lacks access to the expert knowledge that he needs to solve many of our society's complex problems.

Should we then agree that belief in man's ability to use reason in solving his problems is outmoded? If, because man sometimes does not reason, we abandon our assumption that he can, we pave the way for a dictatorship or an oligarchy. Most of us prefer the imperfections of the democratic way to the alternative. We may also agree with Herbert J. Muller, who writes:

> What most plainly and positively distinguishes him [man] from other animals is the power of conscious thought and responsible behavior. If we respect him at all we must treat him as if he were rational, and enlist his free consent in joint enterprises. The argument for liberty and democracy ultimately rests on Pascal's dictum that thought makes the whole dignity of man, and that the endeavor to think well is the basic morality.[23]

THE ROLE OF THE SCHOOL IN A DEMOCRATIC SOCIETY

What is the role of the school in the education of citizens in a democratic society? Thomas Jefferson believed that education's contribution to freedom was simply the formation of a literate, informed citizenry. He said, "Where the press is free, and every man able to read, all is safe." Many modern educators insist that pupils also need experience in living democratically. Methodology, curriculum content, cocurricular activities, theories of administration and other interpersonal relations within the school—all are justified in terms of their democratic orientation. Very few educational leaders or teachers today omit a reference to democracy in their professional writings and speeches, irrespective of the topic to which their remarks are addressed. What accounts for the current concern with democracy in schools? Why do we talk more about democracy than did the men who wrote the Constitution and the Bill of Rights and who originated many democratic practices?

Reasons for Current Concern

In recent decades the United States has become the champion of democracy. Communism's challenge to the free world forced the United States into this position. It is with chagrin, therefore, that Americans admit the Robin Hood appeal of communism that has seemed to win more converts than democracy in many countries. At

[23] Herbert J. Muller, *The Uses of the Past,* Oxford University Press, 1952, p. 363.

home and abroad loyal critics are dissatisfied with our performance as a world leader. Our voters are charged with political apathy and ignorance of world affairs and of their own democratic heritage. Foreigners deplore racial discrimination in a purportedly democratic nation. Our citizens abroad are sometimes branded as poor representatives of a nation of free men. These weaknesses give the Communists an advantage. Thus fear of communism today, as of nazism and fascism a generation ago, adds a note of urgency to the demands that schools inculcate democratic values.

The dangers to democracy in modern American society also add a disquieting note. The growth of special-interest groups and of mass media complicate—some would say jeopardize—the democratic process. Ignorant men become greater liabilities when their questionable political judgments are deliberately fashioned by professional propagandists. The maintenance of a free society under present conditions requires citizens who are well grounded in their social heritage and skilled in critical analysis.

Although only those who are politically active appear to understand the practical connotations of such beliefs as freedom and equality, many agree that in this century democracy has become a "secular religion" uniting all Americans. Its dogma, Herberg says, supplements the religious tenets of the devout, fills the spiritual vacuum of nonbelievers, and serves as a state religion for all.[24] In an era when most Americans agree that religious teaching should be banned from public schools, democracy as a system of values in the abstract meets no opposition. Undoubtedly teachers constantly reaffirm, often with a fervor akin to religious zeal, the virtues of the free society. Most teachers, like most other Americans, refer to the Constitution and the Bill of Rights as if they were sacred documents. They appeal to democratic values as guides for behavior in much the same way that teachers in the religion-dominated schools of an earlier period appealed to religious values. It is therefore reasonable to attribute increased concern for democracy in schools, at least in part, to the decline of religious influence and the elevation of democracy to the status of a secular religion in American society.

Another factor contributing to the emphasis on democratic beliefs and practices in American schools is the influence of philosophical thinking. Philosophers, particularly John Dewey, have popularized the following thesis: "The problem of freedom and of democratic institutions is tied up with the question of what kind of culture exists; with

---

[24] Will Herberg, *Protestant–Catholic–Jew*, Doubleday, 1955, pp. 87–94.

the necessity of free culture for free political institutions."[25] In other words, a democratic government exists where people have developed values, institutions, beliefs, personal relationships, and other aspects of culture consistent with the support of this political form.

Defining democracy as a way of life that is not limited to political institutions expands the concept of training for citizenship. No longer is literacy and acquaintance with governmental structures, forms, and practices adequate; young people must internalize the values of a democratic society and learn through experience in school the behavior of a free people.

If learning to be democratic is part of formal education, how did earlier generations maintain political democracy when schools taught little more than reading and elementary civics? The answer lies in the changes that accompanied industrialization. It is said that Americans lived democratically before they talked about democracy. The community activities of the frontier, the New England townships, the agricultural county seats, the trading centers, and the rural parish gave abundant opportunities for democratic living. In a rural, agricultural society young people share in the work, play, political and social activities of their elders. In an urban, industrialized society the exclusion of children and adolescents from participation in adult affairs denies them the experiences they need to learn democratic skills, attitudes, and values. Therefore formal education is now being asked to do what was formerly done by informal agencies.

Should Schools Teach Pupils to Value Democracy?

Democracy is a theory of human behavior that many intelligent people do not accept. Plato dismissed democratic theory in two pages. Aristotle, Hegel, Hobbes, and even Rousseau (in his concept of the general will) glorified the state and subordinated the individual to it. The majority of the world's peoples are ignorant of democratic beliefs or they reject them. Can we say that the beliefs of democratic societies are useful in all societies? Among democratic societies and within the United States, which is one of these societies, different interpretations of democratic theory exist. Which interpretation has the most validity?

If schools teach beliefs, tenets, theories, doctrines—all of which are open to honest questioning—are they indoctrinating young people? Hitler's schools indoctrinated German youth to believe in nazism; the Soviet schools indoctrinate their pupils to believe in communism. The

[25] John Dewey, *Freedom and Culture*, Putnam, 1939, p. 13.

University of the State of New York issued this dictum to public schools: "We have . . . common ideals of government and civic responsibility, the values of which must be placed at the very heart of the public school program." American educators bristle at the word indoctrinate, but they would not quibble about the goal embodied in the New York statement. Is there a difference between what we try to do and what we call Soviet indoctrination?

This question is important to educators because indoctrination is the antithesis of education that frees the mind, the basis of democracy. It is also sometimes argued, and with logic, that education should not busy itself with beliefs, attitudes, and values because the sole concern of education is knowledge, which, unfortunately, is subject to change.

An important distinction exists between the indoctrination practices of nazism and communism and the American school's attempt to teach pupils to value democracy. In the first place, the dynamic, experimental nature of democracy precludes laying down an inflexible, democratic "line" to which all must subscribe. Even the tenets of democracy cannot be rigidly prescribed. If an agreement could be reached on an exact wording of a creed, differences in interpretation would arise in each new situation. These conflicting interpretations of the so-called democratic theory increase the difficulties of verbalizing what we believe to persons unacquainted with the creed, but the absence of a dogmatic creed helps to assure freedom of the mind within a democratic society.

It is also assumed that teachers encourage critical thinking when democratic beliefs are discussed. They may reward the student who is analytical and creative in his thinking about the theory and its application. In advanced high school history and social problems classes, students may study differences between England's form of democracy and our own. In other words, democracy is not a set of cliches and slogans. Its theory is an intellectual feast.

A democratic country's high valuation of the right to dissent, of human dignity, and of the equal right of all persons to share in making decisions releases the creative capacities of individuals. By way of contrast, nazi ideology rejected the intellectual contributions of Jews, thus losing Einstein's brilliant reasoning that ultimately led to the development of atomic energy. Democracy provides no preconceived blueprint for solving problems. The assumption in democratic societies is that man will use reason and make changes without violence whenever a majority of its citizens decide that change is needed. Democracy includes no "thought control." Teachers are not government agents committed to propagating the government's policies.

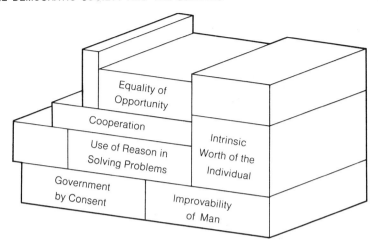

Democratic Ideology

Nevertheless, American education is clearly committed to transmitting democratic values. Whether the schools should or should not inculcate values, they do. Every teacher reveals his own values in his words, tone of voice, deeds, interests, and biases. Because he selects, organizes, and interprets content studied by a class over a generous period of time, the teacher probably articulates his own values more often to pupils than do any other adults except the children's parents. Many people believe that values are "caught," not "taught." Assuming that all factors are conducive to pupils' receptivity, the teacher as exemplar of democratic values or of authoritarian values may be fairly significant in children's lives. Values are concomitant learnings in all learning situations—they do not go away just by being ignored. It is therefore incumbent upon a teacher to be aware of his own values, to ascertain whether they are consistent with the democratic tradition that he is expected to exemplify.

A democratic teacher's job, however, is not to win converts to his own view of democracy. His task is to expose students to varying views in such a way that each student evaluates these interpretations and reaches his own decision as to their relative merits.

Obstacles to a Democratic Education

Even if we could assume that the school is a perfect training ground for democracy, acceptance of democratic beliefs by the young would not be unanimous. A child lives in many worlds and has numerous models other than teachers with whom he may identify—his parents, peers, youth leaders in church and other organizations, stars of the entertainment world, politicians, businessmen, military heroes, gangsters, and a host of others. Each of these does not always present a consistent model of the democratic citizen. One model may not value rational thought, a second may resort to violence, a third may discriminate against persons in minority groups, a tradition-oriented model may reject all experimentation, another may have little or no concern for the welfare of others. In such cases, the failure of the school to produce democratic citizens may be attributable to other agents of socialization who happen to be more influential in the life of a particular child than are his associates in school. A more pervasive influence than the individuals with whom a child may identify lies in the attitudes toward human relationships held by members of his social class. If a child comes from a lower-class home, he is likely to be predisposed toward authoritarianism. Numerous studies have revealed more intolerance, greater civic apathy, less liberalism in noneconomic fields, and less concern for social planning among the working class than among the upper classes.[26]

The world picture of working-class authoritarianism is less gloomy in the United States, where industrialization and labor unions have improved the status of labor and where enfranchisement has given workers a stake in their government.[27] Free, universal education may contribute, too, to reducing the tendency toward authoritarianism among American workers. Nevertheless, children from predominantly lower-class communities do not react to democratic training in schools with the responsiveness of children from middle- and upper-class homes.

Furthermore, the school is itself an imperfect model of democracy. The traditional authoritarian administration of schools is not the theoretically ideal example of a democratic institution. The relationships between principal and teachers and between teachers and pupils are likely to be paternalistic, resembling a benevolent despotism rather than a democracy. Patterns of leadership among individual teachers vary from rigidly authoritarian to excessively permissive. The individual teacher also oscillates in his role as a leader between the two

[26] See Seymour Martin Lipset, *Political Man: The Social Bases of Politics,* Doubleday, 1960, chap. 4, for a discussion of working-class authoritarianism. See also James G. Martin and Frank R. Westie, "The Tolerant Personality," *American Sociological Review,* 24 (October, 1959), 521–528; and W. J. MacKinnon and Richard Centers, "Authoritarianism and Urban Stratification," *American Journal of Sociology,* 61 (May, 1956), 610–620.

[27] Lipset, *ibid.*

extremes. In short, the school does not present consistent models of ideal democratic behavior.

Thus the nature of the total social environment and the subculture of the school may limit the effectiveness of a child's understanding of democracy. Nevertheless, the educational process is shaped to a considerable extent by teachers' and educationists' theories regarding the kind of education needed by young people for effective participation in a democratic society. What then is being done in the name of democratic education, and how successful are these attempts?

EDUCATION FOR LIVING
IN A DEMOCRATIC SOCIETY

Education in countries dedicated to the principle that government is to serve its citizens ought to differ from education in countries in which leaders believe men to be the servants of government. In a free society, the presumptions are that students are treated as persons of dignity and as citizens, and that they have the right to search for truth. They are entitled to equality of opportunity. They are taught how to think for themselves. They also are prepared with the knowledge, skills and understandings that they will need to live meaningfully and fully as free men. Schools in a free society are organized to provide experiences in democratic living. But do American schools usually measure up to such expectations?

Students as Citizens
Worthy of Respect

Irrespective of how a teacher feels about a particular student (and many teachers respect neither trouble-makers nor poor students), in conversations with him, the teacher should use civil language, avoid sarcasm and disparaging remarks, and encourage him to express his view. Such behavior requires the self-discipline expected of democratic adults. Treating children and adolescents with respect provides the "climate" in which a young person can develop the positive self-image that is necessary to both his developing academic competencies and democratic attitudes.

In their disciplining of young people, many teachers and principals not only fail to treat them with respect but also violate their rights. As Earl Kelley points out:

> We do not treat youth as though they were citizens. I imagine there are some adults who do not even know that children are citizens. The United States Constitution, however, is quite specific about this.

Article XIV says that all persons born or naturalized in the United States . . . are entitled to the privileges (of citizenship) . . . it does not say that all those born in the United States will become citizens later on. . . . The Constitution says that government of citizens shall be by the consent of the governed; that a citizen is considered innocent until he has been proven guilty; and that he shall be secure in his person, papers, and effects.[28]

Eric Hoffer also indicts intellectuals. (Let us assume that he classifies elementary and secondary teachers as intellectuals.) He says:

[The intellectual] derives his sense of usefulness mainly from directing, instructing, and planning—from minding other people's business—and is bound to feel superfluous and neglected where people believe themselves competent to manage individual and communal affairs, and are impatient of supervision and regulation. A free society is as much a threat to the intellectual's sense of worth as an automated society is to the working man's sense of worth.[29]

Teachers' "minding other people's business" is more apparent and unnecessary at the high school level than in the lower grades. The average American high school is still a rigid, authoritarian institution in which twelfth graders, like ninth graders, have few if any liberties. School officials rarely see fit to adjust their controls to the maturity level of students or to respect their desires for independence in matters within their capabilities.

Academic Freedom

As defined by McMurrin academic freedom is "the freedom of both teachers and students to engage honestly and openly in the pursuit of knowledge, to enlist fully the instrumentalities of reason and critical intelligence in that quest, and to express and communicate their opinions and ideas without liability, forfeit, or penalty."[30] The importance of intellectual freedom is that it is in truth the cornerstone of a free society. Without it, man cannot make rational and wise choices.

Notwithstanding its importance, academic freedom, like freedom in general, must be viewed in its social context. A teacher in a school, like a man in a free society, is not free to act irresponsibly. He is not free to present his personal opinions as absolutes and to exclude other points

[28] Earl C. Kelley, *In Defense of Youth,* Prentice-Hall, 1962, pp. 59–60.
[29] Eric Hoffer, *The Ordeal of Change,* Harper & Row, 1963, p. 100.
[30] Sterling M. McMurrin, "Academic Freedom in the Schools," *Teachers College Record,* 65 (May, 1964), 658–663.

of view. He is not justified in introducing controversial issues to children in the lower grades of the elementary school before they have the maturity, experience, and knowledge to evaluate such issues. In other words, a wise teacher knows, as McMurrin states, that "a major purpose of schooling in the early years is induction into the culture." Even though social criticism of society is inappropriate in the lower grades, a teacher of young children does have the responsibility to help them understand the evils of prejudice, half-truths, and misrepresentations. He is responsible for helping them learn how to evaluate evidence, to respect contrary opinions, and to seek reliable information before making decisions.

In the upper grades and in college, students should be provided opportunities to examine political, economic, and social matters carefully, responsibly, and critically. Such examination is much more common in college than in the lower schools. Below the college level, several factors have limited the exercise of academic freedom to the detriment of the proper education of free men. The unwillingness of administrators to risk community disapproval, the timidity and conservatism of teachers, and the vindictiveness of many special-interest groups in attacking teachers and administrators (described in Chapter 8) have clearly limited freedom of inquiry in public schools.

A teacher's lack of freedom in areas other than intellectual has contributed to his timidity. In the past, he has often been denied privacy, personal freedom, the right to participate in political activities, protection against slander, and the right to seek redress through due process. One of the praiseworthy outcomes of the increasing militancy of teachers' organizations is that in several instances classroom teachers have been supported by their colleagues in their right to freedom of inquiry.

Equality of Opportunity in Schools

Universal, compulsory education is one of the most important ways in which American citizens try to provide equality of opportunity for all. Equality of opportunity does not necessarily mean identical opportunity, although it has at times been so interpreted by teachers. Equating equality of opportunity with identity of opportunity has undoubtedly resulted in a leveling process, a mediocrity in education for the gifted. It has also led to the neglect of individual needs, particularly those of disadvantaged children. In a system of mass education, it is, of course, difficult to allow for individual differences, but failure to allow the individual to develop his potential is a serious weakness in a society that depends upon individual and collective resourcefulness. Much can be done to break the lock-step, impersonal nature of American schooling and to individualize instruction. Many innovations, such as increased staff, time for student-teacher conferences, and computerized learning, will cost a great deal. Other innovations, such as differential assignments, require nothing more than a teacher who recognizes and is willing to encourage individual differences.

The concept of equality for all has also encouraged conformity. In our eagerness to make people equal, we often try to make them alike. Teachers may be so insistent upon conformity that they iron out differences of opinion. They may reward obedience rather than initiative and self-direction. But the school is also an instrument of social control. A certain amount of conformity is necessary and desirable in an institution dedicated to transmitting a many-sided cultural heritage. The issue is whether a desirable balance between conformity and creativeness is maintained in a given classroom. Equality of opportunity is denied when self-expression is denied.

Schools fail to provide equality of opportunity not only when they do not develop individual abilities, but also when they overlook special needs of some children. For example, poor people who usually do not vote have the greatest need for political skills and knowledge of political processes, yet their children are the least likely to acquire such information in schools. Middle-class children often learn practical politics as well as social skills in cocurricular activities. They have opportunities to be "Mayor for a Day," to assist in "Get the People Out to Vote" campaigns, and to discuss politics with their parents. In such experiences, middle-class youth usually learn that group action can be effective in gaining political ends. Children of the working class, especially of the poor, are unlikely to participate in such activities.

They shun school activities partly because of cost. In 1960 the average cost per pupil of "extras," not including costs of class jewelry and graduation activities, was $238.40 in 197 Oregon high schools. Such costs would be much higher today.[31] The disadvantaged also do not join school activities because they feel uncomfortable about their clothing and social acceptability.

In addition to lacking opportunities to learn from participation in the civic life of the school and community, pupils from disadvantaged homes may not acquire useful political skills and knowledge in classes. Litt charged, after comparing the content of civic education textbooks and programs in three schools, that the material presented in the

[31] Errett Hummel, "Dad, I Gotta Have a Buck," *Oregon Education*, 34 (May, 1960), 12.

working-class school did not "encourage a belief in the citizen's ability to influence government action through political participation."[32] If such practices are widespread, it is not surprising that many Black Power advocates favor violence over sustained political pressure as the means by which they hope to achieve their goals.

Teaching Pupils to Think

The most important job of the school in the service of a democratic society is to teach the young to think critically, independently, and creatively. Outside of school, students may gain political information, democratic attitudes, and the skills in social interaction needed for participating in politics, but they are unlikely elsewhere than in school to learn the techniques of research, critical analysis, and other orderly processes that aid rational thinking.

Although the school is the ideal agent for teaching students how to think, it does not always succeed. One reason for its failure is that many teachers assume that learning the accumulated knowledge in a discipline (the results of others' thinking) teaches a student how to think. Since one must think about something, a certain amount of information is, of course, always needed in the thinking process. Nevertheless, the *way* information is acquired may induce a restrictive attitude toward independent thought that precludes thinking. In other words, when material is presented in such a way as to lead pupils to believe there is only *one* right answer or point of view—usually that of the teacher or the textbook—pupils seek to reproduce this response rather than try to think of other equally reasonable answers. Free-wheeling "thinking" on the basis of inadequate information is, of course, equally dangerous. A question that pupils should be encouraged to ask is "Do we need more information before we can make a reasonable decision?" A wise teacher, then, is one who leads pupils to think independently within the confines of currently available data.[33]

Learning to think, however, involves more than a permissive classroom atmosphere and possession of relevant and reliable evidence. It also involves deliberate use of certain teaching techniques, some of which have greater utility for certain learning situations than for others and none of which escapes criticism from scholars of differing points of

[32] Edgar Litt, "Civic Education, Community Norms, and Political Indoctrination," *American Sociological Review*, 28 (February, 1963), 69–75.

[33] This paragraph is taken from *Urbanization and Oregon's Schools*, 1965, p. 12, a statement of the Educational Policies Commission, Oregon Education Association, written by Grace Graham.

view. Much research has been done in the last decade on theories of learning and thinking, but more must be done before adequate theories can be conceptualized and methods of teaching appropriate in varying situations formulated. In the meantime teachers must make do with available methods. These methods, fallible though they may be in some respects, would promote open-mindedness, critical and creative thinking, and rational decision-making to a greater extent than is common in most classrooms today.

> The ability to think is not only difficult to develop, but it is also diffi-cult for many persons in authority to accept the product of a young person's thinking if it differs from their own. Many parents, teachers, school administrators, employers, community leaders, and government officials do not really want a youth to think. When he thinks, he may ask embarrassing questions, challenge values, make proposals for change, and in general upset the *status quo*. If we say we want our young people to learn to think independently, we must be willing to ac-cept the fact that often their ideas may seem dangerous to us.[34]

Knowledge and Skills

As suggested earlier, students, particularly those in high school, need to analyze democratic theory, preferably through a study of the wisest thoughts of famous theorists. Students need to understand the goals, objectives, and ideals of a democratic society; why they are seldom reached; and what progress has been made toward achieving them. They need to understand what freedom implies and how it can be preserved. They need, of course, to understand the structure and processes of their own government. They must be aware of the role of political parties and pressure groups.

Students also need to learn principles of social interaction, such as the meaning of status and influence (who "rates" and why), the significance of one's role in a group, and the methods of social control used by groups to assure conformity among their members.

Moreover, they need practice in developing the ability to present their ideas effectively in spoken and written form. They need to learn to compromise differences by finding whatever common ground exists between divergent interests and to make decisions consistent with a proper allocation of justice to various factions. They need to learn self-discipline and respect for law and order. They need to develop social sensitivities, such as concern for others, a willingness to listen to divergent opinions, and a belief that everyone is entitled to fair treat-

[34] *Ibid.*, p. 14.

ment. They also need to participate as junior partners with adults in community affairs.

In acquiring skills and attitudes, book learning and didactic teaching are no substitute for direct experience. Such experiences in school and community must be deliberately planned in line with the pupil's level of maturity. In his book *In Defense of Youth*, Kelley demonstrated that disadvantaged youth can assume much more responsibility for their own government than school officials commonly assume they can. Leaders of Job Corps Centers also claim that disadvantaged young people can learn self-discipline.

The tenor of this discussion of the school's role in educating pupils to live in a democratic society may suggest that schools and teachers have failed at this task. Such an appraisal is not fair; some schools and teachers have been highly responsive to the need to educate students for their roles as free men. Notwithstanding such glorious exceptions, practices in many schools do not encourage the kind of behavior designed to develop effective citizens in a free society.

IMPORTANT CONCEPTS

Academic freedom. See pp. 88–89.

Critical thinking. Thinking that questions and evaluates in terms of stated criteria which can, in turn, be questioned and evaluated, and that reaches conclusions as objectively as possible following a consideration of all relevant factors.

Democracy. See pp. 69–79 for a discussion of the meanings associated with this word in Western thinking.

Equality. See p. 73 for a discussion of this term in the context of politics; pp. 89–91, in the context of education.

Empirical theory. Stresses the measurement of individual performance rather than profession of general beliefs.

Freedom. See pp. 78–79.

Liberty. Lack of domination or undue restraint; an essential condition of equality and freedom; sometimes considered a synonym for freedom.

"Natural law" or *"Moral law."* A principle or body of laws considered to be derived from nature, right reason, or religion and to be ethically binding in human society.

"Natural rights." For a discussion of some of the implications, see p. 70 ff.

Normative theory. Assumes an accepted standard or norm. See p. 70 ff. for a discussion of such a theory of democracy.

Popular democracy or *Popular sovereignty.* A theory of government based on the assumptions that one of the natural rights of *all* men is self-government; that every man will be actively engaged in the decision-making process; and that sovereign power lies in the people.

II. CHANGING INSTITUTIONS AND SCHOOLS

5. GOVERNMENT AND SCHOOLS

But today, the implications of national policy make politicians of all of us.

—JOHN F. KENNEDY

Since World War II, particularly since the passage of the Elementary and Secondary Education Act of 1965, the relation of public education to local, state, and federal governments has undergone radical change. Varying interpretations of the separation of church and state have also, in some instances, clarified, and in other instances, obscured the role of the public school in respect to its relationships with religious groups. The first section in this chapter reviews the traditional relationship of schools to governing bodies and the effects of early legislation upon schools. The second section points out how the role of the federal government in relation to schools is changing. The third section explores the complex relationship of church and state and its implications for public education.

FORCES INFLUENCING THE DEVELOPMENT OF PUBLIC SCHOOLS

The educational system of the United States is unique in that its most distinctive structural characteristic is its diversification. In fact, the United States has no system of education. Rather it has 51 different systems in the states and the District of Columbia, and, furthermore, it has hundreds of thousands of different systems at the city, town, and school-district level. The American school is, in a sense, as individualistic as a fingerprint.

Some years ago the Minister of Education in France is said to have boasted that at any hour of the day he could tell exactly what every school child was studying. If the United States Commissioner of Education were asked to describe the activities of an eighth grade pupil, he would not know what courses the child is studying, nor whether the pupil is in high school, junior high school, or elementary school.

The reasons for the proliferation of educational forms and practices within this country lie in the historic local origin of schools, in commitment to the belief that the schools "belong to the people," and in the fact that local property taxes usually pay about 50 percent of school costs. Thus schools have been controlled primarily at the local level. Local control through an elected lay school board or a similar body produces much variety in school organization, curriculum offerings, physical facilities, length of schooling, salaries paid, education of teachers hired, and other policies and practices. These differences are praised from the point of view that an institution tailored to meet the needs of the local community is thought to provide the best education for the community. Experimentation in education, often necessitated by local decisions, stimulates a creativeness, a flexibility, and a dynamic quality, advocates of local control claim; but they also admit that local control has weaknesses. It leads to inequalities of educational opportunity, with poorer states and districts falling short when measured by almost any criterion of educational excellence, to unwarranted responsiveness of schools to local pressures and local values, and to a lack of uniformity in curricular offerings that often places individual students at a disadvantage, particularly children of migrants.

Early in the twentieth century, state governments increased their supervision and control of local schools, and the likelihood is that state and federal direction will continue to grow. Such centralization will undoubtedly result in increasing standardization in American education. In the meantime local control is still important, and the local community is of great significance to schools.

Despite the lack of centralization of American schools and the concomitant variations in school matters, educational institutions are alike in many respects. How can these similarities be explained? Why do we find uniformity within diversity?

Factors Producing Uniformity in American Schools

When the men who drafted the Constitution of the United States did not delegate the responsibility for education to the federal government, education became a state function by virtue of the "all other powers" clause. For several decades in the late eighteenth and early nineteenth centuries the states permitted local school districts to handle school affairs, but in the last century state legislators have promulgated an increasing number of school laws and established state departments of education to lead and supervise local schools. The encroachments of state departments of education into such matters as teacher certification and curriculum (formerly prerogatives of the local school districts), and the requirements laid down by state departments for beneficiaries of state aid have produced uniformity within states. Imitation, exchange of information, and the need for cooperative arrangements among states have also resulted in greater educational uniformity among states.

The state departments of education have also laid a heavy hand on what is taught within a classroom. An important standardizing factor, particularly in elementary schools, is the state curriculum guide, which is often followed slavishly by classroom teachers. Of even greater importance in determining course content are the ubiquitous state-adopted textbooks that in many classes form the core of the curriculum. Both state guides and textbooks cross state boundaries. The guides of other states are studied and emulated whenever new guides are prepared within a state. The same textbooks are usually adopted by several states.

The federal government, too, has become increasingly influential in education through its research, its land and money grants to schools, and its court decisions. The lack of centralized control of education in Washington, D.C., does not mean that the federal government has until recently been impotent in school affairs.

Nongovernmental influences have, of course, also contributed to uniformities in American schools. Educational research, interchange of ideas among members of professional and nonprofessional organizations, such as the Parent Teacher Association, and the development of common theory and methodology in institutions educating teachers have helped to develop a certain amount of consensus about how schools should be operated. Educational journals, books, articles, and conferences as well as writings in newspapers and popular magazines have promoted points of view that are sometimes translated into school practices. Evaluation and accrediting procedures of national educational organizations also tend to standardize educational programs.

Such influences are, however, less demanding and pervasive than laws that relate to education. Because laws set more or less permanent patterns, nineteenth-century legislation still has an impact on today's schools.

Political Events Shaping Education

In 1800 most Americans, except New Englanders, accepted the English tradition that only schools for paupers were free. All other schools were supported by religious or private funds. Changes in the American political situation helped to bring about changes in attitudes toward free schools. Political democracy was extended far beyond the expectations of the writers of the Constitution by Andrew Jackson's "spoils system" that assumed any man fit to hold office, universal suffrage for white males in the 1820s and 1830s, and the gradual abolition of property qualifications for voting and holding office. In the middle of the last century the most powerful argument for free, public schools was that successful democracy depends upon educational opportunities for all children. The last resistance to tax levies for the support of schools folded when court decisions, the most famous of which was the Kalamazoo Case in 1874, upheld the legality of taxation for high schools. By 1875 almost all states and communities had passed laws levying property taxes upon all persons, including those who had no children in school. All children were expected to attend the elementary school and climb as high as they could in the comprehensive high schools and in the colleges. Theoretically, rich and poor alike would receive equal opportunities in a classless school system that was free through secondary school and partially subsidized in college by the state.

Appeals based on the need for an educated citizenry as well as pressure from members of labor unions who wanted to keep children off the labor market led to a further extension of educational opportunities. Compulsory school-attendance laws, passed by some states in the nineteenth century, became nationwide in the twentieth century. Thus, attending school became the civic duty of all American youth, including the sons of immigrants and recalcitrant Americans.

Advocates of public education won other victories in the nineteenth century. First, they fought for the extension of state control over education. The upshot was that by the turn of the century the state was recognized as the final legal authority, with power to set standards and to delegate administrative authority to local schools. In a sense this change, which lessened the control of schools by the local community, might be judged undemocratic, but it was an advance for democracy in that it provided more nearly equal educational opportunities within a state.

The second fight was against religious groups that opposed public schools. Until the middle of the nineteenth century the majority of American schools were religious or private. During the 1830s, 1840s, and 1850s some religious groups tried either to forestall the development of public schools or to get a share of the tax funds. Horace Mann and others fought the diversion of tax monies to religious schools. They believed that giving tax money to religious schools would weaken public schools, that sectarian instruction in the public schools would encourage ideological discord, and that only a secular public school could promote tolerance of religious differences and loyalty to common democratic practices. The advocates of secular public schools supported by taxes found support for their position in the First

Amendment of the Constitution, which clearly separates church and state. By 1860 secular public schools were accepted in principle, but the religion-in-education debate is still alive in the twentieth century.[1]

THE FEDERAL GOVERNMENT'S
CHANGING ROLE IN EDUCATION

That ours is a government "by the people" does not rid government of power nor of possible abuses of power. In truth, our government today is the largest reservoir of power in the nation. It can put a man in jail or execute him, compel him to join the armed forces or go to jail, take a good part of his earnings in taxes, and tell him many things he can do or cannot do in running his business, building his home, getting married, and rearing his children. Despite the precautions of the Founding Fathers, who sought to limit federal powers, and the reluctance of many Americans who see government as the chief enemy of freedom, the power of government, particularly that of the federal government, has grown enormously in recent years.

The phenomenal increase in the power of the national state is matched by that of large corporations and, according to C. Wright Mills in *The Power Elite,* by that of the military establishment. In a constitutional democracy, government is not conterminous with the society, but is merely an institution within the society. Like the strands of fiber in a rope, the institutions of the society are intertwined. When changes occur in one institution, changes are also likely to occur in other institutions. Although Americans lament the expansion of controls by the federal government, they sometimes fail to recognize that "big government" is needed to counterbalance the centralization of powers in other areas. They may also underestimate the influence of wars and the threat of war upon the extension of governmental controls.

Big government is a product of the exigencies of our times. The laissez-faire, "night-watchman state" of the nineteenth century, which was restricted largely to police functions, gave way to that of the "positive state" of the twentieth century for a number of reasons. The inequalities of unlimited competition among persons who had unequal chances, the rise of monopolies to reduce competition among top-level competitors, the plight of consumers at the mercy of monopolies, unfair distribution of limited supplies in times of crisis, and finally the Great Depression, two world wars, the Cold War, and its "brush

---

[1] This historical sketch follows in general the account in R. Freeman Butts, *A Cultural History of Education,* McGraw-Hill, 1947, chaps. 17 and 22.

wars"—all of these have contributed to the development of a planned economy.

How has planned economy been reflected in changes occurring in the federal government? How do these changes influence education in our society?

Structural Changes
in the Federal Government

The structure of the federal government has been significantly modified in many ways, the following in particular:

THE ENHANCED ROLE OF THE EXECUTIVE BRANCH. The office of the American presidency has become a "strong" position mainly because of the recurring crises that have had to be met during this century. The legal powers of the president are not so great as the authority that his mandate from the people, his personal influence and prestige, and the functional view of his office give him. "The Administration," meaning the President, the White House staff, department heads, the Federal Bureau of Investigation, the Central Intelligence Agency, and the National Security Council, usually aided by Congressional leaders of the President's political party, is powerful because it initiates most of the legislation that Congress passes. If there is a "power elite" in this country, it probably consists of "The Administration," leaders of "The Military Establishment," heads of a number of large corporations, and the "Senatorial inner circle."

The United States Office of Education (USOE) has grown in status with the expansion of executive services to the nation. Beginning in 1867 as a minor agency and transferred between departments several times, in 1953 it became a part of the newly established Department of Health, Education, and Welfare under a secretary in the President's Cabinet. For many years the principal contact that most local school officials had with the U. S. Office of Education was through its work in collecting and disseminating educational statistics. It allocated only a small percent of the total federal funds spent for education. In recent years its role of national leadership has been greatly extended as will be discussed later.

A RELATIVE DECLINE IN THE STATUS OF CONGRESS. Congress has traditionally been the law-giving body and the watchdog of the federal government. Members of Congress, elected by local districts, see themselves as close to "the people." Many Congressmen resent the great influence of the executive department in legislation, the presidential power in foreign affairs, and the independence of various executive commissions and agencies in decision-making. Lerner attributes the increased attention in Congress to investigative committees to a relative decline in prestige in its legislative function.

In the 1945–1955 period, Congressional committees were particularly abusive and neglectful of the rights of Americans brought before them. Hapless victims were accused without knowing their accusers or the specific charges against them. They were tried by the press and punished as subversives by economic and social sanctions, but rarely by court action. Several intellectuals in top-flight universities were accused. Several years later, the House Un-American Activities Committee (HUAC) began what seemed to be an effort to stamp out dissent to the war in Vietnam, particularly among college students and Negroes.

Although some Congressional investigations and hearings have been resented by those who are jealous of freedom, Congress does have certain legitimate investigative functions. Many Congressmen also deplore their colleagues' excessive zeal when it jeopardizes intellectual and other citizen freedoms.

THE JUDICIARY AS THE CHAMPION OF FREEDOM. A unique development in American constitutional history is the principle of judicial review by the Supreme Court. Presumably decisions as to the constitutionality of laws and executive orders are reached on the basis of law rather than political considerations, and Mr. Dooley exaggerated when he said, "Whether or not trade follows the flag, one thing is clear: the Supreme Court follows the election returns." In view of the many split decisions rendered by the Court, it seems reasonable to assume that many recent verdicts have been based upon current societal norms and the personal philosophies of the individual judges as well as upon new interpretations of existing law and precedent. At any rate, the tenor of interpretations changes. In recent years Court interpretations have led citizens to regard the Constitution as a "code of freedom."

During the last three decades the most important court decisions that affect education have been the order to desegregate schools and the rulings concerning religious practices in public schools. Prescribing desegregation and upholding the right of the Jehovah's Witness to refuse to render flag salutes in schools are decisions in line with a "code of freedom." The decisions about released-time religious education, prayers and the Bible, and aid to pupils attending parochial schools presume a separation of church and state, but these rulings have not clarified all aspects of church-school relationships. The members of the Supreme Court, like most Americans, hold divergent and perhaps ambivalent opinions on the problem of religious education.

THE RISING INFLUENCE OF SPECIAL-INTEREST GROUPS IN GOVERNMENT. In this century special-interest groups have become an increasingly important element in the "invisible government" wherein much legislation originates, compromises and bargains are made, and consensus is reached. Agents of special-interest groups lobbying in Washington number over 3000. Frequently representing thousands of "constituents" in their organizations, the most aggressive and highly organized groups are undoubtedly very influential. Among the most powerful are the representatives of business and industry, trade, finance, labor, and the professions. Other powerful lobbies are operated by ethnic and religious associations, patriotic organizations, and advocates of various special causes. In 1959 Hunter reported that of 1093 national organizations, the 20 listed below were the most influential policy makers.

U. S. Chamber of Commerce
American Federation of Labor
American Legion
American Medical Association
Congress of Industrial Organizations
National Association of Manufacturers
American Farm Bureau Federation
National Council of Churches of Christ in U.S.A.
National Education Association (NEA)
National Grange
American Bankers Association
Veterans of Foreign Wars, U.S.A.
National Association for the Advancement of Colored People
National League of Women Voters
Council of State Governments
National Congress of Parents and Teachers
Federal Bar Association
U. S. Conference of Mayors
U. S. Junior Chamber of Commerce
Brotherhood of Railroad Trainmen

Hunter says that although the rank order may not be significant, all of these are consistently high-status organizations. Other influential associations that he names are the National Association of American Railroads, National Association of Real Estate Boards, National Better Business Bureau, Rotary International, Automobile Manufacturers Association, Foreign Policy Association, American Petroleum Industries, and the American Jewish Congress.[2] Since Hunter's report, other organizations not identified by him may have gained influence.

The existence of lobbies openly pursuing their special goals is healthier for the maintenance of a stable democracy than are splinter political parties with widely divergent aims. In the United States, where major parties cross special-interest and class lines, the differences between the two parties is blurred, but this lack of clean-cut conflict promotes national unity. Election results are accepted more or less amicably because everyone knows the sky will not fall if his party loses. If the only legal political outlet for special-interest groups lay in the party system, the parties would split and the reconciliation necessary to form a stable government would have to come by coalition. Attempts to corrupt politicians might also be greater if lobbying were illicit.

But lobbying has its evils. The interests of the highly solvent lobby are likely to prevail. Lobbyists may encourage corruption in government, especially when contracts are let. They may resort to flagrantly inaccurate propagandizing. Often they become nuisances to busy Congressmen and other government employees. Almost always they represent the interested few rather than the apathetic many.[3]

Nowhere has the influence of special-interest groups upon legislation been more clearly demonstrated than with respect to federal aid to education. In opposition to the wishes of the majority of Americans, special-interest groups blocked such aid for years, and as we shall see in the discussion that follows, only after special-interest groups had been appeased was the Elementary and Secondary Education Act of 1965 (ESEA) passed.

Post World War II Legislation
Shaping Education

Following World War II, federal aid to education significantly increased both in amount of funds appropriated and in ways in which the money could be used. Legislation, such as the G.I. Bill of Rights, 1944; the National Science Foundation Act, 1950; the Cooperative Research Program Act, 1954; the National Defense Education Act, 1958; the Higher Education Facilities Act, 1963; the Vocational Educa-

[2] Floyd Hunter, *Top Leadership, U.S.A.*, University of North Carolina Press, 1959, pp. 14–16.

[3] This discussion of changes in the structure of the national government was influenced by Max Lerner, *America as a Civilization: Life and Thought in the United States Today*, Simon and Schuster, 1957, pp. 371–464.

tion Act, 1963; the Manpower Development and Training Act, 1963; the Economic Opportunities Act, 1964; and others, greatly expanded the federal government's investment in education, particularly in higher education. Each of these acts demonstrated the federal government's commitment to categorical aid, i.e., aid for specific purposes. In general these bills diverted more money to higher education than to elementary and secondary schools.

Meanwhile federal aid bills to provide public school funds for general purposes had failed to pass Congress in the 1918–1925 period, bills for operating expenses had failed in the 1937–1943 and 1946–1950 periods, and bills for school construction had failed in the 1954–1957 and the 1959–1961 periods. Over the years conservative groups (the Daughters of the American Revolution, American Legion, and the Farm Bureau) and the National Association for the Advancement of Colored People had tended to be against the legislation, Protestant groups had tended to favor the bills (provided Catholic schools did not benefit), and Catholic groups tended to oppose aid if their schools did not share in the funds. Business groups opposed federal aid to schools; education groups and labor favored it. Members of Congress from wealthy states were also unwilling to divert tax monies from their districts to poor states. Three major issues divided opponents and supporters: segregation, aid to parochial schools, and federal control of schools. Faced with powerful opposition and a lukewarm general public, members of Congress seemed to be unable to work out an effective compromise that would allocate funds to public schools.

In 1965 such a compromise was effected. The ingenious device of basing federal contributions on the number of poor families a school district served enabled 90 percent of the nation's school districts to obtain funds. The Civil Rights Act of 1964 had effectively silenced desegregationist Congressmen who had previously attached riders to aid bills forbidding the allocation of funds to segregated schools. Such riders invariably led to southern opposition to the bills. Catholic groups were appeased by being given a share in the spoils, and many Protestant groups, softened perhaps by the ecumenical movement and the memory of a popular Catholic president, agreed that parochial schools should receive a limited share. The NEA approved the bill despite its provision of aid to both parochial and private schools, presumably because it saw the bill as the beginning of a policy of general aid to education. Of course, special-interest groups do not vote in Congress, but members of Congress with an eye on public opinion polls were aware of changed sentiments. Other factors that expedited the passage of ESEA were the predominance in Congress of Democrats, who are more likely than Republicans to support federal aid to schools, and the skillful political leadership of the president.[4]

When President Johnson signed the Elementary and Secondary Education Act of 1965, he said that it was "the greatest breakthrough in the advance of education since the Constitution was written." It was indeed revolutionary in at least two respects: It provided that about 45 percent of the funds would be distributed to school districts in proportion to the number of children from low-income families served. It also provided that public funds may be used for certain purposes (television equipment, mobile educational services, textbooks, library materials, and fees of visiting artists, musicians, and lecturers) to benefit pupils in private and parochial schools. Moreover, these students could take certain courses, such as those in the sciences and languages, in public schools. The sum—$1.3 billion—was also unprecedented and seemed to assure that the federal government had at long last accepted a responsible share in financing public education.

In 1966 and 1967, larger grants, following the same general pattern of emphasis on disadvantaged children as had the ESEA, provided funds to "beef up" state departments of education, school libraries, educational research, and materials of instruction. The purpose of the federal grants was "to strengthen and improve educational quality and educational opportunities" by offering categorical, not general, aid.

Effects of Federal Aid
upon Curriculum

Federal funds have encouraged activities in schools in many different fields. The U. S. Office of Education reported that during the first year of a program to strengthen school libraries, almost 9 of 10 students were provided with new teaching materials. In Alabama, many children who had never before had a chance to take a book home with them were able to do so during the 1966–67 school year. In New York, reporters claimed general improvement in pupil achievement, particularly in the social studies and sciences, as a result of improved teaching materials.[5] Federal grants also stimulated the development of improved programs of counseling and guidance, in-service training, audiovisual aids, remedial instruction, and parent-school relationships. With the aid of federal monies, many schools have

[4] Frank J. Munger, "Changing Politics of Aid to Education, *Trans-action*, 4 (June, 1967), 11–16 and James W. Guthrie, "A Political Case History: Passage of the ESEA," *Phi Delta Kappan*, 49 (February, 1968), 302–306.

[5] Helen M. Gibbs, "Title II of ESEA," *Phi Delta Kappan*, 49 (February, 1968), 323.

been able to increase the size of professional staffs and reduce class sizes in schools for the disadvantaged. Legislation to become effective in 1969–1970 provided $9.3 billion for schools, and included new programs for the deaf, blind, and other handicapped persons.

In the long run, however, the most significant contribution that federal aid is making to education may be its sponsoring of educational research. For the first time in the history of education, a substantial sum is being spent for research. For example, *Pacesetters in Innovation, Fiscal Year 1966* lists over 1000 projects, conducted under ESEA, which experimented with new educational methods. *Office of Education Research Reports, 1956–65, Indexes and Résumés* cites over 1200 significant findings of educational researchers. The *Reports* summarize findings in many diverse fields, such as vocational education, teaching foreign languages and the new mathematics, and methods of teaching disadvantaged and handicapped children.[6]

Although the many improvements made possible by federal funds should not be denigrated, particularly long-range research goals, effects of federal interest in school curriculums have not always been salutary. Under the initial NDEA provisions, federal grants of categorical aid to schools and universities expanded programs in science, mathematics, and languages to the neglect of those in the social sciences and humanities. Subsequent federal legislation boosted the training of counselors and ignored the needs of teacher education. Because of this tendency of categorical aid to distort curriculums, many educators support "block grants" to be used by state departments of education and institutions of higher education as local needs dictate. Since national interests must also be served, however, Congresswoman Edith Green, long-time member of the House Subcommittee on Education and Labor, advocates general aid with limited aid in categorical areas.[7]

Federal grants have also complicated school finance and curriculum development in that school officials are never sure whether their proposals will be funded, whether approved proposals will be funded promptly, or whether grants will be renewed. Such uncertainties make it difficult for administrators to decide whether a program can or cannot be offered within the school year. The need to solicit grants has created a new, onerous, and sometimes unrewarding role for professors and school officials, called "grantsmanship." Successful "grants-

---

[6] Both manuals are available from the Superintendent of Documents, Government Printing Office, Washington, D.C. 20402.

[7] Edith Green, "A Congresswoman Discusses the Politics of Education," *Phi Delta Kappan, 49* (February, 1968), 308.

manship" includes a thorough knowledge of what kinds of proposals are likely to be funded as well as a willingness to spend hours and hours upon the paper work required by USOE. In at least one instance, it cost an institution more money to submit its proposal than the grant award would have yielded. For better or for worse, the entry of the federal government into educational decision-making has created a revolution in the "politics of education."

The New "Politics of Education"

Campbell and Layton point out that since World War II, the augmented roles of the federal government, major foundations, and big business organizations in educational matters have resulted in a major shift in policy-making for the public schools. The impact, they point out, is more comprehensive than the impact of the federal government alone.[8] Although the three-fold impact is indeed significant, the following discussion is concerned largely with that of the federal government.

One way of demonstrating the growth of federal influence is by noting the expansion of the USOE. In 1966 the budget of USOE was eleven times as large as it was in 1961. Although USOE disburses less than half of all federal funds for education, the expanded program in that office alone required the hiring of more than 200 new employees in 1965. In 1947 USOE had about 280 employees; in 1967 it had 2,759.

This expansion of federal educational activities has had several effects. It has encouraged interagency rivalries in Washington, D. C., decreased the influence of professional educational associations upon the USOE,[9] led to the formation of an interstate Education Commission of the States, and radically changed internal educational patterns within the states.

Highly critical rivals of USOE and of public schools are the Department of Labor and the Office of Economic Opportunity, which operates the Head Start, VISTA, and Job Corps programs. OEO officials frequently contend that if public schools would adopt its educational techniques, educational problems would be solved; and they chide officials of USOE for their alleged alliance with spokesmen of the NEA. Although USOE administrators have not reacted by assuming that Job Corps methods and costs can be duplicated in public schools,

[8] Roald F. Campbell and Donald H. Layton, "Thrust and Counterthrust in Education Policy Making," *Phi Delta Kappan, 49* (February, 1968), 290–293.
[9] Russell I. Thackrey, "National Educational Organizations and the Changing Politics of Education," *Phi Delta Kappan, 49* (February, 1968), 314.

they do seem at times to be trying to prove that USOE is not an arm of the NEA.[10]

Apparently the advent of the federal government as a man-sized partner in education was a factor in the establishment in 1965 of the Education Commission of the States, which enrolls representatives from over 40 states and territories. The Commission's main thrust is not yet clear, but the theme of its meeting in 1967 "Power-Play for Control of Education" suggests that it is interested in conflict analysis and in emerging state-federal relations in education. Governors and state legislators, educators, and laymen have joined hands in what they call a Compact for Education. In the words of the Commission's executive director, the Commission is "dedicated to encourage continued effective dialogue between the establishment [meaning educational organizations] and the new-era groups [meaning foundation officials, political action group leaders, and other interested individuals]." The new-era groups, he says, "rattle the bones" of the establishment.[11]

Presumably the heightened interest of state governors and politicians in educational matters, as demonstrated by their response to the Education Commission of the States, is changing educational politics at the state level, but the impact of such change is not clear. Ex-Governor of Oregon, Mark Hatfield, may have indicated the direction of change when he said that educators "must be prepared to prove their case in the court of public opinion." If such a change is in the offing, educators will no longer be able to claim that education is not a political issue. As a matter of fact, it always has been a political issue though not usually a public issue. Researchers have not yet studied the politics of education sufficiently to present much evidence on what has happened or is happening, particularly at the local and state level.

The effects of the expanding role of the federal government upon state departments of education are much more readily observable than its effects upon state politics. Federal aid has both weakened and strengthened state departments of education. In some instances, under the provisions of ESEA and OEO, local districts could—and did—by-pass the state departments and appeal directly to the federal government for grants. Although such procedure continues to undermine the authority of state departments of education, in 1965 Congress did recognize the need to strengthen state authority. Ever since the passage of the Smith-Hughes Act in 1917, federal aid programs have

[10] W. W. Wayson, "The Political Revolution in Education, 1965," *Phi Delta Kappan, 47* (March, 1966), 334.

[11] Wendell H. Pierce, "The Politics of Education," *Phi Delta Kappan, 49* (February, 1968), 335–336.

distorted curriculum emphases in state departments. In 1951 the New York state department of education had in the federally-supported vocational agriculture program one specialist for each 4000 students enrolled whereas in the state-supported English program it had one specialist for each 1,000,000 students enrolled. Congress therefore sought to redress such inequities by providing funds under ESEA to augment the budgets, professional staffs, and programs of state departments. Much of the new money used for strengthening traditional programs has thereby strengthened the departments in general, yet at the same time it has made the departments increasingly dependent upon federal funds. Despite such adjustments, a disproportionate number of state department personnel are still assigned to federally-supported programs. Campbell and Layton found that in one large state department, 16 of its 26 divisions and 64 of its 135 professional workers were devoting all or part of their attention to federally related programs. These researchers charge that state education departments "appear to be simply responding to forces about them."[12]

At the local school district level, federal aid is creating a new role for school superintendents and their assistants, i.e., government affairs specialist. In Nebraska, Budig found that superintendents are spending no less than one-fourth of their time reviewing federally-sponsored programs and implementing provisions of federal legislation. The expertise required to understand and implement federal directives has shifted much responsibility from the shoulders of the local school board members to those of the superintendent.[13]

Federal aid programs, designed specifically to *push* schools into doing their full duty with respect to the underprivileged, are welcomed by districts that wish to expand programs in this direction. Educational leaders in some districts, however, do not concur in the generous support of some programs to the exclusion of others. In these schools, federal aid is seen as undesirable outside control. Such attitudes were particularly prevalent when USOE attempted to enforce its guidelines based on the 1964 Civil Rights Act requiring the desegregation of schools. Commissioner of Education Howe, called by opponents "a commissioner of integration," during his first 18 months in office, spent more than two-thirds of his time on civil rights matters. Although most of the resistance to desegregation guidelines came from educators in the south, school leaders in northern cities such as Chicago also resisted the guidelines. The difficulties encountered in at-

[12] Campbell and Layton, *op. cit.*
[13] Gene A. Budig, "The Government Affairs Person in the Schools," *Phi Delta Kappan, 49* (February, 1968), pp. 350–351.

tempts to hold Chicago to the guidelines, in fact, led USOE to abandon for a time its efforts to desegregate schools in northern cities when desegregation results from housing patterns and not from deliberate intent on the part of school boards to discriminate.[14]

The political implications of ESEA of 1965 with respect to aid to parochial schools will be discussed in the following section. The possible impact upon education of ESEA aid to nonpublic schools may perhaps be that expressed by the title of an editorial in *Phi Delta Kappan*, "Did We Break an Arm Sliding Home?"

CHURCH, STATE, AND THE SCHOOLS

Earlier in this chapter reference was made to the general acceptance by 1860 of secular public schools but of a continuance of the "religion-in-education debate" in the twentieth century. Two major issues in this debate have been whether reverential religious practices should be permitted in public schools and whether parochial schools should be supported, at least in part, by public taxes.

For purposes of discussion, let us define religion as a specific system of belief, worship, and conduct that often includes a code of ethics and a philosophy accepted by an identifiable group, such as Christians, Buddhists, and Mohammedans; and an established religion as an officially designated religious denomination that is usually supported at least in part by public taxes.

In the United States, people accepted the principle of religious freedom for all and rejected an established religion when they adopted the Constitution. The First Amendment to the Constitution forbids enacting laws "respecting the establishment of religion" and "prohibiting the free exercise" of religion. In other words, under the Constitution neither Christianity in general nor any particular Christian denomination can become the established religion of Americans nor can they be denied freedom to worship or not to worship as they please. As an agency of government, the public schools are bound to comply with these constitutional provisions. The chief arguments against reverential religious activities in public schools are that such practices encroach upon the free exercise of religion by all students and violate the "establishment of religion" clause. The United States Supreme Court has defined religion as a private matter and the role of government (including its agencies, such as schools) in relation to religion as *neutral*. In accord with its assigned role of neutrality, schools can neither aid

---

[14] Stephen K. Bailey and Edith Mosher, "Implementation of Title VI of the Civil Rights Act," *Phi Delta Kappan*, 49 (February, 1968), pp. 300–302.

Faith and Knowledge

nor denigrate religion. The Supreme Court has also ruled in the Oregon Case (1925) that parents may send their children to parochial rather than public schools.

Presumably, then, the United States has a tax-supported, secular public school system free of reverential religious activities and several privately-supported parochial school systems that include religious instruction in their curriculums. Neither of these assumptions is well grounded in evidence. For many years parochial schools, especially colleges and universities, have benefited from government grants, and they are presently receiving further benefits under ESEA. This issue will be discussed in detail later. On the other hand, public schools have encouraged many religious activities, and despite court rulings that such practices are illegal, they continue.

Religion in Public Schools

According to Dierenfield, a 1961 survey[15] of the extent of religious activities in public schools in 2183 communities throughout the nation

[15] R. B. Dierenfield, "The Extent of Religious Influences in American Public Schools," *Religious Education*, 56 (May–June, 1961), pp. 175–177.

revealed that the schools sampled were participating in six types of religious activities to the extent shown in the table below.

Religious Activity	Public School Participation —Percent
Baccalaureate services held	86.8
Gideon Bibles distributed	42.7
Homeroom devotional services	50.1
Regular chapel	22.0
Bible readings	41.7
Christmas exercises	87.9

In 1962 when the Supreme Court ruled the New York Regents Prayer in violation of the "establishment of religion" clause in the First Amendment, twelve states were requiring Bible readings by law, five states permitted it by law, seven states permitted it by court interpretation, six states declared it unconstitutional by court rulings, and six others by attorney-general opinions. The other states had no rulings for or against Bible readings in public schools. The use of the Lord's Prayer was not prohibited by law or court decisions in any state.

The Supreme Court's ruling against the use of the Regents Prayer in 1962 as well as against Bible readings and use of the Lord's Prayer in schools in 1963 evoked a strong negative reaction from many Americans. Several weeks after the decisions Gallup Pollsters found only 24 percent of the respondents supporting the Court. In November, 1964, the Michigan Survey Research team reported that 74 percent of its sample favored prayer in public schools.[16]

Three factors seem to influence popular opinion in the Bible reading–prayer cases. First, many Americans believe that a commitment to religious faith is a necessary foundation for a moral life. They attribute an increase in crime and delinquency and an alleged decrease in morality to a lack of religious commitment. Second, advocates of religious activities in schools view public schools, which all pupils not attending private schools must attend, as the place that pupils who are not reached by churches can be given a reverential view of religion. Teaching *about* religion as a part of the cultural heritage, a legal activity in public schools, would not satisfy those people who feel that schools should encourage pupils to take part in church activities and to

[16] Reported in Donald R. Reich, "The Supreme Court and Public Policy: The School Prayer Cases," *Phi Delta Kappan, 48* (September, 1966), 30.

be reverential toward the spiritual view of life espoused by religious groups. Such study does not necessarily build "moral and spiritual values" nor impel students toward religion because the history of any given religious group is not always noble and the study of religion as an intellectual discipline is not designed to win converts.

Finally, many Americans fail to accept the fact that reading the Bible and saying prayers are sectarian activities. They do not realize that in the United States there are about 6 million Jews, more than 100,000 Buddhists, and many other non-Christian faiths as well as an unidentified number of agnostics and atheists who have the same right to freedom of belief as do they. Moreover, Roman Catholics use a version of the Bible that differs from the Protestant version, and Jews read only from the Old Testament.

Thus popular support of Bible reading and prayers in schools has encouraged flagrant violation of Supreme Court rulings. In 1963–1964 the Educational Testing Service asked high school principals, "Are there regular religious observances at your school (e.g., prayer, Bible reading, etc.)? One-fourth of the principals replied, "yes." The percentages ranged from 66 percent in the south and 52 percent in the border states to 19 percent in the Pacific states and 18 percent in the mountain states. A 1965 questionnaire to state superintendents of public instruction revealed that in 29 states permitting Bible reading prior to 1963, only 5 had completely stopped the practice.[17]

Why does such widespread disregard of the law exist in schools? It occurs because state departments of education have in general left the matter of religious observances to local option, law enforcement agencies ignore failures to comply with the law, and very few parents have filed legal protests. There are several questions that teachers and school authorities should consider with respect to their defiance of the law. First, does disregard of the law set young people a good example? Second, should school authorities deny the rights of minorities in respect to freedom of religion? Third, can the public schools maintain that parochial schools should be denied public tax support if public school officials are also permitting religious observances in schools?

Tax Support of Parochial Schools

The issue of whether public taxes should support parochial schools is also muddled by practices that seem to violate the principle of separation of church and state. Such practices have a long history. The association of government and religion in the American colonies is well known. Colonial Massachusetts, New York, Maryland, Virginia,

[17] *Ibid.*, p. 31.

Georgia, and the Carolinas had established churches and tax-supported religious schools. In Virginia conflicting pressures of other religious schools demanding equal financial support with the established Anglican schools were a significant factor in leading Jefferson and Madison to favor separation of church and state. Upon its adoption, the First Amendment was not applied to states. Nevertheless, the constitutions of new states entering the union usually included explicit provisions prohibiting the use of tax funds to finance private and parochial schools. Massachusetts, the last of the original thirteen to do so, did not, however, abandon the legal establishment of religion until 1833. In the nineteenth century, although states other than Massachusetts, New York, and Indiana seldom granted financial support to religious schools, federal aid to religious colleges and universities, Alaskan missionary schools, and Negro schools conducted by religious groups was not uncommon.[18]

In the twentieth century too, federal legislation has included grants to religious schools. Public, private, and sectarian institutions were equally eligible for federal funds made available through the Higher Education Facilities Act of 1963 to pay part of construction costs of educational facilities. The National Defense Education Act of 1958, the Manpower Development and Training Act of 1962 as amended, and, as stated earlier, ESEA provided federal funds for library materials, textbooks, and supplementary materials for private as well as public school teachers and students. Federal grants to parochial schools under ESEA have caused considerable difficulty in several states, first because state constitutions include more explicitly worded prohibitions than those of the First Amendment, and second because the First Amendment was deemed applicable to states by the Supreme Court's decision in the Cantwell case of 1940. In Kentucky, for example, federal funds have to be isolated from the state and local funds in order that federal money can be disbursed through state agencies to parochial schools.[19]

Advocates of such federal disbursements to parochial schools point to the contribution of parochial schools to national welfare, the unfair burden of "double taxation" that parents who send their children to parochial schools pay, and the ambiguity of the First Amendment. To justify tuition payments to parents of parochial school pupils, they cite the example of subsidies paid to individuals using the G.I. Bill to

[18] See William W. Brickman and Stanley Lehrer, eds., *Religion, Government, and Education,* Society for the Advancement of Education, 1961, p. 113; and appendix, "Chronological Outline of Church-State Relations in American Education," pp. 252–269, for a complete listing of laws and court decisions up to 1961.
[19] Edgar Fuller, "Government Financing of Public and Private Education," *Phi Delta Kappan, 47* (September, 1965), 366.

study in religious colleges.[20] They also cite the precedents of Supreme Court rulings in the Cochran case of 1930 and the Everson case of 1947. These rulings permitted states to furnish free textbooks (Cochran case) and offer public bus transportation (Everson case) to parochial school pupils. Both of these expenditures were justified by the court under the theory of child benefits.

Presumably the substantial sums given parochial schools under ESEA are also justified by the same theory. If shared-time programs, which save parochial schools the expense of offering the most expensive curriculums, e.g., science, language, and vocational training, with laboratory and technical equipment, can be justified as child welfare, just what part of parochial schools' activities, with the exception of religious instruction, is exempt from public support?

Opponents to the use of tax monies to aid parochial schools contend that parents who send their children to private schools are not doubly taxed. They argue that all taxpayers including those with no children in school must pay taxes to support public schools. Parents who choose to send their children to parochial rather than public schools are simply paying for their choice. In the past, for a variety of reasons, those advocating a complete separation of church and state have seldom voiced their opposition to government grants to religious colleges and universities or to the inclusion of parochial school pupils in the school lunch program, but they have been alarmed by the authorization of bus transportation and textbooks under the theory of child welfare. Moreover, federal aid to parochial schools under ESEA has led to strenuous efforts among some individuals and groups to test the constitutionality of such aid and to warn public schools of their fate if such aid is further expanded.

The political expediency necessary to win the votes of congressmen from predominantly Catholic districts, they say, has opened a Pandora's box. They charge that parochial school leaders are already politicking for increased aid and cite the English and Canadian provincial experience, in which ever increasing pressures for aid to parochial schools has been the pattern. For example, the English Education Act of 1944 provided 50 percent governmental support for parochial schools; in 1959 the government's share was increased to 75 percent; some Englishmen, among them Roman Catholics, predict that churchmen will soon press for 100 percent governmental support.[21]

If we can assume that parochial schools in this country will also

---

[20] Ernest van den Haag, "Federal Aid to Parochial Schools: A Debate," *Commentary*, 23 (July, 1961), 1–11.

[21] A. Stafford Clayton, "Lessons from Europe on Public Support of Nonpublic Schools," *Phi Delta Kappan*, 47 (September, 1965), 20.

press for and receive a larger share of federal funds, to what extent will public schools be damaged? Edgar Fuller, executive secretary of the Council of Chief State School Officers, believes that federal matching and administrative techniques may eventually force states to allow grants to parochial schools from state and local school funds.[22] In such an event, parochial sharing of all school tax monies would become a *fait accompli*. What effects would such sharing have on public schools?

Fuller says, "Should private schools be tax-financed, the elementary and secondary public schools would be left to educate children from denominations too small to operate their own schools, the unchurched, the culturally deprived, and the rejects and problem students from the private schools which can choose their own pupils."[23] Clearly some splintering of public schools is likely because more and more religious groups would be able to establish their own schools. Again a look at what has happened in other countries may be enlightening. In the Netherlands, the Primary Education Act of 1920 provided for equal support of private as well as public schools. Dutch private schools are almost all parochial schools. During the last half of the nineteenth century—before public money was allotted to private schools—70 to 80 percent of primary pupils were enrolled in public schools; by 1958 only 28 percent of them were enrolled in public schools. Clayton claims that Dutch society, in strengthening religious subcultures through schools, has encouraged marked cleavages between Roman Catholics, Protestants, and general or neutral associations. These divisions occur not only in the social contacts of Dutch people but also in their political and economic life. Clayton says, "an individual may spend practically his whole life in contacts with members of his own religious group."[24]

Whether such changes would take place in the United States is, of course, questionable. Many people believe, however, that only judicial decisions that interpret the First Amendment explicitly can spare Congressmen and the Administration from excessive pressures. The future alternative of not succumbing to such pressures may very well be the failure to pass federal aid-to-education bills, as it was prior to 1965. Many opponents to expanding aid to parochial schools, nevertheless, admit that such schools do contribute to the national welfare. Just how much that contribution is worth in tax dollars and how many tax dollars can be given to private schools without serious damage to public schools and without increasing intergroup tensions in the United States are issues of grave concern.

[22] Fuller, *op. cit.*, p. 371.
[23] *Ibid.*
[24] Clayton, *op. cit.*, pp. 22–24.

IMPORTANT CONCEPTS

Block grants. Unmarked federal aid to be used as the recipients deem fit. See p. 108.

Categorical aid. Federal aid limited to certain named programs such as those in science, mathematics, and language. See p. 107.

Established religion or *church.* One closely associated with the governing body of a state or nation, such as the Church of England. See p. 112.

"The Establishment." Those who collectively occupy positions of influence and power in a society. See p. 110.

"Night-watchman state." A state that exercises little more than police power and contrasts sharply with the modern activist state.

Parochial. Narrow and provincial in the sense that a church parish may be; the term is often used to describe schools maintained by church parishes.

"Positive State." See pp. 101–102.

Religion. A widely and loosely used word, the core meanings of which still refer to the beliefs, attitudes, and behaviors by which men define their relationship to the power and principle of the universe in which they find themselves through a personal commitment to God or a god. See p. 112.

Sectarian. Characteristic of or belonging to a particular group, especially a religious sect.

Secular. Pertaining to and characteristic of activities of a practical, present-day nature not within the purview or under the control of any organized religious group; used to establish a contrast with the term, "sectarian."

Shared-time program. Programs conducted by school districts which are open to, or shared by, students from parochial schools. See p. 117.

6. SCIENCE, INDUSTRIALIZA-TION, AND THE SCHOOLS

What's coming in education by 1980 will have the same effect on education that the automobile had on transportation.[1]

Schools of the United States have been profoundly influenced by the four most powerful movements in the modern Western world: democracy, capitalism, urbanization, and industrialism. These movements are interrelated, but for purposes of exposition their impact on the schools is being discussed in separate chapters. In the twentieth century, the primary impetus to industrialization has been the expansion of scientific knowledge. In this chapter industrialism is presented with emphasis on educating children for work and for leisure.

SCIENCE, INDUSTRIALIZATION, AND CULTURAL CHANGE

Ever since Heraclitus in fifth-century Greece observed that "man cannot step in the same river twice," man has pondered the inevitability of change. Social philosophers have tried since early times to explain why change occurs and how it affects man and civilizations. In this country, because the transition from an agricultural to an industrial society has brought numerous social changes, Americans are likely to assume that all cultural change originates in technological development. The popularity of Ogburn's "cultural lag" hypothesis—that a culture's nonmaterial aspects change less rapidly than do its material components—testifies to this belief. Material change may seem to precede nonmaterial change in this country, but political and ideological revolution antedated industrial development in Russia. In other societies men have resisted material change more or less successfully. Hence a reasonable conclusion is that improved technology depends upon man's inventiveness, his need for inventions, and his willingness to accept change.

Assuming that men have been receptive to technological change, as they have been in the United States, invention is, of course, an important agent of cultural change. Disease, flood and droughts, migrations, natural resources, ideologies, the actions of other societies, and the like may also account for change. To know that cultural change does not necessarily derive from a single source tells us nothing of the force or

[1] *Changing Times, 21* (March, 1967), 24.

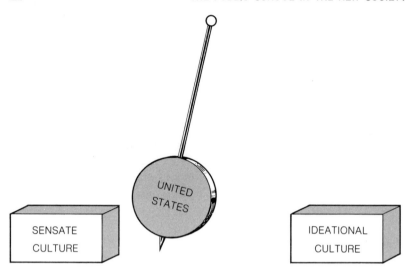

direction of the change, however, and such knowledge is also needed if man is to predict and control change. Although no adequate theory of social change has been formulated to explain the kinds of changes and how they vary from time to time, Pitirim Sorokin, a contemporary sociologist, suggests a conceptual scheme as a hypothesis on a grand scale.

Sorokin and his researchers first examined Western cultures, past and present. They found fundamental changes in all cultural patterns, such as in the arts and in political, economic, and religious systems. From these data Sorokin assumed change to be inherent in society, but he did not attempt to explain why it occurred. Rather he examined the general tendencies that reoccurred at different times in different societies, and from these trends he postulated two polarized or opposing types of cultures, the *sensate* and the *ideational*. In a sensate culture, man accepts sense impressions as truth and is stimulated primarily by things that may be found in a quantity-producing and consuming society like the United States. In an ideational culture, man finds truth in faith or in a "deeper reality behind sense impressions" and has little interest in the material products of culture. Sorokin then advanced a sociological "theory of limits" as a theoretical framework for all repetitive social change. His "theory of limits" is similar to the psychologists' concept of regression toward the mean. The latter theorizes, for example, that the children of geniuses will be intelligent but less intelligent than their parents, and that children of feebleminded parents will be slow mentally but less so than their parents. Sorokin theorizes that when a society is pushed too far in one direction, counterforces emerge to push it back toward the center. For example, a highly sensate culture will in time move back toward the center—the *ideal* culture—where there will be a judicious combination of the sensate and the ideational.[2]

That a self-adjusting mechanism exists within a specific trait of culture, as exemplified in fads and fashions, may be accepted, but that self-regulation is an attribute of culture as a whole is, of course, speculative. Most of the civilizations described in Toynbee's *A Study of History* are no longer extant. Perhaps they fell because the people could not assimilate the nonrepetitive and accidental types of change that Professor Sorokin's theory admittedly does not cover.

The significance of cultural change to a teacher lies not so much in the causes of change but in the fact that change as a constant factor in society must be recognized and children taught how to face its many manifestations. Schools that teach children how to kill saber-toothed tigers when such tigers no longer exist, as Harold Benjamin's satire suggests, do not serve their society. What schools can do to help pupils face a full-scale atomic attack would be minimal at best, but what schools can do to prepare young people for an automated society might be very helpful. If we can embrace the optimism of Sorokin's theory, perhaps the United States is about ready to swing from a sensate toward an ideational culture. If such a change should occur, schools might find altered opinions about "what knowledge is of the most use."

Although American social scientists recognize other agents of change, they agree that industrialization brought about by harnessing mechanical energy to man's use is the principal force that revolutionized American life. The unparalleled expansion of industrialization was achieved, for the most part, by developing fairly simple machines made bigger and more efficient than their predecessors, standardizing parts, breaking jobs down into segments for assembly-line production, and using new sources of power. The industrial changes now in the making are of a different order. To understand recent developments, changing methods of invention must be considered.

Science and Technology

Until well into the twentieth century the "know-how" for industrialization of the United States was the product of practical inventors, not

[2] See Carle C. Zimmerman, *Patterns of Social Change, A Survey of the Main Ideas of the Greatest Sociologists,* Public Affairs Press, 1956, for a discussion of theories of social change. See pp. 30–34 for Sorokin's Theory.

of scientists. The inventors had a smattering of scientific principles, tinkered experimentally, almost by trial and error, and sometimes by luck stumbled on solutions to specific problems. Theoretical scientists looked down on the men who made practical applications of current scientific knowledge. James Clerk-Maxwell, instigator of the electro-magnetic theory of light, called Alexander Graham Bell a "speaker, who to gain his private ends, has become an electrician." But every American schoolboy knows about Alexander Graham Bell and few have heard of Willard Gibbs, an American theoretical physicist of world renown. The heroes we honor are indicative of America's adula-tion of practical inventiveness. Not all civilizations have shared Amer-ican enthusiasm for the practical. The ancient Greeks knew enough basic science to have invented simple labor-saving devices, but be-cause slaves, not free men, labored nobody bothered to invent such devices.

American admiration of industrial production, gadgets, and labor-saving machines has not abated, but the day of the lone inventor and the tycoon who bought his creation is over. The period between the two world wars saw scientists turn inventors, and today teams of scientists and engineers work for big business and big government. Like inventors, scientists may work empirically, but their experiments are carefully controlled. They develop theories to reduce experimenta-tion wherever possible.

In explaining the scientists' reliance upon theory, James Bryant Conant says, "The history of science demonstrates beyond a doubt that the really revolutionary and significant advances come not from em-piricism but from new theories."[3] He illustrates the point that theory reduces empiricism by telling how brewers, who learned to make beer as a cook makes a stew, did not know why some beers became acid or spoiled. After Pasteur advanced the theory that the growth of micro-organisms caused fermentation and putrefaction, brewers knew what steps to take to prevent spoilage. Dr. Conant implies that the so-called "scientific method" taught in public schools is the least significant part of scientific activity. He suggests that the use of conceptual designs that serve as working hypotheses on a grand scale—in short, theory, not empiricism—is that which really distinguishes a scientist from a tinkerer.[4]

The significant difference between science in the nineteenth and the twentieth centuries, Conant says, is a revolution in scientific thought

[3] James Bryant Conant, *Modern Science and Modern Man*, Doubleday, 1953, p. 53.
[4] *Ibid.*, pp. 34–35.

and a changed attitude on the part of scientists. The new theories have already been "enormously fruitful," producing atomic energy and automation, and the end is not yet in sight.

The current stress on scientific theory has implications for public education. The United States has need for more scientists, mathematicians, and engineers who can operate at a higher level of conceptualization than was necessary in earlier years. To educate future researchers and technicians, teachers must encourage theory-making and creative thinking in high school classes more than has been common in the past. They must also stress devotion to truth, for the unforgivable sin of the scientific community is to falsify results or misrepresent one's experiments.

Through its devotion to truth and to testing the observable, communicable, and reproducible, its interest in the natural world, and its improved instruments, the scientific community has greatly expanded technology. "It is hard to think of any advance in pure science which has not opened the door to a new advance in technology," Boulding states.[5] The work of scientists, 90 percent of whom are still alive, laid the foundation of a "knowledge industry" to which social scientists are now contributing. The term "knowledge industry," estimated at 30 percent of the Gross National Product of the United States, refers to the information component of economic activity. The amount of such information is, of course, growing rapidly because the more there is of it, the easier it is to add to. Boulding suggests that in 100 years it may take a student 50 years to reach the "frontiers of knowledge and begin making his own contribution" whereas now it takes about 25 years.[6] If knowledge does indeed accumulate so rapidly, the schools need to redouble their efforts to improve techniques of instruction that will enable a student to acquire more information in less time and to separate the chaff from the wheat of available information.

An Automated Society

The term automation, i.e., automatic production, was first used in the late 1940s. By substituting electronically equipped machinery for labor, automation increases production and lowers costs. The significant difference between mechanization and automation is that man is no longer needed to tend the individual machine. The early machines

[5] Kenneth E. Boulding, *The Meaning of the 20th Century: The Great Transition,* Harper & Row, 1964, p. 53.
[6] Kenneth E. Boulding, "The Knowledge Explosion," to be published in Association for Supervision and Curriculum Development, NEA 1970 Yearbook, *Developing Humane Capabilities,* The Association, 1970.

displaced many farm laborers and craftsmen, such as spinners, weavers, shoemakers, tailors, and bakers, and provided jobs for semiskilled operatives. Later developments substituted machines for unskilled workers. The new automated machinery is now displacing the semiskilled and clerical workers.

Two types of automation are not only changing the nature of available jobs but also rapidly speeding production: first, continuous automation production that links machines and, in many instances, a self-correcting control system; and second, integrated data processing by computers, called cybernetics. The first type decreases the need for semiskilled and sometimes skilled labor and increases the need for high-level technicians. The second type decreases the need for white-collar clerical workers and accountants and creates a need for programmers and technicians.

In January, 1961, in a report to President Kennedy on the effects of automation, Congressman Elmer J. Holland found that the number of office and clerical jobs had dropped by 25 percent since 1955.[7] Ida Hoos estimated that the electronic computer creates only one clerical or office job for every five eliminated. She claims that key-punch operation, a dead-end, repetitive chore, is replacing accounting, bookkeeping, filing, and ledger clerks, and that programming jobs, the new elite positions in offices, are very scarce and require skills unrelated to academic education.[8] Congressman Holland's 1961 report also cited a 25 percent drop in jobs in brewing, liquor, and soft-drink industries since 1950. In New York City alone, 40,000 elevator operators lost their jobs in a period of 15 years; over 160,000 unemployed automobile workers in Detroit have never been rehired; 50,000 jobs in radio and television manufacturing were eliminated in 11 years. Automation has replaced a million men in railroad work between 1940 and 1961 and about 33,000 telephone and 80,000 electrical machinery jobs between 1953 and 1961. In 1961, 12 men could produce as much steel as could 21 men in 1940. Not all these eliminated jobs are semiskilled. In many industries, automation is increasing the number of jobs for technicians, but eliminating those held by other skilled employees.

Meanwhile thousands of industries are being automated in either a single operation, a series of operations, a department, or a whole factory. The petroleum and lumber industries, communications, mili-

---

[7] Reported in the *Eugene Register-Guard,* Eugene, Oregon, February 2, 1961, p. 2.
[8] Ida Russakoff Hoos, "When the Computer Takes Over the Office," in Sigmund Nosow and William H. Form, eds., *Man, Work, and Society,* Basic Books, 1962, pp. 74–75.

tary, atomic plants, and many light industries—facial tissues, light bulbs, toothpicks, matches, breakfast cereals, chemicals, hardware, paper, flour—are either highly automated or becoming automated. Airlines, banks, brokerage firms, government agencies, universities, and schools are using computers in increasing numbers.

How many workers are losing their jobs because of automation? Apparently no one really knows because the employees who had jobs taken by automated equipment are assigned new jobs. The advancing average age of members of labor unions and the extent of unemployment among young workers indicate, however, that the employer does not hire new employees. A Harvard professor said, "If you put in a machine that costs $100,000 a year to rent and it doesn't replace anybody, you should never have put it in to begin with."[9] As a rule of thumb, a computer must eliminate 120 clerks to be worth its rental cost. In 1963, the Bureau of Labor estimated that automation was eliminating jobs at the rate of 4,000 a week; the same year, the chairman of U. S. Industries, Incorporated, which makes automated equipment, estimated the number eliminated at 40,000 jobs a week.[10]

The bright side is that automation creates jobs: the space industry with its satellites, such as Telstar, Early Bird, and weather satellites, the polyethylene industry, the atomic-energy industry, and others were made possible by automation. Moreover, effective use of automation will enable the United States to compete successfully in world markets and to maintain its leadership in technology.

During the next few decades the most rapidly growing occupational categories will be professionals, technicians, service workers (except domestics), salesmen, advertisers, and distributors. Although declining employment in many other fields was predicted, economists are beginning to doubt that automation will, in fact, produce mass unemployment in this country. They predict that consumer demands for goods are far from satiated. "The American economy," Kalachek says, "permits an unparalleled standard of living, but one which still falls considerably short of that retailed by *McCall's* and *Life* or the other tastemakers of our society."[11] If the demand for goods is maintained as he believes it will be, Kalachek says that workers with less than high school education will be able to find jobs. They will earn less-than-average incomes and suffer unemployment more often than others, but

[9] Thomas O'Toole, "White Collar Automation," *The Reporter,* 29 (December 5, 1963), 24–27.
[10] *Ibid.*
[11] Edward D. Kalachek, "Automation and Full Employment," *Trans-action, 4* (March, 1967), 28.

they will not constitute an unemployed class as was predicted in the early 1960s. Both the public and private sectors of the economy are providing greater income and employment security as well as employing various fiscal-monetary policies in an effort to assure continuing high levels of employment.[12]

Kalachek's prediction that workers with less than a high school education will find jobs does not change the fact that high school dropouts, disadvantaged in seeking jobs, are often unemployed during the years they should be in school and that dropouts are prone to delinquency. Since jobs are being created that can be filled only by persons who have developed technical skills whereas jobs for unskilled, semiskilled and clerical workers are declining in proportion to population, keeping youth in school is important to their future success. Changes occurring in occupational requirements and in the social climate in which man works are also significant in planning appropriate school curriculums.

SOCIAL CONDITIONS
IN A TECHNOLOGICAL SOCIETY

Changes in technology are accompanied by changes in other institutions. As Boulding points out, "we must look at pure science, technological change, and social invention as parts of a single pattern of development in which each element supports the other."[13] It has been said, in fact, that the greatest of all inventions was a social invention: organized research and development.

Clearly the development of science and technology has contributed to the growth of big business and of big government. Imperialism is no longer a profitable undertaking because investment in applied science and technological progress at home pays higher dividends than investments abroad. Science and technology have influenced the family structure and the roles played by members of the family. By increasing life spans, science contributed to the population explosion, which will overwhelm mankind with problems if it is not checked soon. Increasing industrialization has given rise to mammoth cities choked with smog and to factories that pollute man's water supply. Whether man can overcome the ill effects of industrialization in order to enjoy its benefits depends largely upon his capacity to make social inventions.

At this point, however, our concern is with changes in man's life style at work that have implications for educating the young for work and leisure.

[12] *Ibid.*, 24–29.
[13] Boulding, *The Meaning of the 20th Century*, p. 11.

The Social Climate
in Modern Man's Work

Ever since the founding of this country, middle-class Americans have placed a high valuation upon work as an activity that gives meaning to life. Not all unskilled and semiskilled workers have shared this point of view. Although craftsmen may have lost their pride in workmanship when they became machine workers in an assembly line, this line was not always the dreary place that middle-class writers depict. Observers have found much horseplay, betting, and "banking" of items so that workmen can rest and chat with neighbors. Among mimeograph operators, file clerks, and other low-paid clerical workers, the same kind of behavior prevails. Such occupations are not a source, however, of high esteem within the community. Rather than identify himself with the unknown machine he tends when he knows the questioner has never heard of it, a worker identifies with a powerful company, "I work for General Motors," he will say. It seems unlikely that such employees seek meaning in life in their jobs. Their primary objective in working is to earn money to find meaning in life elsewhere. Automated jobs do not necessarily promise rewarding activity. Employees in the lower echelons may, in fact, be lonelier than on assembly lines since fewer employees are needed. At least one British labor union thinks so—it has applied for "lonesome pay" for overseers of automatic machines. The alienation of workers described by Karl Marx may indeed take place in automated factories. Marx believed that when a worker did not own the product of his labor, he saw it and his job as alien things. Eventually this estrangement from his work led a man to see himself as worthless and others as hostile and alien, according to Marx. Not many research studies are available to support an assumption of automated places of work increasing feelings of alienation. Early preautomation studies do reveal, however, that where intercommunications among workers is curtailed, workers may react either by becoming very absent-minded, accident-prone, and hostile to authority or by escaping into daydreams.

Champion and Dager studied the effects of a switch to electronic data processing (EDP) upon 31 middle-class bank employees who held responsible positions. Nine employees quit. After several positions were eliminated, a number of employees were transferred to other duties. The work force was divided into shifts, with some persons working from midnight to dawn. Communication among employees was drastically curtailed. The researchers concluded that EDP increased impersonalization, feelings of alienation, anxiety, and job dissatisfaction, which were minimized, however, when work loads were heavy, status was raised, and the employee was an aloof, cool, thick-skinned person, enthusiastic about things. Employees who were friendly, excitable, and dependent made poor adjustments.[14]

Another source of impersonality in places of work that predates the use of automated equipment is bureaucracy. A bureaucracy is a formal, rationally organized social structure designed to achieve the organization's purposes by a clear-cut division of duties and responsibilities.

Many of us think that bureaucracy is peculiar to government, and fail to recognize its presence in business, trade unions, churches, and other agencies *including schools.* Superficial differences should not mask the basic bureaucratic structure of all large-scale organizations in the United States. Among the characteristics commonly associated with bureaucracy are routine paper work and regulations developed originally in the interest of efficiency, but the most important characteristics of a bureaucratic organization are hierarchical structure, spheres of jurisdiction, and qualified experts.

Hierarchical structure means a system of graded institutional authority that assigns to some positions the responsibility for policy decisions of major importance, relegates to others the responsibility for policy decisions of minor importance, and to still others responsibility for job performance only. Authority resides in the position, not in the man holding the position. One foreman may be replaced by another, but the job, its authority, and its specifications remain the same. A chain of command must be followed in which each person's communication range is limited by the dictum that he must not go "over his boss' head" to superior authority. The hierarchical system operates largely through formal written directives defining responsibilities and duties and evaluations of performance. Each segment of the organization has a sphere of jurisdiction, carefully prescribed, sometimes by law in government agencies, such as schools. In an ideal bureaucracy each person holding a position is a trained expert. He qualifies for the job by having passed an examination or having earned a special degree. He holds a license. He receives the same salary as others who possess the same qualifications.

Paradoxically the bureaucratic system generates feelings of security

[14] Dean J. Champion and Edward Z. Dager, "Automation Man in the Counting House," *Trans-action,* 3 (March/April 1966), 34–36.

and insecurity among employees. An employee is secure in his job in that he is not easily fired after having successfully completed a probationary period. But the impersonal atmosphere of bureaucratic places of work may give him a vague sense of insecurity, unworthiness, and alienation from others. In a bureaucracy, personal relationships become formalized, lacking in intimacy, and, for the ambitious, competitive. Supervisory personnel are expected to be rational, impartial, and impersonal in their dealings with subordinates. Proficiency ratings and promotions are presumably based solely on merit. The rules, routines, and rituals establishing rigid discipline enforced by a chain of command do not encourage the creativeness that makes work pleasurable. In *The Caine Mutiny*, Lieutenant Keefer doubtless exaggerated when he said, "The Navy is a master plan designed by geniuses for execution by idiots," but he expressed the sentiments of many whose only job is to carry out the orders of superiors.

Automated equipment, bureaucracy, and division of labor do not create conditions conducive to high morale among workers. A Roper poll found that two of three Americans felt neither "ideally" nor "miserably" adjusted to their jobs. Over half (51 percent) said they would choose another occupation if they had it to do over; fewer than one-third (31 percent) said they would enter the same work. In 1957 NEA pollsters reported, however, that over 80 percent of the nation's teachers said they would choose teaching if they could live their lives over. Professional and managerial people are more likely than wage earners to be satisfied with their jobs.

As school systems throughout the nation, particularly in urban areas, have grown in size, bureaucracies have necessarily expanded their controls. Teachers and students in bureaucratic school systems suffer the same frustrations as other workers in such organizations. The popularity among teachers of *Up the Down Staircase* indicates that many of them enjoy the opportunity to laugh at their superiors in the chain of command. Further effects of bureaucracy in schools are considered in the next chapter.

The Increasing Significance of Leisure

If many workers in bureaucratic and automated places of work are finding little or no personal satisfaction in their work, where can they find self-realization? Increasingly social philosophers and others suggest that the man of the future will develop his potential in leisure, not work activities. If predictions of a workweek of three or four days become realities, the average employees could indeed find more time to devote to leisure-time endeavors than to work. A long workweek of 50 to 60 hours is, however, envisioned for professionals, at least during the next few decades. Thus in modern times the educated man has less leisure than the less well-educated whereas in earlier periods the best educated man had the most leisure. The Greek word *scholé,* from which the English word *school* is derived, meant *leisure,* reflecting the idea that only those who had leisure could be educated.

The recognition of the need to relieve man from routine, mechanical chores in which he finds no meaning, and thus to free him for leisure activities in which he can develop his individuality, has a long history. In ancient Greece a leisure class enjoying the fruits of slave labor developed a democratic form of government and cultivated the arts. Plato thought workers had to be excluded from participation in government and the arts because their energies were exhausted in their work. Many centuries later John Stuart Mill suggested that men can achieve the "Art of Living" only when "minds ceased to be engrossed by the art of getting on."

If leisure then is such a boon to creative, productive activities, why do many Americans fear the expected increase in leisure? Between 1940 and 1965 Americans spent almost a third of their 26 million recreation dollars on spectator activities, such as television, movies, theaters and operas, and sports.[15] Today the average American spends most of his leisure watching television. Notwithstanding a notable increase in the sale of sports and camping equipment, musical instruments and art supplies, and admissions to commercial participant amusements, the average American seems to be using his leisure primarily as a diversion or an escape from life rather than as a time for personal fulfillment. Does this sorry set of facts suggest that schools have ignored the problem of how to use leisure?

EDUCATION FOR WORK AND LEISURE

Scientific and technological changes have been affecting schools in many ways. The most significant influences are the increasing use of technology in teaching and the imperatives to change curriculums in

---

[15] For complete figures on how recreation dollars were spent in 1940 and 1965, see U.S. Bureau of the Census, *Statistical Abstracts of the United States: 1967,* Government Printing Office, 1967, p. 212.

respect to consumer education, vocational guidance and training, and education for leisure. First let us consider the use of technological aids in teaching.

The Uses of Technology in Teaching

Audiovisual aids and closed-circuit televised programs are being increasingly used in teaching. Many school administrators who purchased teaching machines a few years ago have, however, been disappointed in their usefulness. The current and future use of EDP and of computer-assisted instruction (CAI) appears to be much more promising. Computers, the "hardware," are already available for rental, but educational programs, the "software," have not yet been developed to any great extent. Although widespread use of CAI is likely to be deferred until the 1980s, EDP is being increasingly utilized for scheduling students, maintaining personnel records, and gathering data upon which educational decisions are based.

CAI is being tested experimentally by a number of organizations, including the University of Pittsburgh, the University of Illinois, Stanford University, the University of California at Irvine, International Business Machines, Bolt, Beranek, and Newman, and System Development Corporation. The Stanford Project instituted drill-and-practice systems in arithmetic and language arts that are being used by some 2000 students daily in California, Kentucky, and Mississippi. It also initiated a tutorial reading program for first graders in Brentwood School, Palo Alto, California. The students in this school were primarily from culturally disadvantaged homes. After very short to 35 minute CAI periods over the school year, the CAI group performed significantly better on standardized reading tests than did the control group. The computer method of teaching was judged to be very responsive to individual differences.[16]

The difficulties of immediate, widespread use of computers in instruction were also demonstrated in this research. For example, a typical first-grade reading lesson of 30 minutes required the coding of more than 9000 course-writer commands for the computer. The programmer also made a tape recording for all the messages the student might hear during a lesson, and a technician prepared a film strip for each picture the student viewed.[17] The greatest difficulty in develop-

---

[16] Richard C. Atkinson, "The Computer Is a Tutor," *Psychology Today, 1* (January, 1968), 36–39, 57–59.
[17] *Ibid.*, p. 57.

ing the "software" for computer instruction is, however, the lack of adequate learning theories upon which a theory of instruction can be based. (The theoretical breakthrough in biology that seems imminent and new psychological researches may soon vitalize learning theories.) After being written, programs must be tested for effectiveness and for social and emotional effects of CAI upon students.

Despite such difficulties, the potentialities for increasing knowledge that students acquire, for individualizing instruction, and for providing the teacher with aids that will enable him to teach high level processes rather than information, are so great that undoubtedly experimentation and research will be pursued relentlessly. Possible uses of computers in the future include not only drills and tutorial sessions for students but also spoken dialogues between student and computer, improved diagnosis of student successes and failures in learning, computer scoring of essays as well as objective test items, college and vocational counseling, identification of relevant research, cataloging books, and other uses.

What will be the effects upon schools if computers do much of the work formerly done by humans? No one knows, but many make predictions. Among others, Goodlad foresees the day when students will come to school only for discussions and related activities, for they will communicate with the computer at home. An expansion of nongraded classrooms is also anticipated.[18] The most significant change, however, may be in the role of the teacher.

The teacher will become a diagnostician, remediator, coordinator of programs, and director of group activities. The teacher will become increasingly concerned with the highest cognitive processes, such as helping pupils develop abilities to see relationships, stimulating curiosity and creativeness, and encouraging critical thinking, as well as with improving interpersonal relationships. To a considerable degree such changes in the teacher's role are dictated not only by computerized instruction but also by technological and social changes in the larger society.

Influence of Job-Market Changes
upon School Curriculum

For many years American education has been dominated by a concern for vocational preparation and the assumption that man will find self-fulfillment in his work. A concern for vocational education is likely

[18] John Goodlad, "Learning and Teaching in the Future," *NEA Journal,* 57 (February, 1968), 49–51.

to continue, but what the school offers in respect to vocational preparation is due for a drastic change, as is its assumption that a young person should find significant meaning in his work.

Probably the future typical high school will offer very little specific job training for technicians and craftsmen. Such training may be offered in regional vocational high schools or in community colleges. The likelihood that specific job training will decline in most high schools is suggested by the following changes in the larger society. A student can no longer train for a specific job in industry long in advance because the nature of jobs is changing too rapidly. Moreover, the average high school cannot afford to purchase the highly complex machinery used on thousands of different industrial jobs today. Although vocational teachers in most high schools cannot hope to keep abreast of anticipated industrial changes or to negotiate training agreements with labor unions and industries, regional vocational high school and community college officials may be able to do so.

For several common-sense reasons then, prevocational training may become the average high school's contribution to technical training. Such training will include an acquaintance with common tools, safety measures, the rudiments of electronics, and thorough grounding in mathematics and in mechanical and electrical principles. It would teach theoretical principles that underlie families of occupations, acquaint pupils with occupational information and industrial processes, and help them develop job responsibility. It would also develop the communication skills essential in industry—listening and speaking effectively, writing technical reports and business letters, completing application forms, and reading technical reports, blueprints, and instructions.

Work-study programs at the high school level may concentrate largely on jobs in service and distributive occupations since these are expanding fields. Work-study programs and courses in agriculture will decline. A number of high schools will also sponsor work-study programs for mentally retarded students in which they may learn to perform routine tasks dependably.

Guidance counselors may pay increasing attention to the personality needs of a student in helping him choose vocational goals not because they expect work to be all-important in the student's life but because some people are more likely to be alienated by jobs in automated businesses and industries than are others. Teachers and counselors will prepare students to accept the fact that the job they choose may be short-lived, and that they must be able and willing to learn new skills, possibly by returning to school, several times during their lives. They will also help students plan for professional and subprofessional occupations in terms of their needs for humanistic as well as specialized academic preparation. Teachers, counselors, and curriculum developers will need to devote a great deal more attention to education for leisure than they have in the past.

Education for Leisure

Education for "worthy use" of leisure has long been one of the objectives of education. But Americans differ greatly in their interpretations of what is worthy use of leisure. Teachers, parents, and ministers have, in fact, talked so much about "unworthy uses" of leisure—dissipation, gambling, alcoholism, drug addiction, illicit sexuality, and spectatoritis—that they have tended to equate "worthy use" with avoidance of evil. Traditionally, leisure has been defined as time left over from work and the necessary chores of living, during which a person may pursue his personal interests (assuming, of course, that his interests were "worthy"). Perhaps today working time should be defined as the time left over from leisure spent in activities that are purposeful for individual development and possibly for society.

American teachers have not clarified their own values or the school's role in respect to leisure. Should they view leisure as a prerequisite to self-fulfillment? Clearly leisure is necessary for effective citizenship, indispensable for a life-long educational process, and required for the development of individual talents, an appreciation of the arts, and creative expression. It is essential for re-creating the individual by allowing him to alternate physical with mental activities, contemplation with pressured decision-making. In short, it provides variety within routine.

If leisure is viewed in this light, how can the school best educate for leisure?

Education for leisure can be improved if the school's role is clarified. The first step is to distinguish between entertaining students and educating them to use leisure for self-cultivation, social service, creative endeavors, political activities, and contemplation. Inevitably a certain amount of recreation is provided in schools through activities, such as dramatics, athletics, and organizations, which should be viewed in part as exploratory leisure experiences. But, in general, park and recreational districts are better prepared to serve recreational needs than are schools. The main job of the school is to educate, not to entertain.

A second step is to adopt a positive philosophy of leisure. For too long school leaders have used getting a job as a carrot that will attract the industrious student. Employment is a worthy goal of vocational training, but a complete life is the appropriate goal of education. Because he has many interests, an educated man is seldom bored. He is a good workman and more. He is an active citizen, a man who joins with his family in creative pursuits. He is capable of using his talents in ways that increase knowledge and interest in life for himself and others. He is physically fit. He enjoys fun for its own sake, but he does not search blindly for diversions.

The next step is to study how the subject matter taught in school can contribute to the enrichment of leisure activities. Every discipline can make a contribution that will open doors for some pupils if teachers deliberately plan to make their subject relevant to leisure pursuits. A person is rarely interested in anything that he knows little or nothing about. The more history one knows, the more likely he is to enjoy reading history, especially if he has been led to see such reading as an interesting hobby. His interest is whetted as his competence grows. The boy who learns to play tennis well in his physical education classes is more likely to continue to play the game when he is older than is the boy who never played well. The pupil who becomes proficient in the use of tools is likely to enjoy "do-it-yourself" projects.

The school can teach pupils to be selective in artistic matters. Students can be exposed to art, music, literature, and dramatics in such a way that their powers of discrimination and capacities for appreciation are enlarged. To set standards of taste is not the goal. Developing sensitivity to the feelings being expressed by the artist and his artistry and comparing artist with artist enable the student to develop his own standards. The school can cooperate with the community in providing children opportunities to attend symphonies, recitals, art exhibits, and theater productions.

Competitive interscholastic athletics that emphasize winning teams should not preclude good physical education programs for all young people. Keeping oneself physically fit through daily exercise is a habit most easily developed in the young. When physical educators teach pupils to hike, swim, bowl, play golf, tennis, and badminton, they have taught activities that may be continued into adulthood. Intramural sports enable more pupils to participate than do interscholastic athletics. In large urban communities that have little interest in local high school teams, physical educators can stress physical fitness for all and tone down the excessive emphasis on winning teams.

The student activity program can be made a training ground for many leisure activities. Over-involvement of a few capable and willing students should be discouraged; participation by many students encouraged. Pupils often learn more about working successfully in groups, develop more hobbies and creative interests, and gain greater insights into social problems through participation in student activities than they do through class discussions.

School leaders sometimes assume that whatever is good for many young people is good for all of them. Such an assumption may lead to over-organized lives. Social life in many suburbs has over-emphasized group activity and allowed little privacy for the individual. Since urban life provides so many contacts with others, the time comes when the average person wants to be alone or when a family wants to be together. Everybody needs a chance to do something—or nothing—for his own satisfaction, and alone if he prefers. In short, self-fulfillment implies individual growth as well as participation in the social concerns of a society.

If an individual uses his leisure advantageously, his activities are not simply distractions to while away time. They contribute to his conviction that life has purpose, sustain his interest, arouse his enthusiasm, elicit his energies, and provide an outlet for his creativeness. Hundreds of activities in an urban society meet these criteria. Some of these activities involve groups of people, others are restricted to family groups, many may be pursued individually.[19]

IMPORTANT CONCEPTS

Alienation. The state of feeling estranged or separated from one's self and others, and from the known and comforting. See pp. 129, 234, 236.

Automation. The technique of converting a mechanical process to a maximum of automatic operation. See p. 125 ff.

Bureaucracy. See pp. 130–131.

"Cultural lag." See p. 121.

Cybernetics. A science dealing with principles of control and communication applied in the operation of computers and the functions of organisms.

Empiricism. Reliance on observation and experimentation as the bases of knowledge.

"Hardware." See p. 133 for the meaning of this term in an educational context.

"Ideal" culture. See Sorokin's definition of this term on p. 123.

"Ideational" culture. See pp. 122–123.

"Knowledge industry." See p. 125.

---

[19] This section on education for leisure is paraphrased from *Urbanization and Oregon's Schools,* 1965, pp. 25–28, a statement of the Educational Policies Commission, Oregon Education Association, written by Grace Graham.

Leisure. See pp. 131 ff. and 136 ff. for a discussion of the expanding use of this term.

Nongraded classroom. The assignment of pupils from what would usually be two or more school grades to the same classroom for the purpose of reducing the threat of nonpromotion and individualizing instruction.

"Sensate" culture. See pp. 122–123.

"Software." See p. 133 for the meaning of this term in an educational context.

Sphere of jurisdiction. The territory within which or the matter over which a legitimate authority may exercise control.

Theory. See Conant's definition, "the use of conceptual designs that serve as hypotheses on a grand scale," pp. 124–125.

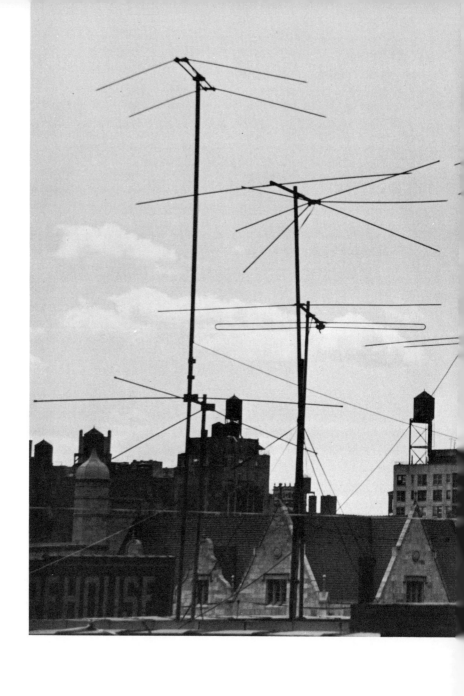

7. EFFECTS OF MASS SOCIETY UPON SCHOOLS

If the nineteenth century was the age of the editorial chair, ours is the century of the psychiatrist's couch.

—MARSHALL MC LUHAN[1]

In recent decades for different reasons, many literary, art, and social critics, as well as journalists and social scientists have described the United States as a "mass culture" or a "mass society." The first section of this chapter explores the cluster of meanings associated with this term. The second section examines aspects of the mass society that the modern school must take into account. The third section deals with the mass media as educational agencies. The final section describes involvement in special-interest groups as a product of mass society.

WHAT IS A MASS SOCIETY?

Clearly a mass society is large and complex, but it also has other characteristics. It has a ubiquitous system of mass communication.

[1] *Understanding Media,* McGraw-Hill, 1964, p. 21.

This characteristic of mass society has engaged the attention of many commentators on the current scene. Writers from literary and artistic fields, using the word "culture" in the sense of refined taste, contrast the "High Culture" of an elite with the "Mass Culture" of the common man as reflected in the output of the mass media. Others inquire into social, personal, and political behavior patterns that may be the outcomes of the drift toward a mass society in the United States. Again such inquiry is often linked with a study of the mass media.

Although social scientists may agree with scholars from the humanities in their low opinion of the popular arts, their interest in mass society stems from different considerations. They define mass society in terms of great numbers of individuals of heterogeneous social origins. The members of a mass are anonymous in the sense that a viewer of television does not know others in the audience of which he is a part. Mass men have no leaders, no plan of action, and few unifying values. Their standards are flexible, and this flexibility accommodates frequent fads and crazes. The unity of the mass is its acceptance of common emotional symbols, a common language, and a historical heritage. Lacking deep roots in social affairs, mass men readily accept suggestions from manipulators of mass movements and of the mass media.

Scientists studying the effects of mass society upon the individual find evidence of increased interdependence, dislocations in community and church, loss of traditional values, and the impersonalization of modern life—all of which lead to striving for status and feelings of anxiety and estrangement. Students of mass society have also analyzed the dynamics of mass or crowd behavior. They find man in mass society prone to both apathetic and extremist reactions. The apathetic fail to contribute to their society; the extremist may resort to revolution, violence, crime, or religious or political radicalism. The chief danger of a mass society, they say, is that it provides a hospitable environment for totalitarianism, should a demagogue with an ideology appear in a time of crisis.[2]

Two theories of mass society are the *aristocratic, conservative theory* that views the extension of equality to all men as dangerous in that the most competent men—the political and intellectual elite—lose their prerogatives in setting standards and in making decisions, and the *democratic theory* that deplores the vulnerability of the mass man to the wiles of totalitarian leaders. Theorists of both schools are concerned with maintaining significant values, particularly freedom, but

[2] Modern writers on this subject were scooped by Plato. See *The Republic,* Book 8, chaps. 32 and 33.

they may disagree as to the interpretation of the values they wish to preserve.

Kornhauser thinks that a combination of both theories gives a more adequate theory of mass society. He points out that both the elite and the non-elite must be protected. The best protection of individual freedoms is the existence of local centers of power, independent social groups, and voluntary associations that can offset the influence of highly centralized, bureaucratic organizations and government. When intermediate groups are active, citizens become concerned with local affairs, develop a feeling of importance through participation, and leave to the specialists the jobs that experts can do best.[3]

When one refers to *the masses,* he usually means the common people, the working classes, the lower socioeconomic levels of society. Chiefly because the lower classes are less well educated and have a smaller stake in the status quo, they are generally more susceptible to mass movements than are middle-class people. Nevertheless, discontented middle-class persons and intellectuals, particularly free-lancers, who are ignorant outside their own specialties, unhappy in their anonymity, and afraid of the unknown are also vulnerable. McCarthyism, the closest approach to a fascist mass movement in the United States, found strong support in Bennington, Vermont, among small businessmen.[4]

Mass movements, which may be encouraged by means of mass communication, are often the result of the activities of influential pressure groups that endanger the ideal of free discussion. Not only is a free society jeopardized when free discussion is curtailed, but also the education of future citizens is imperiled when freedom of thought in schools is denied. Many schools are directly influenced by powerful special-interest groups that seek to determine the social goals of education, win acceptance for certain values, and control the school's policies and practices. Schools are also affected by the omnipresent agencies of mass media that tend to standardize thought, lull sensibilities, and offer simple answers to complex problems. Perhaps, as Aldous Huxley said, the real teachers in the United States today are not the school teachers, professors, librarians, philosophers, ministers, and priests, but the commercial and political propagandists.

Certain forces operating in a mass society may, however, have beneficial as well as deleterious effects. For instance, the voluntary

[3] William Kornhauser, *The Politics of Mass Society,* Free Press, 1959, chaps. 2 and 3, *passim.*

[4] Martin Trow, "Small Businessmen, Political Tolerance, and Support for McCarthy," *American Journal of Sociology, 64* (November, 1958), 278.

associations are the strength of a democratic society; they are dangerous to our social order only when dominated by a remote bureaucracy
that distorts truth. The mass media, too, especially the free press, have
been staunch defenders of a free society. Television and radio have
great potentialities for the education of democratic citizens in social
and political matters, esthetic appreciations, and general information.
The mass media are harmful only when misused to dupe the general
public or when they cater too frequently to the lowest popular level
of taste.

It is clear that the term mass society defies simple definition. But
some of its manifestations can be dealt with. The theme of this chapter
is that certain tendencies in mass society must be checked if American
children are to receive the intellectual heritage to which they are
entitled. Teachers must be concerned about developments outside and
within the schools that tend to create alienated mass men rather than
independent thinkers. Their first concern must be with the dangers in
mass education, which is a product of the population explosion and
other social changes.

MASS EDUCATION

Education in the United States has become mass education in several
ways and for a number of reasons. Student enrollments have grown
because the number of young people to be educated has increased
enormously, and they are staying in school longer. The first part of this
section discusses the so-called population explosion in this country,
and the second part discusses the effect of this explosion on school
enrollments. The final part elaborates upon the implications of the
concept "mass education."

The Population Explosion
in the United States

The birth rate in this country is about average among nations—more
than that of most European countries but less than that of most Asian
and Latin American countries. Nevertheless, our population growth
between 1953 and 1963 was as much as the growth of our population
from the time of the Pilgrims until the beginning of the Civil War
(from 1620 to 1860). According to the United States Bureau of
Census, the population grew from 76 millions in 1900 to 200 millions in
1967. The most conservative estimate of government demographers is
that our population will be 205 millions in 1970, 228 millions in 1980,
and 256 millions in 1990.

What accounts for such rapid growth? The high birthrate during World War II and thereafter is, of course, one factor. Although the birthrate has declined somewhat since 1962, the population will continue to grow rapidly because the number of mothers having babies today is much larger than the number of mothers who bore the "war babies." Factors other than birthrate that account for rises in population are low infant mortality rates and high longevity rates, resulting from improved medical care, sanitation, and nutrition. Earlier marriages than formerly are also a factor in that more generations of children are reared when parents are very young.

The size of our population is still, however, not out of proportion to the size of our country if people were evenly distributed. The reason that the United States has many mass society characteristics is that over half of the people live in 13 major "strip cities." These strip cities are the metropolitan areas, the most densely populated of which lie between Boston and Washington, Cleveland and Pittsburgh, Detroit and Muskegon, Chicago-Gary and Milwaukee, and San Francisco and San Diego.[5]

The choice sites of the strip cities, however, will not be able to contain the population if it continues to grow at its present rate. If the birthrate of 1965 continues until 2065, the United States will have a population of one billion, what it would have today if all the people now living in Europe, Latin America, and Africa moved to this country. Even if the birth rate dropped to its level during the Great Depression, by 2065 the United States would have a population of almost half a billion.[6] Boulding estimates that if world population continues to grow at its present rate for 300 years, the land area of the whole world will be one big city and in 700 to 800 years there will be standing room only![7]

Effects of the Population Explosion in Schools

The most striking change in education, like the changes in production per man-hour, speed of communication, rise in per capita income, can be demonstrated numerically. Table 2 substantiates the claims of increased enrollments in high schools and colleges, where the greatest

[5] See William M. Dobriner, *Class in Suburbia*, Prentice-Hall, 1963, pp. 149–151.

[6] Donald J. Bogue, "Population Growth in the United States," in Philip M. Hauser, ed., *The Population Dilemma*, The American Assembly, Prentice-Hall, 1963, pp. 71–72.

[7] Kenneth E. Boulding, *The Meaning of the 20th Century: The Great Transition*, Harper & Row, Colophon edition, 1964, pp. 124–125.

gains have been made in recent years. Most people attribute the rise in school enrollments solely to the baby boom, but the rise in the birthrate during and since World War II does not account for the fact that a larger proportion of our total population is now in school than was in school in 1900. In 1900 there were proportionately more children in our population than today, yet today the proportion of our population in school is larger than in 1900. Why? An industrialized society requires literacy of all citizens, technical training of a substantial number, and specialized knowledge of many. Child labor is not needed. Therefore the job of modern children is, by law and consensus, that of attending school.

TABLE 2. Secondary School and College Enrollments in Relation to Total Age Groups

Year	No. Enrolled in Secondary Schools per 100 Persons 14–17 Years of Age	No. Graduated from Secondary Schools per 100 Persons 17 Years of Age	No. Enrolled in Institutions of Higher Education per 100 of Population 18–21 Years of Age[a]
1879–1880	—[b]	2.5	—[b]
1889–1890	6.7	3.5	2.99
1899–1900	11.4	6.4	3.91
1909–1910	15.4	8.8	4.99
1919–1920	32.3	16.8	7.88
1929–1930	51.4	29.0	11.89
1939–1940	73.3	50.8	14.57
1949–1950	77.4	59.0	27.22
1959–1960	90.3	65.1	37.2[c]
1965–1966	—[b]	71.9	—[d]

[a] Does not include summer session.

[b] Figures not available.

[c] Based on early fall enrollments. Enrollments for full academic year would be larger.

[d] Figures not available. College enrollments have been increasing about 10 percent a year since 1960.

Source: Adapted from figures in U. S. Department of Health, Education, and Welfare pamphlets: *Progress of Public Education in the United States of America, 1960–61*, pp. 17–18; *Statistics of Higher Education, 1955–56*, p. 8; *Opening (Fall) Enrollment in Higher Education, 1960: Analytic Report*, p. 12; and *Statistical Abstract of the United States, 1967*, p. 131.

Of course, not all pupils and not all parents view this job in the same light. Parents from the lower socioeconomic levels may see the school as a custodian of children who are too young to work, and their children also may feel that they are marking time; but ambitious parents and their offspring know that, as the level of general education rises, individuals who want to improve or keep their social status must attend school longer. Whereas their grandparents might have attained superiority upon high school graduation, the present generation must graduate from college and perhaps even pursue graduate work to achieve the same relative status.

Not only are more pupils attending schools for longer periods of time, but also the schools they attend are larger. Large public schools are the rule in cities. With improved transportation, small schools in rural areas are being replaced by large consolidated schools. College and university enrollments are also growing by leaps and bounds.

The trend in rising school enrollments will continue. In 1955, 37 million Americans were full-time students, compared to 68 million in the labor force. By 1965 the number of students had risen to 54½ million, the labor force to 77 million. Elementary and secondary school enrollments will grow as population increases, but they cannot attract a much higher percentage of children than they now do since almost all children (age 6–17) are already in school. The greatest increases in enrollment in proportion to population will be at the college level. The number of college students is expected to have doubled between 1960 and 1970. Community colleges offering technical training will be well attended in an automated society. Participation in evening classes, university and college extension courses, correspondence studies, and other forms of adult education will show substantial increases. In 1963 pollsters from the National Opinion Research Center estimated that about one-fourth of American adults were part-time or full-time students.

Increased enrollments result in many problems for schools. Problems of finance, budgets, bond issues, school construction, maintenance, transportation, class size, and teacher recruitment plague administrators. Universal education through high school presents trials for the classroom teacher. In "readiness," motivation, and academic interests, the teacher finds many of his pupils wanting. These problems are still unsolved and become more difficult to solve as enrollments continue to grow.

The most serious problem, however, is whether administrators and teachers, especially at the high school and college level, will be able to offset feelings of anonymity, alienation, and rootlessness that develop in systems of mass education just as they develop in mass society.

Hazards of Mass Education

The social climate of the school has been greatly affected by increased enrollments. A rigid, impersonal, inflexible bureaucracy tends to develop as schools increase in size. Rules cannot be set aside to meet individual needs. Teachers as well as students begin to feel that they have no part in making decisions that affect their lives. People become things. Especially in colleges, students are likely to become numbers, not people. The Berkeley revolt and other such protests among college students grew out of such circumstances. The recent militancy of teachers may also be caused in part by similar conditions in public schools.

Ignoring student and teacher protests, critics sometimes say that the young can be taught by fewer teachers. It is indeed true that experimental results have failed to show older methods to be more effective than large classes, television teaching, and teaching machines in respect to pupil mastery of subject matter. Conversely, advocates of small classes claim that attitudes, values, and other intangibles not measurable by tests, are developed in small groups. These contentions are hard to prove. What might be worthy of serious consideration is whether Americans want to subject their children to anonymity in schools. Whatever methods are devised for teaching large numbers of pupils with few teachers will have to be counterbalanced by small-group instruction. Corporations are hiring personnel men to offset impersonality and anonymity in industry. Surely if such conditions are bad for the morale of adults, they must be undesirable for young people.

Students can become school-oriented, teachers know, in one or both of two ways—through involvement in the academic life (which is difficult in large classes) or through participation in the social life of the school. Barker and Gump found, however, that students in large schools are less likely than students in small schools to be involved in student activities.[8]

Another weakness of mass education is that many teachers have not yet been able to adjust to a new type of student and to his needs. Mass education tends to provide the same education for all. The purpose of

[8] Roger G. Barker and Paul V. Gump, *Big School, Small School,* Stanford University Press, 1964, *passim.*

remedial work is to bring everyone up to the same standards. The purpose of counseling is to help everyone fit the established mold. The teacher's lower-middle class tradition stressing the Puritan ethic, respectability, community service, conformity, and responsibility permeates the school. No one is encouraged to challenge the status quo. Fortunately not all schools and all teachers are guilty of impersonality and of lack of concern for individual differences, curriculum revision, and creative thinking. Nevertheless, the dangers of miseducation, lulling of students' sensibilities, and their alienation from society are as inherent in mass education as in mass communications, which will be discussed in the following section.

THE INFLUENCE OF MASS MEDIA
UPON SCHOOLS

A significant characteristic of this century is the prodigious expansion of several communication media—newspapers, comics, paperbacks, periodicals, motion pictures, radio, and television. Each of these serves as a medium for bringing to large numbers of people experiences outside their immediate environment. Everyone can share in the communications cornucopia. As a matter of fact, so ubiquitous are the productions of mass media in the United States, no one can escape them. The short workweek and added leisure give Americans time to consume the media's products, and advertisers pay most of the costs.

The Significance of Mass Media
in Modern Life

Until modern times the average man's geographical space was largely confined to the area he could travel on a horse or in a boat; his communications were limited to the spoken word in face-to-face situations. Gutenberg's invention of the printing press in the fifteenth century encouraged literacy and contributed to the rise of a middle class that could read. Nevertheless, prior to the nineteenth century mass literacy was only an ideal in the United States and books were not printed for popular consumption.

The historical forebear of modern mass media in America was Benjamin Day's *New York Sun,* established in 1833, the original "penny press" that depended upon mass appeal and advertising money. Since that time the advent of each new medium aimed at mass circulation has given promise of expanded educational opportunities for the common man; each in turn has failed to fulfill its potential. The seeds of success and failure lie within the nature of the media.

In this country agencies of mass media are organized as businesses motivated chiefly by the desire for profits. To sell advertising copy or win sponsors for broadcasts, a medium must attain high circulation. Designed to attract mass audiences, a medium's content is likely to be mildly entertaining, trivial, noncontroversial, sensational, ephemeral, and amusing rather than instructive, intellectual, and artistic. The chief criterion of success in its productions is therefore quantitative, not qualitative.

Nevertheless, the mass media are obligated to provide a public service. Freedom of the press and freedom of speech, stoutly defended by Americans as bulwarks of a democratic society, are based on the premise that purveyors of news, ideas, and values are persons of integrity, concerned with truth, accurate reporting, and the welfare of others. The power of mass media in the sense of potential influence is thought to be too great to be delegated to irresponsible agents. Moreover, the air space allocated to radio and television by the federal government is public property. Thus agencies of communication must offer popular fare to stay in business and provide a public service to meet their social responsibility.

Social reformers who worked for shorter hours of labor envisioned a day when the average man would have leisure for creative and intellectual pursuits. In 1966 with abundant leisure, the typical American family watches television programs, at least 75 percent of which are entertainment features, about five and a half hours a day—about six and a half in mid-winter.[9] No other medium draws such large audiences. A poll of 1,722 urban women revealed that 57.6 percent of them had not read a book in the last year.[10] Roper pollsters found that 46 percent of their respondents admitted that they rarely or never read a book that they felt would advance their knowledge in some way.[11] Hence, much of the criticism of the mass media stems from disappointment. Idealists' dreams of leisure used for the ennoblement and intellectual development of man has turned into a nightmare of hours wasted in diversion and emotional dissipation.

Judged only in terms of time spent, the importance of mass media in the life of most Americans cannot be ignored; but the media are also significant because they confer status on many. The prestige of individuals is enhanced by favorable citations in the various media. Many believe that Nixon lost to Kennedy in 1960 because his image as

[9] W. H. Ferry and Harry S. Ashmore, *Mass Communications,* The Fund for the Republic, 1966, p. 30.

[10] Jan Hajda, "A Time for Reading," *Trans-action, 4* (June, 1967), 46.

[11] Elmer Roper, "How Culturally Active Are Americans?" *Saturday Review* (May 14, 1966), p. 22.

projected on television was less attractive to voters than that of Kennedy. In recent years "idols of consumption"—popular entertainers—have replaced the "idols of production" of the early 1900s—leaders in politics, business, and the professions. The earlier heroes were presented in the press as models for identification and imitation, with the implication that the reader too could match their rise in social status. Today's television celebrities are persons very much like the viewers except that they have had lucky breaks. Is television's portrayal of heroes creating popular acceptance of such heroes or is it simply reflecting a change in Americans' choice of heroes? A study made in the early 1940s found a change in magazine heroes prior to the coming of television, which suggests that TV is reflecting rather than creating a change in the type of American hero.[12]

The assumption that the mass media generally reflect existing cultural patterns is reasonable. Control of the media is vested in the hands of wealthy businessmen who have little to gain from change. Two press bureaus and three networks are responsible for most of what is presented in newspapers and on television. The chief sponsors of radio and television broadcasts are commercial advertisers, government bureaus and agencies, and special-interest groups. All of these advocate change only in carefully circumscribed fields. The old way of doing things is less controversial and more acceptable to most people, and the media must win popular approval for survival. Perhaps the most valid criticism of the media is that they usually encourage conformity, fail to stimulate critical thinking, and fail to point out desirable social changes.

Despite the natural conservatism of the mass media, they are viewed as instruments of social change. Much fear is expressed of the media's alleged political, social, and moral influence among persons who sample their wares. The assumption is that when the media present ideas and values vividly and repeatedly to large numbers, the audiences—particularly individuals in their impressionable years—accept them. Research by social scientists neither proves nor clearly refutes the theory that attributes to the media great influence upon individuals in the mass audience.

It can be stated categorically that the mass media play an important economic role in the United States. The media not only give employment to millions but also draw the water that turns the wheels of industry. Through advertising, the media create wants and encourage purchases of industry's products.

[12] Leo Lowenthal, "Biographies in Popular Magazines," in Bernard Berelson and Morris Janowitz, eds., *Reader in Public Opinion and Communication*, Free Press, 1950, pp. 507–520.

Television, the Bane of Intellectuals

Singling out television for special consideration should not be interpreted as a denial of the importance of other media, but rather as an attempt to discusss more fully in a limited space the newest of the media. Television appeals to children as well as adults, attracts the largest audiences for the longest periods of time, and is the most widely discussed in regard to its potential educational use. Television is also the most criticized for its tiresome and trite productions.

Who selects and what criteria mold most of the shows presented on television? TV stations like radio stations are licensed by the FCC and regulated by the Criminal Code, which forbids on the air the use of "obscene, indecent, or profane language," the advertising of hard liquor, and the dissemination of information about lotteries or frauds. It is subject to laws concerning slander and libel. Sponsors of TV programs have much influence upon the content of programs. Their influence might be compared to that of buyers of advertising space in newspapers and magazines if the advertisers had a part in writing both their advertisements and the news stories. These programs must meet the standards of an industry-wide code. The networks also maintain eagle-eyed editing and screening departments. Finally, the local independent and affiliated stations may accept or reject network offerings. Winick says, "A medium so hedged about with restrictions cannot have the powerful negative effects that its critics attribute to it."[13]

An inquiry into what is deleted and for what reasons is less reassuring. Network screeners do not permit spoofing of serious matters. They discourage political satires, disparagement of the military elite, unfavorable comment on our system of free enterprise, and levity about or irreverence for any kind of religion. They look with a jaundiced eye on stories that seem to approve of superstition, suicide, and antisocial or illegal activity unless it is punished. They usually gloss over or ignore controversial national and international issues. Television, then, tries to avoid offending anybody, especially anybody who belongs to a powerful special-interest group.

Stock-in-trade television programs are newscasts of headline news, variety shows of the old vaudeville type, "audience participation" shows where prizes are won through contests or giveaway schemes, popular music, Sunday-morning religious observances, a few new films and many old ones watered down by deletions, cartoons for children,

[13] Charles Winick, *Taste and Censor in Television,* The Fund for the Republic, 1959.

detective and western stories, soap operas, comedy dramas—all generously punctuated throughout with commercial advertising.

It must be conceded, of course, that providing entertainment is a legitimate function of television, and that personal tastes in programs differ. The earthy and slapstick comedians, the sports events, the trite family comedies and "trivia" performers, and the fantasies exemplified in the westerns create diversion for persons whose daily experiences are routine. The school's quarrel with broadcasters is not that they fail to cater to popular taste, but that they do not do enough to elevate it. Persons cannot learn to appreciate artistic productions unless they are exposed to them.

The wise teacher does not indict television. He is alert to first-rate drama when presented. He recognizes advertisers who provide telecasts of public affairs, political events, general informational programs, and good children's programs. He may even use the programs of a clever comedian or satirist to give fresh insight and a touch of humor in the classroom. He calls his students' attention to the network "specials," which include classical music, musical drama, and excellent theatrical productions. He urges them to see opera, how-to-do-it educational shows, programs about research, science, literature, studies of natural history, Shakespearean plays, documentaries, and other programs of educational and cultural value.

Increasingly in the 1960s television newscasts and documentaries have discussed current issues, such as the Negro revolt, and, in fact, they have become primary instruments of Negro progress. TV's portrayal of the war in Vietnam has encouraged the revulsion toward war in general as well as criticism of this particular war. Every year at least one or two programs, none of which survives for many years, deal with pertinent social issues, and even the long-lived, top-rated "Bonanza" occasionally tells a story of social significance. All of these are grist for the mill of an alert teacher.

Television in the Lives of Children

High school and college students usually find movies, radio, and their group activities more interesting than television. Elementary school children are, however, avid television fans. Viewing tends to reach its peak when children are in grades 6, 7, and 8, and to decline during the high school years. In 1966 the television industry estimated that children average about 20 hours a week watching television. After making an intensive study of almost 6000 children in San Francisco, Denver, an American suburb, 2 Canadian towns, and 5 Rocky Mountain communities, Schramm and his associates state that during the first 16 years of his life, the typical child spends as much time with television as he does in school. They estimated that the young child plays less, reads fewer comics and pulp magazines, goes to bed a few minutes later, and listens to radio less than a child his age would have done in the pretelevision era.[14]

Schramm's research indicates that the child's purpose in watching television is to escape into the realm of fantasy. Although the viewer may incidentally learn something, he is seeking only entertainment. He found that bright (over 115 IQ) and below-average (under 100 IQ) first-graders who had watched television since infancy scored a year higher in tests of vocabulary than did nonviewers, but they had lost their initial head start by the time they reached the sixth grade. Among older children and adolescents, "heavy viewers" could name more singers and band leaders than "light viewers," but the latter could name more writers and statesmen. The research revealed that the bright children of well-educated parents see less television and are more discriminating in their choice of programs. These adolescents are among the few who watch Educational Television (ETV) and who are more likely to view reality than fantasy programs. Schramm found no evidence that commercial television markedly broadens a child's horizons or stimulates him intellectually or culturally any more than he would be broadened without television.[15] A carefully controlled English study of 1850 matched children, who either watched or did not watch television, found that only younger, duller children actually gained in knowledge from television. The secondary school pupils who were viewers were a little less knowledgeable in general than the nonviewers.[16]

No one doubts that television promotes fads and fashions in manners, hobbies, dress, and speech, nor that it exalts "stars" and popularizes certain types of music and dance. It gives young people a superficial acquaintance with national and world affairs, other countries, ballet, opera, marital conflict, and a host of other topics. Schramm found, however, that only adolescents commonly view public-affairs programs. Television programs do stimulate use of the library, some librarians claim.

Other effects of television upon children may be less obvious and

[14] Wilbur Schramm, Jack Lyle, and Edwin B. Parker, *Television in the Lives of Our Children*, Stanford University Press, 1961, pp. 12, 70–73.

[15] *Ibid.*, chaps. 4 and 5, *passim.*

[16] Hilde T. Himmelweit, A. N. Oppenheim, Pamela Vince, *et al., Television and the Child*, Oxford University Press, 1958, pp. 20–21.

more disturbing—if they are indeed effects. Does a child really need the amount of fantasy he is getting from television? Is the fantasy draining off the child's aggression in a constructive way or is it encouraging the child to withdraw into a world of make-believe and to forget his problems? Are young people learning to be satisfied with superficial knowledge and to regard only sensational events as important? Do they believe that all learning is easy because TV programs oversimplify complexities? How do youngsters react to the greed exemplified in TV's give-away shows? Do they equate with scholarship the ability to answer miscellaneous questions on quiz programs? Does violence in television drama dull sensibilities?

Easy, exciting, something for nothing, materialistic, glamorous, lucky! When television programs reiterate these themes, can the school convince pupils that learning, the result of meticulous, unglamorous, laborious, concentrated study, is rewarding to an intelligent human being?

We do not know what the impact of television on children is. Research is scarce. That some harm and some good may have come to some children cannot be denied, but direct and immediate effect on behavior of all or many young people cannot be assumed. McLuhan hypothesizes that television "involves us in moving depth, but it does not excite, agitate or arouse." It has the effect upon young people, he claims, of driving them to "total involvement in all-inclusive nowness." Suburban beatniks, he says, have rejected a "fragmented and specialist consumer life for anything that offers humble involvements and deep commitment."[17]

Experimentation indicates, however, that what a person learns in any situation depends upon his personal interpretation of the stimuli. Interpretation depends not only on the content being transmitted (which McLuhan believes to be unimportant) and the receiver's level of intelligence but also on his general frame of reference. The latter in turn depends upon previous experiences, level of formal education, attitudes and values derived from his cultural contact, and emotional needs. Situational factors, such as the credibility of the communicator, the prevailing climate of opinion, and the presence of supporting evidence from other sources, will also influence what is learned.

For these reasons most social scientists discredit the thesis that television programs stressing violence *cause* delinquency. That violence exists does not mean that it is perceived as such by all children. Sadism, horror, and killings may upset parents, who were themselves weaned on gory fairy tales, more than their children. Some psy-

[17] Marshall McLuhan, *op. cit.*, pp. 294, 292, 279.

chologists claim that violence in the mass media may actually be
therapeutic, or at any rate act as a sedative, for children who are
excessively frustrated. The normal child is not likely to identify with
the perpetrator of crime. Children who are predisposed toward delinquency may do so, however, and may in fact learn techniques of crime
from television. Researchers also conclude from recent studies that
some viewers of violence are stimulated to actual violence, especially
if the viewer perceives the violence as justified and if he knows someone he associates with the victim he has just seen. The research on
subtle TV themes is even less definitive than that on violence.

Educational Television

Educational Television (ETV) is noncommercial, supported by
communities, foundations, school systems, or universities. Programs on
these stations stress reality and carry little of the fantasy and virtually
none of the violence that is the major output of commercial TV.
Studies of two ETV stations' audiences revealed that only about 15 to
20 percent of the potential audience, adults and children, chose the
educational station each week. The educational level of the family is
the best clue to whether or not parents and children will watch
ETV.[18]

Expansion of ETV suffers from several handicaps. The most obvious
is its lack of money. When the 1966 estimated cost of a one-hour
"Bonanza" show is just under a half million dollars and of a "Huntley-
Brinkley Report" is $75,000, the possibility of ETV's competing suc-
cessfully with professionals for other than the captive audiences in
classrooms seems hopeless.

The closed circuit ETV used for instructional purposes in school and
college classes is viewed by enthusiasts as one answer to the teacher
shortage. They claim that one teacher can teach thousands and can do
a better job since a master teacher could be presented on television.
They point to experimental evidence that student achievement in
college lecture courses is as high when the lecturer is projected on a
screen as when he is present in a classroom. They offer proof that
certain experiments, lessons in music and art, controlled observations
in child study, and demonstrations of techniques are more clearly
presented on TV than in a classroom. They also point to successes of a
televised master teacher in helping the classroom teacher teach foreign
languages in elementary schools.

Although such claims deserve consideration by those responsible for

18 Schramm, Lyle, and Parker, *op. cit.*, p. 93.

educating young people, objections to closed circuit ETV should also be considered. Finding master teachers who are also successful TV actors is not easy. When such a person is found, he cannot provide for individual differences, encourage discussion, correct misunderstandings, and stimulate the personal interaction that is so important to the teaching-learning process. Just as the mass TV audience cannot respond, and therefore leaves us in doubt as to what they learn, the more restricted audience of ETV also cannot respond except in written quizzes and compositions. To obviate this difficulty, discussion leaders or classroom teachers are often used in conjunction with the television teacher. At best then, ETV is a teaching aid, for if personal interaction is not part of ETV, it encourages the same feelings of anonymity in students that we deplore in mass audiences of commercial TV.

The School's Role in Regard to TV

A significant educational task is developing pupils' capacities for discrimination in respect to the offerings of the mass media. If the average American prefers "Batman" to an excellent documentary, the fault lies not with the commercial medium but with the intellectual level of our society. Analysis and discussion of TV programs and exposure to high standards in literature, art, drama, music, and documentaries will develop discriminating consumers. Encouraging children to view the programs that are good or excellent is as important as any other assignment that a teacher might make.

The school shares the responsibility with home and church for teaching children the wisdom of the Golden Mean. Any pleasure, any activity carried to excess is harmful. Although many entertainment broadcasts are in themselves innocuous, they become harmful when too much time is wasted on them or when they serve as convenient escape from reality.

Educators are justifiably concerned with the amount of trivia in commercial TV programs. Letters of praise to local stations and to networks when good programs are offered may encourage broadcasters to improve their offerings. One sponsor is said to have changed a program because he was "inundated with three complaining letters" from viewers. Teachers and parents waste their breath complaining to each other about the content of mass media; addressing their praise or censure to proper authorities is more appropriate action. It may be possible sometime in the future for teachers' organizations, the P.T.A., the League of Women Voters, the American Association of University

Professors, and other interested persons to persuade the FCC that, in addition to newscasts and occasional documentaries, an hour of prime evening viewing time be set aside by all networks and stations for public service features.

THE INFLUENCE OF SPECIAL-INTEREST GROUPS UPON SCHOOLS

One of the most significant developments associated with mass society is the growing influence of special-interest groups. The average man is anonymous. He works in an impersonal, bureaucratic place of business, lives next door to neighbors who are casual acquaintances or strangers, and finds his recreation in watching television and sports events. Under such circumstances, he finds that by joining organizations he makes desirable contacts with other people. To be heard in community affairs, he must join with others who share his interests and convictions. By joining a group, he can—and does—ally himself with sympathizers all over the nation.

Most persons react negatively to the term *special-interest* or *pressure group*, without realizing that they too are members of such groups. In a sense all groups with which a person is affiliated are special-interest groups and likely to become pressure groups if their interests are threatened. Teachers will readily admit that taxpayers' leagues, veterans' organizations, various business and industrial groups, the temperance societies, labor unions, bird-lovers' societies, and the like are special-interest and, at times, pressure groups; they are less willing to admit this of the intergroup-relations organizations, the child-welfare and health-promotion groups, the PTA, service clubs, and education associations. Nevertheless, the groups that we approve and belong to are also special-interest, pressure groups.

A few decades ago the activities of lobbyists in legislative centers were deplored by many social scientists. Today the label lobbyist is no longer a term of opprobrium; representatives of pressure groups are recognized as necessary and, to some extent, valuable contributors on the legislative scene.

In recent years, however, many special-interest groups have expanded their activities beyond their efforts to influence legislation into obvious attempts to mold public opinion. They employ public-relations experts who devise sophisticated propaganda techniques in an effort to win public support. So successful is the business of mass persuasion that a new type of foundation has been invented in the last 35 years. These foundations, financed largely by contributions and "book sales" to wealthy donors, make a business of selling an economic or political point of view.

The chief ideological interest of major, nationwide pressure groups centers in the major conflicts found in our society: individualism versus cooperative group action, "free enterprise" versus "planned capitalism" and government controls, isolationism versus internationalism, freedom versus security, private versus public welfare. The vast majority of people representing one or the other side of these politico-economic conceptions of Americanism are loyal supporters of public schools.[19] The attempts of such people to introduce their particular ideology, directly or indirectly, into school curriculums is, however, a new development in the history of education. The accusations of certain extremist right-wing groups, especially during the McCarthy period from 1949 to 1953 and in the 1960s that subversive teachers were deliberately undermining the ideals that American parents want their children to live by, is a louder and more militant kind of criticism than ever heard before.

Special-Interest Groups' Methods of Influencing Schools

Because schools contribute greatly to shaping young minds, members of special-interest groups are concerned with what is taught in the school. They believe that as citizens in a democratic society they have the right to help in shaping the curriculum, to inculcate their point of view, and to determine the social goals of the school. To achieve their ends, special-interest groups use several different methods to influence schools, chiefly the following:

FREE MATERIALS. Private organizations, largely in commerce and industry, according to estimates, spend as much for free and inexpensive materials for schools as is spent on textbooks each year. In 1957, the National Association of Manufacturers stated that it gave "at least two million booklets" to the schools every year. Hundreds of other organizations, whose donations are frequently listed in educational bibliographies and journals, also supply posters, skits, filmstrips, and pamphlets at low or no cost to teachers for classroom use. Although some of this material may seem to be remarkably free of propaganda, public-relations experts rarely forget that their basic aim is to make the special-interest group's program appear to be identical with the general welfare.

[19] Association for Supervision and Curriculum Development, NEA 1953 Yearbook, *Forces Affecting American Education*, 1953, pp. 50–51.

An exceptionally naïve attempt to persuade young readers is found in a booklet called *Health and Liquids:*

> Almost everyone likes soft drinks. Having several bottles on hand at all times is a simple way of helping to meet the necessary daily liquid intake requirement. Their effervescent quality stimulates the desire for more liquid and avoids a heaviness or distressed feeling which many people have from drinking plain water.
>
> The carbonation—impregnation with carbon dioxide, the gas which causes bread to "rise"—gives the beverage a pleasant sharp taste. Also, scientists have long recognized that carbonation tends to inhibit the growth of those types of bacteria quite commonly present in ordinary drinking water.[20]

Can teachers identify the kind of propaganda in these materials donated to schools? There is evidence that many do not. A study of 73 teachers' reactions to sponsored teaching aids (see Table 3) showed the teachers to be much less critical of the propaganda contained in pamphlets than was a panel of 8 judges (four political scientists, three school supervisors, and an educational research specialist). The teachers were much less likely than were the judges to be aware of the purpose of the pamphlets. Only a third or fewer of the teachers disliked the pamphlets because of their ideological point of view, and

TABLE 3. **Propaganda Content in Free Pamphlets as Judged by Teachers and a Panel of Experts**

No. of Teachers	Grade Taught	Thought Purpose of Pamphlet Was Propaganda		Disliked Propaganda Found in Pamphlet	Judged Pamphlet on Propaganda Content
		% of Teachers	% of Experts	% of Teachers	% of Teachers
29	6th	31	100	27.6	20.6
32	7th	58.4	87.5	31.2	21.9
12	9th	43.8	75	33	29

Source: Adapted from data in William C. Odell, "Are Teachers Aware of Propaganda in Sponsored Teaching Aids?" *Journal of Educational Research,* 51 (October, 1957), 81–88.

[20] *Health and Liquids,* American Bottlers of Carbonated Beverages, 1943, p. 12.

TABLE 4. **Amount of Propaganda in Free Pamphlets as Judged by Teachers and a Panel of Experts**

Pamphlet Designed for Grade Level	Subjects Taught by Teachers	Mean Ratings[a]	
		Teachers	Experts
6th	all	4.17	8.5
7th	core	5.12	9.0
9th	science	3.42	6.12

[a] Ratings: 1–3, no propaganda; 4–7, some propaganda; 8–10, very much propaganda.

Source: Adapted from data in William C. Odell, "Are Teachers Aware of Propaganda in Sponsored Teaching Aids?" *Journal of Educational Research, 51* (October, 1957), 81–88.

less than a third considered propaganda content as a criterion for judging the materials. After being told to look for bias, the teachers rated the amount of propaganda in the literature lower than did the panel of judges (see Table 4). At the sixth- and seventh-grade levels, where the material contained "very much" propaganda in the opinion of the judges, the teachers detected "some." In fact, the teachers' mean is so low, particularly at the sixth-grade level, that it is obvious that many teachers saw "no propaganda."

CONTEST PRIZES.   Offering prizes to winners of essay, art, and debating contests is another method used by special-interest groups to influence the minds of young people. Sometimes sponsors supply study materials that stress their beliefs and often they select topics which require contestants to adopt their point of view. A national essay contest of the Association of American Physicians and Surgeons had as its topic: "Why the Private Practice of Medicine Furnishes This Country with the Finest Medical Care." The doctors' propagandists undoubtedly assumed that the contest was at least partly responsible for changed attitudes reflected in the Purdue University poll of high school pupils. In 1948, 80 percent of the pupils favored "government providing medical service for all." After three years of the contest, only 53 percent favored a government medical program.[21] Accurately assessing a contest's results is impossible, but the enthusiasm of pressure groups for this method of persuasion indicates that they believe it to be effective.

[21] H. Otto Dahlke, *Values in Culture and Classroom*, Harper & Row, 1958, pp. 475–476.

INFILTRATION.   An ambitious effort of a single company to infiltrate higher education was that of a prominent gambling house in Reno. By providing scholarships with large stipends to one of every fourteen students at the University of Nevada, the image of the gambling casino became that of a generous benefactor. Without impugning the generosity of the donor, it may be said this form of institutional advertising may be expected to pay off, even in the legislature, in a state where until recently there was only one college.

Another way to infiltrate is to persuade the school to devote school time to promoting a group's program. Probably the most successful infiltrations have been made by "worthy causes." The various charity drives conducted in schools, the released-time programs for religious instruction, and the local community projects are illustrations. In Portland, Oregon, a high school principal estimated that over 2000 class periods were devoted annually to the Rose Festival.

LEGISLATION.   Many pressure groups have successfully lobbied for laws that shape the school's curriculum. As early as 1929 every state had a law that required either the observance of a Temperance Day or teaching the evils of alcohol and narcotics in schools. Some such laws are ill-advised, out-of-date, ludicrous, or nonenforceable. For example, teaching the German language, discussing the theory of evolution, and sex education have been banned in some states. In other states designated days, such as Bird Day, Arbor Day, Luther Burbank Day, Susan B. Anthony Day, and Robert E. Lee Day must be observed with ceremonies. Schools in some states have been required by law to teach "kindness to animals" for 15 minutes each week. Recently in California sixth-graders were required by law to study a foreign language along with 19 other special subjects. Many of the laws stipulating curriculum are promoted by special-interest groups, some of which are composed of teachers who want a subject required of all pupils.

LITIGATION.   Pressure groups sometimes use the courts as a means of promoting their viewpoint in school matters. The most successful instance in recent years was the desegregation-of-schools case won by the National Association for the Advancement of Colored People in 1954. Organizations not directly involved in a legal combat may express their opinions through the *amicus curiae* (friend of the court) device. In this way they seek to influence a court's decision. Vose gives the following example:

> In 1943, when a member of the Jehovah's Witnesses challenged the constitutionality of a compulsory flag salute in the schools, his defense by counsel for the Watchtower Bible and Tract Society was supported

by separate *amici curiae* of the American Civil Liberties Union and the Committee on the Bill of Rights of the American Bar Association. The appellant state board of education was supported by an *amicus curiae* brief filed by the American Legion.[22]

BLOCK VOTING. School elections provide prime opportunities for pressure-group activity. Because political parties generally refrain from supporting candidates or issues in the "nonpartisan" elections, pressure groups may be the only organized force present. In the larger school systems in Iowa when no organized opposition existed, 93 percent of all school bond elections from 1950 to 1955 passed. When there was organized opposition, only 31 percent of the school bonds were approved by the voters.[23] The local PTA and teachers usually operate as special-interest groups in school elections to pass bond issues and vote for desired changes in education, such as kindergartens and special education.

PRESSURE ON TEACHERS. Special-interest groups may influence schools by means of sinecures for or intimidation of teachers. The bribes are, of course, called consultant fees, fellowships, or stipends. In Michigan, for example, the United Automobile Workers plays host to about 300 teachers each year at institutes. Intimidation of teachers, particularly of those in the social studies, is not uncommon. For examples of such intimidation and the methods used, see Chapter 8.

CENSORSHIP. Special-interest groups throughout the United States sometimes try to get certain books barred from use in schools. Segregationists complain of stories about black and white rabbits that marry, Negro groups object to *Little Black Sambo*, a right-wing group condemns *Robin Hood* as communistic. Local housewives, clergymen, and businessmen, influenced by national organizations, condemn many books as "obscene," "soft on communism," or written by persons whose politics were suspect.

Special-Interest Groups
and the Democratic Process

The use by special-interest groups of increasingly militant methods of persuasion is clear evidence, in some instances, of feelings of alienation, of extremist reactions, and of conflicts in values that develop among people in a mass society. Nevertheless, the tendency to

[22] Clement F. Vose, "Litigation as a Form of Pressure Group Activity," *The Annals, 319* (September, 1958), 27.

[23] "Clues to Bond Issue Success," *Phi Delta Kappan, 38* (October, 1956), 10.

regard all special-interest groups as vicious and undemocratic, especially when one differs with the viewpoints expounded by these organizations, often prevents a realistic appraisal of the role of such groups in our society. In the interest of free inquiry, the unlimited expression of arguments for and against a particular economic or political stand is essential. That a number of like-minded persons unite to promote their concerns and interests more effectively cannot in itself be construed as undemocratic. Consequently, pressure groups can be undemocratic only when their loud voices are mistakenly assumed to represent consensus and when they distort or misinterpret the stand of those who differ with them.

The crucial question, then, is: Does special-interest group propaganda, which represents a single point of view, influence to any marked degree the thinking of children in school? Since billions of dollars are spent by various groups in dispensing such "information," clearly leaders of these groups think so. Since the late 1930s the National Association of Manufacturers, the most articulate voice of big business, has actively promoted an ambitious campaign to "educate" the public. It employs a large staff of public relations experts who use every technique available to them. Movies, described by the NAM in 1966 as "an educational film series on economics," are distributed by Indiana University. More than 5,000,000 booklets and brochures, continuously revised, are sent to teachers upon request. During the early 1960s almost 4,000,000 sets of *Industry and the American Economy* were given to teachers and schools.

In recent years, as labor unions have become more affluent, they too have sought to present their views in schools. By 1959 the United Automobile Workers had donated the "Labor Book Shelf," a set of five books, to 1300 schools in 30 states. Other materials have been given to schools by various unions, and information about labor unions has been inserted in state curriculum guides.

Numerous writers have hazarded guesses as to the general effectiveness of such propaganda. Most scholars subscribe to the "predisposition theory": that those who accept the values advocated are already predisposed toward them. The successes of NAM propaganda may be attributed to the values it advocates—low taxation and limited government—ideals acceptable to many teachers and students.

The proliferation of articulate pressure groups is changing the schools for better or worse. Recent successes in censoring books and state laws regarding curriculum are cases in point. Alert teachers and administrators, aware of such influences, are developing realistic patterns for evaluating and dealing with pressure groups.

School Policy
and Special-Interest Groups

Many schools are developing policies that help them defend free inquiry in schools; many teachers are becoming aware of the need to be critical of sources of materials. The lure of free materials, for example, can be resisted by teachers. They can learn to inquire closely into the identity of the giver and "beware of the Greeks bearing gifts." That is, they can spot the techniques of propaganda and the politico-economic stands of the major special-interest groups. Teachers also are responsible for educating their pupils in detecting propaganda and in recognizing that its use means "Somebody is trying to sell me a point of view."

Teachers should recognize that textbooks too may present biased points of view. The contents of a text are influenced by the writer's personal interpretation, his selection of data, and the adequacy of his scholarship. Occasionally a writer is paid by a pressure group to present a biased point of view in a textbook. It is important that teachers and pupils learn to spot inaccuracies in textbooks. Teachers may provide supplementary readings to assure a balanced view. They may, either individually or through their teachers' associations, complain to publishers about inaccuracies, omission of evidence, and undocumented or erroneous statements in texts. At the same time teachers and teachers' groups should abstain from censorship of materials that present ideas and opinions in a straightforward manner, and they should resist attempts of other groups to censor writings that state clearly beliefs of which those groups disapprove.

Like other people, teachers and administrators, consciously or unconsciously, are sometimes so thoroughly committed to a point of view that they fail to distinguish opinion from fact. They may therefore encourage infiltration in their selection of biased speakers for student groups, they may refuse to consider opposing arguments, or they may be willing victims of propaganda supporting their own viewpoints. If freedom of thought is to be preserved as the highest ideal in American education, educators must become critical of their own values. But teachers should not try to conceal their values, for they too have the right to express their opinions. Teaching "knowledge" without interpretation is sterile, but teaching without a distinction between fact and opinion is inimical to freedom of thought.

Finally, teachers' associations should, and sometimes do, oppose legislation that determines school curriculums. When the dead hand of the past controls the school, changes in curriculums to meet local needs and changing conditions are difficult to make. School curriculums should be responsive to actual needs of the present and foreseeable future, not to the sometimes whimsical interests of the society of another era.

SUMMARY

Mass education, mass media, and pressure groups—aspects of mass society—are alike, on the one hand, in that each may inhibit critical and independent thinking in the school. They are also alike in that, to

The Ideal Role of Education

an extent, each of them—outgrowths of a large, complex, industrialized society witnessing a decline of face-to-face. intimate relationships—may alienate an individual from his society. All three are characterized by unidentified authorities who engineer consent and affect the thought, attitudes, and values of people who cannot reply directly and immediately. All three encourage a feeling of insignificance in individuals who feel impotent to fight a well-organized establishment or a special-interest group or to solve the conflicts and tensions reported in the media. On the other hand, all three can encourage critical thinking and democratic processes of decision-making and they can teach people to cooperate and to become involved in society rather than alienated from it.

The school is, of course, in a unique position to help young people deal constructively with the products of the mass media and with pressure groups if it can break its own lock-step. How well the school succeeds in individualizing instruction and meeting the needs of all students, how successfully teachers and pupils manage to break bureaucratic controls and achieve close interpersonal relations is the crux of the problem. The way in which the school helps pupils to cope with the complexities of mass society may determine whether citizens in the future are committed or alienated, active or apathetic, extremists or problem-solvers.

IMPORTANT CONCEPTS

Free lancer. One who supports several causes without full commitment to any one cause.

Golden mean. A phrase in circulation since the time of the ancient Greeks that suggests a moderate course of action. See p. 157.

Mass education. See pp. 144 and 148–149 for a discussion of what this term embraces.

Mass society. See pp. 141–144.

McCarthyism. Making public and sensational accusations of disloyalty or pro-Communist activities based on little or no evidence, after the manner of U.S. Senator Joseph McCarthy in the 1950s. See p. 143.

Predisposition theory. An assumption that most people who accept and act upon the views and values advanced by propagandists already hold similar views and values. See p. 164.

8. SPECIAL-INTEREST GROUPS AND THE SCHOOLS

BY C. A. BOWERS

LUCY: *"Are you smarter this afternoon than you were this morning?"*
CHARLIE BROWN: *"Yes, I think I'm a little smarter."*
LUCY: *"But are you a whole lot smarter?"*
CHARLIE BROWN: *"No, just a little smarter."*
LUCY: *"See?"*
CHARLIE BROWN: *"See what?"*
LUCY: *"There are serious flaws in our educational system."*
CHARLIE BROWN: *"Oh, good grief!"*
—*"Peanuts" by* CHARLES M. SCHULZ

In this country education has always been a matter of social policy to be determined by the people, but it has not always been subject to the intense activity of interest groups that exists today in some communities. The influence of interest groups has increased as American society has become more pluralistic. When the Puritans of Massachusetts Bay Colony passed the first laws that led to the establishment of public schools and vested responsibility for the control of the schools with the town selectmen, they did not disagree on what values and purposes the school was to serve. Because all Puritans shared the same religious and social views, they could easily agree on educational policy. When formulating educational policy, the selectmen knew that their decisions would have the support of the community. Persons who might have assigned different objectives to the school were discouraged from living in the colony, and those who persisted in forcing their unorthodox ideas on the Puritans were punished.

The colony's singleness of purpose, however, did not last. As new values emerged, along with increased toleration for divergent views in the community, educational issues could no longer be determined without conflict. The trend from a relatively simple and homogeneous social structure to a more complex one has been continuous, not only in states of Puritan origin but also in the other states, with a resulting increase in the level of conflict between divergent interest groups over educational policy.

LAY CONTROL OF EDUCATION

The idea that the people possess the right to control their own schools—an idea that invites interest groups to exert pressure on the school—was originally established when the Congregationalist principle of lay control was applied to schools. The church members were accustomed to choosing their own ministers and running the affairs of the church; they thought it only natural that they should exercise the same authority over the newly established schools.

The rationale that equated public control of education with the democratic rights of the people came into existence much later with the emergence of Jacksonian democracy and, it should be added, under very different social conditions. The practice of local control of education began within a relatively homogeneous social structure, but American society had already reached a high degree of religious, economic, political and social complexity when the rationale for such control of schools developed. Before examining the problem of control of public education within a highly pluralistic society, as it exists in America today, we should consider briefly the folklore that has been passed on to us as well as the arguments that are currently used to justify the people's right to control their own schools.

Rationale for Local Control of Education

The argument that is the most pervasive and the most difficult to come to grips with is that the people must be sovereign in education and other matters that affect their own lives. This argument is particularly difficult to refute because it is buttressed by the thinking of such political theorists as John Locke and Thomas Jefferson, whose ideas on the sovereignty of the people have become political touchstones of American life. What is less defensible, however, is the idea often used to justify the people's right to determine educational policy: namely, that the founding fathers intentionally left the control of education to local authorities because they feared the possibility of a dictatorship if control were centralized at the federal level. As Myron Lieberman has pointed out, decentralized control of education was not the result of profound political insight but rather a historical accident. When the founding fathers were drafting the Constitution, the problem of who should control education did not arise simply because they had not begun to think in terms of free public education.[1]

When they vote on school bonds or bring pressure to bear on school officials to correct a practice that is considered undesirable, people seldom justify their activities with theoretical arguments about the

[1] Myron Lieberman, *The Future of Public Education,* University of Chicago Press, 1962, pp. 39–40.

people's sovereignty. They will, more likely than not, point out that they pay the taxes for the support of public education, and argue that this burden gives them the right to have a voice in running the schools. From their point of view, which is shaped in part by their role as consumers, it is unrealistic to expect them to pay for a service they regard as lacking in quality or perhaps even detrimental to their own political, social, or religious interests. When this line of argumentation is considered from the perspective of the taxpayer, one can see an element of logic.

But for the educator, the argument creates serious difficulties when it is used by members of the community to justify pressuring school officials. Even when a community agrees in general upon what is expected from teachers, a teacher is confronted with the problem of determining whether these expectations are consistent with his moral responsibility to the student, which is to insure that the educational process does not degenerate into indoctrination. The teacher's task of interpreting and carrying out his responsibility—both to the community and to his students—becomes a nearly impossible one when factionalism develops within the community over educational issues. In a community torn by conflicting groups, each group claims that paying taxes gives it the right to determine educational issues.

Still another justification for asserting the people's ultimate authority over the schools is that parents are responsible for the development of their children and they cannot easily relinquish this responsibility for forty hours a week to school authorities. The contention is that the parents' interest in the well-being of their children is as legitimate as is the interest of the teacher. Parental interest often takes the form of protecting the child from exposure to ideas and values that the parent deems undesirable. When a parent intervenes in the affairs of the school—even to the detriment of his child's education—he is protecting a right that is undeniably his.

Effects of Lay Control upon Teachers

Because formal education touches so closely on the social, moral, political and economic interests of the people, educators have not been entrusted with the same degree of professional autonomy that exists among such other groups as lawyers and doctors. Although the activities of lawyers and doctors also touch on the sensitive areas of social policy, they are less frequently involved in social controversy than are educators. Such controversy is especially likely to occur when the educational process is carried on in a vital and stimulating manner. The teacher who seeks to free the mind of the student by exposing him to the culture so that he is no longer swayed unconsciously by its hidden premises is highly vulnerable. Conversely, the teacher who avoids substantive issues in the classroom is safe because he has not threatened the interests of many groups. The relationship between a vital educational program and the rise of public interest and controversy, and between a bland educational program and an absence of controversy, will be considered later in the chapter. At this point, it is important to identify those aspects of education that are treated as a matter of social policy, as well as the educational policies that have, for the most part, been settled to the point where they are accepted by almost everybody.

The Framework for Educational
Decision-Making

A number of educational principles have been won through long and difficult struggles and codified into law. These include compulsory attendance laws, the principle of taxation for the support of public schools, state control of certification of school personnel, school building codes, and state requirements in the area of curriculum and textbooks. Although interest groups may have differing interpretations of these general principles, they are generally accepted. What the requirements for teacher certification should be is a heated issue in some areas of the country; on the questions of state adopted textbooks and curriculum requirements there are even more divergent views. Such divergence can be expected, because curriculum and textbooks touch on vital interests and thus are more likely to stimulate interest-group activity. Other important issues in education have been settled by the Supreme Court and are beyond the public decision-makers. The most notable decisions of the Supreme Court—the ones dealing with school desegregation and the place of prayers and sectarian religious instruction in the public school—have not won universal approval and, as a result, have become focal points for interest groups who are working to have the decisions reversed.

The policies codified in the form of law represent in many ways the framework within which the public schools operate. In effect such policies insure that the educational process will be carried on in a manner consistent with democratic principles and uniform standards. But the legal framework allows for considerable interest-group activity, especially since the general questions of who will get what, when and how in the allocation of educational resources and services remain unanswered.

Educational decision-making is an integral part of the public process of policy formation. The public decides the amount of money that will be allocated for the schools and how much of the money will come from the local, state and federal level. Decisions about when and where new schools are to be built, what qualifications the school board members will possess, and who will get the business of supplying the school with equipment and services, are also made by the public. Although certain aspects of the curriculum are specified by state law, the school board, educators and citizens in the community must decide whether the curriculum will be supplemented with special programs, e.g., a heavy emphasis on patriotism or a strong program in the fine arts. The school board is legally responsible for formulating educational policy in addition to its responsibility for carrying out the educational requirements of the state, but members of the community participate in the process by bringing pressure on the board members and, in some cases, on the teachers themselves. This process, despite its limitations, insures that education remains within the framework of the democratic process, and is thus responsive to the needs and interests of the people.

EDUCATION AND POLITICS: THE MYTH

Although education is very much a part of the political process, educators, as well as the general public, have perpetuated the myth that education is nonpolitical. The educator is thus faced with a strange anomaly of his own making: he must work for consensus among diverse interests within the community to settle matters of educational policy, yet he maintains that education is above politics and that the community is a unity with common educational needs. The myth that education is nonpolitical performs several important functions. Robert H. Salisbury, in his article, "Schools and Politics in the Big City," observed that the myth has been important in "underwriting equalitarian educational programs, in separating the school systems from the main political process of the city, and in validating middle-class control of the schools."[2] Salisbury is using the term "equalitarian" to refer to the same educational program for everybody in the community. This approach, which is in harmony with the educator's ideology of treating everybody the same, enables him to ignore the disconcerting fact that groups within the community want different things from the school. Thus the myth helps to perpetuate the illusion of school-community harmony that is so important to educators.

[2] Robert H. Salisbury, "Schools and Politics in the Big City," *Harvard Educational Review*, 37 (Spring, 1967), 415.

If educators were to abandon the myth, they would have to face the fact that conflict, with all its unpleasant connotations, is an integral part of education decision-making. If the myth were eliminated, the educator would have to provide differential educational programs to meet the cultural and economic needs of the minority groups within the community, as they are now beginning to do in large urban areas.

In addition to having a detrimental effect on the well-being of minority groups, the attempt to separate education from politics has often served to undermine the educator's effectiveness in achieving his own objectives. In attempting to appear impartial, the educator cannot align himself openly with interest groups that could give effective and powerful support to his cause. An alliance with interest groups would exacerbate conflict within the community and perhaps place the educator in a position where he might be asked to repay the support that had been given to him. Thus, to avoid partisanship, educators attempt to have "governmental decisions affecting public schools made in a routine manner; that is, they desire a process in which all decisions are highly predictable as to their outcome, even if this means the sacrifice of certain policy alternatives or acceptance of less desirable results."[3]

In their study of the politics of education in Missouri, Michigan, and Illinois, Nicholas A. Masters, Robert H. Salisbury, and Thomas H. Eliot found that in

> Missouri, for example, the predominate group, the Missouri State Teachers Association, *avoids* raising certain questions, particularly in the area of teacher welfare, in order to minimize conflict within its organization between teachers and administrators, and, by refraining from raising issues that rival legislators would oppose, to maximize its chances for gaining other objectives.[4]

The authors of the study concluded that in desiring the safety that comes with maintaining professional neutrality the educators were led to maintain that "the less direct and open involvement in *political* decision-making the better."

CONFLICTING PRESSURES
AND THE SCHOOLS

At the local level the school and its officials function within the crosscurrents of pressures that mirror the often conflicting needs and traditions of a pluralistic community. The diversity of these pressures

[3] Nicholas A. Masters, Robert H. Salisbury, and Thomas H. Eliot, *State Politics and the Public Schools*, Alfred A. Knopf, 1964, p. 272.
[4] *Ibid.*, p. 273.

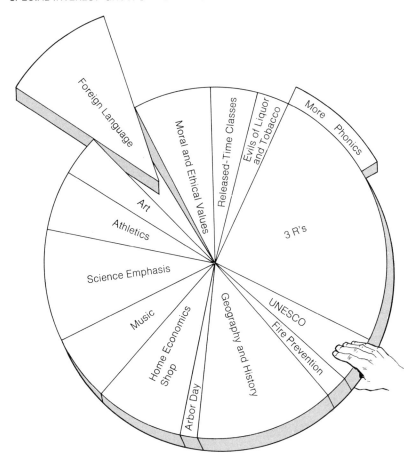

has been clearly shown in Neal Gross' study of the community forces that influence the decision-making of school board members and superintendents in Massachusetts. Although differences in social values and traditions within the states undoubtedly would cause variations in the amounts of pressure applied to school officials, the diverse and conflicting nature of the pressures found in Gross' study is typical of the country as a whole. Interviews with 105 superintendents and 508 school board members, all of whom were chosen randomly, revealed that superintendents and school board members had encountered the pressures listed in Table 5.

The list does not indicate whether the pressures facilitate or hinder the school officials in providing a good educational program, but it does show that people basically disagree over what constitutes the proper social responsibilities of the school. For example, 39 percent of

TABLE 5. **Percentage of Superintendents and School Board Members Exposed to Specific Pressures**

Pressure	Superintendents (N = 105)	School Board Members (N = 508)
Demands that the schools should place more emphasis on the three R's	59	53
Demands that the schools should teach more courses and subjects	64	47
Protests about the views expressed by teachers	49	41
Demands that teachers should express certain views	13	12
Protests against school-tax increases or bond proposals	73	70
Demands for more money for the general school program	66	52
Protests against the introduction of new services (in addition to academic instruction) for pupils	39	35
Demands for the introduction of new services (in addition to academic instruction) for pupils	63	49
Demands for new teaching methods	29	35
Protests against new teaching methods	43	28
Demands that greater emphasis be placed on the athletic program	58	52
Demands that less emphasis be placed on the athletic program	40	38
Protests about the use of particular textbooks	19	19
Demands that school contracts be given to certain firms	46	24
Demands that teachers be appointed or dismissed for reasons other than competence	46	24

Source: Adapted from Neal Gross *et al., Who Runs Our Schools?* Wiley, 1958, p. 49.

the superintendents encountered pressure from those protesting the introduction of new services for pupils, while 63 percent of the superintendents encountered pressures from those demanding new services. Not only is the school official faced with the difficult and often perilous task of mediating between individuals and groups who hold opposing views, but also he must decide which demands are consistent with the best educational interests of the community as a whole.

The school official's task is made even more difficult by a large number of individuals and groups who have a special interest in education. As part of the same study, Gross found that pressure on school board members and superintendents came from numerous sources. See Table 6.

TABLE 6. Percentage of Superintendents and School Board Members Who Said They Were Exposed to Pressures from the Specified Individuals and Groups

Individuals or Groups Who Exert Pressure	Superintendents (N = 105)	School Board Members (N = 508)
Parents or PTA	92	74
Individual school board members	75	51
Teachers	65	44
Taxpayers' association	49	31
Town finance committee or city council	48	38
Politicians	46	29
Business or commercial organizations	45	19
Individuals influential for economic reasons	44	25
Personal friends	37	37
The press	36	19
Old-line families	30	26
Church or religious groups	28	18
Veterans' organizations	27	10
Labor unions	27	5
Chamber of commerce	23	5
Service clubs	20	11
Fraternal organizations	13	9
Farm organizations	12	4
Welfare organizations	3	1

Source: Neal Gross et al., Who Runs Our Schools? Wiley, 1958, p. 50.

In his attempt to distinguish the groups that generally supported the schools from those that did not, Gross's findings were inconclusive and, as he acknowledged, even contradictory. When asked to identify the groups who were the major supporters of the public schools, the superintendents listed the PTA, local government officials and businessmen as the three most important groups. Yet Gross found also that 38 percent of the superintendents identified local government officials as the chief deterrent to improvement in public education; businessmen were named by 36 percent of the superintendents as the second most significant opponents of public education.[5] Similar evidence was reported by the National Education Association's Commission on Professional Rights and Responsibilities in its investigation of the nature and effect of criticism of the schools. Among the ten top groups that teachers listed as helpful to their cause were the PTA, Chamber of Commerce, American Legion, and the Citizens Committee; the same organizations also appeared on the list teachers compiled of the groups that had caused difficulty for the schools.[6]

These findings point to the obvious impossibility of identifying, in the abstract, the individuals and organizations that are the friends and foes of the public schools. Missing in these studies was an attempt to determine the positions taken by various individuals and groups on specific school issues, and this omission helps to explain the seemingly contradictory evidence that was reported. The missing element in the investigation is the key to understanding the inconsistencies: individuals and interest groups within the community change from supporters to nonsupporters of the public schools, and vice versa, when the educational issues at stake fail to coincide with what they see as being in harmony with their own interests.

Interest Groups:
Local, State, and National Level

The majority of interest groups mentioned in the studies by Gross and the NEA's Commission on Professional Rights and Responsibilities represent formal organizations whose main purpose is to achieve for their members social objectives that are in many cases totally unrelated to education. When an educational issue arises, such as a vote on a school bond or an investigation of a teacher's loyalty, organized groups with well formulated policies and established lines

[5] Neal Gross et al., *Who Runs Our Schools?* Wiley, 1958, *passim*.
[6] National Education Association's Commission on Professional Rights and Responsibilities, *State of the Nation in Regard to Criticism of the Schools and Problems of Concern to Teachers*, 1966, pp. 10–11.

of communications have a special advantage in bringing pressure to bear so that the issue is decided in a manner favorable to their interests. Some organizations, such as the American Legion's Americanism Committee, maintain special groups whose express purpose is to keep the organization informed on what is happening in the schools, and thus to facilitate its effectiveness as an interest group in education.

Informal interest groups also come into existence when an educational issue serves as a catalyst to unite individuals in working for a common end. These groups are more difficult to identify because their existence is short, often terminating when the issue is settled. The parents who organized themselves into a pressure group for the purpose of improving the reading program in Berkeley, California, provide an example of an interest group that comes into existence for a specific purpose. In a study of the politics of education in a small town in Oregon, Keith Goldhammer cites an example of a church group that organized for the purpose of electing school board members who would ban dancing in the high school.[7] As such groups are organized in response to educational issues that arise, they are as numerous and varied as the issues that give them life. Although they are often overlooked, they represent an important political force on the educational scene, and one that is not as predictable as are the formal interest groups in the community.

Although the local community is the most closely involved in the affairs of public education, strong political and social forces at both the state and national level also play a vital role in shaping local educational policies and practices. At the state level, for example, the problems of reorganizing school districts and changing the formula of state financial aid to local school districts will precipitate intense interest-group activity in and around the state legislature. Political parties, representatives of organized labor, Chamber of Commerce groups, taxpayers' associations, and ad hoc groups composed of interested citizens will work to bring about policy decisions acceptable to their own groups. Other issues that have in recent years become a matter of urgent concern to interest groups are state textbook adoptions and teacher certification requirements. The handiwork of powerful interest groups—particularly religious fundamentalists and patriotic groups—can also be seen in the teacher loyalty oaths that many states have passed, and in the laws of one state which prohibits the teaching of Darwin's theory of evolution in the public schools.

In recent years decisions by the Supreme Court relating to desegre-

[7] Keith Goldhammer, "Community Power Structure and School Board Membership," *The American School Board Journal,* (March, 1955), p. 24.

gation and religion in the schools, as well as the federal government's investment in antipoverty programs have made the federal government a powerful force in public education. An excellent example of how a branch of the federal government has performed as an effective interest group in the area of public education is the Pentagon's recent success in persuading Congress to pass legislation authorizing a nearly 400 percent increase in the number of high schools participating in the Junior ROTC program.[8]

In addition to the federal government, numerous national organizations, such as the National Association for the Advancement of Colored People, the Daughters of the American Revolution, and the National Association of Manufacturers, exert pressure to influence educational policy-making. The level of their involvement may be the local community, the state legislature, or Congress itself. The textbook publishers and the giant corporations, such as AT&T and General Electric, interested in the knowledge industry, are examples of two more interest groups that exert a powerful and often subtle influence on public education. They are mentioned here not because they will exhaust a list of interest groups that influence education at the national level, but rather because they represent forces that exert pressure on the schools in a distinctly different manner from more visible interest groups such as the NAACP or the John Birch Society. Both the textbook publishers and the corporations that are investing heavily in the burgeoning knowledge industry make their impact on the schools through the services they provide. In the case of textbook publishers, the problem of producing textbooks that can be sold in all regions of the country has very often been solved by eliminating material from the textbooks that would be objectionable to state officials who must approve them if they are to be sold in profitable quantities. Furthermore, ideas and values that are not in harmony with the ideological position of the textbook industry itself are not likely to be given full and impartial treatment in school textbooks. The computer knowledge industry, which is just beginning to make its impact on public education, is concerned with supplying schools with electronic learning devices and thus will not only influence how learning takes place but also what is to be learned.[9]

Although educators still cling to an ideology that maintains that education is above politics, they have nevertheless organized them-

[8] William H. Boyer, "Junior ROTC: Militarism in the Schools," *Phi Delta Kappan,* 46 (November, 1964), p. 117.
[9] Michael Harrington, "The Social-Industrial Complex," *Harper's Magazine,* (November, 1967), p. 57.

selves into interest groups that have become increasingly effective in exerting pressure at all levels of educational decision-making. Thus they must be included in any discussion of educational interest groups. In addition to the formal and informal organizations that exist at the district level, every state has a state-wide teachers' organization. Often there are close ties between the local teachers' organizations and the National Education Association. Many cities and states also have organizations that are connected with the American Federation of Teachers, a powerful rival of the NEA. These organizations have fought for such basic issues as tenure, improved salaries, sick-leave benefits, higher certification requirements, improved working conditions, and academic freedom. Through the militant leadership of the AFT, teachers are now pressuring for a greater voice in shaping curricula and educational policies that were once the sole prerogative of school boards. As ironic as it may seem, the increasing involvement in the politics of education is winning for teachers the rights that go with professional status.

Destructive and Constructive Use of Pressure

This general survey of interest groups and the many different levels at which they operate makes it abundantly evident that the schools are influenced, in terms of both goals and procedures, by the multiple social pressures that surround them. But an acknowledgement of this fact, which is not very different from saying that the people control the schools, leaves unanswered the important question of how and when interest groups become a destructive rather than a constructive force in education—and ultimately in society. This question cannot be answered by determining whether the pressure has been applied in a legally acceptable manner, because the question of legality is vague and thus generally ignored. The legal procedure that has been established for running most schools provides that periodically, through the election of school board members, the people will have the opportunity to express their opinion on how the school is being run. Strictly interpreted, interest-group activity in the area of education is legal only insofar as it takes place during the election of school board members. But this restrictive use of the term "legal" does not reflect the political habits of the American people; moreover it is impossible to legislate in advance for social pressures that may build up and be expressed, because the pressures themselves arise in response to the emergence of social issues. It is a political reality that if school board members and school officials are to have the public support necessary for carrying out their job, they cannot afford to ignore the opinions of individuals and interest groups in the community. As school officials are continually sensitive and responsive to these pressures, they cannot discriminate between destructive and constructive pressures on the basis of legality—except, of course, those cases that involve direct bribery, physical threats, or intimidation.

Criteria for Judging Pressure

It is necessary, therefore, to identify more useful criteria for distinguishing constructive from destructive use of pressure. There are many examples of pressure that represent a basic difference in values between the interest group and school. A difference of opinion between an individual who wants the school to emphasize mastery of a fixed body of subject matter and school officials who want the students to learn to think inductively would be a case in point in which it would do little good to identify the pressure as either constructive or destructive in the educational process. Such a case simply represents an honest difference of opinion on a basic educational question that cannot in the final analysis be resolved to the satisfaction of both parties.

To settle such conflicts, it would be necessary for a criterion to be so broad that it would lose its special meaning, and perhaps leave the erroneous impression that complex issues can be judged simply. It should be possible, however, to distinguish on the basis of a criterion between pressures that result in the voting down of a school bond and the kind of pressure that is directed at the removal of books from the school library. Both are examples of pressure activity that has the effect of diminishing the educational program. Yet nobody would want to say that the interest group working for the rejection of the school bond did not have a right to pursue its objective; that would be saying that pressure-group activity is legitimate only when it is in harmony with what is desired by school officials.

On the other hand, it should be possible to say that exerting pressure on school officials for the purpose of having books removed from the classroom or school library is not legitimate, and that it represents a destructive use of social pressure. The criterion for making this decision *is that any pressure that has the effect of crippling free inquiry of teachers and students in the classroom by placing constraints on them or the materials they use to achieve their educational objectives, undermines the purpose of the school.*

A related criterion is that social pressures cease to be legitimate when they infringe on the teacher's right to exercise professional judgment in the classroom. Both criteria are predicated on the proposition that the teacher is competent in professional skills and subject-matter area, and that he is not using the classroom to indoctrinate the students. Without these protective criteria the educator must surrender the value of free inquiry in the classroom and accept the principle that educational policies are an expression of the dictum which holds that "might is right."

Why Criteria Are Needed

That educators need to create new institutional arrangements embodying these criteria is shown by the growing number of attacks on the schools made by extremist groups. Not only have they questioned the loyalty of teachers, but they have also criticized books as subversive and immoral. In a study of censorship and its effects on the public schools in Wisconsin, a researcher found nearly 120 episodes involving censorship of school books. Among the books removed from the schools were MacKinlay Kantor's *Andersonville,* J. D. Salinger's *A Catcher in the Rye,* Sinclair Lewis' *Main Street,* T. S. Eliot's *The Wasteland,* John Steinbeck's *The Wayward Bus,* and the *Dictionary of American Slang.*[10] Extremists successfully censored *Androcles and the Lion* on the grounds that it was written by an atheist. In another case a policeman recommended that Erich Remarque's *A Time to Live and a Time to Die* be removed from the school library, and the librarian complied.

A much larger study of criticism and censorship in the schools by the NEA's Commission on Professional Rights and Responsibilities revealed equally ominous findings. Although it was found that the total number of cases involving criticism and censorship decreased from 364 in 1960 to 357 in 1965, the study showed that extremists groups had been the chief source of the attacks. The attacks in 1962 resulted in the removal of 17 percent of the books that were criticized; in 1965 the percentage of books removed nearly doubled.[11]

The past indifference of teachers to maintaining high intellectual standards has partly undermined the public's confidence in their competency and in their right to determine the suitability of school books; consequently teachers themselves must be held partly responsi-

[10] George L. Williams, "School Censorship in Fascist Italy and the U.S.," *School and Society,* 95 (March 18, 1967), 186–187.
[11] NEA's Commission on Professional Rights and Responsibilities, *op. cit.,* pp. 8–9.

ble for the vulnerability of textbooks and school libraries to outside attacks that exist today. During the 1940s and early 1950s, when "Life Adjustment" philosophy permeated the educational scene, many textbooks degenerated to surprisingly low standards. During this era science and mathematics textbooks sometimes dealt with the problem of "life situations"; some books dealing with history, literature and government underwent similar oversimplification for the purpose of teaching "democratic living." University professors and concerned parents understandably reacted to the low intellectual standards in school books when students began arriving at universities with little knowledge of academic subjects. What Richard Hofstadter called the "appearance within professional education of an influential anti-intellectual movement" provoked a number of academicians such as Robert M. Hutchins and Arthur Bestor to criticize severely and sometimes unfairly the teaching methods and textbooks used in classrooms across the country.

In addition to the appearance of numerous books that were critical of anti-intellectualism, organizations such as the Council for Basic Education (CBE) were formed for the purpose of strengthening academic standards in the public schools. Part of the CBE's self-appointed mission was policing the intellectual standards of school books: it focused public attention on books that it regarded as unsuitable. The CBE attack on low academic standards was a different kind of pressure than that to which the schools are exposed to today. Nevertheless the CBE was an outside interest group challenging the competency of teachers to make professional decisions.

Extremists and the Schools

Many of the attacks on the curriculum and on teachers appear to begin over a single issue, but often such attacks are quickly expanded until the whole school system and its educational philosophy are brought into question. In Scarsdale, New York, for example, a small group of local citizens became disturbed over books in the school library that these citizens thought were contributing to the domestic menace of communism and the lack of spiritual awareness in the classroom. Their attempt to eliminate the threat involved the community for nearly two years in a bitter controversy over such basic questions as the loyalty of the teachers and the subversive content of books.[12] The controversy in Pasadena, California, was, of course, the classic

[12] See Robert Shaplen, "Scarsdale's Battle of the Books," *Commentary,* (December, 1950), pp. 530–540.

example of opposition to the schools beginning over a single issue—in this case over a budget and assessment tax for the next school year—and becoming a general attack on the schools and their administration. Before the Pasadena incident ended, powerful factions within the community forced educators to repudiate progressive principles even though these principles had been applied only moderately in the schools. Over the last two decades, controversies similar in bitterness if not in the exact nature of the issue at stake have taken place in Denver; Houston; Eugene, Oregon; Englewood, New Jersey; and Montgomery County, Maryland. Since these represent only a few of the incidents involving extremists and the schools that received wide publicity, one can only speculate on the number of attacks that have gone unnoticed by the press.

The extremist's use of pressure on the school can be clearly seen in the attack that was made on a high school social studies teacher in Paradise, California. The teacher had won an award from the Freedom Foundation in recognition of her outstanding ability to train students to make up their own minds, yet such recognition did not prevent her from being accused by extremists of subverting with leftist ideas the patriotism of the students. The attack began in 1961. An anonymous warning printed on the wrappers of candy was given to the children at Halloween. It charged that the social studies teacher was weakening the "souls and minds of our children" by taking them to the Human Rights conference that was sponsored by the American Friends Service Committee.

This bizarre use of pressure was followed by a letter-writing campaign in which the patriotism of the school officials was also questioned; in addition, a list of school books whose authors were identified by the extremists as un-American was circulated throughout the community. The extremists continued to create an atmosphere of suspicion and fear by sending letters to new teachers in the district warning them against using un-American teaching methods. In September, 1962, a letter to the editor of the community paper urged that the people vote against the forthcoming school bond issue; the bond issue was subsequently voted down. It was nearly a year after the attacks began that members of the American Legion Post in Paradise, who had been among the chief instigators of the attacks, appeared at a school board meeting to present formally their charges of subversion in the schools. But when the school board met a week later to answer the charges, the Legion members failed to appear.

The attacks nevertheless continued in new forms—telephone calls that were intended to harass school officials, letters to the editor, the formation of youth study groups on anticommunism—and reached a climax in April, 1963, when the three school board members who had backed the accused teacher ran for reelection. Supported by members of the John Birch Society, the local Legion Post and other embittered townspeople, the opposition ran their own candidates for the contested school board positions on the platform of teaching the fundamentals, economizing in running the schools, and eliminating "Life Adjustment" classes and psychological testing in the schools. As part of their tactics to discredit the social studies teacher, the extremists planted a tape recorder inside a hollowed out textbook, and had a student bait the teacher by asking whether the mock U. S. Senate hearing, which the class was enacting, should not start with a prayer. This tactic, as well as the others used by the extremists, eventually enabled the school partisans to rally sufficient support to reelect their candidates to the school board.

Aside from the fact that the school supporters eventually won, this incident is significant in that it shows that the school was caught in a struggle between interest groups who were separated by basic ideological differences on the meaning of democracy and its implications for the educational process. Their intolerance, unwillingness to communicate on a rational level, authoritarianism, and general hostility to the open society and anyone who defends it, make extremists especially dangerous to the school. No institutional safeguards will protect the school from the pressure extremists can skillfully exert. In fact the school is more vulnerable to their pressure tactics than it is to the parent who wants the school to add substance to its literature program. When pressure is exerted on the school, as in the case of Paradise, the teachers and school officials must divert their time and energy away from the task of carrying on a viable educational program in order to function as a counter-pressure group. If they are successful in disproving the charges made against the school and in rallying the supporters of the school, they may win as they did in Scarsdale, New York, and Paradise, California; but for these victories, the supporters of freedom of inquiry in the classroom pay a tremendous price in time, energy, and emotional tension. The unfortunate thing, however, is not so much that they have to divert their resources to protect the schools from pernicious elements in our society, but that their efforts frequently are unsuccessful.

One of the school's perennial sources of difficulty has been the anti-intellectualism that has often been the underlying source of motivation for interest groups bent on pressuring the schools into becoming a pipeline for transmitting orthodox ideas and values to the younger generation. With the emergence, about 1960, of numerous and power-ful organizations on the Radical Right, the anti-intellectual forces have been joined by, and in many cases fused with, the extremists who have dedicated themselves to fighting communism in all its manifestations. The union of these forces has further clouded the atmosphere sur-rounding the school by fostering mistrust among people regarding the loyalty and ability of educators. The schools have been charged with subversion and immoral practices prior to the recent growth of the Radical Right, but the early attackers used somewhat different tactics.

During the 1950s, for example, numerous books were written by individuals who set out to prove that progressive education was based on "un-American and anti-American atheistic philosophies," and that both the Progressive Education Association and the National Educa-tion Association were subversive organizations.[13] E. Merrill Root's *Brainwashing in the High Schools,* Verne P. Kaub's *Communist-Social-ist Propaganda in American Schools,* and Kitty Jones and Robert Olivier's *Progressive Education Is REDucation* were typical of the books that became "authoritative" source material for a generation of zealots who have dedicated themselves to restoring the schools to the American Way, as they understand it. As the Radical Right grew in strength during the 1960s, the books and pamphlets containing re-dundant examples of what extremists regard as subversive practices of teachers, school librarians, and textbook writers multiplied.

John A. Stormer's *None Dare Call It Treason* (published in 1964 by the Liberty Bell Press) is an example of this kind of book, which reached a surprisingly large audience. In its first year of publication 800,000 copies were sold or given away at political rallies and conven-tions of the Radical Right. Such printed charges of disloyalty as well as materials on alleged social ills and school finance are used by members of national right-wing organizations in local communities in attacking an individual or an institution suspected of being un-American. The national group also supplies outside speakers, moral support, and financial help. The presence of local members of right-wing groups in the community makes them far more effective in disrupting and turning the community against the school than did the antischool literature of the fifties.

Nearly 500 right-wing organizations have been identified in recent years. To support their activities, which are carried on at both the national and local level, tax-exempt foundations, large corporations,

---

[13] Verne P. Kaub, *Communist-Socialist Propaganda in American Schools,* American Council of Christian Laymen, 1953. In particular see his chapter en-titled "Following the Communist-Socialist Line."

utility companies, and wealthy individuals have annually donated the sum of 14 million dollars. Whereas most of these organizations have concerned themselves with the school as only one among many sectors of American society that require their constant policing, several of them have made schools a matter of central concern: the National Education Program, which is based at Harding College in Searcy, Arkansas, and the John Birch Society are the most notable. The NEP produces textbooks, pamphlets, school study outlines, and motion pictures designed to extol the virtues of the free enterprise system and to discredit socialism. In addition to being used by nearly 600 business firms for the purpose of "educating" their employees, these materials have been used in more than 3000 public schools in 35 states.[14] The NEP's propaganda has also been used by extremists in attacking schools.

The impact upon schools of the NEP and other Rightist organizations is to create a climate of fear and hostility within the community, but the John Birch Society attempts to gain control of the schools. The Society members have followed their leader Robert Welch's advice to direct their efforts at gaining control of school boards, city colleges, local business and the local clergy—the "soft underbelly" of American democracy, as Welch put it.[15] In a more specific reference to the schools, Welch urged his followers in the September, 1960 issue of *Bulletin*, to "Join your local PTA . . . and go to work to take it over . . ." His followers were sufficiently successful in carrying out his instructions to cause Jennelle Moorhead, ex-president of the National Congress of Parents and Teachers, to say that "the capture of the PTA may seem a limited goal, but the larger goal of the extremists is to dominate the school system." She clearly understood the destructive nature of their pressure when she wrote: "Extremism usually ignores the real problems of the schools—understaffing, lack of financial support, the educational needs of the disadvantaged. Instead, it raises ghosts of its own creation, shadows of its own imagining. . . . It shakes public confidence in teachers and school administrators and in the PTAs, which are the school's staunch allies."[16] Although John Birchers have declined in strength in the last few years, as recently as 1966, the President of the California State Board of Education charged that the Society was "overtly or covertly at work" in ten school districts in the state and that in at least one district their influence had reached

[14] Arnold Forster and Benjamin R. Epstein, *Danger on the Right*, Random House, 1964, p. 88.

[15] Daniel Bell, ed., *The Radical Right*, Doubleday, 1964, p. 251.

[16] Jennelle Moorhead, "The Danger of Extremism," *NEA Journal*, 54 (September 1, 1965), 17.

"poisonous proportions."[17] That same year, the NEA revealed that teachers rated the Birch Society as the chief source of difficulty for the schools.[18]

In contrast to the highly visible tactics of the Right Wing, Leftist groups have traditionally accorded the public schools only minor political importance. Karl Marx believed that the schools were an instrument of the bourgeoisie and that only after the revolution had succeeded in destroying the capitalist class would it be possible to utilize the schools to give the masses a truly proletarian education. Many on the extreme Left accepted this idea. Hence they generally ignored the school as a possible instrument of revolutionary change.

The major exception occurred during the height of the depression in the thirties, when a group of influential progressive educators argued that the schools should be used to reconstruct American society along socialistic lines.[19] The chief significance of their activities lay in the fact that they were functioning as a politically-oriented interest group within education itself. Their efforts to use the school as a vehicle for overturning capitalism have subsequently been interpreted by Rightist groups as evidence of subversion in education, and thus these reforming educators are partly responsible for Right Wing attacks on the schools today. Having used the schools for partisan purposes themselves, it is now very difficult for educators to tell interest groups on either the Right or the Left that it is morally wrong to transform schools into agencies of political indoctrination.

The recent appearance of the New Left has plunged universities across the country into turmoil and controversy, as students have challenged the morality of the close ties that have developed between universities and the industrial-military complex. But the New Left has seldom exerted organized pressure on the public schools. The schools are not, however, entirely free from Leftist pressure. Parents and other concerned citizens have sought to achieve greater harmony between the purpose of the schools and their own ideological position by pressuring school officials to de-emphasize chauvinism and militaristic values in the curriculum, and instead to stress the importance of peace and world government. Occasionally the Left's ideological position has been represented in the classroom by teachers whose own deeply felt

[17] Benjamin Epstein and Arnold Forster, *The Radical Right,* Random House, 1966, p. 170.

[18] NEA's Commission on Professional Rights and Responsibilities, *op. cit.,* p. 11.

[19] See George S. Counts, *Dare the School Build a New Social Order?* The John Day Co., 1932; Committee on Social-Economic Problems of the Progressive Education Association, *A Call to the Teachers of the Nation,* The John Day Co., 1933; also see the editorial statements that appeared in 1934 and 1935 in *Social Frontier.*

commitments have led them to confuse indoctrination with the process of representing impartially all relevant sides of the issue. The influence of these few individual teachers has, however, been more than offset by their more conservative colleagues who unconsciously indoctrinate their students with great effectiveness and subtlety.

VULNERABILITY OF EDUCATORS
TO SOCIAL PRESSURE

Attacks by powerful and fanatical interest groups within the community make teachers and administrators aware of the vulnerability of their positions. And this awareness can undermine the learning process in the classroom by making teachers feel less inclined to deal with "unsafe" ideas. When a teacher is forced to conform to the dictates of an interest group, every teacher becomes aware that he too can be "reached" if he steps out of line. In too many instances, this sense of vulnerability has caused teachers to comply willingly with the demands of interest groups and even to eliminate material from the curriculum because they feared that it might provoke controversy.

In her study of the critics of the school, Mary Anne Raywid cites the example of an art teacher who had been given the task of selecting suitable paintings for the new school building. Although the teacher admired the work of Picasso, none of his paintings was selected because the teacher found that Picasso's political opinions would involve the school in controversy.[20] The actions of school officials in Fullerton, California serves as a good example of how professional ethics are sacrificed to appease angry critics. A unit on human reproduction had been taught successfully in the high school for thirteen years, but when a group of citizens—many of whom were from outside the community—objected to teaching the unit on reproduction, the principal forbade the use of the textbook, *Understanding Sex,* and modified the content of the unit.[21] Within a short time the subject disappeared entirely from the curriculum. Some teachers, however, do not compromise their professional ethics to placate irresponsible critics. In answering the charges, these teachers may nevertheless be forced to expend human and financial resources that can only be made up at a cost to the student.

[20] Mary Anne Raywid, *The Ax-Grinders,* Macmillan, 1963, p. 159.

[21] NEA's National Commission for the Defense of Democracy Through Education, *Fullerton California: Report of an Investigation,* National Education Association, 1961, p. 10.

Freedom of Inquiry:
The Problem of Control

The public schools are, in effect, caught in a dilemma created by the conflict between the ideological framework within which the school operates—the idea that the people have the right to control their own schools—and the educational process itself, which thrives only when the teacher is free to deal with ideas regardless of how controversial they might be in the community. In commenting on the limitations inherent in a populist form of democracy where the people refuse to recognize agents of authority, legally constituted and otherwise, T. S. Eliot touched on a disturbing truth when he said, "A democracy in which everybody had an equal responsibility in everything would be oppressive for the conscientious and licentious for the rest."[22] The nature of the dilemma is demonstrated also when a parent or interest group exerts pressure on the school for constructive purposes. For even in such instances the autonomy, and thus the professionalism, of the teacher is diminished. The ideology of local control thus serves to keep the teacher in a subservient relationship with the community.

The conflict between the liberalizing purpose of the school and the political process by which it is controlled has other implications of a practical and theoretical nature. The first implication concerns the criteria used in making decisions about how the school should be run and what resources will be made available to it. The question that must be asked is whether the economic and social criteria that are generally used by the public in making decisions affecting the schools are relevant to the educational issues being decided. When an individual votes against a school bond or for a board member who promises greater economy in running the schools, his vote may reflect an attempt to preserve his economic interests rather than his concern for a good educational system. Because the people in the community are not involved in the day-to-day problems of teaching—and thus are not burdened with the same kind of responsibility as teachers—they approach the process of educational decision-making from a perspective reflecting their social interests and involvements. For example, people who are deeply concerned about high taxes are often more concerned with making a decision that will check a further increase in taxes than they are with the effects upon schools. Similarly, an indi-

[22] T. S. Eliot, *Notes Toward the Definition of Culture*, Faber & Faber, 1962, p. 48.

vidual who is troubled by what he sees as the growing immorality in society will tend to evaluate the school within the framework of his special concern rather than in terms of the traditional idea of a liberal education. As it is impossible for anyone to transcend his social values, interests, and commitments and be objective when voting on matters affecting education, laymen will seldom use the same criteria for reaching decisions on educational issues (e.g., a bond issue) as teachers who are responsible for the educational process. When the teacher has professional integrity, it should be possible to trace the motive for his educational decision back to his concern with developing the mind of the student. Yet the people in a community can by their vote or the pressure they apply on school officials be more important in terms of deciding educational issues than can teachers. This problem raises the difficult question of how power should be allocated between the public and school officials for the latter to be sufficiently autonomous to exercise professional judgment in the classroom.

A second implication of local control of education is that it contributes to neutralizing the school by placing restrictions on what will be acceptable as a life style and, in some communities, the race or religion, of teachers. As most communities are made up of individuals who hold a wide and conflicting variety of religious, political, and social beliefs, the school is continually in danger of arousing opposition from interest groups who may find the ideas or life style of the teacher threatening to their own. Given such a potential threat, the easy way to minimize pressure on the school is to hire teachers who do not openly hold unorthodox ideas or deviate from the dominant expectations of the community. As paradoxical as it may seem, control of education within the context of pluralism has the effect of creating a degree of uniformity among teachers, particularly in terms of basic social values, which does not reflect the complexity and richness of the society that the school has been designed to serve. If a teacher is an atheist or a socialist, to take two examples that are extremely relevant today, he will have to hide his belief if the school is not to be embroiled in controversy by individuals in the community who think that teachers must believe in God and capitalism. This constraint on the expression of the teacher's views neutralizes the intellectual atmosphere of the classroom and at the same time undermines the pluralism of the community by preventing students from being exposed to intellectual positions that stand as alternatives to the dominant orthodoxy of the community. The safest way to avoid controversy, therefore, is to hire teachers whose ideas on politics, religion, sex, and the good life are such that they will not offend any interest group capable of exerting pressure on school officials.

The vulnerability of administrators' positions understandably has led them usually to hire teachers who are "safe." An administrator is highly sensitive to modes of behavior, ideas, and activity that he thinks may provoke a negative reaction from the community. His concern for good public relations can and does contribute to greater harmony between the school and the community, but it also comes in conflict with the purpose of education when he limits the exploration of ideas and roles to what he thinks the community will tolerate without discord. When the administrator attempts to anticipate the level of public tolerance, a problem arises as to whether he can indeed judge what the public expects of its schools or whether his attempts to place constraints on behavior and ideas are in fact an expression of his own prejudices and anxieties. The examples of expulsion of students for wearing long hair, short skirts, peace buttons, etc., are numerous and sobering reminders that the current system of controlling the public schools has not contributed to clarifying the kind of authority that may be properly exercised by the school.

IMPORTANT CONCEPTS

Chauvinism. Glorification of one's country, race, or cause, as practiced by N. Chauvin, an ardent supporter of Napoleon.

Extremist. A person who holds extreme views or advocates extreme measures, especially in political matters. He may aggressively deny the rights of others to express opinions contrary to his own.

Indoctrination. Instruction in partisan or sectarian dogmas, beliefs, or practices.

Lay control. Control of an institution by nonprofessionals or laymen.

Open society. A society which permits and encourages the expression of opposing points of view and the implementation of points of view that are not in conflict with the public good.

9. THE FAMILY AND THE SCHOOL

To a considerable degree what a school should do and can do is determined by the status and ambitions of the families being served.
—JAMES B. CONANT[1]

The family is generally recognized as the primary agency of socialization, the process by which a child learns through interacting with others the behaviors and values approved by his social group. In becoming socialized most children accept family standards because relatives make suggestions and also praise, reward, criticize, threaten, and punish them. Since the behaviors and values of children are shaped to a large extent by the family, a teacher's understanding of the family background of his pupils is important to his success as a teacher.

Family backgrounds of pupils vary widely, however, because differences in ethnic origin, religious and philosophical assumptions, social-class status, and other factors influence the patterns of behavior and values accepted by a particular family. Although results of research do not support many generalizations about family systems in this country, certain characteristics seem to be associated with certain groups of families. In the first section of this chapter, we discuss presumed characteristics of the dominant American family system; in the second, variations from this pattern; and in the final section, Negro families.

THE DOMINANT FAMILY SYSTEM

A prevailing middle-class family system, just as the middle-class life style in general, is said to be the dominant pattern in the United States. Presumably its patterns changed as an accommodation to technological change. As man's principal source of livelihood and his place of residence changed from farm and countryside to factory and city, his family system changed. According to one analysis, the family is ceasing to be an institutional system, characterized by rules, routines, and defined roles, and becoming a companionship system, characterized by individually determined behaviors and equalitarianism.[2] Soci-

---

[1] James B. Conant, *Slums and Suburbs: A Commentary on Schools in Metropolitan Areas,* McGraw-Hill, 1961, p. 1.

[2] Ernest W. Burgess and Harvey J. Locke, *The Family,* American Book, 1953; and Carle C. Zimmerman, *Family and Civilization,* Harper & Row, 1947. Other books with somewhat the same theme are Robert F. Winch, *The Modern Family,* Holt, Rinehart and Winston, 1951; Ruth S. Cavan, *The American Family,* Crowell, 1953; and William F. Ogburn and Myer F. Nimkoff, *Technology and the Changing Family,* Houghton Mifflin, 1955. The following description is largely in line with discussions of the modern family described in these books.

ologists often refer to the American family as "the family in transition." Rural families, upper-class "old families," lower-class families, and families of recent immigrants and various ethnic groups are thought to be moving in the direction of the companionship, or individualistic, family system less rapidly than are urban middle-class Americans, who also vary in their speed in assimilating the new pattern.

The chief characteristics of the modern family system are that it is nuclear (consisting of husband, wife, and children), small in size, and mobile. The large extended family, admirably suited to a rural society, is inappropriate in an urban society in which the family moves often. Often the father's work requires such moves. Widely scattered grandparents, uncles, aunts, and cousins are not viewed as part of the immediate family circle, and children leave home when they marry. Despite the rise in the birth rate during and after World War II, the average American family has declined in size from slightly over 5 persons in 1870 to about 3.7 in 1967. The small size of the family increases the likelihood of close interpersonal relations among members. The modern family is therefore likely to stress love and affection as unifying forces and equalitarianism as its *modus operandi.*

When the average American family left the farm, it lost many of its functions. In the city the father seldom employs his sons, nor can he teach them vocational skills and academic competences. To a large extent commercial entertainments supplant family fun. Although the family has to care for children through a prolonged adolescence while they learn marketable skills, it cannot take care of its own in prolonged illnesses, periods of unemployment, and old age.

As family functions declined in an urban setting, the relative importance of the family as an affectional unit giving emotional security to its members increased. Love became the primary basis for marriage, the reason for procreation, the underlying disciplinary force in child-training, and lack of love, compatibility, and understanding the explanation for the high divorce rate. An outstanding characteristic of the American family system is its emphasis upon romantic love. In a highly competitive, impersonal world, marriage has become "an island of security in a sea of insecurity." In marriage Americans find, or think they find, someone who accepts and loves them as they are. Throughout his life the middle-class child is urged to "be somebody," to prove himself through successful competition. It is therefore very important for a young person to feel that he has a partner, an insulator against the cruelties of a competitive society. Americans marry more often for love than for any other reason. Because they marry to prolong a romantic relationship that may not survive the vicissitudes of married life, one-fourth of them are later divorced.

Child-bearing and child-training are extensions of the love relationship between mates. When a man and a woman have a child, usually they have it because they want offspring as an emotional investment. If they have practiced "planned parenthood," they feel a particularly strong sense of obligation to do their best for the child. This attitude is in marked contrast to that of rural parents of an earlier period who thought God sent the child partly to help them on the farm and aid them in their old age. Under such circumstances, both parents and children had duties to each other.

The modern mother, who carries the burden of child care, sometimes interprets "doing her best" for the child in ways that may be har~ᶠ to the child's development. She may overprotect the child by
him from real or imagined dangers or spur him to accom-
; beyond his abilities. With society's approval, such a "good
ay show her excessive concern for her children in many
·pect little in line of duties and responsibilities from them.
ιsis on love in the modern family may also color parental
tle children are conditioned to depend upon parents for
ι   l security. Being a "bad" boy or a "naughty" girl, they
ι.   ɔst them parental affections. Not all American children
aι   ch hazards; many children, secure in the knowledge
thι   love, understand, and trust them, develop poise, self-
coι   tiative beyond their years.

T.   ly tends to be equalitarian: husband, wife, and to a
limit   ren share in making decisions. The middle-class
male ι   relinquished his patriarchal role when he had to
go awa   ɔr work, when his wife sometimes earned part of
the fam   assumed major responsibilities for the children,
and wheι   came smaller. In most families he still retains
the power oι   ses it sparingly. Each member of the family,
including the chilu…..,   expected to develop his personality, to make
many of his own decisions, and to be heard as well as seen. The family is presumably united in its pursuit of happiness, which is equated with warm family relationships and parents' and children's successes in terms of education, prestige, and income. Despite its materialistic goals, the family is often more concerned with the psychical than the material welfare of its members.

The modern, middle-class family prizes individual achievement and social service. Satisfaction in one's job, particularly among middle-class professionals, is a focal concern, but self-expression and success in one's work do not preclude empathy with others. Persons who make up the larger society are seen as friendly, cooperative, and worthy of help.

This so-called democratic family system is often criticized, as democratic government is criticized, for its failures. Its lack of success is reflected in the high incidence of divorce and poor mental health. A family system based on love, understanding, self-control, self-discipline, and individualism presents formidable challenges to participants, many of whom have not yet learned how to meet them. Nevertheless, this family pattern may offer a better environment for the development of free men than did the authoritarian family system of the past.

Do researchers agree that a "democratic" family system has developed the characteristics described in the preceding paragraphs as an accommodation to modern conditions of living, particularly industrialization? Some of them suggest that industrialization rather than being a causal factor in bringing about change in the family system may be simply an independent but interacting variable. Others distinguish between a family living in a closely knit network of relatives and one living in a loosely knit network separated by distance, as is customary among families of professional people. In the closely knit network husbands and wives divide household and child-rearing responsibilities more sharply, spend more time apart in recreation and visiting, and invest less emotion in their relationship than do married couples in loosely knit networks. Both groups of families, however, are more likely to spend their vacations visiting relatives than in any other way, a fact which suggests that the extended family is still important to them both.[3]

Investigators also doubt that many modern families are truly equalitarian. The husband who helps with household chores, they say, may be gaining authority in that area rather than losing his headship of the family. They find no clear trend in the direction of greater influence in family decision-making by wives who work. Although the majority of researchers find that a mother has more influence on a child's knowledge, values, and companions than does a father, perhaps mothers have always had more influence in these matters.[4]

Despite the uncertainties of researchers, the emerging family system

---

[3] Marvin B. Sussman and Lee Burchinal, "Extended Kin Networks in the United States," in William J. Goode, ed., Readings in the Family and Society, Prentice-Hall, 1964, pp. 170–175; and William J. Goode, The Family, Prentice-Hall, 1964, pp. 51, 73–74.

[4] Goode, The Family, ibid., pp. 74–75; and James M. Rollins, "Two Empirical Tests of a Parsonian Theory of Family Authority Patterns," The Family Life Coordinator, 12 (January–April, 1963), p. 19. Rollins' article contains a detailed summary of research done between 1930 and 1961 pertaining to family authority patterns.

seems to be a reality in that common characteristics are shared by a growing number of families. Undoubtedly the well-educated, upper-middle class family is the exemplar of the pattern. Whether it will spread or is spreading to other social levels is a debatable question.

In any event, the hazards to child development in the modern family are real enough to concern teachers. Over-protecting children or expecting too much from them influences their behavior and what they learn in school. On the one hand, overprotected children often lack initiative and are unwilling to work very hard at a task. They expect a great deal of help from a teacher. They may have difficulty in relating to other pupils. On the other hand, children of whom too much is expected may become so frustrated by their inability to please their parents that they may not try to succeed in school. They may develop strong feelings of inadequacy. They may even cheat in their school work. In such cases, teachers should strive to compensate for the home influence by setting realistic goals and by helping pupils attain some measure of success in assuming reasonable responsibilities. They may also encourage parents to recognize the kind of expectations that are in line with the norms of child development.

Many teachers express more disapproval of women who work than they do of stay-at-homes who expect too much or too little of their children. In this respect, teachers share the lay belief that mothers who work tend to neglect their duties as mothers. Despite such criticisms, approximately one-third of all American mothers, many of whom are middle class, work outside the home. Researchers find that, contrary to popular opinion, children of mothers who work do not necessarily suffer.[5] Such children may, of course, be poorly adjusted psychologically but for reasons other than that their mothers are working.

OTHER FAMILY SYSTEMS AND SCHOOLS

A product of the cultural diversity that characterizes this country is a diversity in family patterns. Such diversity, rather than the patriarchal pattern usually described by novelists and early social scientists, was probably always the rule.

Social Class Influences
Family Patterns

At any rate, modern researchers find many variations among families. The majority of them conclude, however, that in the upper classes,

[5] F. Ivan Nye and Lois Wladis Hoffman, *The Employed Mother in America,* Rand McNally, 1963, chaps. 4–8.

the father tends to be the authority figure and that in the lower classes, either the father or the mother may be the head, whereas, as we have already seen, joint authority is often shared by mother and father in the middle class. In the lower classes, mothers who work, especially if they earn more than their husbands, are likely to have a dominant position in the home. In the middle class, whether a mother works outside the home appears to be unrelated to her position of authority in the home.[6]

In all social classes, parents usually urge their children to seek mates from their own social class and indoctrinate them in the value system of this class. Since lower-class and upper-class values differ appreciably from those of the middle class, the values that children from higher or lower socioeconomic levels assimilate may differ markedly from the individualism and achievement orientation of the middle class.

The primary or at least the most visible difference between the working class and the middle-class family, according to Gans, is the role of the family circle. The working-class family circle may vary in many ways and even include friends, but it is usually larger than the nuclear family of the middle class. Work is seen by the working class as the means for earning money to maximize pleasures within the extended family circle. The larger society is evaluated and often judged to be hostile, especially by poor members of the working class and the lower-lower class, because of its effects upon the family circle.[7]

The distinguishing characteristic of lower-lower class homes, Gans states, is the marginal status of the male and the female-based family. The family circle includes only female relatives. The male, a casual provider who is often absent in pursuit of thrills and action, has little responsibility for the rearing of children. The woman, usually more working class in values than her mate, wants her children to do better than their father. Boys from such homes rarely do.[8]

Ethnic and Religious Affiliations
Influence Family Patterns

Not only social class but also ethnic origin and religious affiliation may influence the family system. Among first- or second-generation

---

[6] Goode, *The Family, op. cit.*, p. 76; and Rollins, *op. cit.*, p. 12.

[7] Herbert J. Gans, "The Subcultures of the Working Class, Lower Class, and Middle Class," in Harry L. Miller and Marjorie B. Smiley, eds., *Education in the Metropolis*, Free Press, 1967, p. 146.

[8] *Ibid.*, pp. 147–148.

Jewish working-class families of Eastern European descent, for example, the male is dominant in theory, yet frequently a middle-aged or elder matriarch makes the day-by-day decisions. If the man wishes, he may overrule her decisions, but generally he uses his authority as a threat or a veto rather than actively. The same kind of relationship is common among recent immigrants from Greece and Italy. The chief reason that Jews have been more mobile than Greeks and Italians is that they emphasize contact with the larger society, education, and professional and white-collar occupational goals. In such cases, family values seem to be more important to mobility than either social-class status or family structure.[9]

Some families in other ethnic groups (such as, Polish, Oriental, Mexican American) and religious groups (such as, Roman Catholic, Mormon, Christian Scientists, many other small Protestant groups) may depart in various ways from the "dominant" pattern. Each departure is likely, in some way, to influence child-rearing practices and the personal characteristics of members of the family and their relations with persons in the larger society, especially in the school.

Jehovah's Witnesses, an Example of a Deviant Family Pattern

A rapidly expanding religious group that has a family system of interest to teachers is the Jehovah's Witnesses. The Witnesses carefully socialize their young people by absorbing their energies and shielding them from contact with the larger society. Groups of Witnesses meet several times a week—often on Tuesday and Thursday evenings, Saturdays, and Sundays in addition to a private family study hour and the ministerial duties that all members, including teenagers, perform. Often children eight to ten years old as well as older children and adults are assigned to make six- or seven-minute speeches in their congregations. Such talks may require several hours of preparation. The Witnesses also have church socials in which the whole family may participate. With such a rigorous schedule and close associations within the church, children seldom find time for, or interest in, school and secular social activities.

In their daily devotions children absorb the basic beliefs of the Witnesses. These beliefs are grounded in a literal interpretation of the Bible. Witnesses, therefore, reject the theory of evolution and do not celebrate holidays not mentioned in the Bible. They do not vote for the election of school or community officials because they argue that only

[9] *Ibid.*, p. 145.

God can judge who is best among humans. They do not salute the flag because they say one pledges allegiance only to God. They usually refuse to serve in the Armed Forces on the grounds that the Bible forbids killing others. They are not concerned with problems of the world or with personal advancement. Unable financially to establish their own schools as many other divergent groups have done, they "render unto Caesar" by sending their children to public schools, but they do not encourage them to attend college. Children are expected to obey their parents unconditionally. In theory if not always in practice, the family has a patriarchal organization based on the assumption that man is subordinate to Christ and woman to both man and Christ. The father conducts the family study hour, the aim of which is the children's understanding their roles and the Witnesses' beliefs and practices.

Parents imply that they leave decisions up to their children. They say "We encourage them to . . ." or "We don't encourage . . ." They believe, however, that among them are the select few who will be saved at the Millennium. The motive of salvation (and the possibility of punishment for deviation) coupled with a thoroughgoing system of socialization assures a high level of compliance with parental encouragement.[10]

In school young Witnesses refuse to run for office, vote in school elections, and participate in holiday celebrations and school assemblies. The children of recent converts sometimes donate Christmas decorations, but they take no part in decorating the classroom. They rarely take part in school activities, often for reasons of conscience or because the children are too busy elsewhere. Their practice in making speeches and in studying Witness literature tends to help them in reciting and reading in school. Their home training in obedience is likely to make them well behaved in their classes. They stand respectfully when the flag is saluted.

Witnesses met resistance in schools for refusing to salute the flag until a Supreme Court decision confirmed their right to refrain from taking part in this ritual. Of course, teachers and principals recognize the constitutional right to object on religious grounds and usually excuse pupils from activities to which such objections are made. Less clear-cut and unavoidable conflicts between the teachings of the religious group and those of the school are not so easily resolved. The

---

[10] For additional information on the Witnesses, see "Witnesses," *Time,* (June 30, 1961), p. 47; Everett C. Parker, "Jehovah's Witnesses," *Christian Century,* (July 19, 1961), p. 886; Albert Muller, "These Jehovah's Witnesses," *America,* 105 (June, 1961), 464; and Edgar R. Pike, *Jehovah's Witnesses: Who They Are, What They Teach, What They Do,* Watts & Co., 1954.

school, for example, is charged with educating citizens for a democratic society, which involves the act of voting and a knowledge of and
concern for community welfare. Teachers therefore encourage pupils
to assume the responsibilities of citizenship, whereas parents of young
Witnesses encourage them to avoid such responsibilties. In line with
the constitutional provision for religious freedom, teachers encourage
pupils to be tolerant of religious differences, but many parents who are
Witnesses teach their children antipathies for Roman Catholics.[11]

Such conflicts between values established in the home and those
promulgated by the school raise several crucial issues. When children
accept family values in conflict with the dominant values of the larger
society, are the interests of the larger society at stake? Are family
values having a class or a traditional basis entitled to the same respect
as values based in a religious conviction? One may argue that values
other than religious are also derived out of a group's experience and
represent the group's philosophy of life. When members of the working class view their jobs as merely a means to an end (pleasure with
their family circle) and when they see education as useful only in job
preparation, do teachers err when they try to instill in working-class
children some of the middle-class attitudes toward work, the family,
and education? When working-class people lack organizational and
political interests as well as skills that they need to achieve their own
working-class ends, should the school teach pupils these skills? Under
what circumstances should teachers decide what are the best values
for children to hold? At what point are the interests of the so-called
larger society at stake?

Answering such questions seems simple enough at a theoretical
level. A liberal thinker will quickly point out that in a democracy an
individual has the right to make choices and to live with the consequences of his choices so long as they do not interfere with the rights of
others. He will say that to the extent a teacher or a school administrator denies the exercise of this right, he diminishes democracy. He
believes that if education is indeed a leading-out process, what best
promotes the student's growth will become clear to him and through
experience and example he will learn how to make better choices.

In the context of families whose values differ from those of other
Americans because of their religious beliefs or because of working-
class acceptance of a pragmatic attitude toward work and education,
most educators would readily agree with the liberal thinker. Teachers'

---

[11] Much of the information herein was gathered through interviews with
Witnesses in Eugene, Oregon. Their activities and expressed values may vary from
Witnesses in other areas.

actions may, of course, be inconsistent with what they say they believe. In other situations, the answer is less obvious. In the case of the lower-class Negro family, discussed in some detail in the next section, teachers may face a real quandary as to what action should be taken when the values of the home and those of the school are in conflict.

NEGRO FAMILIES

For a long time the Afro-American family has been described as a matriarchy, an institution ruled by mothers. During the days of slavery and for some time thereafter, Black families were often, perhaps usually, headed by a woman. Toward the end of the nineteenth century and the early part of this century, the number of formal marriages among Negroes increased markedly and the number of children born in wedlock rose to about 89 percent.[12] Since 1950, the number of female-headed families and the number of children born out of wedlock have, however, increased to almost 25 percent in cities, yet during the same period, the numbers have decreased in rural areas and in the South. As a result of divorces, separations, and illegitimate births among Negroes, no more than half of the Negro children at age 18 have lived all their lives with both parents. Notwithstanding these startling statistics, one cannot accurately describe the Negro family as a matriarchy.

Jessie Bernard describes two Negro family systems: one that she calls "acculturated," the other "externally adapted." Because the differences between the family systems are not based on income, a lower-, middle-, or upper-class family may fall into either category. Members of the "acculturated" group have internalized the moral norms of American society. They strive to maintain a stable family life, to conform to conventional sexual behavior and the Protestant ethic, and to live respectably. Members of the "externally adapted" group are described as essentially hedonistic and pleasure-loving. Their behavior is relatively free and uncontrolled by convention and at times even by law. They are likely to value warm, affectionate relationships more highly than a marriage vow, leisure more highly than a job, and present gratifications more highly than future rewards. In calling such families "externally adapted," Bernard admits that like the so-called "acculturated" they are, in fact, "acculturated" but to the "fun morality" point of view. Presumably members of the "acculturated" group

[12] Jessie Bernard, *Marriage and Family Among Negroes*, Prentice-Hall, 1966, p. 5.

are largely descendants of house slaves; members of the "externally adapted" group descendants of field slaves.[13]

Bernard maintains that there is no such thing as a "typical" Negro family. Like Caucasians, they differ as to social class and religious, or lack of religious affiliation, but they also differ in respect to the two clusters of values she describes. She is unable to estimate the proportion of Negroes in each category. Some "acculturated" Negroes are very poor and live in slums and rural poverty areas. Probably a large percentage of middle- and upper-class Negroes are "acculturated," but some "externally adapted" people have acquired enough money in various ways to move up the social scale.

Bernard's terms are useful because they suggest that particular families in all social classes may cherish one of two different clusters of values. Since, used in this way, the terms are probably as applicable to whites as to Blacks, one wonders why Bernard restricts their usage to Negroes.

In 1965 Daniel Patrick Moynihan's report, *The Negro Family: The Case for National Action,* pointed to the deterioration of families among disorganized, disadvantaged lower-class Negroes (Bernard's "externally adapted," lower-class Negroes). Citing the high divorce, separation, and illegitimacy rates and the number of families headed by women, he called for Federal programs designed to strengthen the Negro family.[14] Using this report as a basis for his 1965 speech at Howard University, President Lyndon B. Johnson said, "So, unless we work to strengthen the [Negro] family, to create conditions under which most parents will stay together—all the rest: schools and playgrounds, public assistance and private concern, will never be enough to cut completely the circle of despair and deprivation."

Moynihan's report has been widely criticized by government officials, journalists, and Negro leaders as being somewhat inaccurate and as providing fodder for white racists who say the weaknesses of the Negro character cause his current status.[15] Although such was clearly not Moynihan's intention, critics say that his report may lead people to impute the characteristics of a minority of the Negroes to all Negroes. Such false generalizations may indeed be made by people who do not know that similar conditions prevail among a smaller percentage but

13 *Ibid.,* pp. 27–66.
14 U.S. Department of Labor, *The Negro Family: The Case for National Action,* Government Printing Office, 1966.
15 See Herbert J. Gans, "The Negro Family: Reflections on the Moynihan Report," *Commonweal,* (October 15, 1965), pp. 47–50 for suggestions to educators in regard to interpreting the report.

still a substantial number of white families. Moynihan's contention that the plight of the slum Negro family has its roots in the low status of Negro males, unemployment, substandard wages, poor housing, inadequate education, and widespread poverty should not be overlooked and his appeal for social and economic reforms should not be ignored.

With the exception of the family role of women, none of the conditions described by Moynihan or the value-systems described by Bernard is uniquely Negro. If Black families are distinctively different from white families, the differences are found primarily among lower-class Negroes with respect to their reactions to racial discrimination, the role of the woman in the home, and the large number who are poverty-stricken.

Reactions to Racial Discrimination

As Lee Rainwater's contrastive hypothesis suggests, the reaction of "externally-adapted" ghetto Negroes to racial discrimination is not a direct but an indirect cause-and-effect relationship:

$$\text{White cupidity} \xrightarrow[\text{Not}]{} \text{Negro suffering}$$

But
White cupidity
creates

Social and Personal Responses which serve to sustain the individual in his punishing world but also generate aggressiveness toward the self and others

which results in

Suffering directly inflicted by Negroes on themselves and on others.[16]

Thus not only the pathological influences of a disorganized social environment but also feelings of frustration growing out of the refusal of many whites to recognize Negroes as humans worthy of respect lead to aberrant family life among slum Negroes. Because they suffer as employees, recipients of welfare, losers in competition, users of drugs and alcohol, husbands inflict suffering on wives and wives on husbands. Their children suffer in the unstable homes they provide.

Realizing that his parents and other Negroes he knows are not respected, a Negro child begins at an early age to doubt whether they really deserve respect. He begins to develop a self- and group-hatred

[16] Lee Rainwater, "Crucible of Identity: The Negro Lower-Class Family," in Talcott Parsons and Kenneth B. Clark, eds., *The Negro American*, Houghton Mifflin, 1966, p. 164.

and to believe that Negroes are, in truth, inferior. A vicious circle begins. Because he feels inferior, he lacks self-confidence in his ability to learn especially in school. Because he does not think he can succeed there, he does not learn very much. Because he does not learn in school, he has few marketable skills. Because he has a poor job or no job, a poor education, a poor self-concept, he in turn becomes a poor father in an unstable family. Although such feelings and behavior patterns are also common among poverty-stricken whites, they are not discriminated against because of race. "To the [American] Negro child," says Kenneth Clark, "the most serious injury seems to be in the concept of self-worth related directly to skin color itself." The "obsession with whiteness," he adds, "stays with the Negro all his life."[17]

A Negro child's fantasies and comments often reveal his obsessions with his dark skin. When asked to color a figure to look like themselves, very young children will sometimes use a light color or a dark purple. Cottle reports a teenage girl's terror lest the Boston Strangler enter her home and her strange fear that the Strangler wouldn't stop to kill her because she was a Negro. He quotes a teenage boy to the effect that "All of us are dark specks on a policeman's badge."[18]

Although Negro children feel that the police more than other adults discriminate against them because they are black, they are also likely to distrust anyone in authority especially anyone who is white. The teacher is an authority figure. When a little child first enters school he is told to obey the teacher and that he will be punished if he does not, but he is seldom encouraged to view the teacher as one who will help him learn. His expectation that adults will treat him unfairly begins in early childhood and often leads to his withdrawing from or rebelling in school.

Closely allied to the distrust of white authority is the fairly common belief especially among lower-class Negroes that they have "soul" whereas whites do not. "Soul" has many meanings, even among "street people" who "hustle" (steal, gamble, sell dope, etc.), but basically it seems to imply honesty—the opposite of hypocrisy, deceit, and phoniness.[19] A former president of the National Association for the Advancement of Colored Peoples (NAACP), the late Walter White, in a *Saturday Review* article entitled "Why I Remain a Negro" rested his case on the assumption that Negroes are better people than whites.

[17] Kenneth B. Clark, "Explosion in the Ghetto," *Psychology Today, 1* (September, 1967), 36.

[18] Thomas J. Cottle, "Encounter in Color," *Psychology Today, 1* (December, 1967), 24.

[19] John Horton, "Time and Cool People," *Trans-action, 4* (April, 1967), 5–12.

Roles of Parents in the Lives
of Their Children

Although a common problem in Negro ghettos is families without
fathers, statistics show that fatherless families are not characteristic of
the majority of American Negro families. In 1960 both husband and
wife were present in 61 percent of the Negro households. Nor is a
household with a mother, a succession of lovers, and many children
typical. The latter type has been estimated at about 11 percent.[20]
Among the poverty-stricken lower strata of Negroes, far too many
children are, however, held together as a family by a poorly educated,
overworked mother.

Even among families with both parents present, the Negro female
may dominate decision-making. Unlike lower-class white women, who
are likely to be intimidated by their husbands, Negro women feel
equal or perhaps superior to their husbands. They are often the
primary financial support. As indicated previously, there is historical
precedence for the dominant role of the Negro woman in the home,
but the situation continues to exist largely because the Negro male has
been so consistently demeaned in American society. If he cannot support or protect his family, he may desert it. If he cannot provide
support, his wife may feel that she is better off without him.

Before a Negro couple marries, the way is paved for family disinte-
gration. Males usually see all Negro girls as fair game. Most girls from
poverty-stricken homes expect to be seduced, but they do not want to
be taken advantage of or to become pregnant. As a consequence,
intercourse occurs much less frequently than is often assumed, but
pregnancy is likely to follow when it happens because the partners are
ignorant of contraceptives. When pregnancy occurs, a Negro girl, like a
Danish girl, does not feel compelled to marry her partner. Many Negro
girls, in fact, marry after they already have a child who has been cared
for in their own home by their mother. When a girl decides to marry,
however, she may feel ambivalent about her decision because she
doubts that the man will be able to support a family. The young man
may also feel ambivalent about marriage because he is likely to doubt
that the girl will be true to him. Once married, however, the girl
attains "respectability." If she is later parted from her mate, she may
with impunity take other "boy friends."[21]

The absence of a strong father-figure in the home is thought to be

[20] Bernard, *op. cit.*, p. vii.
[21] Rainwater, *op. cit.*, pp. 172–180.

especially harmful to the psychic growth of a male child. He finds identification with a male role difficult because he has no suitable model in the home. In seeking such a model, he sometimes identifies with older boys and young men (school dropouts) who hang out on slum streets seeking excitement and "bread" (money), which they often obtain by illegal activities.

Boys from fatherless homes usually dress, talk, and act like men, yet at least one psychological study of white and black boys found them to be less analytic and aggressive and more passive than boys who had fathers at home. Not only did the boys from fatherless homes have more "feminine" scores than did those with fathers at home but also the Negro boys had more "feminine" scores than white boys. The researchers concluded that the demasculinization of Negro males in their subculture influences Negro boys even if they have fathers at home. Other researchers found a boy from a fatherless home is more likely to dream of someone giving him money rather than of his earning it.[22]

Very little research examining the influence of fatherless families upon white or Negro girls has been undertaken. A Negro girl's attitude of distrust and sometimes disrespect for males may, however, have roots in such a family. Gisela Konopka, studying institutionalized delinquent girls and unwed mothers, few of whom were Negroes, found that many of them came from fatherless homes. Most of them were economically deprived. When a mother has to be everything, Konopka concludes, frequently she can be nothing because she too has no support.[23]

Held together with a woman domestic's wages and occasional help from an absent father or aid to dependent children, Black families headed by lower-class women are generally poverty-stricken. Providing food and clothing is a continuous problem. Little time or money is available for education. Many of these women also have little or no knowledge of how to help children learn.

In Kansas City, organizers of a nursery program for four-year-olds from poverty-class, fatherless Negro homes found they had to pay the mothers for "their trouble" of bringing the children to school. They also found that rewarding the children with food was the best way to encourage them to learn because they had not learned to respond to praise. Many of these children were inarticulate. Teachers taught a

[22] Allan G. Barclay and D. R. Cusumans, "Testing Masculinity in Boys Without Fathers," *Trans-action*, 5 (December, 1967), 33–35.
[23] Gisela Konopka, *The Adolescent Girl in Conflict*, Prentice-Hall, 1966, pp. 49–51.

child to imitate sounds and helped him increase his vocabulary and the length of his sentences by asking him many questions. Another program under the same leadership tried to teach "upwardly mobile" mothers how to teach their children. The teachers found the mothers were inclined to give little instruction and to punish errors with nagging or threats. After training, the mothers learned to be more effective in teaching and more generous in praise, particularly when teaching children not their own.[24]

Educational Disadvantages of Children from Poverty-Stricken Negro Homes

In 1966 a group headed by James S. Coleman reported statistics supporting the conclusion that on the average Negro, Indian, Puerto Rican, and Mexican American children trail white children in academic achievement when they enter school and even more so during the last year of high school. Coleman found little variation in Negro pupils' achievement among schools irrespective of condition of libraries, age of buildings, and experience level of teachers. He concluded that the sources of inequality of educational opportunity lie primarily in differences in family background and in the social composition of student bodies; they lie in the school's ineffectiveness in helping pupils to achieve despite their environments.[25]

In light of such findings, a reasonable conclusion is that if children from underprivileged homes are to have equal educational opportunities, their education must start earlier than it now does and it must include experiences beyond their immediate families and neighborhoods. Specific proposals designed to achieve these ends are considered in Chapters 12 and 13. Another reasonable conclusion is that if the lower-class Negro family is to become more stable, its members need not only more education but also more money. In short, the War on Poverty has only begun; to win it will require billions and billions of dollars. Finally, prejudice among Americans of different skin colors can be unlearned and an understanding of different values encouraged in schools and throughout the land. When people learn to be sensitive to the needs of others, racial discrimination, already illegal, may become obsolete.

At this point, let us return to the questions as to the role of the

[24] Todd Risley, "Learning and Lollipops," *Psychology Today,* 1 (January, 1968), 28–31, 62–65.

[25] James S. Coleman *et al., Equality of Educational Opportunity,* U.S. Government Printing Office, 1966, p. 325.

teacher in promoting values that differ from those held by the families and neighborhoods of pupils. Social scientists assert that the adaptations of lower-class Negroes are sensible. First, because the young desperately need love, affection, and acceptance, sex becomes very important for them even if it involves no long-time commitment. It is, Clark claims, "innocent" in the sense that the girl is not trying to trap the male into matrimony. Second, "hustling" is not considered immoral. It is necessary to survival. After a young man acquires "knowledge" of the street, he uses a great deal of initiative and ingenuity to get what he wants. And third, desertion of the family by the father may improve the family's chances of getting help from welfare and other sources. Such behavior, then, is to be understood rather than condemned. If it is condemned by a teacher on the grounds that the individual as well as the larger society suffers from such marked deviance from social norms, how does a pupil react? Does he forego committing the acts or does he simply acquire a feeling of guilt about doing the things that his needs justify?

Since the lower-class black (or white) family is reacting, not necessarily unintelligently, to the social situation in which it finds itself, its value system is not likely to change unless the social situation is changed. An improvement in the social and economic situation of the underprivileged is clearly justified on the grounds of relieving human suffering. It can also be justified as a way to reduce welfare costs, racial tensions, and crimes of violence. Obviously the school cannot change the social environment of disadvantaged people, yet it is expected to educate children from disadvantaged homes.

Bruno Bettleheim says that to educate these children "we will have to free ourselves of a few of our most widely held prejudices—that the child is the private property of his parents to do with as they please, that we are therefore powerless to change the environment he grows up in, and that human beings are infinitely improvable, at any age, no matter what the home environment of their childhood."[26] He supports his thesis with findings of psychoanalysts and educational psychologists, particularly Benjamin Bloom. Bloom found that children's intelligence quotients, depending upon their environment, may vary as much as 20 points (the difference between a feeble-minded person and one who can live a normal life or between a person who can succeed in a semiskilled job and one who can become a professional). The most significant finding, however, pertains to the importance of early environment in the development of intelligence. Children in

[26] Bruno Bettleheim, "How Much Can Man Change?" in Daniel Schreiber, ed., *Profile of the School Dropout*, Random House, 1967, pp. 215–224.

impoverished homes may score 10 points lower on intelligence tests in their first four years, 6 points lower in the next four years, and only 4 points lower in the next 10 years (between ages 8 and 17) than they would have if they had lived in normal homes.[27] In general, then disadvantaged children are exposed to educative stimuli too late for schooling to be effective.

Although Bettleheim is not specifically discussing family values, he is suggesting that in some instances the rights of some parents to rear their own children as they now do may be questioned by members of society. Perhaps the social situation leading to educational deprivation can be changed without directly attacking family values. In other words, impoverished Negro and white mothers could be paid to attend classes in which they learn how to care for and to teach children and, in some cases, how to read and write themselves. Very young children can be given educational experiences in Day Care Centers. Methods of teaching and curriculums in school and preschool classes can be improved. Even with such innovations, successful assimilation into the larger society of lower-class disadvantaged families, particularly those headed by women, cannot be assumed. The neighborhood environment must be changed and jobs provided for those who take advantage of educational opportunities. The value system of children from fatherless homes is not likely to change if they find no suitable models with whom they can identify and if they have no reason to believe that education has rewards.

IMPORTANT CONCEPTS

Equalitarian Family. See p. 197.
Extended family. A social group consisting of several related individual families, often living in a single large dwelling or a cluster of small ones.
Matriarchy. See p. 204.
Nuclear family. See p. 196.
Patriarchy. See p. 202.

---

[27] Benjamin Bloom, *Stability and Change in Human Characteristics*, Wiley, 1964, p. 72.

III. THE LOCAL COMMUNITY AND SCHOOLS

10. SCHOOLS IN RURAL COMMUNITIES

Great economic and social forces flow with a tidal sweep over communities that are only half conscious of that which is befalling them.

—RICHARD COBDEN[1]

Census-takers in this country characterize all areas as either urban or rural. Any place with 2500 or more inhabitants and any area with a population density of 1500 or more per square mile are categorized as urban; all other areas are rural. Hence the densely populated fringe of cities, commonly called suburbs, and many very small cities, commonly called "small towns," are classified as urban.

Urban areas differ from rural areas in ways other than density of population. An urban community's occupational and economic activities usually center in industry rather than in agriculture. In urban areas fertility rates are lower, more women are in the labor force, more adults are unmarried, the educational level is higher, and residents are more cosmopolitan in outlook than in rural places. The rural community is, however, rapidly acquiring many of these characteristics.

All American communities are adopting the way of life of persons who live in a large city. A growing number of Americans, about 70 percent in 1967, live in urban places, and people who live in rural areas are becoming more and more like city dwellers in their occupations, outlook, and life style. Nelson says that even the "farmer in the United States can in a sense be regarded as a suburbanite."[2]

In terms of life style, the degree of urbanization varies greatly, depending in part upon the relative proximity of large urban centers. Hence villages and towns (terms used interchangeably to describe places of 500 to 2500 population), hamlets (under 500 population), and communities in the open country—all of which are classified as rural may, in fact, sometimes be more highly urbanized in life style than isolated small cities.

Traditionally the chief occupation in rural areas has been farming, but today three-fourths of those who live in rural places are not farmers. Heads of nonfarm families, like many part-time farmers, are local business and professional men or they are commuters to jobs in the city. Most residents of rural areas, then, have occupations much like those of city dwellers.

Urban-rural differences persist in fertility rates, numbers of women

[1] *Life of Richard Cobden.*
[2] Lowry Nelson, *American Farm Life,* Harvard University Press, 1954, p. 171.

in the labor force, proportion of single persons, and average educational level of adults, but changes in statistics upon which these generalizations are based show that rural areas are moving in the same direction as urban areas. The average size of rural families is declining, the income and educational levels of rural adults are rising. New outlooks on life, encouraged by improved transportation and communication, are accompanying these occupational and social changes.

CHANGES IN RURAL LIFE
THAT INFLUENCE SCHOOLS

To understand what has happened in the rural community, one must consider how technological changes have influenced the social environment of farmers and townspeople in villages.

The internal-combustion engine, scientific methods of farming, and electrification have revolutionized rural life. Before they had motorized transportation and good roads, most American farm families (most rural dwellers were farmers) were more isolated than farm families in other countries because they had lived in scattered farmsteads rather than in villages. Their isolation encouraged individualism coupled with mutual aid, a feeling that cities were evil and dangerous, and local autonomy in such community institutions as the schools.

Isolation ended when the farmer bought an automobile or a truck. These vehicles enabled the farmer to transport goods to markets and his family to social gatherings and jobs in nearby cities and towns. No longer dependent upon a single trading area, he could buy commodities in different centers. The importance of improved transportation can hardly be overemphasized, for at the same time that it brought town and country together, it led to the decay of many rural institutions.

Mechanization and electrification lightened the family's work load, and along with improved methods of farming, increased the farm's yield. Many farms became "factories in the fields" requiring scientific and technical knowledge, capital, and expert management.

A young farm boy, attending a conference in 1963 sponsored by the National Committee for Children and Youth, said:

> First it takes capital to get started [farming], and that is not too easy to get. Where I come from, Sidney, Nebraska, the price of land is high—$100 to $200 an acre for good farm land and $36 for prairie land for grazing. Your modern machinery is more efficient—it doesn't take as long to do the work—but it costs more now.
>
> But the main problem I face in getting started in farming is lack of

education. I don't have a good background in agriculture except what I learned from my father, and he was not a college man.[3]

Thus not all would-be farmers and farmers have benefited from advances in scientific agriculture and mechanization. For several decades the trend has been toward large farms of 250 to 1000 acres or more, and very small farms of 10 to 20 acres or less. Numerous farms with inadequate capital, poor land, and small acreage have had to be abandoned. Between 1930 and 1964, the index of farm output per man-hour rose from 28 to 137, which means that one man in 1964 could do the work done by five men in 1930. Many farmers and farm laborers lost their means of livelihood. Millions of sharecroppers, farm laborers, and small-farm owners either crowded into cities to seek jobs in industry or became migratory farm workers. Some of the latter live in cities and during certain seasons work under contract on farms. Others became subsistence or part-time farmers. Still others, relatively uninfluenced by new agricultural practices, eke out a miserable existence in such areas as Appalachia and other isolated places. The standard of living of these marginal farmers and of farm laborers is far below that of the prosperous farmer.

Many full-time farmers, however, now live much like their city counterparts. Almost all of them have a television set, electrical fixtures, and an automobile or truck or both. The majority have a telephone and such modern appliances as a home freezer. The average farmer's land and buildings were worth $51,000 in 1964. He sold farm produce valued at $20,000 or more. With comfortable incomes and increased leisure, farm families in upper income brackets travel widely at home and abroad.

The farmer's neighborhood at the turn of the century included families scattered throughout the countryside. It has been weakened by the loss of the country store, church, and the "little red schoolhouse," by the lack of communion between rich and poor farmers and between farmers and those who do not farm, and by the disappearing borders between town and country. Even though today farmers may trade in more than one place, their social contacts are usually stronger in one of these places. Some farmers have moved to town. As a result the rural community is becoming town-centered. Frequently, in fact, the community's boundaries are defined by those of the consolidated schools usually located in a village.

In like manner, rural towns have changed. They once were service-station communities whose economy depended upon supplying farm-

---

[3] National Committee for Children and Youth, *Rural Youth in a Changing Environment,* Ruth Cowan Nash, ed., 1965, pp. 129–130.

ers' needs. Consequently the effect upon them of farmers using their improved transportation to buy in distant centers was sometimes disastrous. In other instances, the change led to increased interdependence among centers, as in Nebraska where "market towns" or "farm cities" flourish, surrounded by satellite villages.

By and large, these changes have evoked a general air of pessimism in many residents of small towns. Accustomed, like many other Americans, to judge progress in terms of rapidly increasing population, townspeople rued the passing of the days when their communities were thriving. As a matter of fact, only hamlets are actually deserted. Most villages have grown in recent decades, and towns and cities dependent upon agricultural income have shared in the big farmers' relative prosperity. The prosperous communities have made adjustments. Retailers learned to stock the commodities that their customers continue to purchase in local communities rather than in cities. For many towns, however, the most promising future is tourism. An expansion of rural recreational facilities, encouraged by federal grants, helps not only in bolstering the rural economy and providing jobs for rural young people but also in supplying needed recreational facilities for urban centers.

Despite these adjustments, small towns have suffered the loss of young adults who have moved to the city, and the towns are apparently unable to stop this drain. The possibility of good paying jobs, varied amusements, and personal freedom in cities holds great allure for small-town progeny, and young people leave homes, never to return except for brief visits. These young villagers, between ages 16 and 30, joined by young people of the same ages displaced by technology on farms make up the overwhelming majority of migrants to cities. The typical rural community, therefore, has a disproportionate number of children and people in older age brackets.

Rural life is being profoundly affected by the fundamental dislocations of an ever-declining need for farmers and farm laborers, an increasing social distance between the rich and the poor in rural areas, and a weakening of community ties.

These changes are significant to residents of urban as well as rural areas. The roots of many big city problems are entwined with problems of rural areas, for displaced rural youth of lower-class origins are the new immigrants to city slums. Ill-prepared for industrial jobs and urban living, they contribute to the ranks of the unemployed, delinquent, and alienated. These young people have been found to have less chance of rising occupationally in cities than have natives of cities from the same social backgrounds. The disadvantage of rural origin is not so apparent, however, among middle-class migrants. They do as well or better than natives.[4]

For this and other reasons, the increasing social distance between rich and poor in rural areas has serious social implications. Although rural areas have long been praised for their democratic acceptance of all residents, as early as 1955 a researcher found that social-class lines are, in fact, more rigid in small towns than in cities[5] and that the small-town middle class is smaller in size than that of the city. Because "everybody knows everybody," all possible candidates for middle-class status in small towns are included in middle-class activities and subjected to the pressures of conforming to middle-class norms of behavior. The result is that few of the middle-class lose status in small communities. Likewise working-class persons, easily identified as lower-class since "everybody knows everybody" and excluded from middle-class activities, find rising into the middle class more difficult in a small community than in a city.

Social differences between middle-class and lower-class people are being augmented by greater differences in income, especially along the east and west coasts, as the family farm is being replaced by the factory farm. Therefore the chances are lessening for lower-class children to associate closely with middle-class children from whom they could learn the social skills and vocational aspirations necessary for mobility. As will be explained in the next chapter, the gap is also widening between social classes in cities. A lower class excluded from close contact with the middle class, from legitimate social rewards, and from adequate income is a serious menace to a society.

In time, but not without much conflict, unionization of the farm factory may raise the income of farm laborers, but only through proper guidance, schooling, and associations can the young develop skills they will need when they move to cities. These migrations give urban dwellers as large a stake in providing improved educational experiences for rural children as rural dwellers have.

RURAL PERSONALITY AND ATTITUDES
TOWARD SCHOOLS

Until recently, persons who lived in rural areas were often described by city residents as "hicks," "hayseeds," or "rubes." Perhaps the declining use of such epithets indicates that urbanization is erasing super-

[4] Seymour Martin Lipset and Reinhard Bendix, *Social Mobility in Industrial Society*, University of California Press, 1959, pp. 224–228.
[5] Godfrey Hochbaum *et al.*, "Socio-Economic Variables in a Large City," *American Journal of Sociology*, 61 (July, 1955), 31–38.

ficial differences, such as manners and fashions in clothing, between rural and urban residents. Whether real differences in personality and norms of behavior are associated with ruralism is, however, an important question to teachers.

Evidence about the existence of such differences is scarce and often inconclusive. Whatever differences are reported are usually greater between the extremes in the rural group than between the rural and the urban.

Assertions that simple, rural surroundings promote mental health of residents have not been supported with evidence. Although statistics show that fewer rural than urban families are broken by death or divorce and that rural families tend to be larger, studies of the personalities of rural children fail to indicate that these or other possible characteristics of their family life produce better adjusted boys and girls. Studies comparing social adjustments of rural and urban pupils that used the California Test of Personality reached contradictory conclusions. A study of 15,000 ninth graders' responses to the Minnesota Multiphasic Inventory revealed significant differences in a few characteristics. Rural more than urban children are likely to be shy, self-deprecating, and suspicious of others. Urban more than rural children are likely to rebel against authority.[6] Results of another study showed rural boys more withdrawn, submissive, and nervous, and less optimistic about man's ability to control events than urban boys.[7]

Two national surveys conducted by the Survey Research Center at the University of Michigan revealed dramatic differences between farm boys and girls and adolescents in urban centers. Farm children were described by the Center's interviewers as less "poised," "confident," "organized," and "articulate," and as more dependent upon parental authority than urban children. Adolescents who live on farms are "as deprived," these researchers said, "as those from the meanest urban environment." They have few leisure activities and organizational memberships. They have little opportunity for part-time employment and friendly relationships with adults.[8]

The belief that rural children enjoy better physical health than urban children is also questionable. Many children in rural communities drink raw milk and untested water. They live in places where sanitary inspections are lax or nonexistent and medical care is scarce. A researcher found that rural residents are less likely to exercise regu-

[6] Stark R. Hathaway, Eli D. Monachesi, and Lawrence A. Young, "Rural-Urban Adolescent Personality," *Rural Sociology, 24* (December, 1959), 336–346.
[7] A. O. Haller and Carole Ellis Wolff, "Personality Orientation of Farm, Village, and Urban Boys," *Rural Sociology, 27* (September, 1962), 275–293.
[8] Elizabeth Douvan and Joseph Adelson, *The Adolescent Experience,* Wiley, 1966, pp. 315–316.

larly than city dwellers.[9] The armed forces reject for physical reasons more young men in rural than in urban places. Although relatively low family incomes and below standard health services undoubtedly increase the number of young men who are disqualified, a study of military statistics does not support the assumption that living in the country is necessarily healthful.

The likelihood of self-deprecation, poor health, and little exposure to enriching experiences in poor homes may account for the consistently lower ratings of rural than of urban children tests of mental ability and of academic achievement. These ratings, in turn, are related to higher rates of dropouts from rural than urban schools. A number of researchers have found also that the level of aspiration of rural youth, excepting those from middle-class homes, is lower than that of urban youth.

The situation is, however, getting better rather than worse. Mental and achievement test scores of rural students are rising and dropouts are declining in rural places. An analyst of a recent Roper poll, based on interviews with a random sampling of 1794 rural and a control group of 720 urban youths, reached this conclusion: "There is a possibility that no longer is there a significant difference between rural and urban youth as to their problems, attitudes, and aspirations."[10]

This poll found negligible differences between the two groups of young people in their opinions about jobs, morality, civil rights, future opportunities, juvenile delinquency, and the like. Its findings tend to refute the belief that rural youth are committed to individualism, hard work, and unrestrained enterprise. Although farm parents, more often than nonfarm parents, stress that young people learn by working and give them jobs,[11] the Roper poll reported that only 1 percent more rural than urban youth (67 compared to 66 percent) said "hard work" gets you ahead faster. The same poll found little evidence that rural youth are more individualistic than urban youth although a few more of them want to run their own businesses. Among the future entrepreneurs, however, urban youth are more adventuresome than the rural.[12]

The findings of a study of Texas rural and urban adolescent attitudes also support the conclusion that place of residence has little influence upon youth's orientation to society. Young people from large families in cities more than from those in the country were, however,

[9] Saxon Graham, "Social Correlates of Adult Leisure-Time Behavior," in Marvin B. Sussman, ed., *Community Structure and Analysis,* Crowell, 1959, pp. 344–345.

[10] National Committee for Children and Youth, *op. cit.,* p. 31.

[11] Murray Strauss, "Work Roles and Financial Responsibility in the Socialization of Farm, Fringe, and Town Boys," *Rural Sociology,* 27 (September, 1962), 257–274.

[12] National Committee for Children and Youth, *op. cit.,* pp. 26–81.

critical of education; young people in the country more than those in the city disapproved slightly more often of peer groups, yet found opposing the demands of peer groups more difficult. Another conclusion of this study is that in Texas the range of differences between poor and middle-income families was not so great in rural as in urban communities.[13]

Although rural teenagers, influenced no doubt by the mass media, may indeed seem remarkably like city teenagers, conditions in rural communities support the assumption that older people have resisted change except in agricultural technology. There the celebrated "grassroots" democracy has led to very few changes in community institutions. The consolidated school, for instance, has more often been imposed upon rural communities than initiated by them. Service organizations find fewer active members in proportion to population as the size of the community decreases. Community support of schools and the PTA and its interest in educating children are also likely to decline with rurality.

Until recently many farmers believed that their sons could learn more about farming by working on the farm than they could by attending high school and college. Resistance to children's attending school was greater among farmers of some religions and cultural origins than among others, but villagers of the same social backgrounds as these farmers were more likely than farmers to approve higher levels of education for their children.[14] Nevertheless, rural as well as urban children complete more grades in school than their parents did, and more of them go to college.

SPECIAL PROBLEMS
OF RURAL SCHOOLS

Only 10 percent of farm boys can hope to make a good income on the farm. Most of the others and most boys from villages have no alternative but to emigrate to cities to find work. Rural schools are therefore faced with the incredibly difficult task of preparing young people to live and work in a society different from that in which they have lived all their lives. Many rural schools have failed to recognize the urgency of this task.

Although an urban life style has spread to many rural communities, teachers in rural schools need to prepare pupils for persisting rural-

[13] Bernice Milburn Moore and Wayne H. Holtzman, *Tomorrow's Parents: A Study of Youth and Their Families,* University of Texas Press, 1965, pp. 86–90.
[14] Nelson, *op. cit.,* pp. 93–95.

urban differences. For example, the urban society more than the rural is:

HIGHLY VERBAL.   A farm boy discovers that you apply in writing for a job, unemployment compensation, or welfare. You read a city map, street sign, or perhaps a bus schedule to find an address in a city.

CONTRACTUAL.   He learns that you sign a lease for an apartment or a contract when you buy appliances.

IMPERSONAL.   He finds that you meet many people, yet know few intimately. You may find a friendly stranger is a "confidence" man or a slick salesman. You get a job by making a "good impression." You feel lonely in the crowd.

TIME-ORIENTED.   He realizes that everybody expects you to be on time. The pace in the city is so fast that people don't have time to waste waiting for you.

SPECIALIZED OCCUPATIONALLY.   He finds people have thousands of different jobs, many of which require special technical skills.

Not only do urban ways create problems for emigrants, but also their rural customs that are inappropriate in cities cause them trouble. For instance, throwing garbage out the back door in the city is very different from throwing it out the back door in the country. Hanging around the corner store is part of the social life in the country; it is loitering in a city. Shooting a squirrel in a city will bring the police.

Obviously the extent of deprivation within a rural community as well as the extent of migration from it determines its needs. Even the prosperous communities have not usually adjusted their schools and community organizations to meet current needs. Almost any rural community has some disadvantaged children, and throughout the United States there are pockets of rural poverty. Many children in rural America are as socially disadvantaged as those in city slums. The problems there have not, however, been so widely advertised.

Rural schools have other problems. Securing parental cooperation, particularly of parents who live farthest from school, is not an easy undertaking. Since rural communities often have no local newspaper and rural residents are likely to reluctantly participate in the PTA and to be conservative about educational matters, school leaders have difficulty in explaining to the public the need for changes in schools. In some places, very small, inferior schools still exist. Although consolidation of rural schools has proceeded rapidly in recent years, in some communities farmers and villagers have successfully resisted those who would "take their school away."

Conservative rural residents also often resist raising teachers' salaries. As one farmer put it in a letter to the editor of a local newspaper, "Why the teachers already make almost as much as my best hired hand." But alleged provincialism, poor living conditions, and limited social opportunities as well as low salaries deter many young teachers from accepting positions in rural schools.

The foregoing discussion suggests that rural schools like many urban schools have not been able to provide the best education for all their students. The blame for this inadequacy must be shared by state departments of education, teacher-education institutions, and legislatures, for none of these agencies has aided the rural community much.

Curriculum Changes Needed

A thorough overhaul of the curriculums of rural schools is long overdue. A critical examination of courses of study in many schools may reveal too much emphasis on agricultural training and college preparation and not enough on social skills, technical education, and occupations related to agriculture, sometimes called agribusiness. Work-study programs, urban-rural student exchanges, field trips to industries, study beginning in elementary schools of occupations, use of resource speakers from industry, mobile vocational facilities, area or regional service agencies that provide specialized educational services, expansion of library resources, extensive counseling and guidance, remedial programs, opportunities to study art, music, dramatics, simple carpentry skills, and the like, and a comprehensive program of health education would up-date rural education. Area vocational-technical high schools and community colleges established throughout the country would be able to offer specialized technical training.

Revised teaching methods designed to provide practice in the kind of reading, speaking, and writing that is used in everyday affairs, to train students in techniques useful in getting jobs, and to acquaint them with legal procedures and labor union practices would prepare rural students to compete in national marketplaces. Cocurricular programs that include lower-class as well as middle-class students would develop the initiative, social skills, and self-confidence of students.[15] If community agencies, such as service clubs, hospitals, and retirement homes, would use student helpers, work of this sort would encourage student attitudes of cooperation and discourage feelings of alienation.

The kinds of programs suggested above are too ambitious for most

[15] Many of these recommendations for curriculum change were also made by participants at the National Conference sponsored by the National Committee for Children and Youth, *op. cit.*, pp. 140–152.

rural schools to undertake without help. Nor should they have to do so. Public organizations, such as the federal Departments of Agriculture, Labor, and Health, Education, and Welfare, and the Children's Bureau and state employment agencies, agricultural extension services, departments of education, and teacher-education institutions can and should provide expertise and financial support. Likewise, private organizations, such as the National Education Association, American Federation of Teachers, the American Medical Association, labor unions, industries, foundations, and other national organizations can help. Nevertheless, the rural community must take the initiative in organizing its resources for action.

The chief help that teacher-training institutions can give is technical advice and aid in recruiting teachers. Student teachers and interns should be placed, whenever possible, in rural as well as in urban schools. The challenge of up-grading rural education is as great and, in some respects, more attractive than the challenge of up-grading schools in urban ghettos. A young teacher will usually find his classes smaller, his pupils more tractable, responsive, and appreciative, and his relationships with colleagues and residents of the community friendlier in a rural than in an urban community. He has unlimited opportunities for creativeness because he is largely free of bureaucratic restraints. Most of the prohibitions once put upon the teacher's conduct have been removed. Improved transportation enables him to combine the rewards of teaching in the country with the excitements of city living on weekends. The satisfactions of teaching in rural areas, especially for young married couples, are much greater than most young teachers today realize.

IMPORTANT CONCEPTS

Cosmopolitan. Marked by interest in, familiarity with, or knowledge and appreciation of many parts of the world; not limited by the attitudes, interests, or loyalties of the local scene.

Open country. Sparsely settled agricultural areas, including farming, fishing, mining, and forest areas.

Provincialism. The state of being concerned mainly with a local area and marked by its limitations.

Rural. See p. 215.

Urban. See p. 215.

Urbanization. The process of becoming urban: the movement of people and industries to urban centers; the increase of population and processes in these urban centers.

11. SCHOOLS IN URBAN COMMUNITIES

Those who make peaceful revolution impossible will make violent revolution inevitable.

—JOHN F. KENNEDY

In 1966 Senator Abraham Ribicoff referred to the problems of cities as "our biggest domestic crisis ever." Although nobody has used these exact words to refer to school problems, many people feel that the problems of schools in slums is the biggest educational crisis ever. In 1967 when the NEA urged that federal funds be provided for purposes of general education rather than specifically for disadvantaged children, its recommendation was overruled by a Presidential committee of laymen and educators. More and more studies, articles, and books about disadvantaged children have been published lately. Clearly education of children in urban ghettos is of national concern, even though it may not be the biggest educational problem ever.

In the first section of this chapter the patterns of urban growth that have created problems for school systems are described; in the second section the so-called "urban way of life," its problems, and its effects on children are discussed. In the third and fourth sections, special problems of schools in the inner city and in the suburbs are examined.

PATTERNS OF URBAN GROWTH

The phenomenal growth of American cities during the last two centuries was made possible by the size of the population, developments in organization (a strong central government, expanded markets, specialization of labor), and technical improvements in agriculture and industry. At the time of the American Revolution about 90 percent of the people in this country were engaged in agriculture, whereas today less than 10 percent are so employed. About 90 percent of Americans, most of whom live in cities, now devote their energies to tasks other than producing food. For many years, persons in rural communities have migrated to cities seeking jobs. Since 1820, except during the decade of the Great Depression (1930–1940), the urban population has, in fact, grown at a more rapid rate than the rural population. The large number of migrants to cities, not natural increase by births, accounts for most of this growth.

Growth of Metropolitan Areas

Since World War II urban growth has been largely concentrated in Standard Metropolitan Statistical Areas (SMSA's), cities of 50,000 or more inhabitants and their suburbs. Between 1950 and 1960, increases in metropolitan areas accounted for 85 percent of the nation's growth in population; yet with few exceptions the large cities of over 250,000 inhabitants grew slowly within the city limits or not at all. The 1960 census showed that 18 of the 40 largest cities actually lost population. Many people, mostly middle-class families, moved to the suburbs, and other people, largely rural Negroes and whites, Puerto Ricans, and foreign immigrants, migrated to the centers of cities. Between 1950 and 1960, each of the 50 largest cities increased its proportion of non-white residents. Statistics for most SMSA's showed the same pattern of growth during the same period except in the South where the proportion of nonwhites declined in the smaller SMSA's.

Statistics for the 1960s show a continuation of such trends. Between 1960 and 1966, the number of persons residing on farms declined by 12.6 percent. During the same period, the number of whites in central cities (i.e., within the city limits) of metropolitan areas declined by 2.5 percent and the number of Negroes increased by 24.4 percent. The number of whites living in the suburbs increased by 20.2 percent and the number of Negroes by 8.9 percent. Notwithstanding large increases in Negro populations of cities, in 1966 the percentage of non-whites (which includes groups other than Negroes) living in central cities seldom exceeded one-fourth of the population. Outside of the South, the only cities of over 100,000 population with more than 25 percent nonwhite populations were Baltimore, Cleveland, Detroit, Gary, Grand Rapids, Manhattan Borough of New York City, Newark, Philadelphia, and Washington, D.C.

Socially Homogeneous Neighborhoods

Another characteristic of recent urban growth is the increasing homogeneity of urban neighborhoods. People who live in the same neighborhoods, even though strangers, are likely to have similar incomes, educational levels, occupations, preferences, prejudices, and other characteristics. The rich and poor have always to some extent lived in different residential districts, but never to the extent that is common today. Never before have people who lived in the same neighborhood been so uniformly alike in income and life style. Such . homogeneity has been encouraged by modern zoning regulations, the development of housing tracts, and discriminatory clauses in deeds to property.

By and large, life style more than income seems to influence where

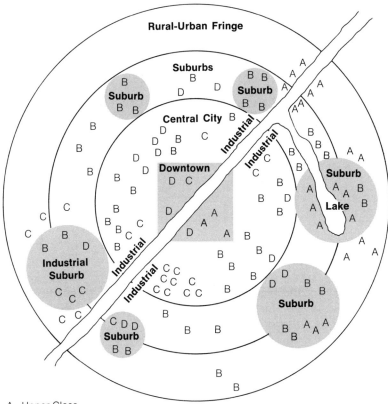

A—Upper Class
B—Middle and Working Class
C—Lower Class
D—Heterogeneous

people live. Researchers find that clerical workers who earn less money
are more likely to live in high-prestige, middle-class neighborhoods
than are the more highly paid blue-collar craftsmen and foremen.[1]
Income and discriminatory housing practices as well as cultural preference, however, determine where many members of minority groups
live in urban areas. The suburbs are peopled largely by whites; subcultural islands in the centers of cities are mostly Negro or colonies of
immigrants. White people move to the suburbs because they want to
and can afford to; ethnic groups live where they must. Although many
writers point out that Caucasians move to the suburbs when a large

[1] Otis Dudley Duncan and Beverly Duncan, "Residential Distribution and
Occupational Stratification," *American Journal of Sociology*, 60 (March, 1955),
493.

influx of Negroes move into the inner city, Schnore found no relationship between the extent of racial change and rapidity of settling
suburbs. Between 1950 and 1960, cities receiving many Negro newcomers and those receiving few of them developed suburban areas at
comparable rates.[2]

The homogeneity of urban neighborhoods has a great impact upon
school populations, particularly at the elementary level. In most places,
elementary schools are neighborhood schools. High schools in certain
sections of a city and its suburbs may also draw pupils primarily from
similar socioeconomic and ethnic backgrounds. The impact upon
schools of predominantly white middle-class student bodies in the
suburbs and of predominantly Negro and white lower-class student
bodies in many schools in the inner city is readily apparent in descriptions of suburban and slum schools.

THE URBAN WAY OF LIFE

Classic sociological theory has assumed an "urban way of life," more
or less applicable to metropolitan city-dwellers of all social levels.[3]
According to the theory, urbanites have physical contacts with many
individuals, intimate relationships with few. They meet one another,
for the most part, only in highly specialized roles—the barber cuts
one's hair, the checker totals the grocery bill, the service attendant
comments on the weather as he cleans the windshield. Persons are
freed from the social controls of the gossipy neighbor, the pastor concerning himself with their spiritual growth, and relatives and intimate
friends influencing their actions. Family ties are not very binding
except in the affectional relationships of husband, wife, and children.
Thus urbanites lose the sense of community participation, the belongingness of the rural society. Durkheim, a famous French sociologist,
called this rootlessness, this collapse of rules of conduct, the state of
anomie, to which he attributed the social disorganization of technological society. In an effort to compensate for the loss of primary face-
to-face relationships, the urban dweller joins organized groups devoted
to his special interests. In these voluntary associations, where relationships are rational and impersonal, he presumably acquires status and
expresses his personality. Uninhibited by the restraints of the local

[2] Leo F. Schnore, *The Urban Scene: Human Ecology and Demography,* Free
Press, 1965, pp. 290–291.

[3] See Louis Wirth, "Urbanism as a Way of Life," *American Journal of Sociology,*
44 (July, 1938), 1–24 for a full discussion of the theory.

community and stimulated by a heterogeneous society, varied recreational outlets, many diverse ideas from the mass media, and his own mobility, the city man is said to be cosmopolitan in outlook, blasé and sophisticated, competitive, individualistic, and tolerant of differences. The larger the city, the more typical of the "urban way of life" are its inhabitants assumed to be. Recent research casts doubts on facets of this theory of urban life.

To describe an "urban way of life" that would be valid for all cities or all men in any city is an impossible undertaking. Smaller, independent cities are quite different from the central cities of the large metropolitan areas and from the satellite cities on the urban fringe. Cities differ, too, for reasons other than size and location. They differ also in ethnic composition, principal occupations of residents, and regional subculture.

Only a few valid generalizations apply to people who live in large cities. The generalizations are notably applicable to residents of cities in the three biggest "megalopolis" areas—the regions between and including Boston and Washington, around the Great Lakes, and in southern California.[4] In these metropolitan areas adults are usually better educated, more likely to be Roman Catholic, of recent immigration, and of varied ethnic origins, and somewhat older than are rural inhabitants. In large urban centers the number of white-collar workers is growing and the number of workers in manufacturing industries is decreasing. The proportion of the labor force in service, administrative, distributive, and clerical occupations is high. Women outnumber men. The larger the place, the more broken homes, the more women who work outside the home, and the lower the fertility rate. Urbanism and familism are said to vary inversely.[5]

Despite their validity, such generalizations do not reveal the very real differences among the urban subcommunities. All urban areas have places where ethnic or religious groups cluster; where rich, middle-income, or poor people live. The metropolis is, as Louis Wirth said, "a mosaic of social worlds." While all residents are affected by certain patterns of industrialized urban living, those who live in the suburbs or in middle-class enclaves within the city limits and those who live in the slums represent grossly different life styles.

[4] The term *megalopolis* is used by Jean Gottmann to describe the urbanized northeastern seaboard of the United States, which he says "may be considered the cradle of a new order in the organization of inhabited space." Jean Gottmann, *Megalopolis*, The Twentieth Century Fund, 1961.

[5] Otis Dudley Duncan and Albert J. Reiss, Jr., *Social Characteristics of Urban and Rural Communities, 1950*, Wiley, 1956, chap. 11.

Urban Neighborhoods

Wendell Bell, studying economic, family, and ethnic characteristics by tract analysis in the San Francisco Bay area, gives numerical indices to 244 tracts. He believes that each of these tracts maintains fairly consistent social patterns for relatively long periods, has certain distinctive social problems, and that the neighborhood sets certain expectations for its inhabitants to which they tend to conform. He says that it is possible to hypothesize

> many relationships between neighborhood differences and the attitudes and behavior of individuals ranging from suicide, voting behavior, religious preferences, mental disorder, personal morale, and type of crimes to such things as frequency and nature of participation in formal organizations, amount of close contact with neighbors, local community identification, extent of kinship ties, child-rearing practices, and patterns of courtship.[6]

Greer and Kube suggest other revisions in the classic theory about what is typically urban. They find that kinship groups, friends, and neighbors are much more important in urban life than has been assumed. Using an urbanization index based on the proportion of women working in the labor force, the proportion of the population living in single-family dwelling units, and the fertility ratio, Greer and Kube investigated four residential sections in Los Angeles that were inhabited predominantly by Caucasian, white-collar workers in the middle-income range. The difference among them was the degree of urbanization, with the least urban being a tract which in cities less successful than Los Angeles in extending their city limits would be a suburban development. Although the "least urban" dwellers visited others more frequently than "most urban" dwellers, visiting was common among both groups. Once a month or more, two-thirds of the "most urban" dwellers visited relatives, over a fourth of them visited work associates, and three-fourths of them visited "other friends."[7] In the peninsula area of San Francisco, Hodges found almost half of the lower-lower class people had close relatives living within a four-block radius of their homes. Lower-lower class males "neighbor" more fre-

[6] Wendell Bell, "Social Areas: Typology of Urban Neighborhoods," in Marvin B. Sussman, ed., *Community Structure and Analysis*, Crowell, 1959, pp. 61–62.
[7] Scott Greer and Ella Kube, "Urbanism and Social Structure: A Los Angeles Study," in Sussman, *op. cit.*, pp. 93–112.

quently and intimately with brothers, brothers-in-law, or same-sex cousins than do males in any other class.[8]

Jane Jacobs, a staunch opponent of high-rise public housing that eliminates the sociability of crowded streets, relates an incident that occurred in her mixed tenement and small-business neighborhood in New York City. A man, she said, seemed to be molesting a child on the street. Within minutes, the locksmith, the fruit man, the laundry proprietor came out of their shops; other "eyes" watched from windows. "Nobody was going to allow a little girl to be dragged off . . ."[9]

Greer and Kube agree that the local community has not disappeared in the city. They found, however, that their "most urban" middle-class respondents were less frequently active in local groups, read local newspapers less often, and were less likely to be able to name local leaders than were their "least urban" respondents. Nevertheless, they concluded that anomie was much less common in urban life than had been assumed.[10]

Thus we find that researchers disagree with Wirth's conclusions that urban living provides few intimate contacts, rejects the extended family, or drives the "most urban" residents into voluntary associations. Probably urban living restricts only interaction with persons who live in a different "social world" from their own. One may, therefore, doubt that inhabitants of the many "social worlds" in urban areas, walled off by ethnic and socioeconomic differences, are particularly tolerant of people who are different from themselves.

Problems of Urban Areas

Notwithstanding such caveats, Wirth's analysis is useful in helping students understand the urban way of life. Many factors in American urban life do contribute to social disorganization. Bureaucracy and specialization in occupations, the inevitable concomitants of industrialization, encourage individuals to feel that they have little personal responsibility or influence. Impersonal, contractual relationships with others and high rates of residential mobility engender feelings of rootlessness. Although extremely interdependent, city dwellers are also extremely vulnerable to forces beyond their immediate control—smog, power blackouts, crime, and the like. Discriminatory practices cause

[8] Harold M. Hodges, Jr., "Peninsula People: Social Stratification in a Metropolitan Complex" in W. Warren Kallenbach and Harold M. Hodges, Jr., eds., *Education and Society,* Merrill, 1963, p. 394.

[9] Jane Jacobs, "Violence in the City Streets," *Harper's Magazine,* (September, 1961), p. 40.

[10] Greer and Kube, *op. cit.*

persons in minority groups to feel hostile toward society, and the poor, constantly exposed to an affluence they cannot share, feel isolated and abused.

Anomie in the sense of normlessness or a breakdown of cultural values may indeed be an important factor in alienation among urban residents. Clearly many people in urban societies share feelings of estrangement from others and from self, which we call alienation. Whether such feelings are more common in modern urban societies than in earlier rural societies cannot be substantiated, but the incidence of suicide, delinquency, crime, and drug addiction in industrialized, urban societies suggests that alienation is one of the chief problems of residents of urban centers.

Other urban problems of vital concern to the welfare of this country, which are related to alienation, are minority rights, poverty, and social disadvantages. The Black Revolution has generated interest in these problems, but, as Dr. Martin Luther King pointed out, more whites than blacks stand to benefit from the elimination of poverty and educational deprivation. The people of our sick cities, of course, face other problems, such as unemployment, welfare costs, increasing delinquency, sprawling slum housing, inadequate transportation, and overcrowded schools.

The problems of alienated youth, and of poor, socially disadvantaged Negro and white pupils are, however, of immediate concern to educators. On the one hand, many people have accused school personnel of being responsible, at least in part, for not having solved these problems. For instance, Kenneth Clark, a Negro psychologist, said:

> It is not necessary for even the most prejudiced personnel officer to discriminate against Negro youth, because the schools have done the job for them. The massively gross inefficiency of the public schools has so limited the occupational possibilities of the Negro youth that, if not mandatory, a life of menial status or employment is virtually inevitable.[11]

On the other hand, school leaders and others have recognized the school's limitations in solving such acute social problems. These people say that Negroes need help in many ways unrelated to education, that the poor who can work need jobs, that the aged and mothers with dependent children need a redistribution of income, and that families

[11] Kenneth Clark quoted in Nat Hentoff, "Making Public Schools Accountable: A Case Study of PS 201 in Harlem," *Phi Delta Kappan*, 48 (March, 1967), pp. 332–333.

need an economic "floor" beneath which they cannot drop. Education cannot provide such a floor but it can be insured by a reverse income tax, rent supplements, or a guaranteed minimum income.

Effects of Urban Living upon Children

Children, including those who are disadvantaged, who grow up in large cities or their suburbs are likely to be precocious. Perhaps, as Douvan and Adelson suggest, they are eager to become adults because a city "offers most of its advantages to adults."[12] Be that as it may, the early social maturity of children seems to be a by-product of urban living. Exposed to constant stimulation from competing attractions, they tend to become blasé and worldly-wise beyond their years. Less likely than children in sparsely populated places to be supervised by relatives and community elders who are not related to them, they develop independence and outward manifestations of self-assurance. The lessening of dependence upon adults strengthens the influence of peer groups.

The emergence of delinquent gangs as well as of a "teenage sub-culture," a "subculture of student activists," and a "hippie subculture" demonstrates the decline of mature adult influence upon adolescents and young adults. (A discussion of youth subcultures follows in Chapter 15.) Such developments also suggest that an urbanized, industrial community has effectively barred adolescents from meaningful participation in the work of adults. Subcultures of young people are rarely found in nonindustrialized, rural societies, where induction into adult roles follows quickly on the heels of childhood.

Another characteristic of urban living that affects children is occupational specialization. To become a specialist, one must acquire skills which, in this country, are usually acquired in school. Thus a child's failure in school becomes tantamount to his failure in life to a much greater degree than in the small, agricultural communities of yesterday. A big-city student is less likely than a small-city or town youth to have a part-time job while in school.[13] Cut off from the workaday world, an urban adolescent may feel that school is unrelated to life. For young people who have little motivation to achieve in school, their teachers' claim that education will have future advantages for them may not only fall on deaf ears but may also increase their alienation

[12] Elizabeth Douvan and Joseph Adelson, *The Adolescent Experience,* Wiley, 1966, p. 312.
[13] *Ibid.*

from school. A low level of motivation, found among some pupils in all social groups, is common—though not universal—among socially disadvantaged pupils.

Many of the socially disadvantaged, delinquent, and Negro pupils are also more likely than other young people in cities to be alienated from society as well as from school. The alienation syndrome seems to be related to low self-esteem, low social interests, and egocentrism.[14] An alienated person does not identify with a group to help him interpret the world, thus his self-image is low because he lacks group identification. As Cooley said, a person tends to see himself as he thinks others see him. If others reject him or treat him impersonally, he develops a low self-concept. The frequent moves made by poor families and the instabilities of poverty-stricken homes contribute to egocentrism in a child because the people he knows are constantly changing. He is therefore less willing to trust others. He feels rootless and unable to change his lot. Like a bicyclist who falls off if he does not move forward, the alienated child or adult, consciously or unconsciously, drops out of contact with others if he has not found such contacts rewarding.

Feelings of alienation are probably more common among Negroes than among whites for several reasons. They feel a social stigma associated with their race. Even some middle-class Negroes find it difficult to accept the fact that they are Negroes, a state of mind which is damaging to their social interests because acceptance of self and of one's heritage are essential components of acceptance of others. Some Negroes seem to lose their self-identity in their group identity as the title of James Baldwin's book, *Nobody Knows My Name* suggests. Many Negroes who have lost faith in others decide they have few if any opportunities for success. They feel isolated and insecure in an impersonal, contractual urban environment. A number of experts in social psychology point out, however, that feelings of alienation among Negroes have declined in recent years because of their active involvement in sit-ins, picketing, and other civil rights activities, including rioting.

SPECIAL PROBLEMS OF SCHOOLS
IN CENTRAL CITIES

Much of the discussion that follows pertains to education of the socially disadvantaged pupils. The problems of schools in central cities

[14] Ziller, Robert C., "The Alienation Syndrome: A Triadic Pattern of Self-Other Orientation," a paper read at the American Educational Research Association Convention, Chicago, 1968.

are, of course, by no means restricted to educating poor whites and unassimilated Negroes in the inner city, but ghetto school problems are the most urgent at this time. In some large cities (with populations of 250,000 or more), the schools serving such groups account, in fact, for no more than 10 to 20 percent of the schools; in other cities, the percentage is much higher. As an overall average in large cities, the proportion of schools engaged in teaching disadvantaged pupils is about one-third of the total.

Schools Serving the Urban Poor

Amid the plenty in America lies an "economic underworld," in which millions of families (about one in five of all Americans) are too poor to maintain anything near a decent standard of living. Harrington calls the culture of these poverty-stricken people "The Other America." Some of them live in rural areas, others in the inner city. The urban poor are unseen, he says, because the freeways bypass their filthy, crowded homes and because their clothes are not so shabby that they are immediately observable. (One can dress reasonably well for little money, he points out.)[15] The urban poor are the unskilled, the alcoholic, the rural Negroes and "poor whites" dispossessed on farms, industry's rejects, the aged, the sick, and the unemployable. One-third of them are children. Unlike immigrant slum-dwellers who shared the American dream, hoped to rise, and often did, the present residents of slums have little or no hope. They are poor because they were born poor, and they will probably remain poor because they started poor. To call children born in these families the "socially disadvantaged" is to understate the case.

In 1961 Conant reported an average of 40 professionals per 1000 pupils in city schools for the underprivileged compared to 70 professionals per 1000 pupils in wealthy suburban schools.[16] These 40 professionals worked with pupils who placed well below national norms in tests of mental ability, reading skills, and academic achievement. Their schools were desperately over-crowded. During the 1950s and 1960s school enrollments had grown because thousands of rural Negroes and whites with large families had moved to cities, large Catholic and immigrant families clustered there, and more children were going to school and staying in school longer than ever before. Meanwhile school construction, delayed through the war years, was not able

[15] Michael Harrington, *The Other America, Poverty in the United States,* Macmillan, 1962, pp. 5–6, 10.

[16] James Bryant Conant, *Slums and Suburbs: A Commentary on Schools in Metropolitan Areas,* McGraw-Hill, 1961, p. 67.

to meet the need for new buildings. Urban schools were overcrowded, classes were too large to teach, special services were too few.

During this period a few experimental programs, such as New York City's "Higher Horizons," the Benneker program in St. Louis, and the Ford Foundation's Grey Areas Projects in several cities, tackled some of the problems of the disadvantaged. The big push to alleviate conditions in city schools, especially for those serving disadvantaged persons, came, however, in the 1960s from the federal government. The Manpower Development and Training Act and the Vocational Education Act of 1963, the Economic Opportunity Act of 1964, and the Elementary and Secondary Education Act of 1965 helped to provide sorely needed money for city schools and for improving to some extent the quality of city life.

The Office of Economic Opportunity (OEO) has approached the problem of educating the disadvantaged from the vantage point of the family and the community. It has sponsored health and birth-control clinics, counseling for poor families, Head Start preschools, remedial reading programs and training for school dropouts in Job Corps, Neighborhood Youth Corps, and other programs, projects for migrants, Upward Bound for would-be college students, VISTA Volunteers (Volunteers in Service to America) who aid people in poverty-stricken communities in appropriate ways, and work experience for fathers on relief rolls. OEO tried without much success to tap the local poor for leaders to help plan and direct its War on Poverty.

Critics say that many of these programs are too expensive. In the long run perhaps they will prove to be, as *Time* phrases it, "more boon than doggle." Unless conditions in homes of the poor can be upgraded, the school's success in educating the children of the poor may always be limited.

Meanwhile encouraged by federal funds, large city school systems, after extensive study of conditions in the ghettos, instituted special programs for disadvantaged pupils, sometimes called Model School Programs. Such programs usually provided for remedial and guidance specialists, additional staff to insure small classes, audiovisual and library equipment, opportunities for pupils to work-study, in-service training of teachers, and personnel for involving parents in the work of the school and for working more closely with other community agencies. Field trips and curriculum revision were encouraged. Such programs report some but not enough progress.

Critics charge that changes that have taken place in schools have not been sufficiently radical. They deplore the middle-class stance of teachers and the school's attitude that some of these children are uneducable. Accounts published in such books as *Pickets at the Gates,*

Walk the White Line, and *Death at an Early Age*[17] suggest that the attitudes of many teachers toward their charges is such that special programs though helpful will never solve the problems of socially disadvantaged children.

The attitude of a teacher is a highly influential factor in determining what a child will learn. That some teachers fail to give every pupil the respect due him as a human being (student respect is an essential ingredient in effective teaching) is demonstrated in the excerpts below:

> Now, how would you like a Negro teacher to tell you . . . "You Negroes," . . . really, she calls us niggers . . . "You niggers, you don't have no right on the street . . . those white people owned you and you let yourself be enslaved and that's what you deserved."[18]

> And if, if you made a little mistake she's quick to call you stupid and especially me.[19]

> I left school last week because . . . they make me doubt myself, you know, they show me so much to doubt . . . They tell me, my dean told me, he said: "You can't even read . . . you're not going to get a diploma so I don't know why you even come to school anyway."[20]

> A cry goes up as the teacher pulls Allen by the ear over to the wastepaper basket where he must spit out his gum. She shouts at several other children, "You want me to get John? Let me see you act up once more and you'll be in trouble." She hustles another boy off to the corner to stand with his hands on his head.[21]

> I asked, soon after I had started teaching and observing the acts of other teachers, whether it was within the rules to strike a child or whether that was against the law.
> "Don't worry about the law. You just make damn sure that no one's watching."
> From a teacher at my school: "The ones I can't stand are the goddamn *little* buggers. The First Graders. And the Second Graders. There's nothing you can do to them—you can't even lift up your goddamn hand."[22]

[17] Estelle Fuchs, *Pickets at the Gates,* Free Press, 1966, chap. 7; Elizabeth M. Eddy, *Walk the White Line: A Profile of Urban Education,* Doubleday, 1967; and Jonathan Kozol, *Death at an Early Age,* Houghton Mifflin, 1967.

[18] Fuchs, *op. cit.,* p. 144.

[19] *Ibid.,* p. 145.

[20] *Ibid.,* p. 149.

[21] G. Alexander Moore, Jr., *Realities of the Urban Classroom,* Doubleday, 1964, p. 63.

[22] Kozol, *op. cit.,* p. 16.

In several large city schools the practice of homogeneous grouping by ability levels begins as early as the primary grades. In ghettos the lowest-ability group is then often assigned to an inexperienced teacher, who sometimes is a substitute teacher with no formal teacher training. Several researchers have found that teachers in schools in slums have had fewer years of teaching experience than have those in schools serving more privileged children. Such a difference does not, however, necessarily mean that teachers in ghettos are less able than other teachers. A more pertinent argument is that they need to be more highly competent than other teachers because the difficulties of teaching disadvantaged children are greater than those of teaching more privileged pupils.

Whatever their training and abilities, new teachers in schools for the urban poor find their work difficult for several reasons. Many of the children are emotionally disturbed, below average in academic skills, and hostile toward the teacher and the school. Physical facilities may be crowded and suitable library and audiovisual equipment scarce. Often the teacher's skills are inadequate to enable him to work successfully with slow and recalcitrant learners. His work exhausts him. Much of his trouble stems, however, from failure to understand and accept the children, some of it from the manner in which he perceives his duties and roles. Initially he may suffer from "culture shock," later he may become callous and feel that he can do little or nothing to change what seems to him to be a hopeless situation.

Anyone living within a culture alien to his own is likely to experience "culture shock." He is bewildered and sometimes repulsed by the strange behavior of people he cannot understand. Sometimes he simply withdraws and reacts apathetically, at other times he becomes unsympathetic and punitive. In a sense, the new teacher in a ghetto school experiences something akin to "culture shock."[23] He is unaccustomed to obscenity on the lips of little children, repelled by stories of their home life, appalled by their short-comings, and frustrated by his own inability to keep order among children unsocialized in the ways of the school. He may begin to see his pupils as undisciplined, unfeeling, unteachable, and even immoral. He may begin to think of his job as custodial and of his pupils as people who understand nothing but force. He may not understand the adage, "Rob a man of respect and he will have no self-respect."

Of course, many changes in administrative procedures and teaching techniques, among the most important of which is involvement of parents, may improve the learning climate of the inner city school. But

[23] Moore, *op. cit.*, pp. 3–5.

none is more important than a change in attitude of the ineffective classroom teacher. Unless he treats his pupil as a person of dignity worthy of respect, he is likely to fail as a teacher. If pupils do not see him as a person who likes them, they team up against him. To treat his pupils with respect, a teacher has to understand why they behave as they do. To understand their behavior, he must know their parents and their social environment.

In ghetto schools both pupils and parents are likely to see the teacher as an enemy. To win their support, he has to show that he does not condemn their values or criticize their adaptations to their environment and that he is able and willing to help children prepare for successful living. The teacher has to be aware that all the nuances of lower-middle class subculture are not necessarily components of a good life for his pupils. He has to inculcate "survival skills," described in Chapter 12, that will enable those pupils who wish to "defect" to the working or middle class to do so. At the same time, he has to provide a climate of acceptance of all his charges irrespective of their capacity to acquire anything more than minimal "survival skills." If a teacher would combat rather than contribute to feelings of alienation, he has to convey to each child his concern for him as a person while holding reasonable expectations in respect to his academic performance. Expecting too little may be an insult and expecting too much may be frustrating to a child.

Problems of Segregated Schools

In many big cities there are schools composed largely of pupils from Negro, Puerto Rican, lower-class, or Jewish families, or from families of some other ethnic, national, or religious origin. Occasionally school-district lines are gerrymandered to isolate children of some of these groups. Usually the segregation of a group results from the location of their homes in the same neighborhood. Large cities are not the only places where pupils are separated by social class in elementary schools, for neighborhood schools are common also to smaller cities, but the extremes of social-class, ethnic, and cultural differences are more likely to be found in separate schools in the metropolitan centers.

Between 1963 and 1966 the de facto segregation of Negroes in neighborhood schools was protested vigorously by civil rights groups. Outside of the South, under pressure from such organizations, various attempts were made to integrate schools. Such efforts included open enrollment and transfer policies, enabling pupils to attend the school of their choice; the Princeton plan, by which adjacent white and Negro districts are combined, in the sense that all pupils from both districts attend one district's school for the first three or four years and the other district's school for the next three or four years; transporting pupils by bus to schools not filled to capacity or transporting some white children to previously all-Negro schools and some Negro pupils to previously all-white schools; and the educational park or plaza plan that eliminates neighborhood schools and creates a central school that accommodates children from all districts within a specified radius.

The first three plans have not been notably successful, especially in cities where the Negro population is so large that keeping a "racial balance" in schools is impossible. The educational park plan is being instituted in a number of cities, but it will not be completely implemented for several years. Potentially it shows promise of reducing segregation not only by race but also by social class.

Although a Supreme Court decision of 1954 ruled that separate public schools designed especially for Negroes were illegal, desegregation of southern schools was very slow as southern whites sought ways to circumvent the Court's decision. By 1965 about 7 percent of the Negro children in the South were attending white schools; about the same percentage of Negro pupils attend white schools in cities outside the South. By 1965 southern faculties and county-wide in-service training programs were also being integrated in some areas.

Problems of Finance

In addition to problems of integration, many large city schools have desperate financial problems. School buildings tend to be old and in need of replacement. Equipment in vocational schools is often outmoded. The schools have been expanded by various makeshifts to house far more pupils than they were designed to accommodate. Urban education is mass education. There is not enough money or classroom space for small classes, adequate remedial instruction, or individual guidance.

Money problems have been accentuated by shifts in residential and industrial locations from city to suburb of many wealthy taxpayers. While robbing the city of persons who paid high taxes, the suburbs have strained the city's financial resources by requiring improvements of transportation facilities, highways, and parking areas. (Streets, freeways, parking facilities, and garages take up two-thirds of the space in central Los Angeles.)[24] Welfare and law enforcement costs have mounted with increased social disorganization in the center of cities. Schools have not always fared well in competing for the taxpayer's

[24] Lewis Mumford, The City in History, Harcourt, Brace, 1961, p. 510.

dollar. The friends of the schools are fewer proportionately and less influential in city politics than in less densely populated places.

The billions of federal dollars poured into schools since the mid-sixties have not materially changed the financial situation of city schools. Most federal money has gone into "lighthouse" programs for experimentation designed to show what can be done if local schools had the money to support such programs. In university circles, federal funds are referred to as "soft money," a term that means that they cannot be depended upon on a continuing basis. Neither a university or a school system can plan to meet its recurrent needs with "soft money."

THE SUBURBAN COMMUNITY AND ITS SCHOOLS

The so-called "flight to the suburbs," though dating back to the colonial era, accelerated after World War II to such an extent that now almost a third of all Americans live in areas adjacent to cities. Between 1950 and 1960 the population in central cities increased an average of 10.6 percent and the metropolitan population outside central cities increased 49 percent. This sensational expansion caught the attention of popular writers, journalists, comedians, and sociologists. A plethora of magazine articles in popular and quality periodicals heralded suburbia as a way of life. And some sociologists have called this mass movement a "major social development of the twentieth century."

"Suburbia," as popularly depicted, is upper-middle class living—ranch homes, barbecue pits, swimming pools, martinis, gardens, frequent informal visiting, multiple memberships in organizations, flourishing PTA's, college preparatory schools, car pools, many children, active church interests, kaffeeklatsches (coffee gatherings) at which knowledge of child psychology is aired, Republican political affiliations, status-striving, transiency, conformity, and homogeneity. Both parents are college-bred; the fathers are commuting "organization men." The stereotyped picture, more or less true, of certain suburban residential developments is far from an accurate description of other subcultures found in suburban areas.

Differing life styles are found in the two general areas that surround the central city. The inner ring directly outside the city limits of the central city—the suburban zone—is urban in character and an integral part of the metropolitan structure. In this inner ring are two types: the "employing suburb," usually an industrial center and sometimes a center of higher education, mining, or fishing, and the "residential suburb," inhabited primarily by people who work in the city. The employing suburb, called a satellite city by many writers, differs from the residential suburb in that it is usually larger, older, farther from the central city, and growing less rapidly. Its residents are characteristically working-class people. They are less well educated, younger, more likely to rent homes, and more apt to be foreign-born whites than are the residential suburb's inhabitants. The two basic types may be further divided into mixed types—working-class residential tracts, upper-class suburbs of satellite cities, suburbs with a wide spread in the social class of residents, and other variations. The second general area of the suburbs is the rural-urban fringe; it forms an outer ring beyond the suburban zone. In this area urban and rural forces collide, suburban industrial and residential developments thin out and intermingle with rural villages and agricultural interests. Rural-urban fringe areas, particularly near small cities, are in no sense homogeneous in social class, income level, or individual aspirations.

Social scientists do not find that middle-class or working-class people necessarily behave differently simply because they live in the suburbs. In fact, few differences among people can be attributed directly to suburban living. It may be useful, however, to clarify how suburban communities differ from one another. A description of three of the several styles of suburban living will help us see these differences: suburbia as it exists in a middle-class residential suburb, a working-class residential tract, and in the rural-urban fringe.

Middle-Class Suburbia

Mowrer and Mowrer studied families in 19 communities near Chicago. The new homes in these suburban developments varied in value from about $15,000 to $65,000. The families were more likely than other families throughout the United States to have at least one child, but the number of children in the communities in proportion to population was only slightly higher than that in the United States as a whole. Eighty percent of the people had moved out from the city or from another suburb, and 20 percent had moved in from outside the metropolitan area. Most of the husbands were businessmen, that is, managers and executives, 18 percent were professional men, and 9 percent were craftsmen in the upper wage brackets. They averaged 15 years of schooling and their wives averaged 14 years. Their socioeconomic characteristics are those usually attributed to residents of suburbia.

The Mowrers found the following characteristics that distinguished these families.

Husband and wife are markedly equalitarian in their relationships, but the fiction of male authority is maintained. In practice the wife may assume the husband's role as handyman, gardener, and chauffeur; the husband may help with household jobs.

The family is child-centered "to a greater degree than elsewhere in contemporary America." The most common reason given for moving to the suburbs is that it is a good place to rear children.

Family activity is home-centered. Parents rarely go out together more often than one night a week. Only 9 percent of the wives have jobs outside the home and 60 percent of these have only part-time jobs, whereas in March, 1960, married women constituted 31.7 percent of the national labor force.

Commuting fathers and their families participate less in the residential community's organizations than do noncommuters and their families. The commuters cling to many of their associations in the central city.

Suburban families talk about one another in an impersonal way, but they do not pry into pasts. They are, in fact, much friendlier during the pioneering stage than later.

The Mowrers conclude that the initial stage of settlement is a "temporary mask to the basic urban pattern." Eventually secondary relationships more typical of city apartment-house dwellers than of rural inhabitants largely replace the initial intimacy.[25] Other studies corroborate the Mowrer's major findings that suburbia, even when used as a term including all suburban communities, is basically urban in character. A study of cosmopolitan tendencies among old-timer and newcomer residents in Huntington Village, Long Island, suggests that the suburbanites are more cosmopolitan in outlook than the original settlers. They are more likely to identify with and relate themselves to issues, events, and organizations outside the local community.[26]

Another study found a difference between residents of suburbs and those of the city in the suburban emphasis upon familism. The researcher postulated three life styles or combinations thereof: *familism,* meaning to place highest values on family life and children; *upward vertical mobility* (or career), meaning to devote time, energy, and money to a career; and *consumership,* meaning to find satisfaction in consuming goods and services. Investigations in two Chicago suburbs

[25] Ernest R. Mowrer and Harriet R. Mowrer, "The Family in Suburbia," in William M. Dobriner, ed., *The Suburban Community,* Putnam, 1958, pp. 155–156, 158.

[26] William M. Dobriner, "Local and Cosmopolitan as Contemporary Suburban Character Types," in Dobriner, *op. cit.,* pp. 132–142.

revealed that 81 percent of the residents mentioned their children as a reason for moving to the suburbs, and that 31 percent gave no other reason. Only 9 percent expressed a reason for moving there that could be equated with social striving, and only 10 percent gave consumership as the sole reason. When more than one reason was given, consumership was mentioned by 43 percent, and another theme, "quest for community"—the desire to belong and neighborliness, was mentioned by 73 percent. The researcher then compared two matched suburban and urban communities with respect to life style. The results showed that familism was the first choice of more suburban than urban residents.[27]

It is fairly conclusive that suburbanites are cosmopolitan in outlook, and that they are prone to give higher priority to family relationships than do city dwellers. They also have a slight edge in income and educational level over persons who live in cities. They are predominantly white and middle-class. Some suburban residents are ardent advocates of grass-roots democracy and are active participants in civic and community organizations. They may see such activity as a creative use of leisure and as a status-conferring activity. The apparent middle-class, white homogeneity is, however, dispelled by social cleavages, often created by organizational memberships.

Many residents of suburban developments rarely conform to the popular "suburbia" stereotype mentioned earlier; nor do they fit the mold depicted here. The working-class suburb as described by Berger in the section that follows differs in life style from middle-class suburbia.

The Working-Class Suburb

When the Ford Motor Company moved its assembly plant from Richmond, California, to a site a few miles north of San Jose, California, many workers moved from industrialized Richmond to a San Jose suburb of mass-produced, inexpensive tract homes. Others who lived there were very small businessmen and a few white-collar persons, such as postmen, bank tellers, and supermarket checkers. Berger studied 100 of the 120 Ford families to determine how their way of life and values were influenced by this move. Eighty-five workers were semiskilled and skilled workers, 12 were foremen, and 3 had other jobs. Fifty-four percent of these men had been born on farms and 11 percent in small towns. The men had little formal schooling: 39 percent had left school by the end of the eighth grade, 35

[27] Wendell Bell, "Social Choice, Life Styles, and Suburban Residence," in Dobriner, *op. cit.*, pp. 225–243.

percent had dropped out before reaching the twelfth grade, 20 percent had finished high school, and only 6 percent had had a year or so in college. (Their wives were usually better educated, 40 percent of them having finished high school or better.) The fathers of these men had been either farmers or unskilled or semiskilled laborers. On the bases of their own educational level, of their fathers' occupations (assuming that most of these farmers were not farm owners), and of their own jobs, these men could be categorized as members of the lower class. Would they and their families change their working-class characteristics and values when they moved to more attractive homes in a suburban development?

The pattern of family life seemed to change very little following this change of residence except that all were proud of their new homes. Their home furnishings were of the overstuffed, inexpensive, bargain variety. They entertained very little, and when they invited others for meals the guests were usually relatives. They drank beer occasionally or perhaps whisky in moderation. There was little change in their political activities. They remained Democrats and were not very active in politics. The workers and their families had little interest in community organizations: 70 percent belonged to no clubs or associations. As many belonged to organizations in the city before their move as now belonged to similar groups in the suburbs. Only 20 percent of the mothers and 9 percent of the fathers belonged to the PTA. The wives did belong to more organizations than they had in the city, but 64 percent of them still belonged to no organizations. These figures do not reveal either church or union membership, but 56 percent of the families rarely or never attended church, and the local union had not had a meeting for a year because it could never get a quorum. The family's principal form of entertainment was television, and their favorite programs were westerns and sports events. They tuned out the favorite middle-class musical, variety, and domestic-comedy shows. The only semblance to what is usually portrayed as middle-class suburbia was the wives' participation in neighborhood "coffees."

These people were not social strivers. They seemed to think that they had climbed about as far vocationally and materially as they could expect to go. Many of them classified themselves as middle class because they called persons who are not quite respectable "lower class," but the investigator found only 5 percent who saw themselves as middle class for the reason that they now lived in more pretentious surroundings. Some of those claiming middle-class status based their reasoning on the fact that their income was in the middle of the working-class range.

Although these workers and their families would be classified as upper-lower by Warner's scale, they were respectable, hard-working people with a decent standard of living. Most of them expected to live permanently in their present homes, which they owned. What hopes they held for the future were likely to be centered in their children, but they were not excessively concerned about the young ones. Forty-three percent of the mothers admitted they had read nothing on child-rearing. Of those who said they had read something, almost half could not remember what they had read nor who had written the book. Even if they discussed what they read with neighbors, they were likely to conclude, "I don't go by the book; I go by the way my parents raised me." A father would say that he wanted his son to go to college "if he wants it" or "if I can afford it," but he did not seem to be making plans nor saving money for a college education. He was also vague about occupational goals for his offspring. Almost a third said it's "up to him," and 11 said "don't know."[28]

The Rural-Urban Fringe Community

Census data are not readily available for comparing the rural-urban fringe inhabitants to those in other areas. It is assumed that about 10 percent of all Americans live in the rural-urban fringe, and "in some respects, the fringe experiences a type of residential selection distinct from that of the suburbs, though in many characteristics the two resemble each other in their differences from the central city." In a study of the Chicago rural-urban fringe, Duncan and Reiss found the rural nonfarm population to be primarily urban-oriented. As in the suburbs, most people who lived in the fringe were married, except for unmarried males among the farmers. The socioeconomic level of fringe residents was lower, in general, than the level of suburban or city dwellers. Many craftsmen, operatives, foremen, and laborers lived in this zone.[29]

The fringe, an area of rapid population growth, is probably the most dynamic of all living areas. Unhampered by zoning restrictions, it is often the site of jerry-built homes. It may also include a cluster of expensive homes. It attracts settlers from both the city and rural areas. New industries often choose the outer ring as plant sites. Poultry, dairy, and crop farmers are being eased out, but horticulturists and truck farmers remain.

The adjustment of migrants both from the city and from the country to their new surroundings, to each other, and to old-timers usually

[28] Bennett M. Berger, *Working-Class Suburb*, University of California Press, 1960, pp. 1–123 *passim*.
[29] Duncan and Reiss, *op. cit.*, p. 149.

produces frustrations and tensions. Difficulties increase with the rate of mobility, which is thought to be very high in fringe areas. Few organizations flourish in the fringe areas. Whereas urban children have many organizations such as the Scouts and rural children have organizations such as 4-H Clubs, the rural-fringe has few of these. Adults who participate in organizations are likely to be more active in those located in the city than in the few that exist in the fringe. Nor are the muddled lines of local governmental authority in the fringe conducive to feelings of community loyalty.

What can be said about the rural-urban fringe is more conjectural than factual. The census term *urban fringe*, which includes well-established suburbs, is not analogous to the sociological term, *rural-urban fringe*. Not many sociologists have studied this area. From what is known, we assume that the life style of the fringe differs from that of suburbia, the city, and the rural area. Cleavages are rife, community conflict over all community undertakings including schools is likely, and the feeling of community is low.

Developments beginning in the mid 1960s suggest that the balance between well-to-do and poor in the suburbs is becoming more like that of cities and that by the late 1970s the discrepancies in average income level of the two areas may disappear.[30] Evidence of this trend is found in the spread of inexpensive housing projects and trailer camps in the suburbs and the number of nonwhites who are settling in slumlike suburban communities. The suburbs are also becoming similar to the city in another respect. An increasing number of Roman Catholic schools have been established in the suburbs as more and more Catholics have moved there.

Special Problems of Suburban Schools

The problems of schools in the rural-urban fringe, the industrial suburb, and the residential suburb are quite different. Community conflict over schools between oldtimers and newcomers in the rural-urban fringe and in suburbia are more common than in an industrial suburb. The industrial suburb has fewer school money problems than either the low-cost residential suburb or the rural-urban fringe school. Problems of curriculum differ in these schools. Teachers in rural-urban fringe schools like those in inner city schools are less likely to live in the community in which they teach than are teachers in residential and industrial suburbs. In general, commuting teachers are less well ac-

[30] Robert J. Havighurst, *Education in Metropolitan Areas*, Allyn and Bacon, 1966, pp. 69–71.

quainted with the school's community, and therefore in some respects less effective in their work. Such differences between different kinds of suburbs preclude generalizations about all suburban schools. The special problems discussed below are admittedly those of the residential suburbs.

The surburban curriculum is likely to reflect the interests of many, but not all, students. Its middle-class orientation assures that college-preparatory courses will be given a high priority. Despite their academic orientation, suburban schools are likely to include an extensive cocurricular program and to utilize methods of teaching that stress group work, pupil initiative, and problem approaches. The pupils want good grades in order to get into the "right" colleges, thus their interest in grades does not necessarily reflect deep-seated academic interests. They want to develop "good personalities" too. As a consequence of their parents' interest in the schools and their own eagerness to develop socially, pupils in middle-class suburban schools tend to be school-oriented. It is interesting that these pupils, who because of home training have the least need for learning social skills, attend schools where they have the most opportunities to gain such experiences.

In describing the Park Forest, Illinois, school, William H. Whyte charges that the philosophy of the school, which stresses "the pragmatic," "the social," and the "concept of adjustment," is a "fair reflection of the community." It is the proper education for "organization children," he says. By implication, he deplores the emphasis on social activities.[31] James Coleman also believes that the middle-class homogeneity of a community encourages the stress on social skills. "It is as if the parents, whose children must compete with many others of the same educational and intellectual background, want to make certain that their child can compete socially, on equal terms, without material disadvantages, and without shyness or clumsiness of gesture and speech." The early social maturity of children in suburban and other urban upper-middle class schools leads to a weakening of controls by parents and teachers, Coleman says. Adolescents resist prescribed "scholastic exercises" and the role of "passive learners." "If intellectual activities remain passive exercises, while the excitement of *doing, exploring, creating,* and *meeting a challenge* is left to the athletic field, the yearbook office, and the back seat of a car, then interest in academic directions will certainly decline," he states.[32]

[31] William H. Whyte, Jr., *The Organization Man,* Simon and Schuster, 1956, pp. 382–391.
[32] James S. Coleman, *The Adolescent Society,* Free Press, 1961, pp. 290–293.

Middle-class dominance in setting the curriculum of many suburban high schools may result in a failure to provide adequately for those children who will not go to college. The new schoolhouses built by suburbanites may have few or no facilities for vocational courses. In Nassau County, New York, only 777 high school pupils out of 25,052 were enrolled in vocational courses, but over 5,000 said they wanted to take vocational work. In this area over 40 percent of the pupils do not go to college.[33]

Parent-teacher relations in middle-class suburbia may cause teachers to react ambivalently to ambitious parents. These parents reinforce the school's work. They give their children educational advantages, try to motivate their academic interests, and provide good conditions for home study. They usually encourage experimentation and up-to-date teaching methods. Part of the stereotype of suburbia is that parents are staunch supporters of the PTA. Nevertheless, suburban middle-class parents are harsh critics of schools and teachers when the latter fail to measure up to their expectations. Unlike rural parents and urban working-class parents, they grant teachers no institutionalized respect, for they are often as well or better educated than the teachers. Their excessive concern for their child's welfare may be a help or a hindrance to the school. Conant says that the chief problem in the wealthy suburban school where 80 percent or more of the pupils go on to college is the pressure put on pupils and teachers by parents who are excessively ambitious to have their children enter top-flight colleges and universities. He thinks that the guidance staff should pull no punches with parents who set goals beyond the intellectual capacities of their offspring.[34]

The increasing rate of delinquency in suburbia is also a matter of concern. Although many of the forms that delinquency takes in slum neighborhoods are uncommon in suburban communities, some suburban students do commit crimes of vandalism, theft, and truancy. Wise found that two-thirds of the middle-class boys in a Connecticut suburban community admitted having been truant, half of them confessed to minor forms of vandalism, and about 60 percent said they had been guilty of petty theft and of "breaking and entering" homes and buildings.[35] Most middle-class delinquency occurs outside the realm

[33] Benjamin Fine, "Educational Problems in the Suburbs," in Dobriner, *op. cit.*, p. 324.

[34] Conant, *op. cit.*, p. 144.

[35] Nancy Barton Wise, "Juvenile Delinquency Among Middle-Class Girls," in Edmund W. Voz, ed., *Middle-Class Juvenile Delinquency,* Harper & Row, 1967, pp. 182–187.

of the school, however, and is quietly hushed up by protective parents. Until recently traffic offenses, automobile thefts, drinking parties, and sexual misconduct were the most common forms of such delinquency. In the last few years, the use of narcotics seems to have spread to some extent in suburban and urban middle-class high schools. The roots of alienation found among hippies also usually lie in such communities and schools.

Suburban schools have financial problems. The newcomers to suburbs are generally willing to support schools and to pay teachers well because they want superior instruction for their children. The difficulty is that only suburban developments with high assessed valuations on residential or industrial property can meet the demands for public services of all kinds without heavy tax levies. The tax rate in Levittown, for example, was 8⅓ times higher in the 1957–1958 school year than in the 1947–1948 school year. Other tracts with mass-produced housing of lower value than Levittown's residences and with no industry to tax may face what seem to be unsurmountable financial problems. Lack of adequate space has forced suburban communities more often than other communities to resort to double shifts. The financial difficulties are worsened by conflicts in old communities overrun by suburbanites. In Old Harbor, as described in an interesting case study by Dobriner, oldtimers resisted increased school expenditures that were demanded by newcomers.[36]

Significance of the School's
Community Location to the Teacher

Perhaps for somewhat the same reasons that others move to the suburbs, teachers may seek positions in suburban schools in preference to teaching and living in rural or city schools. Often they do not analyze the assets or the liabilities involved in teaching in these new communities.

A teacher who lacks enthusiasm for PTA activities, pampered and protected children, and anxious parents may want to avoid suburbia, unless his pleasure in teaching academically oriented pupils offsets the other factors. A teacher who enjoys the slower pace of rural living and the comparative warmth and docility of children in rural schools may feel compensated for whatever disadvantages he meets. Another teacher may like the impersonality of the city, the variety of resources available for enriching his teaching, and the sophistication of city children. Although few teachers prefer the slum schools as assign-

[36] William M. Dobriner, *Class in Suburbia*, Prentice-Hall, 1963, chap. 5.

ments, Becker's study of teachers in these schools in Chicago revealed that some teachers learn to like their jobs there. They learn new teaching and disciplinary techniques, adjust their expectations to what they can accomplish, come to understand the children, and gain a reputation that enables them to operate successfully.[37] Teachers in the slum schools in which experimental programs are now underway are undoubtedly challenged by the opportunity for substantial acomplishments in these schools. The wise teacher analyzes all of the factors that make schools different, as well as his own talents and preferences in deciding where he will apply for a position.

IMPORTANT CONCEPTS

Anomie. A French word meaning normlessness, demoralization, a sense of social and personal disorganization. See p. 230.

"Culture shock." The impact of an alien way of life which often results in temporary or permanent frustration. See p. 240.

De facto segregation. Separation of groups (usually Negroes from whites) in fact, with or without legal sanction. See p. 241.

Egocentrism. The tendency to regard oneself as the center of the universe and to ignore the rights and needs of others. See p. 236.

"Megalopolis." An urban complex encompassing several major cities.

Rural-urban fringe. An area of interaction of rural and urban elements.

Satellite city. A separate political entity which is a subordinate center in a metropolitan area or within the zone of influence of a large city.

Suburbia. A popular term connoting a life style with definite characteristics, i.e., upper-middle-class residential suburban living.

Standard metropolitan statistical area. See pp. 227–228.

[37] Howard S. Becker, "The Career of the Chicago Schoolteacher," *American Journal of Sociology,* 57 (March, 1952), 470–477.

12. PUPILS OF MINORITY GROUPS IN PUBLIC SCHOOLS

Do not unto others as you would others do unto you. Their tastes may not be the same.

—GEORGE BERNARD SHAW[1]

A new interest in educating children of minority groups has been kindled during the last 30 years or so. In earlier years educators saw their job as that of Americanizing children of foreign parentage. In short, pupils were encouraged to forget their alien origins and to behave like Americans. Now that immigration is restricted and most pupils of minority groups are native born, educators see the job of educating these pupils differently. Their current goals are twofold: (1) the *integration* of children of minority groups into the school culture, and (2) the *acceptance of cultural differences* in others by pupils and teachers.[2]

In many cases, these goals have not been successfully achieved. Prejudice against certain minority groups has curtailed integration and misunderstanding of differences has limited acceptance. The prejudices (prejudgments) held for years by many Americans are often reflected in the culture of the school. On the one hand, teachers and pupils of the dominant group, consciously or unconsciously, tend to limit the opportunities for children who are different to participate fully, especially in the school's social activities. On the other, pupils whose orientation to life is different are at a disadvantage in that they may lack the skills and attitudes for successful integration. Moreover, teachers as well as pupils may fail to accept cultural differences because they do not know what these differences are. The victims' possible reactions to prejudicial treatment are also imperfectly understood by pupils and teachers.

The first section of this chapter deals with differences in social status and value orientations of various minority groups. In the second section the Mexican American subculture is described in some detail as an example of the kind of knowledge that teachers need to acquire if they would understand children who cherish a subcultural heritage. The third section is devoted to a discussion of common reactions among children to their minority group status.

[1] George Bernard Shaw, "Maxims for Revolutionists," in *Man and Superman,* Penguin Books, p. 257.

[2] These goals are somewhat contradictory in that integration tends to encourage pupils to be alike rather than to be different or to accept differences in others.

MINORITY STATUS AS A FACTOR
IN SOCIAL RELATIONS

A minority group is a subdivision of a society sharing certain characteristics, such as race, nationality, religion or other cultural affiliations, that mark it as different from the dominant group. In the United States the dominant social group, an estimated one-third of the population, has been called the WASPs (white, Anglo-Saxon, Protestants). The core of the group are of "old-American" stock. Presumably the values, standards of behavior, and life style of these "old Americans" set the dominant cultural patterns in this country.

"Old Americans" speak without a foreign accent; repress emotions in public; refrain from excessive gesturing; extol the virtues of free enterprise, individualism, and freedom; and claim to be Protestant even when they are not active Protestant church members. In some regions their social status is unchallenged; in others their road to social acceptance is paved. Their preeminence in most communities obscures the fact that many persons of "old-American" origin are of lower- and working-class status. Nevertheless many "old Americans" are pacesetters in their communities and arbiters of the social status accorded outsiders.

The status of persons who are unlike the WASPs in any one of three characteristics—religion, national origin, and race—is low in the eyes of prejudiced people. Even when no economic or political discrimination is involved, questions of social equality and particularly of intermarriage demonstrate how people feel about those who are different. Many members of minority groups are equally reluctant to marry persons in the dominant group. Since Americans agree upon freedom of choice in the selection of a mate, miscegenation is a matter of personal choice except in states where there are strong sanctions against it, but the lack of substantive equality under the law, in housing, in job opportunities, in politics, and in education is a matter of national concern.

Religion and Status

In 1966, 55.6 percent of church members in the United States were Protestants, 37.2 percent were Roman Catholics, 4.5 percent Jewish, and 3.2 percent Eastern Orthodox.[3] Membership in Protestant churches follows social-class lines, with upper-class and middle-class people

[3] Percentages derived from figures quoted by National Council of Churches of Christ in the U.S.A., *Yearbook of American Churches*, March, 1966.

belonging to the old established churches. New Protestant groups generally attract working-class and lower-class members. It is not uncommon for persons to change from one Protestant church to another, presumably at times as a move in the checker game of social status. In recent years several Protestant churches have widened the range of social classes among their members, thus escaping the label "upper-class church" or some other designation. Perhaps the militant involvement of some of the Protestant clergy in movements designed to help disadvantaged people is in part their way of compensating for the parochialism of their churches.

Roman Catholics are bunched, for the most part, in urban areas. The Catholic Church is said to embrace all social classes, a generalization that is true to the extent that Catholics have not met economic discrimination. But relatively recent Catholic migrants from southern Europe are usually members of the lower classes and therefore many metropolitan Catholic congregations are predominantly of these classes. Non-Catholics mingle freely with Catholics, but many object (as do Catholics) to interfaith marriages. Prejudice against Catholics is largely in terms of the rituals and dogmas of the church, the alleged subservience of members to priests, and the power of the church hierarchy. Rumors of and books about a "Catholic conspiracy" are evidences of the fear with which some Americans regard the Roman Catholic Church. Recent ecumenical councils and conferences may have allayed such fears, and the election of John F. Kennedy as president may have assuaged the anxiety. The efforts of the Roman Catholic Church, however, to receive tax monies for the support of parochial schools remains a bone of contention between Catholics and non-Catholics.

Since anti-Semitism seems to focus on stereotypes of Jews as people, whereas anti-Catholicism centers in the hierarchy and beliefs of the Roman Catholic Church, social discriminations against Jews as individuals have been much more common than against Catholics. Americans are more tolerant of religious differences than they are of differences attributed to a stereotype. Jews are barred from or admitted on a quota basis to a number of private colleges and universities. They are sometimes ineligible, in practice if not by regulations, for fraternities and sororities except their own and for exclusive clubs and other private groups. Until recently they were refused admittance to certain hotels and housing areas. Like Catholics, Jews experience few if any real economic difficulties because of their religious affiliation, and both groups move readily into the middle class, with a few of each group winning acceptance in the upper class.

National Background and Status

One of the paradoxes of American society has been that on the one hand it said, "Give me your tired, your poor, your huddled masses yearning to breathe free," and on the other it denied equality to newcomers. Thus the latest wave of immigrants (excepting a few middle-class groups such as the Germans in 1848 and persons who have come here since World War II) has always started at the bottom socially. In general, immigrants have not been embittered by this treatment, for most of them have been readily assimilated and "worked their way up" in a generation or two.

Whereas assigning newcomers to the bottom of the social ladder merely demonstrated bias against poor, unassimilated foreigners, the Immigration Act of 1924 established a national policy that discriminated against certain national groups. The quota restrictions established by this act reflected the distinctions commonly made in the United States in respect to countries of origin. Because they are more like WASPs, persons from northern and central European countries have won acceptance more readily than those from southern and eastern nations; persons from Europe and Canada have been more readily assimilated than those from Latin America, Asia, and Africa (excepting immigrants of European origin from these countries). Despite discrimination, however, many individuals from "less preferred" nations who acquire education, money, and the social skills of classes above their own become socially mobile.

The quota system of immigration, replaced in 1965 by new legislation effective in 1968, asks, President Lyndon B. Johnson has said, "not where a person comes from but what are his personal qualities." Although departing from the maxim inscribed on the Statue of Liberty by excluding unskilled immigrants, the new legislation eliminates discrimination on the basis of national origin. Since legislation in a democracy should, and sometimes does, follow changes in public opinion, the new immigration policy may reflect a lessening of prejudice in this country against certain national groups.

Racial Origin and Social Status

Census statistics for racial groups in the United States in 1960 are based on self-reports and do not include dark-complexioned Spanish Americans commonly regarded as nonwhites. Persons of Mexican ancestry who were "not definitely Indian or of other nonwhite stock" are therefore included in the white population. The 1960 census reported the populations of nonwhite Americans of different ethnic

Ethnic Origin	Number
Negro	18,871,831
Indian	523,591
Japanese	464,332
Chinese	237,292
Filipino	176,310
All others	218,087
Total	20,491,443

origins as listed above. The "all others" category includes Asian Indians, Koreans, Polynesians, Indonesians, and other nonwhite races. Negroes constitute about 10.5 percent of the total population of the United States and about 90 percent of the nonwhite Americans.

Persons who are not Caucasians meet the most rigid bars to social mobility, and of all the nonwhite groups, Negroes have faced the severest deprivations. The status of the Negro is such that it has been described as castelike. When the caste system was legal in India, marriage within one's caste was required, status was hereditary, segregation was practiced, and eating habits were prescribed. In the past, especially in the South, the Negro's lot has resembled that of a low caste with a very important difference: Americans rationalized the separation of the Negro from the mainstream of American life on the grounds of his alleged hereditary inferiority, but most of them found no support for such segregation in their religious or democratic values. "Caste" is much less descriptive of the Negro's status today. Jim Crow laws have been invalidated, interracial marriages are becoming more common, and Negroes are rising somewhat in educational and occupational levels. Since World War II Negroes have made remarkable strides toward equality, but the goal is far from won.

The unhappy story of the Negro in America has been told and retold many times. The account herein is a sketch of recent events of particular pertinence to schools. The most sensational of these events was, of course, the Supreme Court decision of May 17, 1954, which outlawed compulsory segregation by race in public schools. Since 1954 public schools and colleges have been desegregated in many of the southern states, whereas other states continue to fight a delaying action. Meanwhile southern states have been losing thousands of their Negro population to industrial cities in other parts of the country. In these cities, de facto segregation of Negroes in neighborhoods and schools is common.

TABLE 7. **Percent of Employed Persons, by Occupation and Color 1950 and 1966**[a]

Major Occupational Group	White		Nonwhite	
	1950	1966	1950	1966
White-collar workers	40.3	47.9	10.2	20.8
Professional and technical workers	8.0	13.3	3.0	6.9
Managers, officials, and proprietors, except farm	11.6	10.9	2.5	2.6
Clerical workers	13.8	16.8	3.5	9.4
Sales workers	6.9	7.0	1.2	1.9
Blue-collar workers	39.3	36.1	37.5	41.7
Craftsmen and foremen	13.7	13.6	4.8	7.5
Operatives	20.6	18.3	18.6	22.4
Laborers, except farm and mine	5.0	4.2	14.1	11.7
Service workers	8.5	10.9	33.8	31.4
Private household workers	1.6	2.0	17.7	11.8
Other service workers	6.9	8.9	16.1	19.6
Farm workers	11.7	5.1	18.4	6.1
Farmers and managers	7.3	3.0	7.5	1.6
Laborers and foremen	4.4	2.1	10.9	4.5

[a] 1950 statistics exclude Hawaii and Alaska.

Source: U.S. Bureau of the Census, *Statistical Abstracts of the United States, 1967*, Government Printing Office, 1967, p. 231.

Racism, prejudice, and segregation have spawned ugly social realities. Nonwhites, most of whom are Negroes, are more likely than whites to hold less prestigious jobs and to earn less money. The distribution of jobs to whites and nonwhites is reported in Table 7. One may look at such figures with both hope and despair. For instance, between 1950 and 1966 the percentage of nonwhites in white-collar jobs doubled, whereas the percentage of whites in such occupations increased by only 7.6 percent, but the percentage of nonwhites in white-collar jobs is still less than half that of whites. During the same period, the percentage of nonwhite laborers and household workers declined 8.3 percent, whereas the percentage of whites in such jobs declined only .04 percent, but the percentage of nonwhite workers in these unskilled jobs was still almost four times that of whites.

But statistics on employment reveal only part of the story of the nonwhite in the market place; the number of unemployed workers is the other part of that story. In March, 1967 only 3.0 percent of white males, 16 years of age and older, were unemployed compared to 7.1 percent of nonwhite males.[4] At the same time among the younger workers (16 to 21 years old) in all races, the rate of unemployment was two and a half times that of older workers. The nonwhite rate was twice that of whites. Labor union practices, employers' prejudices, and the low educational level of many nonwhites, especially Negroes, . account for these high rates of unemployment. The median number of school years completed in 1966 for all persons 25 years and over was 12 compared to the Negro median of 9.1.[5]

Since occupation and education are factors in determining social status, the majority of Negroes are in the lower classes. Lacking a remembered common cultural heritage because members of Negro tribes were deliberately separated when they were brought in as slaves, the subculture of the Negro is American lower class. This sub-culture is accentuated by the frustrations and hostilities of minority status. Much of the idealism of the "do-gooder" is lost when he first comes in contact with the lower-class Negro. The behavior of the lower-class white is much the same, but because of his low "visibility" he is not so easily stereotyped as the Negro. Often middle-class and upper-class Negroes reject the lower-class Negro and sometimes blame him for the present plight of the Negro in America. One cannot, however, understand the hostilities, aggressions, fears, withdrawals, compensa-tions, rationalizations, anxieties, and sensitivities of the majority of Negroes unless he understands the effects of both social-class and minority-group status upon behavior. Most social scientists agree that the "social dynamite" piling up in big cities has begun to explode because not enough has been done to relieve the frustrations of lower-class Negroes.

Although a larger proportion of nonwhites than of whites are in the lower classes, many Negroes and other nonwhites are middle and upper class. Such Negroes exemplify their acceptance of middle-class values in many ways, including pressuring their children to do well in school. Nor do the patterns of behavior and value-systems of the lower classes apply to Jews, Japanese, Czechs, Scots, Armenians, and the Parsees and Jains from India even though they may hold low-income, manual jobs and live among the lower classes in this country.

Lipset has tested theories of upward mobility by speculating upon the characteristics of Jews, Japanese, and Scots living in the United

---

[4] U.S. Bureau of the Census, *Statistical Abstracts of the United States, 1967,* Government Printing Office, 1967, p. 223.

[5] *Ibid.,* p. 114.

States. According to theories he cites, the upwardly mobile are likely to come from families dominated by the mother, to have had many opportunities for interaction with adults, to have learned to defer present pleasures for long-term goals, to deal with others objectively, and to have higher rates of certain mental disturbances. Jews, Scots, and Japanese-Americans stress early independence in their training of children. Jews have a strong-mother, weak-father family system. Aspects of the value-system of Japan are significantly compatible with the American middle-class culture, especially in regard to attitudes toward education and authority. Members of these groups frown on extramarital sex relationships. They emphasize the importance of education and motivate their children to do well in school. The religious training of the Jews and of the Scots encouraged them to read the Bible, and they were among the first literate Europeans. Jews in America score higher on intelligence tests than do Gentiles; Scots in Great Britain score higher on these tests than do the English. Because they are bilinguals, most Japanese-Americans do not score as high on mental tests as would be expected from their better-than-average school achievement. From what we know about the three groups, Jews seem to have several of the characteristics needed for mobility, and there is evidence that Jews as a group have attained higher status socioeconomically than have other groups.[6] About one-third or more of the persons in the Jewish labor force are proprietors or managers and another 10 to 20 percent are professional-technical workers. Jewish women in the labor force are typically clerical or sales workers. One would expect higher rates of mobility among Scots, who are readily assimilated, than among Japanese-Americans, who have a racial barrier to hurdle.

These brief comments about certain minority groups may help the reader to understand that there are wheels within wheels (social class, cultural traits, color, religion, and national origin). Such factors influence the social status and the patterns of behavior of members in a particular minority group.

In the next section, the subculture of Mexican Americans is discussed in some detail to illustrate the contribution that ethnographic studies can make to understanding the behavior of children. Similar studies of the subcultures of Puerto Ricans, American Indians, Filipinos, and other groups are equally useful to teachers who work with children from these backgrounds. Each such subculture is, in some ways, unlike any other.

[6] Seymour Martin Lipset and Reinhard Bendix, *Social Mobility in Industrial Society*, University of California Press, 1959, pp. 255–259.

Occasionally the same trait may be found in different ethnic cultures, but usually the reason for its existence is very different. For example, both Mexican Americans and Negroes tend to be fatalistic in philosophy. In the case of Mexican Americans, fatalism is a product of their form of Catholicism. The Negroes' belief may have a grounding in a Protestant faith but is more likely to be derived from their inability in the past to change their fate very much.

The somewhat generalized and comprehensive descriptions of Mexican Americans that follow are normative statements, not applicable in the same degree to all Mexican Americans. Norms are standards, expectations, ideals. For example, a norm among Christians is to attend church on Sunday, but church attendance by individual Christians varies from infrequent to regular attendance. Likewise the extent to which Mexican Americans accept various traits in their culture may vary widely. Nevertheless, ethnographic studies are useful to teachers because they supply hypotheses about human behavior to be tested.

MEXICAN AMERICANS

Most Americans of Mexican descent, the third largest minority group in this country, live in Arizona, California, Colorado, New Mexico, and Texas. A number of them live in midwestern cities such as Chicago, Detroit, Kansas City, and Gary, and a few live in almost every sizable city in the nation. Some Mexican Americans,[7] especially those living in Texas, travel to other communities as migratory farm laborers. In 1960, however, according to Heller's estimate, 80 percent of the Mexican Americans were permanent residents of urban areas.[8]

In addition to not being very geographically mobile, except as migratory workers, Mexican Americans have not been very mobile socially. In 1959, Bogue stated that they constitute the "only ethnic group for which a comparison of the characteristics of first and second generation fails to show a substantial intergenerational rise in socioeconomic status."[9] Although 85 percent of the Mexican Americans in the United States were born in this country, they are also among the

---

[7] Mexican American is not hyphenated because persons in the group resent the hyphenated term. They prefer being called Spanish. In this section, Heller's term, Mexican American without the hyphen, is adopted rather than that of "Spanish-speaking," used by many writers. As Heller explains, many Spanish-speaking peoples come from countries other than Mexico.

[8] Celia S. Heller, *Mexican American Youth: Forgotten Youth at the Crossroad,* Random House, 1966, p. 7.

[9] Donald J. Bogue, *The Population of the United States,* Free Press, 1959, p. 372.

least "Americanized" of all ethnic groups. This resistance to acculturation, this failure to accept American ways and to become like other Americans eager to improve their lot, has discouraged do-gooders and frustrated school teachers.

The assimilation of Mexican Americans into the dominant culture has been impeded by several factors. First, Mexican Americans are fiercely proud of their heritage and do not wish to lose it. Even political refugees, middle class when they entered this country, and those who became middle class after arrival by accepting much of Anglo-American (non-Mexican white) culture, retain identification with their own folk culture. Second, the size of the Mexican American family tends to impoverish it and to prevent individual members from seizing opportunities for advancement. Third, about three-fourths of the Mexican Americans live in *colonia,* ethnic ghettos, separate from Anglo-Americans except for minimal, necessary contacts. Although this segregation is not so complete as that of Negroes, by living together Mexican Americans have not had to speak English or change their ways very much. Finally, attitudes of superiority on the part of Anglo-Americans toward them have led many Mexican Americans to have ambivalent attitudes about their own worth, i.e., their feelings of inferiority are counterbalanced by racial pride. Such attitudes lead them to withdraw from contacts with Anglos. Pride in race makes them very sensitive to insults and discrimination, real or imagined, but it also unites them. Social class differences among members of their group are unimportant to them in comparison to differences between members and nonmembers of *La Raza* (the race).

Notwithstanding the slow rate of acculturation, many Mexican Americans, especially since World War II, have become thoroughly Americanized. Others are attempting to have the "best of both worlds." Still others caught in the conflicts between cultures have rejected Americanization and embraced their own culture, or they have sought to relieve their tensions through alcoholism or crime. For the most part, as children in American schools, Mexican Americans for the first time face the conflict between their home and the Anglo community. Some of the difficulties in adjustment could be averted if their teachers understood their cultural background.

Mexican American Values

Any discussion of Mexican American values must be prefaced with a word of caution. The Mexican American culture is neither Mexican nor American; it is rather a combination of both.

Holland's study of the language handicaps of 36 Mexican American pupils is an excellent example of the effects upon children of mixing two languages. After administering, in English and Spanish, the Wechsler Intelligence Scale for Children to these pupils, he determined the extent of language barrier suffered by individuals. He concluded that 8 pupils had a very serious language barrier, 7 a serious one, 18 a moderate one, and 3 no language barrier at all. In the case of these pupils, he judged that their bilingualism handicapped them academically because their low socioeconomic background deprived them of conceptual tools in Spanish, yet their initial introduction as young children to Spanish rather than English retarded their learning English.[10]

In like manner, studies show that Mexican Americans spread along a continuum in respect to degrees of acceptance of other traits of Anglo-American culture. Some of them, for instance, cling tenaciously to certain values of Mexican culture, but others have accepted many American values, and still others have well nigh abandoned their heritage. Ordinarily younger Mexican Americans, especially those in the middle class, and those who are of the third generation in this country are more likely to be Anglicized than older people, those of lower socioeconomic status, and those of recent immigration. Even among those of the third generation differences exist. The Americanization of rural Mexican Americans who lived in the patron-peon system until recently differs markedly from that of urban Mexican Americans.[11] With this range of differences in mind, we can now describe what researchers find to be the dominant values of Mexican Americans.

Central to the Mexican American value-system is belief in *La Raza*.[12] Mexican Americans see themselves as united by cultural and spiritual bonds derived from God. The spirit of Spanish-speaking people, they believe, is divine and infinite. They attribute their failure to have attained a glorious destiny to human weaknesses among their own people, yet individuals who succumb to temptation do not suffer great anxiety even though God punishes the whole society for their sins. Therefore, Juan was drunk because too much whiskey was served at

[10] William R. Holland, "Language Barrier as an Educational Problem of Spanish-Speaking Children," *Exceptional Children, 27* (September, 1960), 42–50.

[11] Clark S. Knowlton, "Patron-Peon Pattern Among the Spanish Americans of New Mexico," *Social Forces, 41* (October, 1962), 12–16.

[12] For a full account of *La Raza* and other Mexican American values and practices described in this section, see William Madsen, *The Mexican Americans of South Texas*, Holt, Rinehart, 1964, pp. 15–23 and 44–109, *passim;* and Heller, *op. cit.*, pp. 16–23, 32–41, 45–52, *passim.*

the party, not because he was too weak to refuse drinks. They reason that human weakness is universal. Furthermore, good and bad fortune are products of God's Will, and "one has to suffer to deserve."

Their view of life leads many Mexican Americans to reject planning for the future. God, not man, plans. Thus man should live each day to its fullest and appreciate things as they are. Man is subjugated by nature, he is not its master. The only way man can change God's Will is by prayer, sacrifice, and making promises to God, through saints, if He will grant a petition.

Although a large majority of Mexican Americans are Roman Catholics, some of their beliefs are the despair of their priests. In Latin fashion, men, particularly those in the lower class, believe that church attendance is unnecessary because their wives go for them, yet they staunchly defend their faith. Mexican Americans are likely to have altars in their homes and to transact their business with God by direct supplication to saints rather than through priests, and some of these "saints" are not recognized by the Roman Catholic Church.

Lower-class and many middle-class Mexican Americans also believe in supernatural diseases and witchcraft. They respect certain members of their group called *curanderos* (curers) who are believed to have divine power to heal the sick and to remove the hex of witches. Madsen, who studied Mexican Americans in Hidalgo County, Texas for four years, concluded that many *curanderos* unwittingly relieve psychosomatic symptoms by social manipulation and psychotherapy at less cost than physicians and psychiatrists would have charged for their services. Unfortunately, however, the *curanderos* sometimes mistake a contagious or malignant disease for a folk disease. When they do, they fail to refer patients to physicians in time for the latter to help them.[13]

Another folk belief of Mexican Americans is that certain people unknown to themselves have an "evil eye." Madsen cites the case of a public health nurse who irritated Mexican Americans with her "bustling authoritarianism." She was said by gossips to bring sickness to children with her evil eye because she commented on their beauty without removing the baleful effects by touching them. Juana said, "She is either stupid or inconsiderate to admire so many kids when she has strong vision and then not even try to prevent the sickness by touching them."[14] The same nurse could not convince her clients of danger from germs which they could not see.

Speaking Spanish fluently is a symbol of loyalty to *La Raza*, and the

[13] Madsen, *op. cit.*, p. 105.
[14] *Ibid.*, p. 76.

family teaches its children to speak Spanish as well as to observe other behavior appropriate for *La Raza*. In the home, children are taught to be obedient, dependent, courteous, and respectful of their parents. They also learn the "do's and don'ts" that govern their relationships with outsiders, which may be categorized in this fashion:

Do's	*Don'ts*
Acknowledge authority only of God and one's father.	Belong to organizations that weaken your self-reliance or family loyalty.
Be loyal and affectionate to your family.	Get involved in the affairs of others.
Be careful in expressing opinions because you must stand and defend them. Think as you please.	Question another's methods or motives, criticize his beliefs, or try to impose your ideas on him. Avoid controversial subjects.
Repay debts and obligations promptly.	Accept charity or favors outside the family.
Conceal personal gains or advancement.	Make others envious of you; compete.
Defend your honor (manliness).	Work for people who insult you.
Be polite as a sign of self-respect.	Make your family ashamed of you.
Reserve confidences for your family.	Trust others. They are likely to be greedy, dishonest, and treacherous.

The Mexican American Family System

The Mexican American family commands the individual's highest loyalty. He receives social recognition, love, and understanding from his family for which he must give up material possessions and at times personal ambitions. The family household usually consists of husband, wife, and children, but it may also include in-laws and other relatives who need shelter. Relatives usually live nearby and are ordinarily the only welcome visitors in the home. Sex and age determine family roles. The father is the undisputed head of the household. The perfect wife may manipulate her husband into doing what she wants him to do, but she never nags or orders him to do it.

The parents are relatively permissive and affectionate with small children, but after puberty the father avoids demonstrations of affection, demands respect and obedience, and punishes his children when they need correction. Teen-age girls are carefully supervised because "purity" is essential for a suitable marriage and sexual "looseness" brings shame to the family. Boys, however, are relatively free to spend most of their time with their *palomilla, amigos,* or *camaradas* (gang). The family believes that a boy will attain *machismo* (manliness) in his gang.

Achieving *machismo* makes a boy proud, self-reliant, and virile. Just as conserving one's virginity is the highest value for a girl, proving one's virility by seduction is the highest value for a boy. "The better man," one of Madsen's informants told him, "is the one who can drink more, defend himself best, have more sex relations, and have more sons borne by his wife."[15] Thus boys in gangs boast of their conquests, engage in verbal dueling while drinking with friends, and if they or their family are insulted, take their revenge in fierce fighting. Members of some of these gangs, especially in large cities, become delinquent. Then the gangs are called *eses, batos, cholos,* or *chucos.* Gangs of delinquents adopt a distinctive dress and speech, part Spanish and part English. Nondelinquent boys in a gang, like delinquents, may resent their father's authoritarianism and put their gang before their family, but after they marry the primacy of one's obligation to family is usually reestablished.

Mexican Americans and Schools

The Mexican American family ill-prepares its children to do well in American schools. These children know little or no English when they enter school because Spanish is spoken at home. The family's pride in fluency in Spanish has not, however, enabled the children to attain anything approaching mastery of that language. Since Spanish has only recently been taught in elementary schools, lower-class Mexican Americans cannot usually read or write Spanish. Even their speech is imperfect; often those who are American born speak Spanish with an English accent and English with a Spanish accent.

Primary age pupils must, then, learn to speak as well as read and write English. From the outset, they are "linguistically handicapped." Throughout their school years, they are likely to be reluctant to recite because they are sensitive about their language handicap.

An indication of a family's aspirations for social mobility is the presence of books in the home, but the majority of Mexican American homes have no books other than school books, no magazines, and

---

[15] *Ibid.,* p. 20.

frequently no newspaper. Most families have television sets and ra-
dios, but they are likely to prefer programs presented in Spanish. The
lower-class father tends to view school as unimportant except as a
place for his child to learn English so that he can defend himself
against Anglos and avoid being cheated. Parents often point out that
Juan's graduating from high school or Ricardo's graduating from college did not help them get better jobs. There is truth in such statements because successful Mexican Americans usually move away from
the ghettos to live in distant places. A few families, ambitious for their
sons, are likely to consider educating a daughter a waste of time and
money.

The differences between the Mexican American subculture and that
of the school create further difficulties for these pupils. At home they
have learned not to compete with others, not to plan for the future,
and not to be dissatisfied with their lot. They are not convinced that
planning and productive work will pay off in the future. Instead they
have learned that leisure is dignified and productive, for then a man
has time to think. Doing something on time is not very important. In
school, inadvertently or directly, they are encouraged to compete, to
plan for the future, to be punctual, ambitious, and responsible, and to
work hard. If they yield to pressures to study in school, their peers
ridicule them. As a consequence, they are much more likely to be
ashamed of succeeding than they are of failing in school. They are not
likely to believe that a teacher, who so often does and says the very
things that they think are rude and impolite, can help them improve
their standards of living.

Helping Mexican American Pupils Learn

An awareness of the cultural background of Mexican American
children may help teachers work with them. Such knowledge may
keep a teacher from prying into pupils' private lives, criticizing their
beliefs, and trying to impose his ideas upon them. It may lead him to
develop the habit of touching a child when admiring him to a parent,
just in case the parent thinks the teacher has "strong vision." (After
all, does not the teacher himself avoid walking under a ladder?) An
understanding of Mexican American culture may make a teacher
wonder whether a visit to a pupil's home might do more harm than
good and whether urging parents to speak English with their children
would help. It may serve to warn a teacher that Mexican Americans
are easily insulted and that they may drop out of school or not try to
learn if they feel that a teacher has insulted them. One high school

teacher said she could gain the cooperation of Mexican American boys by using, in her words, "extra-polite" language.

Understanding the cultural background of his pupils may also lead a teacher to reconsider his function as a teacher. Is it his job to "Americanize" pupils whose cultural backgrounds are different and to change the way of life in the community? At one time the teacher was the chief agent of the "melting pot," but today educational leaders urge that teachers "respect cultural differences."

After teaching for a year in a school for Indian children, Wolcott concluded that a teacher should direct his energies toward improving pupils' competencies in necessary skills rather than overloading a class with concepts of goodness and badness that may be at variance with beliefs held by the children. He found that by setting specific goals, such as, "teach Walter, Tommy, and Leslie how to divide by ten," arithmetic and other subjects became acceptable to his charges. The pupils knew what was expected of them and could judge how well they had succeeded. Wolcott learned that values necessary to acceptability in the larger society can be taught as skills rather than as values. In short, pupils can learn to be responsible by being given tasks for which they are responsible. They can be taught punctuality and cleanliness, for example, as highly regarded "survival skills" in an industrial society without the teacher's moralizing about the value of punctuality and cleanliness.[16]

Wolcott also suggests that a teacher who succeeds in teaching culturally different pupils will attempt to meet their functional needs. In the case of Mexican Americans, the teacher would first ask himself, "What do these pupils really need to learn? Familiarity with a standard dialect of spoken Engish and standard written English? Computational skills? The advantages and disadvantages of political organizations and labor unions for workers? Vocational opportunities? Educational opportunities? An American's civil and political rights?

Obviously if the curriculum is centered solely in the functional needs of a predominantly Mexican American community, ambitious Mexican Americans who plan to graduate from high school and perhaps attend college will not have their needs met. They will need special encouragement and help in social as well as academic areas from teachers and counselors. As a matter of fact, a number of these mobile young people now in college point to a teacher, counselor, or principal as the person who inspired them to attend.

According to Heller, this group of ambitious Mexican Americans

[16] Harry F. Wolcott, *A Kwakiutl Village and School*, Holt, Rinehart, 1967, pp. 127–130.

may be larger today than it was even a few years ago. From a study of the aspirations of senior boys in Los Angeles, she concluded that Mexican Americans resembled Anglo-Americans of the same social class in their educational and occupational ambitions. She further concluded that a significantly larger ratio of Mexican Americans in integrated schools aspired to nonmanual occupations than did those in schools that had a predominantly Mexican American student body.[17] For the reasons discussed above, Mexican American youth, however, need more empathetic understanding and guidance than do most Anglo-Americans if their aspirations are to be realized.

CHILDREN'S REACTIONS TO MINORITY-GROUP STATUS

Generalizing about the reactions of groups of children as different as those in minority groups can be pointless. About all that some of the children in these groups have in common is that they differ in certain respects from the children in the dominant group. They differ in reactions because they are are not all of the same social class, religion, racial origin, or cultural heritage. They do not experience the same treatment as victims of prejudiced people nor do they necessarily perceive in the same way such discrimination as may exist. Nevertheless, in some situations children of minority groups tend to react similarly.

Reactions to the "Core Culture"

Assuming that an American "core culture" exists, Fishman reviewed research conducted in segregated religious and racial schools to determine the extent of "biculturalism" developed in such schools. By "biculturalism," he means that children select values and patterns of behavior from their minority-group culture and from the "core culture" and synthesize the elements selected. In general he found that the influence of the pervasive "core culture" was stronger than the influence of the minority-group culture of the schools.[18] Because the dominant culture is so influential, minority-group children conform to social pressures to adopt it. They also want to be like other Americans for they want to be accepted by children of the dominant group.

The evidence shows that all teen-age groups, for example, irrespective of minority-group affiliation, share in teen-age culture. The lower-

[17] Heller, *op. cit.*, pp. 81, 87.
[18] Joshua A. Fishman, "Childhood Indoctrination for Minority-Group Membership," *Daedalus, 90* (Spring, 1961), 329–347.

class Negro in the Deep South wants a transistor, a record player, an automobile, and faddish clothes (different from the national mode, perhaps, but like clothes of other teen-agers he knows). He listens to the same music and admires the same television stars.[19] The Italo-American, no longer a member of a street-corner gang as his father was, thinks, believes, and wants the same things as other American teen-agers. Like the third-generation Greek, Ukrainian, or Pole, he may still be considered "different," however, and excluded from equal participation in American peer groups.[20] The middle-class Jewish teen-ager, especially if he is in early adolescence, likes "rock and roll," buys teen-age consumer goods, and dresses in approved teen-age style. If his family is well-to-do, he gets more expensive things from his indulgent parents than do most teen-agers. He may be less sharply set off from adult life than most teen-agers because Jewish family life is more cohesive, but he does not see himself as being different from other teen-agers except that he is a Jew.[21]

Like other teen-agers, the child of a minority group wants to be like his peers. With few exceptions, the Jewish teen-ager has abandoned Orthodox Judaism, has become relatively indifferent to religion, and feels that his religious heritage is not very different from that of a Protestant or a Catholic.[22] Such an attitude is far from the belief that Jews are the Chosen People. The Negro, the Jew, and the young person of Oriental descent try their best to look like run-of-the-mill Americans, not only in dress but also in physical features. Negroes, with the exception of Black nationalists, straighten their hair; other groups sometimes resort to plastic surgery. In his efforts to conform as well as in his lack of acceptance by the dominant group, the non-white faces the toughest situations. Unlike the third-generation American of white descent who has largely lost his foreign heritage and become assimilated into the dominant culture, the nonwhite, even the Negro who is as American as apple pie, is seldom completely accepted because he is visibly different.

The minority-group child usually accepts the values and behavior patterns of his American social class. (Exceptions have been pointed out in Chapter 3.) Because he is a member of a minority group as well as of a social class, he sometimes seems to exaggerate the typical patterns of his class. The lower-class Negro boy, like the lower-class

---

[19] Joseph S. Himes, "Negro Teen-Age Culture," in American Academy of Political and Social Science, *The Annals, 338* (November, 1961), 91–101.
[20] Francis A. J. Ianni, "The Italo-American Teen-Ager," *The Annals, op. cit.,* 70–78.
[21] David Boroff, "Jewish Teen-Age Culture," *The Annals, op. cit.,* 79–90.
[22] *Ibid.*

white boy, believes that physical fighting, profanity, obscenity, and overt sexual activity are expressions of masculinity. Subjected to greater discrimination than his white counterpart, and therefore harboring stronger feelings of hostility, he may react with violence. For the Negro adolescent the open street in the Negro section, free of police controls, becomes the scene of loud talking, raucous laughter, and abusive relations among peers. The lower-class Negro feels rejected. He knows by the time he is 10 or 11 years old, with even more bitterness than the poverty-stricken white child, that the American dream is not for him. He sees a "distorted, frightening, and cruel world," and he is apprehensive about the future and distrustful of adult authority. (Even Negro adolescents of high IQ and middle-class status are likely to have similar feelings of apprehension and distrust of adult authority.)[23] The lower-class Negro does not believe that he has a chance or that school will improve his chances very much. He has no enduring goals; he just hopes for an easy job and quick money from a lucky windfall.

Children from middle-class and certain lower-class minority groups are often excessively middle class in their attitudes toward education. Believing that schooling will improve their life chances, Jews, Chinese-Americans, Japanese-Americans, and upwardly mobile children of recent European immigrants study very hard in school. Their parents make all and more of the sacrifices that middle-class parents of the dominant group make for their children. The educational and occupational aspirations of these minority-group parents for their children are high; their children are strongly motivated to succeed.

Reaction to Discrimination

Young people tend to respond to prejudice against them to the extent that it is perceived, felt, or inferred to be discriminating. They may, in fact, become hypersensitive about their group, seeing insult where none is intended. They may refuse to meet proffered friendships halfway because they doubt the sincerity of the dominant-group person. They may identify excessively with the successes and failures of their group, exulting with the achievements of a Martin Luther King or an Einstein and suffering when headlines about Negro delinquents or Jewish traitors are printed.[24] They may try to disprove by their own

[23] Elihu Katz, *Conflict and Harmony in an Adolescent Interracial Group,* Research Series No. 1, New York University Press, 1955, p. 19.

[24] Adults in minority groups may seek to escape the minority status altogether by changing their names, their religion, or (in the case of nonwhites) by "crossing the color bar." It is estimated that each year about 10,000 light-skinned Negroes move to a new location and pass as whites.

actions whatever stereotyped characteristics are attributed to their group, or they may settle for the stereotype, adopting the attitude "I might as well be what everybody thinks I am." They may rationalize their failures by convincing themselves that they do not have a chance because they are Negro or Indian or Oriental.

Perhaps the most common individual reaction to discrimination is hostility expressed in some form of aggression. Aggression may be defined as attacking others or one's environment to attain personal goals or to find release from one's own tensions. Aggression takes many forms, some bad and some good. A lower-class Negro youth may find a release for his feelings of hostility in fighting, swearing, name-calling, joking, or malingering as well as in uncooperative and delinquent behavior, looting and rioting, religious emotionalism, musical expression, or athletic prowess. The middle-class Negro youth may utilize leadership in racial conflicts. Black Student Union protests, demonstrations, sit-ins, and strikes serve as outlets for members' aggression. Many minority-group persons, especially those of the middle class, may sublimate their aggressions by criticizing society or the arts, by becoming activists in reform movements, by competing in sports or intellectual activities, or by producing artistic creations in drama, literature, music, and art.

Sometimes aggression is displaced to one's own minority group. In such instances, children as well as adults reject their own families and others in their group. Quarreling and fighting among Negroes may be attributable to displaced aggression. Aggression may also be displaced to other minority groups or to individuals of a lower social status within one's own group.

Besides contributing to aggressive acts, the beliefs and feelings of some minority-group members encourage them to be unwilling to accept personal responsibility for their own welfare. We have already seen that many Mexican Americans are likely to believe that their God wills whatever happens. Negroes are more likely than whites to subscribe to a fatalistic philosophy. Battle and Rotter found that lower-class Negroes are more likely than middle-class Negroes to see fate, chance, or powerful people as responsible for their lot.[25] Minority status, especially that of Mexican American, Indian, or Negro, may also lead children to underestimate their own abilities. They learn from the attitudes of their teachers and white classmates, from their report cards, and from the number of their nonwhite peers who drop out of

[25] Esther S. Battle and Julian B. Rotter, "Children's Feelings of Personal Control as Related to Social Class and Ethnic Group," *Journal of Personality, 31* (December, 1963), 489.

school that they are inferior in academic ability. Wylie found that among 823 junior high school pupils of comparable mental ability, Negroes made more modest estimates of their ability than did whites, and children of lower socioeconomic levels made more modest estimates than did children of higher socioeconomic levels.[26] When a child does not hold himself responsible for his actions and underestimates his own abilities, he is not likely to improve his performance.

Reactions Within Minority Groups

When one learns that reactions to prejudice and discrimination are diversified, he still has not fully grasped the intricacies of minority-group status. Not only is each minority group different from every other group and divided along American social-class lines, but each group (with the exception of the Negro) is also divided within itself by cleavages that are carried over in their own unique heritage. Japanese-Americans, for example, include two out-groups. First, the Kibei (rhymes with Libby), a minority group within a minority group, are Americans of Japanese descent who were visiting Japan at the outbreak of World War II and who were detained there during the war and for several years after the war. Often a Kibei was only 5 or 6 years old when he went to Japan and he did not return until he was 15 or 16 years old. In the meantime he learned Japanese ways. Upon his return to this country he was often rejected by his own ethnic group just as he had been ostracized in Japan. His knowledge of English was poor, he did not know American ways. The Kibei today are adults who may have children in school. Their children face problems of acculturation that a second generation child faces. (Most Japanese-American children are now third- or fourth-generation Americans.) A second group of outsiders among Japanese-Americans are the descendants of the Eta, a traditional, unskilled, pariah class in Japan. Lingering prejudice against the Eta still exists among some Japanese-Americans.

A further group division occurs between recent immigrants and ethnic groups who have been in this country for many years. Although the percentage of foreign-born has declined from 14.5 percent in 1910 to 5.8 percent in 1960, approximately 10,000,000 persons living in the United States in 1960 were born abroad. The children among them face the same problems of acculturation as did earlier immigrants, and because of their differences, the possibility of rejection by children of older American settlers, including those of the same ethnic origin.

[26] Ruth S. Wylie, "Children's Estimates of Their Schoolwork Ability as a Function of Sex, Race and Socioeconomic Level," *Journal of Personality, 31* (June, 1963), 204–224.

Thus we see that the status of different minority groups and the reactions of individuals within each group are very complex. Many, though not all, of the undesirable reactions of minority-group children would be eliminated if prejudice directed toward them were eliminated and if teachers and children of all social groups learned to accept others who are different.

Acceptance of Minority-Group
Pupils in Schools

Although the problems of minority-group children in public schools are by no means the same, they do share one overriding concern: *they want to be accepted* as individuals of worth by their teacher and classmates. A Negro college student, writing a description of cliques in her high school, said, "I looked through my annual and found not a single intimate remark under the pictures that were autographed. They left me alone, and I left them alone." Later she commented that one of her teachers "always made me remember that I am a Negro and should keep my place." Children of minority groups do not want to be thought of as a Jew, a Chinese-American, or a Negro but as "a person—just like anybody else."

For such children to be accepted as casually as children of the dominant group accept one another, teachers and pupils have to learn to regard persons who are different as suitable associates. In some cases, persons develop a willingness to accept individuals of different religions or cultural backgrounds by learning more about their religions or their cultural heritages. Young children particularly may be repulsed and even frightened by the strange, the unknown, the different that they do not understand. They have not learned that differences are interesting and add spice to life. In other cases, knowledge of a group's heritage is not enough, for unfavorable attitudes toward members of the group have already been learned. Such prejudices seem to be especially deep-rooted in respect to persons in groups that are *visibly* different from the dominant group. Prejudice against minority groups is also most intense in areas where these groups are heavily concentrated.

A great deal of research has been done and findings published about the causes and prevention of prejudice. Suggested programs and methods of mitigating hostile feelings among various groups have been incorporated into the social studies curriculum in many schools. Attitudes toward persons who are different have been improved, at least at the verbal level, as a result of these educational efforts. It is difficult, however, to determine exactly what methods have been effective since so many different approaches have been simultaneously used.

The first step in helping pupils accept those of minority-group status is, of course, that the teacher demonstrates his respect for individuals irrespective of their group affiliations. Before a teacher can be a model, he has to admit his own prejudices rather than deny them. If he can raise his own prejudices to a cognitive level, squarely face the stereotypes he has developed, and analyze them, he has taken a first step toward a healthy regard for individuals.

Beyond being a model for his pupils, a teacher may help his pupils unlearn prejudices by using some of the recommended methods. Perhaps the first such method tried in schools was that of recognizing contributions of members of minority groups to American society. This method has been found to be more useful if such contributions are merely mentioned in context, such as a remark during a study of explorers that Columbus was probably a Jew, rather than if special units on "Contributions of Jews" are developed. A more meaningful approach than citing contributions is helping a person who is prejudiced learn how it feels to be in the shoes of his victim. To this end, films, books, and role playing that enable pupils to identify with persons of minority groups and that appeal to their sense of fair play can be provided. The most commonly recommended method is ostentatiously called "equal status participation," i.e., intermingling of persons of dominant and minority groups. Using representatives of minority groups who do not reinforce a stereotype as teachers and as speakers in classes may help to counteract stereotyped thinking about a minority group. Teaching such facts as are available about differences between races is also recommended.

None of the recommended methods is likely, however, to be effective with pupils who have psychological needs for a scapegoat. Researchers have found that such persons who may overcome their prejudices against one group will shift their prejudices from that group to another. The person who has to have a scapegoat is, of course, very insecure emotionally and needs to blame others for his own inadequacies. If his aggressions can be directed into socially acceptable channels, he may be helped; but if his insecurities are deep-seated, professional therapy may be required. Teachers are likely to be more successful in mitigating the prejudices of pupils who have simply learned to make certain erroneous prejudgments about groups than they are those of pupils who are psychologically maladjusted.

Since the causes of prejudice are highly complex, the eradication of prejudice is not an easy undertaking. Prejudice is widespread, if not universal. It exists among people in minority groups as well as among people in dominant groups. As a consequence, teachers also need to help members of minority groups overcome feelings of hostility toward other groups.

Besides overcoming their own prejudices, pupils of minority groups need to learn how to avoid the self-defeating responses that they sometimes make to their status. They need help in learning to be proud of their group membership, yet not to identify to such an extent that they become ethnocentric. The teacher has to provide acceptable channels into which a child's aggressions may be sublimated. He has to discourage a pupil from rationalizing his failures and underestimating his abilities. He has to encourage a pupil to accept responsibility for his actions and to develop feelings of friendliness toward pupils of the dominant group. Whatever the teacher may do to improve the self-concept and the ambitions of a minority-group pupil from an educationally disadvantaged home will help him win acceptance from his classmates. He frequently needs praise, successful experiences, and encouragement as well as help in reducing his social and academic deficiencies. Nevertheless, he is unlikely to modify his attitudes toward himself or others unless such changes seem likely to help him attain acceptance. He does not want to be "all dressed up with no place to go."

Whenever children of any ethnic, religious, or racial group have feelings of rejection arising from experiences in school, their personal development and our society suffer. American society can afford neither the tensions created by WASPs who refuse to recognize the dignity and worth of all human beings nor the loss of undeveloped talents of children who fail to grow scholastically because of their emotional blocks to learning and self expression.

IMPORTANT CONCEPTS

Americanization. The assimilation of American cultural patterns by people of foreign birth or heritage.

Caste. Any rigid, exclusive social group in which membership is based on heredity, wealth, religion, or other common factor. See p. 259.

Ecumenical Councils. Roman Catholic Church assemblies that were worldwide in Christian representation. Recent councils included Protestant observers as well as Roman Catholic participants. See p. 257.

Ethnocentric. The attitude that one's own ethnic group is superior to other such groups.

Ethnography. A branch of anthropology concerned with the classification and description of cultures. See p. 262.

Fatalism. A belief that events and conditions are predetermined and inevitable. See p. 263.

Minority group. See p. 256.

Miscegenation. Intermarriage of persons of differing racial origins. See p. 256.

Normative statement. A description of the expected or ideal behavior of a group. See p. 263.

Prejudice. A judgment or opinion formed before carefully examining all relevant facts and issues. See pp. 255, 267 ff.

Racism. An unfounded belief in the superiority of a given group of people, usually one's own, on the basis of physical differences. See p. 260.

Stereotype. A simplified, even caricaturized conception, of the qualities or characteristics attributed to a group from which the individual member of the group is not expected to differ. See p. 257.

"Survival skill." Proficiency that enables one to survive in the environment in which he finds himself. See p. 270.

13. THE SCHOOL'S JOB IN THE COMMUNITY

Be not the first by whom the new are tried,
Nor yet the last to lay the old aside.
—ALEXANDER POPE

Any first-grader can tell you that he goes to school to learn; but the wisest philosophers disagree as to *what* he should learn and *why* he should learn it. In this country what the school has tried to teach has been gradually expanding ever since schools were established in colonial America. The enlarging concept of the school's duties has led to changes in curriculums, methods, and rationale as well as to conflicts among people who disagree about what schools should undertake.

As pointed out in the discussions of the Traditional School and the Modern School that follow, changes in curriculums and in methods of teaching tend to reflect the problems faced and the values subscribed to by Americans in different generations. If we assume that such a relationship is likely to continue, then we may conclude that schools of the future will also reflect changes in social problems and perceptions of values.

THE TRADITIONAL SCHOOL

Three elementary school primers, each of which was remarkably popular for a century or more, reveal the kind of service rendered by American schools prior to this century. First published in 1690, the *New England Primer* reflected the colonials' conviction that children learn to read so that they may read the Bible. It has been said of the *Primer* that "It taught millions to read, and not one to sin." In the concluding poem in the first edition, Death, in grisly language, threatens youth with hell for disobeying their parents and preachers. If a Puritan child could be frightened away from sin, the *Primer* was indeed the ideal textbook.

In the eighteenth century editions the "fire and brimstone" theme and readings were replaced with patriotic precepts, readings with moral implications, and secular material praising the practical values of learning. Pupils were told:

> He who ne'er learns his A.B.C.
> Forever will a blockhead be.
> But he who learns his letters fair
> Shall have a coach to take to air.

Not long after its appearance in 1784, Noah Webster's "blue-back speller" replaced the *Primer* and remained a favorite for another hundred years. The speller, revised over the years, consisted of spelling words, a system of standardized pronunciations, moral readings about such characters as a boy who stole apples or a milkmaid who counted her chickens before they hatched, patriotic and moralistic maxims, American geographical and historical names, and fables. The popularity of the text suggests that Americans at that time interpreted the school's service to the community as teaching fundamental skills, concepts of patriotism (probably equated with citizenship), and standards of moral conduct.

McGuffey's Eclectic Readers, better books in respect to content and teaching aids than Webster's Readers and Spellers, also accepted the view that education is primarily a moral and secondarily an intellectual enterprise. An estimated 122,000,000 of McGuffey's books were sold in six editions between 1836 and 1920. Henry Steele Commager describes these books as "deeply religious" (in the Protestant style), yet markedly materialistic and worldly. An honest boy gets a handsome reward; a disobedient boy drowns. That is, virtue and evil are promptly rewarded and punished. Commager admits that the Readers stressed an ardent Americanism and gave nineteenth-century children "a common body of allusions, a sense of common experiences and of common possessions," but he denies that they were chauvinistic. They were, he maintains, cosmopolitan rather than parochial in that selections from the literature and history of western civilization gave pupils "a sense of membership in a larger community."[1]

Changes in school readers reflected modifications in the value-system of Puritan thinking that had dominated the earliest schools. Calvinist views of the child, which influenced religious thinking of Americans for the first 150 years of our history, assumed the innate evil of the child's nature. The writings of John Cotton, Cotton Mather, and others set forth clearly the belief in a vengeful God who had no mercy on children. To be saved from torment, anyone, including children, must learn of their sins, feel guilty, and be obedient. The rod was not spared in teaching the child. Only a few voices were raised in protest against this stern doctrine. A handful of Quakers, Anglicans, Mennonites, and others from small Protestant groups dissented, but their pleas for gentleness, admonition, and reason in teaching children were not widely accepted until the nineteenth and twentieth centuries.

Jonathan Edwards and other religious and intellectual leaders who

[1] Henry Steele Commager, "Foreword," in *McGuffey's Fifth Eclectic Reader*, 1879 Edition, A Signet Classic, New American Library, 1962, pp. xii–xiv.

dominated education in the colonial period had agreed unquestioningly upon the importance of the classics in the education of leaders for church and state. They believed that "humanistic learning was as necessary for development of human reason as revelation and grace was necessary for faith and salvation."[2] The Latin Grammar Schools, forerunners of the modern secondary schools, concentrated upon classical education because they were designed to feed the colleges. Benjamin Franklin's proposals for an academy, a new kind of school that would combine the practical arts with classical education, though applauded by many educators and other interested persons, met with little success in his day.

Although a high school offering a relatively wide selection of subjects was founded in Boston in 1821, high schools did not immediately supplant the Latin Grammar Schools devoted to the study of Latin and Greek classics. Not until after the Civil War did the high schools gain widespread acceptance, and not until 1874, after a Michigan court's decision in the Kalamazoo Case, were they commonly viewed as an extension of the free public schools. Advocates' arguments for free high schools stressed that such schools would end inequalities and train the masses to be useful and productive members of society.

The establishment of free common schools throughout the land began in the early nineteenth century with the creation of a new republic. A powerful argument for the establishment of such schools was the need for literate and loyal citizens. Hence the colonial emphasis on education as preparation for religious literacy was replaced by a new stress on education for citizenship. Notwithstanding the loss of influence by religious leaders on nineteenth century schools, moral education based on the "common elements of Christianity" was still a major objective of schools. New subjects in school, such as history, geography, and government were, however, justified as preparation for citizenship. Demands for more vocational education were common, but those who wanted practical education at this time had in mind "learning-from-books-more-about-useful-things." Their proposals were opposed by those who embraced the new faculty psychology that provided the justification for mental discipline. One best attained mental discipline, it was said, through the study of the classics, mathematics, and philosophy. Nevertheless, early in the nineteenth century people began to think of education in terms of its cash-surrender value.

[2] See R. Freeman Butts and Lawrence A. Cremin, *A History of Education in American Culture,* Holt, Rinehart, 1953, pp. 66–81, for a full discussion of education in colonial America.

During the latter part of the nineteenth century and the early twentieth century many changes in ways of thinking and living transformed the nation and influenced the schools. General acceptance of free high schools was one of the most significant of these changes, but to a considerable extent the traditional school persisted. Butts and Cremin state:

> While one is able to find numerous examples of fundamentally new school programs here and there before 1918, and while modifications slowly entered most curricula, by and large, traditional aims continued to dominate education. Those who built educational programs continued to assume . . . that the school curriculum consists largely of a body of previously discovered facts and principles which must be communicated to the young.
>
> In spite of growing attacks on traditional conceptions of human nature and learning, religious-moral development and mental discipline remained paramount aims well into the twentieth century . . . In the minds of most educators, the good citizen was the man who could read and write, whose mind had been disciplined, and who had received appropriate character education.[3]

There were, of course, some changes in curriculum and methods. The tendency to value schooling in dollars and cents had increased; the number of vocational-training programs had grown; the rest of the curriculum had changed a little, especially in the high school where modern languages had replaced the classics, business courses had multiplied, interest in science was more evident than in earlier years; and some new teaching methods had been developed.

Good Morning, Miss Dove, a popular novel of the 1950s, presents a somewhat overdrawn and sentimentalized description of a teacher of geography who was still teaching during World War II. The popularity of the story suggests that many persons had known a teacher like Miss Dove, the "public conscience" of a small town who froze the "marrow of sinners." According to the story, parents, remembering their own experiences in her class, still feared her and regressed into childlike gawkiness in her presence. Miss Dove was respected as well as feared because she never stooped to anger, never raised her voice, and never "bribed her class to good behavior or reduced learning to the level of entertainment." She maintained rigid standards of right and wrong, decorum, and honor. She gave no leeway to personality; of all pupils she demanded obedience, work, and "a complete suspension of [their] will."[4]

[3] *Ibid.,* p. 433

[4] Frances Gray Patton, *Good Morning, Miss Dove,* Dodd, Mead, 1954, pp. 11–12, 93–94.

Miss Dove was very much like the ideal teacher of the mid-nineteenth century, who was, in the words of Butts and Cremin, "intellectual or literary, moral and religious, and patriotic." Miss Dove saw her duties as those of teaching geography thoroughly. She was largely self-taught in her specialty but she knew geography well. Pupils memorized definitions (which they might later recall while flying a navy plane across the Pacific) and the products of faraway places, studied maps, and learned to spell esoteric words. In the course of her instruction they acquired the manners and morals acceptable to the community. Not all traditional teachers were as studious nor as literate as Miss Dove; not all of them were such strong characters, and few of them made such a lasting impression upon their pupils.

Like Miss Dove, the teacher in the traditional school interpreted his duty within a limited frame of reference; his service to the community lay in imparting mental training to children, being a model of deportment to his pupils, and requiring his charges to accept certain intellectual and moral standards.[5] He might influence the community, but only indirectly through the lives of his pupils and former pupils. The school, although located within the community, was separate and apart from the community in many ways. Its teachers were likely to be isolated from community affairs, little concerned with the learnings that seemed irrelevant to the fairly rigid school curriculum, largely committed to textbook and recitation methods of teaching, and more often than not, glad when parents and other adults left the school to its own devices.

THE MODERN SCHOOL

In this century ambitious and far-reaching objectives of education, among them the famous Seven Cardinal Principles of Education, have been formulated. By mid-century, delegates to the White House Conference of 1955, representative of many occupational and social groups, discussed the topic "What Should the Schools Accomplish?" Rejecting in part the traditional approach, they spelled out in detail what schools should teach pupils:

1. The fundamental skills of communication.
2. Appreciation for our democratic heritage.
3. Civic rights and responsibilities.

[5] "This doctrine [that schools are concerned solely with the intellectual] was adequate, even inevitable, as long as the village and rural community provided all the other fundamentals—work, play, social life, emotional enrichment, the sense of community, and the framework of a personal career." Joseph K. Hart, *A Social Interpretation of Education*, Holt, Rinehart, 1929, p. 6.

4. Respect and appreciation for human values and for the beliefs of others.

5. Ability to think and evaluate constructively and creatively.

6. Effective work habits and self-discipline.

7. Social competency (as contributing members of family and community).

8. Ethical behavior based on a sense of moral and spiritual values.

9. Intellectual curiosity and eagerness for lifelong learning.

10. Aesthetic appreciation and self-expression in the arts.

11. Physical and mental health.

12. Wise use of time, including constructive leisure pursuits.

13. Understanding the physical world and man's relation to it.

14. An awareness of our relationships with the world community.

By 1955 these objectives were not new. The delegates at the White House Conference simply agreed with earlier theorists when they stated that they expected schools to be concerned with the social, aesthetic, psychological, and physical development of children as well as with their character and intellectual development.

Reasons for Expanding the Objectives of Education

Three factors resulted in broadening the scope of educational objectives in the twentieth century.

First, societal changes brought about by the industrialization and urbanization of American life led to new demands upon schools. Increased enrollments, especially in high schools where numbers practically doubled every decade from 1890 to 1950, lowered the general level of academic aptitude, and created a need for curriculums appropriate for less-talented youngsters. During the depression years of the 1930s, numerous studies of the needs of youth demonstrated that many pupils found little of value in traditional curriculums. Furthermore, the rapidity of cultural change increased the problems and instability of the American family, with the result that many functions of education formerly under familial direction were virtually turned over to the school. At the same time that American parents transferred many responsibilities from the home to the school, the public often expressed an almost naïve faith in education as the answer to increasingly complex social problems and as a means to social mobility.

Second, modern psychologists developed and tested hypotheses and theories about how we learn. They discredited the theory of formal discipline and thereby dealt a staggering blow to the traditional school's insistence that children's minds are strengthened by learning mathematics, Latin, and the like. The new psychology, doubting assumptions of automatic transfer of training and emphasizing individual differences, encouraged experiments that related what was learned directly to pupils' daily lives.

Third, educational theorists in the United States began to envisage formal education as concerned with the social, emotional, and physical as well as with the intellectual and moral development of children. They talked of the "whole child" and noted the influence of out-of-school activities and environments upon learning. Experimentalists among them advocated problem-solving activities, direct participation, use of sensory experiences in learning, and the importance of facts as tools and not as ends in themselves.

Schools as Microcosms
of American Society

As a result of these new social demands, psychological insights, and philosophical concepts, the attitudes of educators, with varying degrees of alacrity, changed appreciably in respect to the school's role in

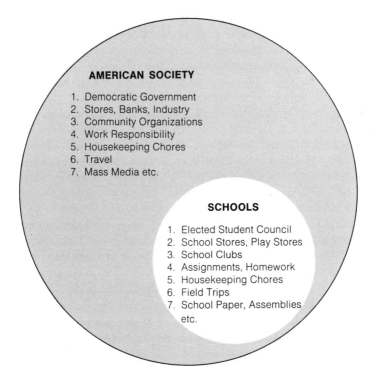

AMERICAN SOCIETY

1. Democratic Government
2. Stores, Banks, Industry
3. Community Organizations
4. Work Responsibility
5. Housekeeping Chores
6. Travel
7. Mass Media etc.

SCHOOLS

1. Elected Student Council
2. School Stores, Play Stores
3. School Clubs
4. Assignments, Homework
5. Housekeeping Chores
6. Field Trips
7. School Paper, Assemblies
   etc.

the community. The world outside the school walls took on new meaning, not only in terms of interpretation of pupil behavior but also as a model for life within the school. Although today teachers vary widely in regard to departure from traditional practices in education, most of them attempt to relate what is learned in classrooms to happenings in the larger society. They seek to reproduce real-life situations within the school to give pupils experience in solving problems similar to those they may face as adults.

The "model of the community" school seeks to determine pupil needs and devise curriculums and teaching techniques that will enable pupils to learn what they need to know for living in modern society. For example, elementary school pupils operate "stores" and "banks," care for pets, grow plants, practice good health habits, learn to eat nutritious meals, act out simple plays, listen to music, paint pictures, work with crafts, and participate in committees at the same time that they are acquiring academic skills and knowledge. High school pupils, too, are given varied opportunities to develop their interests and talents in the arts and athletics, to learn vocational and social skills, to demonstrate initiative, leadership, and good citizenship, and to select school courses in line with their interests and abilities. Classes in elementary and secondary schools study the local, national, and world society, take occasional field trips to learn about community affairs, and sometimes import speakers from the community as "resource persons" who present their experiences or points of view.

An important philosophical assumption of the modern school is that young people will become better citizens if they learn the skills of democratic living within the school. In some elementary schools hazing of younger children by older pupils has been replaced by the older children's helping and protecting the younger children. In classes pupils may aid those who have been absent to catch up with their work. The elementary school child is given many jobs in the school for which he may assume responsibility: he may operate the movie projector or the filmstrip machine, answer the school telephone, carry messages, guide visitors, act as host during lunch, take duty as a safety patrolman, assist the teacher in counting money on "bank day," and the like. Elementary children usually like school because they feel that they are helping to run the school. Presumably they are learning to be responsible and cooperative within a school that gives them more freedom than did the traditional school.

Much of the theoretical justification of the cocurriculum lies in its potential contributions to good citizenship. Part of the school's training for citizenship includes such activities as students making house-to-house calls urging people to vote, serving as "Mayor and Council for a Day," collecting money for charity drives, or working at chores to earn money for welfare agencies. In general, however, most of the civic training in modern schools occurs *within* the school with little actual participation at the community level.

Not only does the school aim to provide experiences in civic activities but also it tries to help students learn to make wise decisions. Schools, especially high schools, usually permit pupils greater freedom to make decisions in planning the cocurriculum than in the curriculum. Given freedom, young people tend to imitate their elders: School political campaigns often seem unintentionally to be satires of adult politics; elections of school queens and kings, mock United Nations assemblies, and the use of parliamentary procedure follow adult practices. The pupils' freedom to make independent decisions, even in student council and in other cocurricular matters, is subject to administrative and faculty veto. For this reason much of the democratic procedure in schools is likely to be regarded as make-believe by pupils.

Suggested Changes in Modern Schools

Surveys of community opinion of modern schools indicate that a substantial majority of the citizens approve the schools' philosophy and practices. Like principals and teachers, laymen think that schools can be improved in ways that are usually related to specific practices, not to basic objectives. There are, however, a small but vocal group of educational theorists who feel that schools have not changed enough and an equally vocal minority who believe that modern education should reassess traditional objectives and practices.

Critics who believe the school is still too traditional deplore its "lock-step" treatment of pupils, its concern with haircuts and dress of students, its invasion of privacy, its middle-class stance. They see teachers as insensitive to the needs of the majority of their pupils. They refer to an "establishment" that, they say, "pushes out" the nonconformist and "locks out" the socially disadvantaged from society's rewards. They urge that testing of mental ability be discontinued because findings are used to "discriminate" against the disadvantaged. They suggest that if a poor student had a proper self-image, he would remain in school and do acceptable academic work. The goals of the War on Poverty have added fuel to the fire of these reformers.

Tradition-oriented critics of modern schools are especially antagonistic toward including social skills, athletics, arts and crafts, dramatics, family-life education, the cocurriculum, and other activities that they call "frills" in the work of the school. They contend that the school often teaches what pupils should learn at home or what they would learn anyway. Henry Steele Commager, one of the friendlier and more constructive critics, denies that a primary duty of the schools is "adapting the young to the society." He writes:

> [Schools] should offer not a repetition of experience but a challenge to, and an extension of, experience. They are not a tranquilizer but a conscience for society.
>
> When almost every agency proclaims the merits of "private enterprise," the schools, all too often, weakly yield to pressures from filiopietistic or business organizations to beat the academic drum for private enterprise. When almost everybody reads *Reader's Digest* and *Life* and *Look* and *Newsweek* anyway and the young can be trusted to see them outside the schoolroom, students read these magazines in the schoolroom or the school library, rather than the less popular and less readily available magazines which they may otherwise never come to know. When the discussion of current events commands the daily press, the radio and television and most conversation at home, the schools, instead of diverting the young to a contemplation of the affairs of Greece and Rome or of medieval England, meekly concentrate on current affairs.[6]

Others are alarmed about the school's emphasis on smooth interpersonal relations, for they believe that the school should offset society's penchant for conformity and "getting along with others" by encouraging creativeness and original thinking. But the primary assumption of those critics, sometimes called essentialists, is that schools neglect academic subject matter. The "beefing-up" of curriculums since Sputnik has allayed some of the criticisms.

THE SCHOOL OF TOMORROW?

If present trends continue, it seems likely that one overriding objective of schools in the near future will be that of providing equality of opportunity to all young people. In a sense, this objective has always been held by both teachers and laymen in that free schools in and of themselves were assumed to provide everyone an equal chance to succeed. In the nineteenth century, each child had an "equal opportunity" to learn the same subject matter. If he did not master it, he had

[6] Henry Steele Commager, "A Historian Looks at the American High School," *School Review*, 67 (Spring, 1958), 1–18.

at least had a chance to do so. In this century, educators have interpreted "equal opportunities" differently. They have assumed that children who are unequal in interests, aptitudes, and social backgrounds have been given equal opportunities only if they have been provided learning experiences relevant to their interests and needs. The most recent interpretation is that integration of pupils of all social classes, subcultural groups, and races is essential if "equality of opportunity" is to be achieved.

Certain subsidiary objectives, less clearly dictated by social pressures in American society, are also likely to become especially important. These objectives are that schools provide students with experiences designed to improve their ability to think and evaluate, to increase their sensitivities in all affective areas, and to develop their creativeness. In effect such objectives are similar to those suggested by the White House Conference of 1955 (see p. 285), but social changes accompanying technological changes in the last ten years make these objectives imperative now. Moreover, the possibilities of their being realized are somewhat greater. Improved technology may free teachers to devote time to achieving these objectives, and advances in knowledge of social psychology and of the learning process may provide the necessary guidance.

In this section the emphasis will be upon ways to improve equality of educational opportunity.

The Rationale for Integrated Schools

As long ago as 1897, Jane Addams, addressing the National Education Association, pointed out that public schools were not successfully educating the children of Italian immigrants in urban slums. Although the inhabitants of ghettos have changed, some of the reasons she cited for the schools' failures are as valid today as they were then.[7] In subsequent years, numerous social reformers and sociological and educational researchers have also found the schools wanting in their efforts to educate the "socially disadvantaged." Scores of books have documented the low achievement scores, high drop-out rates, and other indicators of inadequacies in slum schools.

By 1967 everyone was convinced that poverty—or some would say Negroes—was the nation's most pressing domestic problem. Schools received more than a fair share of the blame. Although a long-time advocate of neoclassicism, a form of education hardly appropriate to

[7] Jane Addams, "Foreign-Born Children in the Primary Grades," *Journals of Proceedings and Addresses,* National Education Association, 1897, pp. 104–112

the education of the underprivileged, Robert Hutchins, for example, referring in his syndicated column to the 1967 Detroit riots said, "As long as the schools are used to produce and reproduce the cycle of poverty, we may expect more long, hot, dangerous summers."

Because Americans, while roundly criticizing schools and teachers, firmly believe that education can solve social problems, the federal government has spent millions in educational research, counselor and teacher education, and special educational programs for the disadvantaged. The Office of Economic Opportunity has also devoted a large portion of its resources to educational activities. Almost all of the federal aid to education has, in fact, directly or indirectly helped schools in the slums to the extent of improving teaching strategies and curriculums. In spite of the upgrading of public school education in recent years, the problem of educating the socially disadvantaged is a long way from being solved. Skirmishes in the War on Poverty may have been won, but no major battles can be cited as having turned the tide that will lead to victory.

Perhaps the War on Poverty can never be won by present tactics. Being impoverished means not having enough money for essentials. One is not impoverished simply because he cannot spell, speak correctly, or demonstrate other academic skills. He may be able to do all of these, and still be poor if he is ill, underemployed, unemployed, poorly paid, too young or too old to work. Obviously education may be the magic key by which some poor children escape from poverty, but it does not guarantee success for all of the disadvantaged because children learn more in the slum neighborhoods from friends, parents, and other associates than they do in schools.

Furthermore, pupils in schools that enroll only disadvantaged pupils suffer from the "cumulative disadvantage of their classmates," a report of the U.S. Commission on Civil Rights states.[8] These pupils measure their accomplishments by the standards set by their classmates. They have no models representing different kinds of behavior with whom to identify. Coleman's extensive survey revealed that Negroes attending schools in which most of the students were white scored higher on achievement tests than did Negroes attending schools in which most of the students were Negroes.[9] Moreover, in the case of predominantly Negro schools, students and their parents tend to believe that because they are judged to be inferior they are provided with inferior schools.

[8] *Racial Isolation in the Public Schools,* Report of the U.S. Commission on Civil Rights, Government Printing Office, 1967.
[9] James S. Coleman, *Equality of Opportunity,* U.S. Office of Health, Education, and Welfare, Government Printing Office, 1966, pp. 330–331.

The assumptions that their schools are inferior and that perhaps others are right in attributing to them inferior academic potentialities lower the self-concepts of Negro students. When they believe they cannot learn, they do not learn.

The Supreme Court's decision of 1954 that schools segregated by law (de jure segregation) were not providing equal educational opportunity was based in part on the evidence of social scientists that segregation breeds feelings of inferiority. In recent court decisions in Massachusetts and Washington, D.C., lower court judges have ruled that schools segregated by housing patterns (de facto segregation) were not providing equal opportunity.[10] The Supreme Court has not, however, ruled on this issue. In the judgment of many educational leaders, the most promising plan for achieving equality of educational opportunity for lower-class whites and other minority groups as well as Negroes is to build educational parks or plazas.

Advantages and Disadvantages of Educational Parks

An educational park or plaza is a large campus set aside in a small city or several large campuses in large cities on which many educational buildings serving large numbers of students are located. In East Orange, New Jersey, for example, plans are underway to locate the whole school system from kindergarten through community college on a central site called a plaza. Boulder, Colorado, a city of about 80,000, has a similar plan that calls for an educational park. Variations of the plan are being put into effect or are in effect in the Lewiston-Porter school near Niagara Falls, New York, as well as in Evanston, Illinois, the Orange district near Cleveland, Ohio, Syracuse, New York, Pittsburgh, Pennsylvania, Berkeley, California, Seattle, Washington, Little Rock, Arkansas, and Albuquerque, New Mexico.[11]

Advocates of an educational park cite the following advantages that accrue from consolidating educational services:

First, a large, centrally located school can support the best educational program. Advanced academic and highly specialized vocational courses that are of interest to only a few students can be made avail-

[10] Barksdale v. Springfield School Commission, Massachusetts, 1965, and Hobson v. Hanson, Washington, D. C., 1967.

[11] See "The Park Way," *Newsweek,* (July 18, 1966), p. 48; Robert G. Lamp, "Educational Parks for Twentieth Century Schools," *CTA Journal,* 62 (October, 1966), 10–15; Max Wolff, "Educational Park Concept," *Wilson Library Bulletin,* 42 (October, 1967), 173–175; and David F. Sine, Max Wolff, and Lucile Lindberg, "Opinions Differ: Educational Parks," *NEA Journal,* 57 (March, 1968), 44–47.

able in a school that brings together all students who may want such courses. Clearly better and more modern facilities for vocational training, language courses, and science education can be provided in one large school than in many smaller schools.

Second, a large school plant is efficient because audiovisual centers, remedial and guidance staff, nurses and health clinics, libraries, facilities for the blind and deaf, and other services are nearby. Such services and facilities are equitably spread. No longer, for example, will schools farthest from a central library use the library less often than do those nearby. Various specialists shared by schools will not need to spend a part of the day commuting from school to school.

Third, many pupils who now transfer to different schools every year will no longer change schools. Although about 20 percent of all Americans move each year, two-thirds of them move to other houses within the city limits. Under existing systems many of these local moves require pupils to transfer to different schools. Changing teachers, friends, and schools disrupts the education of children. Pupils who transfer make extra work for guidance counselors, clerical workers, and teachers. If local moving did not require school transfers, about two out of three of these transfers would be eliminated.

Fourth, in a consolidated system, teachers in special subjects and at different grade levels would be readily available for in-service training and for free exchange of ideas about improving programs.

Fifth, this plan offsets the disadvantages of ecological patterns in the city. Socially homogeneous neighborhood schools that tend to separate children along socioeconomic lines would be eliminated. Children from middle- and upper-class families would learn to be sensitive to the needs of others by associating with children from less privileged homes. Except in our largest cities, socially disadvantaged children could be readily assimilated in an educational park because they constitute at most only a fifth of our population and less than half of them are Negroes. These children would escape the feelings of apathy, resentment, and hopelessness that permeate their neighborhoods and learn different attitudes from their classmates.

But a large urban school of this sort brings problems of its own. Children may suffer from feelings of rootlessness and anonymity in a mammoth school. They may feel pressures from bureaucratic rigidity and specialization. Even young adults in American colleges, better able to fend for themselves than children, react negatively to the impersonality and inflexibility of the multiversity. The response of younger students in a similar situation is likely to be withdrawal rather than rioting, but a negative reaction is not conducive to learning.

The dangers inherent in a large school can be obviated by dividing it into small schools. A high school of 10,000 pupils would then become 15 high schools of 650 pupils, who live in various neighborhoods in the city. Each of the 15 schools would have its own faculty, administration, classes, and activity program. A pupil would go to the high school next door only if it offered a course not available in his own school. The elementary school would be similarly divided. The so-called "Oxford Plan" or "House Plan," modeled on the system at Oxford University, has been instituted in Newark, Ohio, in Parker School near Portland, Oregon, and other high schools as well as in a number of colleges and universities. This plan gives students the social climate of a small school while providing them with the academic benefits of a large school.[12]

Assuming that the house plan solves the problem of the social climate in the large school, what is the cost of such a school? School boards find that costs depend upon the condition of available local facilities, land values, and future space requirements. The East Orange School Board's estimates show that building entirely new facilities over a period of time will cost no more than renovating the old buildings now in use. If the population of the United States doubles within the next twenty years, as demographers predict, some modification of the educational park plan may be practical in most American cities. Certainly locating new school buildings centrally is not more costly than building them in widely separated places.

A major obstacle to educational parks is lack of adequate transportation. How would children in a city get to school? Community leaders have wrestled with the problem of public transportation for a long time with little success. The only sensible answer in cities is mass transit, but Americans have been reluctant to give up their automobiles or to subsidize local transportation. Robert Somerville, president of the Atlanta Transit System, said a $1 monthly charge added to the water bill could provide no-fare transportation for his city. Tokyo has a fast and safe monorail. Even if no such bold scheme is adopted, school leaders who already bus pupils living more than one mile from school would probably not find the additional costs prohibitive.

The last but by no means the least difficult hurdle for advocates of a consolidated school is winning parental support. Parents like neighborhood schools. Sometimes they move to a neighborhood because they like its school. Wouldn't these same parents like a consolidated school if their children could get a better education there? Perhaps,

12 See "How to Make a Big School Little," *School Management, 6* (February, 1962), 59–63.

but experience in consolidating rural schools suggests that much persuasion, education, and possibly coercion will be needed.

Parents like what they regard as traditional. Actually, the socially homogeneous neighborhood school is not traditional. Prior to World War II when neither tract housing nor zoning regulations were common, the population of the neighborhood school represented a cross section of American society.

Parents say they like to live within walking distance of their children's school, yet they often drive their children a few blocks to school and almost never walk that distance themselves. When they have a child in elementary school and another in junior high school, often at least one of these schools is not nearby. And, if they choose to send their children to a parochial, private, or special school miles away from their homes, they somehow reconcile themselves to the greater distance.

Although the educational park plan is assumed by many school leaders to be a better solution to urban educational problems than the neighborhood school, others believe that revitalizing the neighborhood school would better serve slum areas. The latter propose a Community School. In a sense almost any public school is a community school in that it serves a particular community, but the Community School concept implies more than simply a geographical location.

The Community School Alternative

The originator of the Community School concept has never been clearly identified. Several chroniclers of the history of the Community School suggest that the idea came from Joseph K. Hart, who wrote in 1918:

> The problem of democratic education is not the problem of training children. It is the problem of *making a community* in which children cannot help growing up to be democratic, intelligent, disciplined to freedom, reverent of the good things of life, and eager to share in the tasks of the age. A school cannot produce this result; nothing but a community can do so.[13]

Undoubtedly the Community School is an outgrowth of pragmatic theory as expounded by John Dewey. Although Dewey's experimental school at the University of Chicago was, in fact, a "model of the community" type, he gave his blessing to the Community School work

[13] Joseph K. Hart, *Democracy in Education*, Appleton-Century-Crofts, 1918, p. 372.

of Elsie Clapp. When Miss Clapp consulted him about undertaking the experiment at Ballard School in Kentucky, Dewey said, "I cannot urge you to do it, because I think it would be difficult, but . . . I would like to see such a dream come true. Before long we are going to need community schools in this country, and someone must learn by doing it just what a community school is and does."[14]

The chief innovations of the Community School are its insistence that the primary function of the school is to "improve the quality of living here and now" and its assertion that the school should lead in community coordination. This means that the school is as concerned with the education of adults as with the tutelage of children and that the school assumes a leadership role whenever community improvement is needed. What is learned in school is related to what goes on in the community. The "essential characteristic" of the Community School is its "real-life activities" that engage students in cooperative efforts with community adults and teachers.[15]

The Community School, then, has the following characteristics:

It improves the quality of living here and now. The school works with the community in solving problems of immediate concern, such as unemployment, intergroup relations, mental health, divorce, crime, juvenile delinquency, labor-management disputes, sanitation, beautification, and scientific farming.

It uses the community as a laboratory for learning. The school makes use of field trips, resource speakers, community materials, and work experience. It encourages pupils to assist with community projects.

It makes the school plant a community center. School facilities are available to all for study, work, and play.

It organizes the curriculum around the fundamental processes and problems of living. The required, or core, curriculum deals with such problems as adjusting to people, exchanging ideas orally and in writing, making a living, sharing in citizenship, maintaining health, improving family living, finding a life philosophy, and utilizing the natural environment.

It includes lay people in school policy and program planning. Laymen are not only members of school boards and of the PTA, but also of advisory councils and study committees.

It leads in community coordination. The Community School not

---

[14] Elsie Ripley Clapp, *The Use of Resources in Education*, Harper & Row, 1952, p. 8.

[15] Edward G. Olsen, ed., *The Modern Community School*, Appleton-Century-Crofts, 1953, pp. 201–203.

only cooperates with other community agencies, but also accepts responsibility for bringing these agencies together.

It practices and promotes democracy in all human relationships. Citizens, parents, teachers, pupils, and administrators work together in the formulation of policy. Democratic ideals are encouraged, and undemocratic behavior is discountenanced. The teaching method is problem-solving.[16]

Ever since 1919 when Evelyn Dewey described the remarkable work of Mrs. Marie Turner Harvey at Porter Community School near Kirksville, Missouri, reports of successful Community Schools, usually operating in rural or slum areas, have appeared periodically in educational publications. Little has been added to the Community School concept since Mrs. Harvey's day. Mrs. Harvey transformed a dilapidated one-room schoolhouse into a clean, well-heated, attractive school by persuading the school board to invest small sums and by soliciting labor from parents and others in the community. The school's flexible curriculum grew out of community needs: students planted gardens at school, raised pigs and poultry, learned to beautify their homes and school with vines and shrubbery, waged war successfully against the blister beetle and other pests, tested corn for seed, and read agricultural bulletins published by the government and the state college. Their spelling and writing lessons grew out of talks about their agricultural work. Mrs. Harvey found time, too, to help the older boys organize a band and to teach her pupils about happenings outside the local area. During World War I the community was ready with the right kinds of produce needed in the war effort. All this took place in the face of stubborn opposition from conservative farmers who distrusted scientific methods of farming advocated by state-college professors, but who grudgingly accepted their children's successes.[17]

By 1938 other studies of Community Schools were published. Often hailed as the pioneer study, *The Community School* describes two community programs of high schools in underprivileged areas—Welles High School in Chicago and Benjamin Franklin High School in New York City, two programs in small high schools—Dalton in New York City and the Glencoe, Illinois, High School—and five programs in rural areas.[18] The same year Clapp describes programs in the Ballard School in Kentucky and the Arthurdale School in West Virginia.[19] In

[16] Edward G. Olsen, *et al., School and Community*, Prentice-Hall, 1954, chap. 1.

[17] Evelyn Dewey, *New Schools for Old*, Dutton, 1919, *passim.*

[18] Society for Curriculum Study, in Samuel Everett, ed., *The Community School*, Appleton-Century-Crofts, 1938.

[19] Elsie Ripley Clapp, *Community Schools in Action*, Viking, 1939.

the late 1930s the Sloan Foundation financed attempts to improve diet, housing, and clothing in rural communities in Kentucky, Florida, and Vermont through teaching children better practices. Most of these programs were developed in places that were hit hard by the depression and in rural and underprivileged areas.

Although there seems to have been a lull in Community School activities during World War II, numerous other descriptive accounts of Community School programs appeared in the literature of the 1940s and 1950s. The National Society for the Study of Education's 1952 yearbook on the Community School begins with the statement, "Americans are becoming more and more interested in the community school."[20]

The oldest Community School in a city is in Flint, Michigan. Begun with a $6000 gift from an industrialist, the Flint plan has stimulated widespread citizen participation in educational and recreational programs. The Charles Stewart Mott Foundation, established soon after the initial grant in 1926, continues to pay a fraction of the costs and the taxpayers pay the remainder for a remarkably successful program. Schools are equipped as community centers in which thousands of adults study high school and other courses; civic clubs, theater casts, and dance groups meet; and young people engage in recreational activities. Adults assist in many phases of the school's programs. Every year people come from all over the world to observe the Flint Community School.[21]

Less successful Community School programs were sponsored by the W. K. Kellogg Foundation in the late 1940s and early 1950s in Michigan and in Texas. The accounts of Community Schools do not explain why some of them have been very successful and others have failed.

Many of the current programs for the disadvantaged are modeled on the Community School. Federally financed programs under ESEA and OEO have solicited the active involvement of adults in improving the school and community. In big cities, teachers have led students in clean-up campaigns. Efforts have been made to make the school a community center for the activities of adults as well as children. Schools have hired professionals who serve as liaison agents to coordinate the efforts of schools with those of other community agencies. In such schools, the curriculum has been geared more closely than in former years to "real-life activities."

[20] National Society for the Study of Education, 52nd Yearbook, part 2, Nelson B. Henry, ed., *The Community School*, University of Chicago Press, 1953, p. 1.
[21] See Leo E. Buehring, "New Pattern: Community Schools," *Nation's Schools*, (January, 1958), 35–39, for an enthusiastic account of the Flint school.

Increasingly popular with many Negro leaders is support for schools of their own rather than integration of colored children into white schools. They insist that leadership of Negro communities and schools should be the responsibility of Negroes. If they have in mind making their schools Community Schools, they may succeed in vitalizing their communities. Much can be said for community and school action in terms of its effects upon group morale and individual growth. In Philadelphia, for example, Negro leaders have established cooperative businesses that have provided jobs and bargain prices for Negroes. Nevertheless, the element of separatism and violence in the Black Power movement poses a threat to national unity.

Our principal concern here, however, is the relative merits of educational parks and Community Schools with respect to equality of educational opportunity and the development of the intellectual and affective capacities of all children, irrespective of color.

Educational Parks and
Community Schools Compared

As indicated above, both educational parks and Community Schools display features that are desirable in a highly urbanized society. Which type will probably provide greater equality of opportunity for all? If Coleman's tentative conclusion as paraphrased in the bitter words of Floyd McKissick, leader of CORE, "mix Negroes with Negroes and you get stupidity," is correct, Community Schools in Negro neighborhoods will not achieve the equality of opportunity Negroes seek.[22] When McKissick added, "A school *can* achieve excellence [even] if the community is poor and black," he spoke the truth, for some Community Schools in impoverished districts have indeed been markedly successful.

Community Schools in ghettos may succeed for several reasons. Since Negro parents are more likely than white parents in the lower class to show concern for the education of their children,[23] the school's chances of reaching these parents and teaching them how to help improve their children's school work are good. The new feeling of pride in race may also be an asset. Since Community Schools tend to engage the idealism, energies, and enthusiasms of young people working with adults in constructive community improvements, delinquency may be reduced and concern for the welfare of others increased.

[22] Coleman, *op. cit.*
[23] *Ibid.*, p. 302.

On the other hand, implementing the Community School concept requires an exceptional teaching staff dedicated to the concept, an extensive school plant, and solutions to the problems of legal liability and school costs when students are not on the school premises, yet under the school's supervision. Obviously the Community School, which draws from a neighborhood, is not able to promote interracial and inter-class understanding through interaction to the extent that is possible in an educational park. Furthermore, the Community School is less likely than educational parks to be able to provide an extensive educational program and a wide variety of readily available resources.

Earlier discussion identified problems of an educational park system. Its chief disadvantage from the point of view of both equality of opportunity and student growth is that it is less likely to succeed in involving all students in school work and in eliciting parental support from lower-class parents who may live some distance from the park. If experience in comprehensive high schools is repeated in the park plan, middle-class cliques of young people will not usually associate with children of the lower classes. To achieve close interaction among all students, school faculties in educational parks will have to become much more concerned with the quality of school social life than most faculties in comprehensive schools have been in the past.

IMPORTANT CONCEPTS

Essentialists. Persons who hope to reduce the content of school curriculums to so-called essentials. See pp. 289–290.

Experimentalists. Followers of John Dewey whose prescribed educational methods derive from their philosophical assumptions about knowledge and values. They hold ideas and values as tentative until tested in experience. See p. 287.

Theory of formal discipline. The theory that particular branches of study, such as mathematics, Latin, and logic, give a general mental training or discipline that favorably affects ability in other branches of learning. See pp. 283 ff.

IV. SCHOOL CULTURE

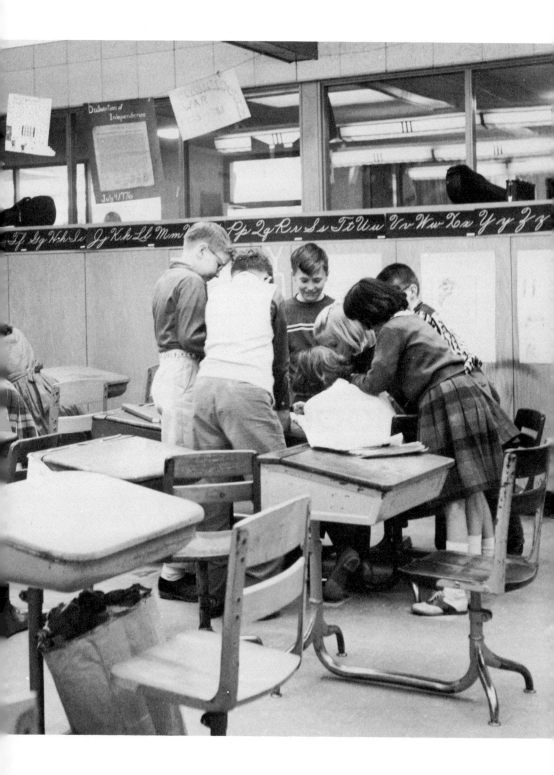

14. ELEMENTARY SCHOOL CULTURE

In short, a substantial body of evidence justifies two conclusions: 1) Teachers differ reliably from one another . . . 2) These reliable differences among teachers are, by and large, consistently related to various desirable things about teachers.

—NATHANIEL L. GAGE[1]

Culture, in its anthropological meaning, entails the notion of an overall design for living, a mode, or as Ruth Benedict describes it, a pattern of life.[2] School culture, then, is the pattern of life found in the school. Pupils, who acquire this culture as knowledge accumulated through experience, learn to accept certain values, attitudes, and ways of behaving as right and appropriate. If an observer would understand why pupils choose one way of behaving rather than another, he has to know what values, attitudes, and standards of behavior the pupils have accepted.

Each school, even each classroom, has its own culture, its own agreed-upon values, attitudes, and behavior norms. Because this culture is representative of that of the United States yet different in certain ways, it is called a subculture. Thus the term subculture applies to any group whose pattern of life overlaps and yet conflicts with our society's culture. For example, adolescents may share a teenage or a delinquent subculture; persons living in New England or Texas may share the New England or the Texan subculture. Individuals may also share the subculture of their kinship group, their social class, their religious affiliation, their country of origin, and their leisure or occupational group. Classrooms in the elementary school, more than classrooms in high school, provide an environment in which a subculture develops.

The subculture of a school or classroom is influenced not only by national and local culture but also by the public's expectations of schools, by other subcultures to which pupils and teachers belong, and by the school's characteristics. But school culture is ever-changing—a mosaic of the cultures carried into it by individuals and modified by encounters of pupils and teachers with new problems and circumstances. New values emerge and old ones persist. Analyzing such a dynamic subculture is not an easy undertaking.

Note: This chapter was written by John Connelly and Grace Graham.

[1] Nathaniel L. Gage, "Can Science Contribute to the Art of Teaching?" *Phi Delta Kappan,* 49 (March, 1968), 402.

[2] Ruth Benedict, *Patterns of Culture,* Mentor Books, 1934.

ANALYSIS OF SCHOOL CULTURE

Culture in the school, as in any other social group, can only be inferred from observing the behavior of individuals in their day by day activities. An untrained observer needs guidelines pointing to facets of the culture that furnish clues useful in a systematic analysis. We are, therefore, suggesting 11 factors to consider in analyzing a subculture, whether of a school, a classroom, or a special group such as teachers, students, or administrators. These 11 factors are as follows:

Location—the physical surroundings in which the group operates.

Composition—personal characteristics of individuals who belong to the group.

Purposes—how the group defines its objectives; the things the group seeks; the group's raison d'etre.

Functions—activities carried on to sustain the group in its purposes.

Values—the shared possessions and ideals of the group; the things the group prizes.

Structure—the relatively permanent organization within the group.

Kinship—the internal relationships within the group.

Associations—relationships outside of the group that influence its internal behavior.

Change—alterations and modifications of the group.

Continuity—values, attitudes, and behavior norms that persist in the group.

Equipment—tools, supplies, and facilities available for use by the group.

To illustrate how applying these factors aids analysis, three third grades are described in the section that follows. Some of these factors cannot be definitively explored within the confines of a single chapter. For example, the short description of the composition of the class is admittedly inadequate to explain how the cultural patterns that each individual brings from home to the classroom are modified by the ethos of the classroom.

The pupils and the teacher are the central figures in the classroom subculture. The world in which third-graders live may be described as a separate subculture just as can the teen-age culture. Nevertheless, the teacher has a key role in molding the culture of a third-grade classroom, which is usually more influential than the dispersed effects of the multiple-teacher influences upon high school culture. Because the teacher is so important in the three third grades, use of the 11 factors for analysis brings to the fore personality descriptions of the teachers and an account of each teacher's interaction within the classroom and within the school.

As you read the descriptions of these third grades, you may benefit from thinking through the following questions:

What values does each teacher demonstrate in her choice of teaching methods?

In what respect was each of these groups of children learning a version of democracy?

To what extent does each of the 11 factors account for some of the differences found in these classes?

THREE THIRD GRADES

The third-grade classes of Catherine Jordan, Mary Anton, and Martha Cope are located in Jefferson Elementary School. The community served by Jefferson School is predominantly "common man" American. The heads of families are engaged in small trades and service businesses or they are skilled workers. They are neither rich nor poor.

Catherine Jordan and Martha Cope came to the school in 1935 and stayed there. Mary Anton came in 1966 as a beginning teacher. All three teachers are keenly interested in teaching and conscientiously concerned for the learning of their pupils. A testing program revealed the three classes taught by them are at a high level of academic achievement.

The culture of each classroom is, however, distinct, due not only to the different methods and personalities of the teachers but also to the other aspects of culture listed earlier. Let us apply these factors to each of the three classes.

Catherine Jordan's Class

Location. Miss Jordan's classroom is adjacent to the main entrance of the main corridor of the building. Its windows face the street. From the room the entrance walk is clearly visible. The entrance, the main corridor, the front lawn, and the driveway adjoining the auditorium effectively isolate the room from other classrooms and their activities.

Composition. The class has 40 children, 25 girls and 15 boys. The children are all of Anglo-American descent. All of them were 8 years of age at the end of January of this school year. There are only slight differences in height among the girls, and all of the boys tend to be short.

Purposes and Functions. In addition to accepting the common purposes for all three third grades as expressed in the state course of study and the local school guide, Miss Jordan stresses detailed excellence. Children are frequently seen checking each other's papers, looking for and pointing out small details in handwriting, making distinctions between assertedly correct forms. The children are almost brittlely individualistic and competitive since neatness is also highly stressed by teacher. The children, especially the girls, are highly responsive to this charge in their dress, fussing with straightening their clothes as well as their desks. Memorization is encouraged by the teacher, but the children spur each other into competitive memorization of poetry, the competition being based upon length of poem or number of poems. There tends to be a degree of satisfaction in seeking out unusual arithmetic problems or lengthy and unusual words for spelling contests. Speed is another pronounced emphasis within the group, and children can be observed shifting their eyes toward the work of others to check how far down their papers they have written, or how many problems they have done. Although finishing an assigned task first is a prized accomplishment, a student loses first place if the task is not also exact and correct in detail.

This group and other classes in the school interact very little, even on the playgrounds. The group seems to be proud of its insularity and its solidarity. This pride does not appear as contempt for other groups, but rather as a search for distinctiveness.

Values. Miss Jordan's group demonstrates that it values teacher approval and success in competitive achievement. Miss Jordan manages to give each child tasks at which he can succeed and win approval. The children seem to be aware of the situation, but nevertheless each child strives for such success and approval. The primary student avenue for such gains is through attention to order and accuracy, which become valued in themselves. Democracy is taught as a thing of value and is accepted as a value in the sense of parliamentary rule and regulation. Democracy as a value expressed in behavior becomes a well regulated system of fairness.

Structure. The structure of Miss Jordan's group is formal and traditional. The teacher role is superordinate and conspicuous. The teacher is authoritarian and directive of the group. The pupils accept the traditional position of subordinates and seldom question the authority of the teacher.

Kinship. The interpersonal relations within the group are highly individualized and competitive, but consolidated against outside groups or individuals. The group solidarity, however, is superficial in that it does not function internally; sub rosa cliques, divisive though secret, develop to contain excessive satisfactions in the form of successes and approvals. Internally the group is marked by a hypersensitivity that places individuals in a position of anticipating threat. Gossip and lying emerge as restraints to aggressions that become intolerable.

Associations. This class is strongly influenced not only by the family groups of its members, but also by the school office staff, the secretary, the record clerk, and the principal. The interaction with the office staff is on two levels, that of Miss Jordan and that of the pupils. This dualism leaves both the teacher and the students without some of the knowledge gained: i.e., the students are more likely than the teacher to be acquainted with other children's parents who visit the school; the relationship of Miss Jordan to the adults in the office group gives her information not available to the students. The limited and discrete exchanges of information within the classroom tend to intensify the attention of the class as a whole on the affairs of the school office. The main entrance to the school is in clear view of the room and few entries are made that escape the notice of some members of the class.

Change. Miss Jordan strongly resists changes in her physical environment, her role as a teacher, and in her methods of teaching. Although she subscribes verbally to the popular view that change (often interpreted as progress) is a cultural good, her influence in selecting pupils of homogeneous ethnic and socioeconomic origins demonstrates her unwillingness to accept pupils who are different from those she has always taught. Her mind set against change, including alteration or modification of her position in the school order, has repercussions upon the behavior of her group of third graders. Exact, detailed attention to assignments marks the behavior of the children. Dependency upon her approval gives Miss Jordan the power to hold to a firm, definite course of action, thus maintaining group behavior within bounds and holding deviations to a minimum.

Continuity. Miss Jordan has scheduled a definite time for each activity. The group clearly recognizes that at certain times in the day, week, and month of the year specific activities are scheduled to take place. Thus pupils anticipate the occurrence and recurrence of learning experiences.

Equipment. The usual supplies and furnishings of a typical schoolroom are found in Miss Jordan's room, as in the other third-grade rooms. In this room everything has a designated place to which it is promptly returned after use. Misplaced equipment provokes irritation that can be observed in Miss Jordan's instructions to replace equipment in its proper place or in the admonitions of the children to each other to "put things where they belong." The children are constantly reminded of the equipment and their privilege in having it. Equipment is highly regarded as a possession in and of itself, with use of it being minimal and preservation of it maximal.

Mary Anton's Class

Location. Mary Anton's room is located in the far end of what is known as the primary wing of the school. It has windows facing the street and front lawn, but is too distant for the main entrance walk to be observed from the classroom. The end wall, adjoining a section of the playground has small, high windows. Even when they are closed, playground noises can be heard. The opposite wall separates the classroom from a room occupied by a kindergarten. Ordinarily the noises of the kindergarten group do not penetrate the wall, but occasionally the sound of the piano and singing can be heard. Across the corridor is the third-grade classroom of Martha Cope.

Composition. Miss Anton's class has 40 children, 21 girls and 19 boys. In the class are two boys and two girls from Spanish-American families, and in both cases the boys are 9 years old and the girls 8. Two girls and three boys, all 8-year-olds and from different families, are Negroes. One 10-year-old boy is from a family of recent Italian immigrants. He has a friendly open personality, but he spoke no English prior to coming to school this year. He has learned English rapidly and is well liked by the other children. Two children, a boy and girl, both 8 years old and unrelated, are foster children living in a home designated by the court. A girl in the fifth grade and another in the sixth grade, also foster children, live in this home. The 16 girls and 12 boys comprising the rest of the class are Anglo-Americans. Two of these boys are recent arrivals from Texas, and one girl came from Indiana after the opening of school.

Purposes and Functions. This group does not seem to seek out distinctive chores or assignments but rather gives great emphasis to its search for relationships. The teacher places strong emphasis upon making use of what is learned, and the children spend considerable time in experimenting with alternatives. For example, they look for varieties of uses for a given thing even to the point of the ridiculous; one youngster stated that a ruler could be used to prop up a window sash if its cord was broken. Competition, although evident, is not strongly individualized; it is more often intergroup, with great flexibility and ease for individual movement from one group to another. The pupils demonstrate a sense of fair play, but they do not hesitate to make up new sets of rules or to change old ones. Anger is not unknown in the group, but there seems to be general pride in what the children express as "Aw, forget it!" At times appearing to be fairly raucous, the group also seems adept at leaving off playfulness and quickly moving toward serious tasks set for them. Restraint is almost immediate. To the oppositional values of freedom and security is thus added the value of balance, or consistency. The salient value, however, appears to be the excitement of being able to explore radical ideas and to suggest far-out as well as sensible solutions to problems.

Values. In Miss Anton's group the chief value seems to be the experiencing of both freedom and restraint, with a resultant understanding of how a balance is achieved. The children express great satisfaction in making suggestions, even wild ones, and experimenting freely, knowing that they can do so because their teacher will bring them down to earth when they get too far out of line. On occasions when youngsters fail to respond as quickly as their peers deem satisfactory, they are given severe scowling stares by the others. The children are verbally impulsive and they convey an impression of disorder, yet the room has an orderly appearance. The pupils use books and materials freely, but with an attitude of conserving them. Their attitude toward the use of things is similar to those toward their use of time—a balance of freedom and restraint.

Structure. Here, as in Miss Jordan's class, the teacher is central and demonstrates traditional authoritarianism in her role as teacher, strongly modified by democratic ethics. Her authority must be recognized, but is utilized sparingly. The teacher role emerges then as one in which individual freedom is encouraged without losing sight of the need for protection of individual rights through restraining authority. The student's role is clearly subordinate but allows a highly tolerant range of freedom.

Kinship. In Miss Anton's group interpersonal relationships are open and friendly. The impulse is to aid others and to trust others. There is little need here for protecting bruised confidence. Trust in obtaining help is as habitual as the impulse to give help. Successes and failures being shared experiences, members of the group have little feeling of threat.

Associations. The major outside influences upon the class, aside from the families of the class members, come from the two kindergartens— the one in the adjoining room and the one across the hall from it. The teacher has exploited the seniority sense of her class in promoting a protective interest in the children in the kindergartens. This interest has, in turn, a reciprocity facet in the admiration of the younger children for the older. A second influence is Miss Cope's third-grade group across the hall. This influence promotes some degree of ambivalence in Miss Anton's class as well as some common enterprises that tend to enhance the group. They feel the other third grade to be, in a psychological sense, their seniors. These classes do not have common interests in play activities because the other third grade does not share their team-activity interests. The primary influence of Miss Cope's group is in joint sharing of scientific experiments and activities. The two grades frequently borrow materials and exchange information.

Change. Miss Anton is confident and open. The children of her group demonstrate a similar kind of behavioral pattern. As she reaches out for new ideas to assess and utilize, so do the children. In both instances, however, there is a recognized limit to experimentation. Change in group experience is positive in that it is encouraged and at the same time moderated. Miss Anton does not fear experimentation by the children, but neither does she lose sight of where it may lead. When it threatens the integrity and stability of the group, she injects the restraint necessary to keep the group from disintegrating. Change in the group is not rejected nor is it disrupted by unleashed individualism. Miss Anton's stress upon controlled relationships tends to facilitate cooperative, interdependent behavior.

Continuity. Mary Anton's time schedule for classes is not rigid. Her scheduling provides general time allotments subject to modification as events suggest. The children may recognize that, if circumstances make change advisable, spelling could take place after arithmetic or even be skipped today and "made up" later. The flexibility in the management of the time periods encourages a flexibility in the nature of the pupil behavior in the learning activities.

Equipment. In this group equipment is valued for its use. It is regarded as expendable as long as it is not wasted or abused. At times, but not ordinarily, material or equipment may be adapted to uses other than those for which it was originally intended.

Martha Cope's Class

Location. Miss Cope's classroom, across the corridor from Mary Anton's classroom, has windows facing the main play yard of the school. The end wall of this room, like Miss Anton's, has small high windows. The adjoining room, occupied by a kindergarten, has a second entry leading to the playground, but Miss Cope's room does not.

Composition. The class has 40 children, 31 boys and 9 girls. Four girls and three boys are Negroes. One boy is Spanish-American. A girl and a boy, first cousins, arrived with their families from England shortly before the opening of the school year. The other four girls in the class are Anglo-Americans whose families have resided in the neighborhood for many years. Four boys in the class are American Indians, one Pueblo and three Navajo. The Navajo boys have never attended Indian schools on the reservation, but all have visited relatives there. The Pueblo boy has spent 2 years in an Indian school near his home village in New Mexico. All four boys speak English well. The Navajo boys declare they know no Navajo, yet on various occasions they have been heard to use it; the Pueblo boy speaks his native tongue and seems proud to speak it. He discusses freely the language with his classmates and teaches them words at times. The other 22 boys in the class are of Anglo-American families, all but one of whom have been long-time residents of the neighborhood. In four cases both the mothers and fathers were once pupils of Miss Cope. In two cases the mothers had been, and in seven cases the fathers had been. The one recent arrival is a boy whose family came from Vermont during the past summer.

Purposes and Functions. The most emphatic purpose of this group is to promote freedom to inquire and experiment. The inquiry and experimentation are not limited to matters of science, although from the standpoint of equipment, science seems to command the room space. Art work is also experimental, and the children demonstrate what seems to be a high degree of musical capability for 8- and 9-year-olds. In both of the other third grades the children are shifting from manuscript (often called printing) to cursive writing; no attention is being given to this matter in Miss Cope's class. It is interesting to observe the children's record-keeping on projects, because in their use of manuscript writing their letters are almost as precise in appearance as those of the children who made studied effort for accuracy of detail. Their handwriting has a quality of maturity because it is a recording skill rather than a writing skill. The over-all purpose in this group seems to be learning by experimenting.

Values. The prime value of this group appears to be enjoyment of its increasing maturity in its ability to explore and to command. The group's classroom behavior reveals a maturing, steadily accumulating interest, but outside the classroom the group seems to explode in

physical activity. It shows little interest in acquiring skills for organized team competition. Simple running, shouting, and throwing
mark the playground activity of the group and express the exuberance
that the children do not demonstrate in the classroom.

Structure. In comparison with the other two classes, Miss Cope's
class appears to be highly disorganized. The small group of nine girls
among the 31 boys appears to band together and function as a group
matriarchy, protecting itself with a manner of aloof confidence. In a
sense, this is a purpose of a group within a group. This little group's
manner is not antagonistic, nor does it appear to provoke antagonism.
The four Negro girls seem to hold leadership jointly but without
excluding the other girls. Maturational differences between boys and
girls appear most pronouncedly in this class. The girls are almost
womanly in manner, and the boys childish. The girls seem to cultivate
and enjoy this role of differentiation.

Miss Cope is almost lost in the classroom and has to be looked for.
In both of the other classes the teacher is always conspicuous and
filling the position with enough assertion to elicit attention from pupils.
In this situation Miss Cope seems deliberately to avoid any expression
of authoritarianism. She seems, upon close observation of her movement in the group, to have chosen to become a teacher who provides
continuous individual attention. The group provides its own leadership
positions, but one by one and one after another, individuals move to
and from the teacher as she also moves to and from them. Pupils can
be observed approaching her as emissaries of several other youngsters
working together. Individualism here, as in Miss Anton's class, seems
to be of a cooperative rather than a competitive character. Whereas in
Miss Anton's class there is a clearly recognizable contrast between
freedom and restraint, the restraint in this group does not appear in
Miss Cope's overt actions. The students tend to establish internalized
personal controls to provide restraint. Release from this self-control on
the playground is unorganized in its expression and highly explosive.
The freedom of the pupils is obvious to an apparent point of confusion, but this appearance is deceptive. If a visitor quietly asks a
student what he is doing, he looks surprised. Whether working alone
or with others, the individual or individuals of the group are quite
clear and confident about the purpose of their activity.

Kinship. In Miss Cope's group, interpersonal relations are highly
trusting, but they are sustained only through periods of common
interests. Excepting the strong ties between the small group of girls,
there is no indication of group solidarity of a continuing nature. The

trust that all members in the group have for others is individual-to-individual rather than individual-to-group. A friend is whoever is working with you, and the emotional focus is more upon the common interest than upon the person.

Association. Not only is this class influenced by the families of the children and the third-grade group across the hall, but it is also influenced by the high school science and art departments. Several field trips have been planned in which the class visits those departments of the high school, but of particular importance is the number of activities that high school students in those departments conduct with this grade.

Change. In this group Miss Cope is not afraid of change. She tolerates almost any change the children want to make within the classroom. She trusts the children thereby not to create a chaotic situation. Not much if anything is said about the children's working together, but they do so when cooperation in the use of materials and equipment seems to be of mutual benefit. In this class modifications and alterations, occurring as needed, result in apparent disorder. In remarking that she does not know where things are "but the children do," Martha Cope is simply recognizing that what may appear to others as disorder is in fact a flexible form of order. Fundamentally Miss Cope is more interested in how children learn than in what they learn because she believes that when children know how to do a job they also understand what the job involves. She thinks children learn by their mistakes, but she does not let children think they failed because they made an error. She questions rather than corrects. When a child makes a mistake, she helps him carefully retrace and evaluate what he did that may have led to the error. Thus in this class, change is a realistic product of the teaching technique and therefore always present.

Continuity. Miss Cope uses class time in a drastically different way from the way in which Miss Jordan uses it. Whatever amount of time is needed for individual or small-group projects is the amount given to them. Sometimes the period allotted is exact; usually it is variable. The only definite regulation of time comes from the school bells. When the bells ring for recess, lunch, or the end of the school day, they are observed. More often than not, the bells come as a surprise to the children because they are too absorbed in their work to anticipate the sound of the bells. Nevertheless, time perception is highly developed in the children because consideration of time frequently influences how thoroughly and how rapidly they decide to work.

Equipment. In this classroom, all equipment is moved about and used in many different ways. Extra equipment of all sorts—jars, metal cans, wire, buckets, bits of cloth, two washing-machine motors, dry batteries, a small kiln, a small scale—have been brought in by the children. When the children finish projects, they take out the equipment used and bring in new. As a result the room takes on different aspects from time to time. But at any time it looks cluttered because seeds are growing, plants are being tested, and weights, wires, and webs are strung about the room. Experiments are always underway. Books are crowded into a smaller space than in the other rooms, but they are readily available and well organized.

Personalities of the Three Teachers

Catherine Jordan has been at Jefferson Elementary School for 34 years. "Several times," she has a way of saying quietly but pointedly to people, "they wanted me to go into administration, but I prefer my third grade."

On two occasions Miss Jordan served as principal on temporary assignment at Jefferson. "Never again," she declared at the time and repeated ever since. "They can have that job. All it is is complaints, complaints, complaints—a real headache. Complaining parents, complaining children, complaining teachers, even complaining custodians! It's a continual headache. Everybody is short of something, wants this, wants that, can't manage this, can't manage that. Of course, it was war time, but even so, the way everybody feels the principal of a school can work miracles. . . . If children don't have the IQ, they can't learn, I tell parents. It's amazing what parents think a school can do with a child! You would almost think they felt the school was responsible for the intelligence *they* gave their children! And teachers—they always want the principal to handle the children *and* the parents! Well, it opened my eyes, I can tell you. If parents of my children have any complaints, I handle them. I just tell them not to bother the principal, he has enough to do. And I have not sent a pupil to the office to be handled in 18 years."

Miss Jordan has a technique for getting her own way. She never makes a frontal demand, but she downs alternatives by lengthy comment and questioning and repetitious references to her experiences at Jefferson. Whenever Miss Jordan begins such a tirade, Martha Cope, who has taught every grade in the school, shrugs her shoulders and remarks, "Yes, Catherine, life's a misery."

Miss Cope, who has been at Jefferson as long as Miss Jordan, is briefed on all of Miss Jordan's references. She just smiles when Miss Jordan snaps, "Now, Martha, I'm not being negative, just questioning," and then goes into a pout disguised as resigned acceptance of whatever decision is to be made. Generally the staff agrees with what Miss Jordan wants. The other teachers are disinclined to suffer her avoidance, which she can prolong for months.

The folklore of the faculty includes a story of how Charles Austin, a seventh-grade teacher, was subjected to the avoidance. It happened in 1941 just after the Martin Junior High School had been completed. Charles was to go along with his seventh grade to the new junior high school, but he was asked to help with the plans for new room assignments in Jefferson, and herein lay the cause of the clash with Miss Jordan.

Miss Jordan had selected her room several years earlier while she was still principal. She liked the room for its location and convenience. There was a place where she could park her car so that she could step out of it directly into her room. Although the room was in the wing occupied by the upper-grade classes, Miss Jordan merely smiled and said, "Well, we are just on the edge, just a step over the boundary; and I know my little ones won't hurt those great big boys and girls." After she had repeated this defense in many variations, to end the discussion, the staff resigned itself to her occupying the room of her choice.

Now that the upper grades were leaving the school, however, the faculty agreed to place grade groups in proximity to each other and to convert Miss Jordan's room into a library. Apparently Miss Jordan had heard that a room change was in the offing.

"Oh, I see," she said, looking at a newly posted colored chart in the faculty room, "the plan of the building." Then turning to Mr. Austin, who was chairman of the Planning Committee, "But what do all the colors mean?"

"The red," said Charles, "are the kindergarten rooms. The blue, the first grades; green, second; yellow, third; purple, fourth; orange, fifth; and brown, sixth."

Miss Jordan smiled sweetly, "Oh, yes. I see now. I'm glad you left my room white. I never did like yellow."

Charles walked over to the chart. "We plan to put the library here, Catherine," he said putting his finger on the square representing the room she occupied. "All the third grades will be together in this area over here."

"But, Mr. Austin," Miss Jordan responded frigidly, "I was not *asked* about changing my room."

"You have been here at the planning sessions all year, haven't you,

Miss Jordan? This proposed room arrangement grows out of the needs of the shared teaching program we have been planning."

"That is beside the point," she argued. "At no time did we discuss changing rooms. I like my present room, have it arranged to serve my teaching, and I don't intend to change." Then hesitating, she added in a raised voice calculated to reach the ear of Mr. Mitten, the principal who was just joining the teachers. "Unless, of course, I'm ordered to by the principal."

"Nobody is ordering anybody on these matters," he said steadily. "All along this proposal has been the result of cooperative planning."

Miss Jordan smiled and said brightly, "Then if I am not ordered to move, I will stay where I am in Room 14. If the discussion is to be on room selections, I won't be needed, so I'll just go along and complete grading papers."

As she started toward the door, Charles Austin held up his hand and stopped her. "Hear ye! Hear ye!" he called out. "Queen Catherine has spoken. Her Majesty retires now to her castle." He bowed low and, throwing open the door, said, "Exit the Queen."

Catherine Jordan, red with anger and embarrassment, left the room.

The incident had, of course, left the staff somewhat stunned.

"I'm sorry," said Charles Austin humbly, "but I'm fed up. I should have kept my mouth shut, but after all those meetings—not a peep out of her, and now she pulls this kind of an act."

"Forget it, Charles," Mr. Mitten replied. "I'll see if I can talk to her. Let's postpone this meeting for now." All the teachers except Martha Cope left quietly, some murmuring approval to Charles as they left, others simply smiling their agreement with him.

"Well," said Charles, "I guess I fixed this plan. Do you think the queen will change her mind?"

"No," replied Martha, "she won't. That's our Miss Jordan. Sweet on the surface, good, too, in many ways, but hard when she once gets her mind set."

"Then where do we go from here?" asked Charles.

"Just as we've planned—*sans* Catherine. She will remain, just as you said, a queen in her castle. They would have to transfer her out of the school to change her, or fire her, which of course they won't. She won't participate, but she won't cause trouble either."

"Oh," murmured Charles, as much to himself as to Martha.

Martha continued, "Someone has concocted the idea of 'life space.' You know—the range of life a person can handle. Well, Catherine is the kind of person who can manage only a small range. It's thorough, but it's tight. There are people like that, afraid to move, afraid of people and so she jumps them before they can jump her. Forget her, Charles. It won't do any good to push her."

During the remaining months of the school year, Miss Jordan so thoroughly ignored Charles that it became a staff joke. Some teachers said to him, "The Queen doth not yet speak?" Catherine made no apparent effort to avoid Charles, but wherever they met it was as though he were not present. At first he felt a bit awkward, but as time went on he began speaking to her whenever they passed in the hall and ignoring her lack of response. Years later Mary Anton remembered the story of Queen Catherine and her private parking spot as she hurried to school, for she was anticipating Mr. Mitten's expected comment about parking. No matter what the cause or occasion of anyone's being late to school, he always made some joking comment on parking. Well, it was a problem finding a spot, especially since the construction crews had moved in. The high school pupils were now parking increasing numbers of cars, farther and farther down the street from the high school, which was four blocks up the hill. Construction was going on up there too. For whatever else they might say about Charles Austin, he certainly was getting buildings up since he had become superintendent. Mary had heard that the old members of the board (five of seven were still on the board) were amazed at the change in Charles. Mary decided that after school she would ask Martha Cope for her impression of Charles, as Martha and Charles were good friends.

Shortly after the children left for the day, Miss Anton, as planned, sought out Miss Cope and asked her if Mr. Austin had changed.

"He hasn't changed a nickel's worth," laughed Martha. "He's a little older, wiser, but the same old Charles. . . . Well, yes, I guess you could say he knows his way around a little more nowadays, but he learned most of what he knows from Matt.

"Of course, Mary, you didn't know Matt Colter, our former superintendent, but he was a wonderful person. The youngsters everywhere adored him."

"That is what I've heard, but I never met him," Mary agreed.

"No. He left before you came. Died the next year."

"Then Charles came in?" Mary asked.

"Yes! And he knew what he wanted in schools. He had learned a lot from Matt."

"And Catherine?" ventured Mary. "How did she take it?"

Martha chuckled, but did not answer directly. "Catherine thought there was no one in the world quite like Matt. You know how firm she is with her youngsters—never a peep, everything in order—a place for everything and everything in its place? Well, you know, Mary, Matt would walk into Catherine's room and have it stirring from top to bottom in no time and Catherine would be in the thick of it. He would get them so involved in a project in science, or politics, or almost anything."

"But now Charles doesn't ever go to her classroom?"

Again Martha chuckled. "Not very often—but then he doesn't do much class visiting anyway, with all the building going on."

"You know, Martha, I often wonder about Catherine. You say she admired Matt Colter and he was so free with people. If she approved of him and his ideas of schools, why is she so rigid, so formal with her own teaching?"

"Well, the truth of the matter is that she is not so formal as she appears. She just doesn't know how to be free. She's one of those people who has to have everything in order, so that she'll know where it is all the time. Now look at this room; it's a mess, and I haven't any idea where lots of things are. The children know, but I don't. Actually Catherine starts out with everything tight—shipshape—and the kids don't touch a thing without being told. But you know her room isn't cold. It's a warm, friendly place, colorful, and the things in it are for children. It isn't things for things' sake with Catherine, or things just for show. I suppose you'd say I teach by ear and Catherine does it by note. Catherine scares easily, but once she feels safe with a situation, she relaxes the reins quite a bit. Of course, she tightens up if things seem to get out of hand in her view of things. That's it; she doesn't want to lose her grip, but her grip isn't always tight."

"Hm-m," Mary mused, "I hadn't thought about it like that. But still it bothers me. I couldn't teach like that. I have rules, and so do you, but with me they don't come before everything else."

Martha nodded, "With Catherine they do. The first thing she does when she comes in here is to straighten things up. And chattering away all the while. I think the chattering covers up her inability to cope with people."

"But she can make people so uncomfortable. In all that chatter there are always little jabs that reach out and cut you, while she goes on and on. Frankly, I can only take so much of it."

"Of course," Martha agreed. "You wouldn't be human if you didn't feel that way, and let's not fool ourselves. Catherine has it down to a technique. The thing I'm getting at is that she doesn't do it with the purpose of hurting people, but to ward off getting hurt herself."

"Yes, I can see that. But it doesn't make me any more comfortable around her. You are more charitable than I am, Martha."

"Probably I've just been living with it longer and don't let it get under my hide any more."

Mary Anton always valued her conversations with Martha Cope. Martha appealed to her as a person and as a teacher. At times things did seem "pretty messy" in Martha's room. As for herself, she did not let things go so far, but she felt she would rather be like Martha than move in Catherine's direction.

That night Mary Anton and Marc, her fiancé, talked "shop"— school shop, that is, because Marc was going into law. Ordinarily he teased her about being a "school marm," but that evening he seemed unusually curious about school. He asked her whether she knew Charles Austin.

"Of course. He's my boss, don't you know?" she had replied airily. "Why, what's he done?"

"Oh, I just met him. A friend of Dean Joseph introduced us. But I took a liking to him. He seems like a good man."

Mary talked a great deal about schools and education with Marc that evening, and was rather surprised at the hoops he put her through with his questions. Before long she realized that she was becoming rather defensive. She even found herself making quite a case for Mr. Mitten, something she had never done before. Not that she disliked him. He was accommodating enough, undemanding, a little tedious at times, such as with his little sallies about parking, but on the whole he left you alone. She realized, however, that the picture of Mr. Mitten's experience, training, understanding, and competency that she was drawing for Marc did not ring quite true. When Marc suggested that he would like to meet her principal sometime, she realized what a shock it would be for Marc to compare his impressions of Mr. Austin and Mr. Mitten.

At that point she backtracked, and in correcting her description of Mr. Mitten, she realized that she could never visualize Charles Austin as ever having been like Mr. Mitten, nor could she admit the possibility of Mr. Mitten's ever being superintendent of anything. Actually Mr. Mitten was some 15 years older than Charles Austin, and she had heard that over the years he had held a number of positions in the school system. Mr. Mitten, she realized, was an innocuous, ineffective person.

But Charles Austin was no less a teacher or a principal for being a superintendent. Even though he did not presently have time for visiting classrooms, he was perfectly capable of walking into any classroom and teaching most subjects without any to-do. Imagine Mr. Mitten's taking over her third grade or even Miss Jordan's well-oiled third grade—and his taking over Martha's would be impossible. As usual, Martha had been right. Catherine, despite her chatter and her order, gave identity to what she was doing. She knew that if she had a child she would prefer a Catherine as his teacher rather than a Mr. Mitten who had neither vigor nor direction.

Thinking of Mr. Mitten and Mr. Austin and trying to explain to Marc their impact in the school system fascinated Mary Anton because as she moved along in the discussion, especially after she got beyond defending the profession with an imaginary Mr. Mitten, her defensive feelings about the profession and her own teaching evaporated. She felt no need to compare her teaching with Martha's or with her conception of Charles Austin's, nor even to bolster her confidence by contrasting her teaching with Catherine's or with her conceptions of Mr. Mitten's. She knew she was competent. She recognized her lapses without fear—embarrassment perhaps, but not fear. Marc nodded when she expressed this confidence, "Fear can be two things," he said. "There is fear of a specific situation. Any of us can be frightened of a given thing that happens or might happen. But some people pick up a feeling of failure somewhere along the line. Such people aren't necessarily actually failures, but the prospects of their being failures become greater than their prospects of not failing. They meet a situation not as it is but as their fear makes them think it is."

As she listened Mary thought not only of Catherine and Mr. Mitten but also of little Joey in her third grade.

VARIABLES INFLUENCING
PUPIL BEHAVIOR

In the preceding section the emphasis upon teacher personality may suggest that it is the only important factor in determining school culture. Many other factors, such as the 11 listed on page 306 and still others that may be subsumed under them, influence the school subcultures. In many instances pupils refuse to accept teacher domination. For example, it is a mistake to assume that the values that permeate a class are necessarily those held by its teacher. Part of the difficulty of raising the level of academic performance in the upper grades arises out of the values of the teen-age culture that are at odds with sustained scholarship. It is well known that the mores of pupils prevail over those of teachers in respect to cheating and reporting one's peers for dishonesty in school work.

It is perhaps less well known that teacher effectiveness is related to the climate of opinion among the pupils and their parents. A teacher as permissive as Martha Cope may have difficulty winning respect in communities where families stress obedience as a prime virtue. Her lack of authoritarianism may be interpreted by pupils and parents alike as weakness, indecision, and incompetence. Even Mary Anton may have disciplinary problems with those pupils who if given an inch by a teacher take a mile. The statement has been made that all of these teachers are considered good teachers. One may wonder, however, if they would be rated as good teachers by the same pupils, the same parents, and the same co-workers.

At the high school level the influence of other teachers in the school affects the subculture of a particular teacher's classroom. That is, what happens in one class may have repercussions in another. If Miss Cope taught in high school, the pupils, moving from a class like hers (where concentration and self-control explode in boisterous playground activity) into a second teacher's classroom may create untold difficulties for the second teacher.

Furthermore, the relationship between a teacher's personality and her own performance in a classroom is probably not always so fully demonstrated as suggested here. Many of us know a "Catherine Jordan type" of teacher, although she may not be old, contentious with her colleagues, nor even traditional in her teaching methods. She may be just as rigid as Miss Jordan in her acceptance of the "progressive methods." Even if she does not resemble Catherine Jordan in personality at all, she may then use the same teaching methods that Catherine does because she teaches as she was taught and knows no other methods. Or she may be like Catherine Jordan in having difficulties in relating amicably to adults, yet she may behave differently with children by being accepting, understanding, and patient.

Spindler presents evidence of a teacher of the Catherine Jordan type who was well liked by his colleagues and rated highly by his supervisors. This good-looking, socially pleasant young man prided himself upon being fair to all his fifth-grade pupils, but a series of observations and other methods of evaluation indicated that he was unconsciously biased against children who were not middle class. Therefore, he was far from fair in his relationships with the majority of his pupils. He was, in fact, rigidly committed to traditional values in general and inflexible in opposing change. His classroom manner was as unbending as that of Miss Jordan.[3]

[3] George Dearborn Spindler, *The Transmission of American Culture,* Harvard University Press, 1959, pp. 29–38.

The Principal's Influence
upon School Subcultures

Miss Anton reasoned that a pupil in a class taught by Mr. Mitten would suffer because he lacked "vigor and direction." One may wonder how his ineffectiveness affects the operation of the school. At least one study found that the morale of the faculty is influenced more by the principal than by the salary scale or any other single factor. Does the incompetence of a leader like Mr. Mitten lower the morale of teachers in a school or does his indecisiveness provide greater freedom for his teachers than would be possible with a vigorous, forceful leader?

The composition of these third grades suggests that Miss Jordan's preference for girls and Miss Cope's preference for boys were honored. It also suggests that Miss Jordan did not want and thus was not assigned children from minority groups. The unusual tolerance in Miss Cope's classroom and Miss Jordan's success in resisting a room assignment further suggests a highly permissive principal. But permissiveness without support and guidance seldom provide leadership for faculty growth. Nevertheless, the structure of the school enables a weak principal to survive. How?

If Mary Anton and Martha Cope were to admire Mr. Mitten as much as they do Charles Austin and if Catherine Jordan were to admire him as much as she did Matt Colter, how would their feelings influence their behavior as teachers? Is a respect bordering on hero worship of a principal common among many teachers? Is such an attitude healthy from the point of view of the profession? Why, or why not?

Analyzing Class Behavior

As an aid in clarifying and analyzing the contrastive behavior in the three classrooms, study the accompanying chart. The data shows, for example, that "location" was a factor in the associations of Miss Anton's class and Miss Cope's class in that they were able to exchange materials and information. "Location" also was a factor in Miss Anton's class's association with the kindergarten, but it does not account for Miss Cope's class's association with the high school art and science classes. The "location" of Miss Jordan's class doubtless contributed to its insularity and to its gossipy interest in the front office and in visitors. One may hypothesize that location of the classroom provided an easy and distracting access to information that, in turn, contributed to the class's feeling of "distinctiveness" because they were "in the know."

After studying the composition of the three classes, do you conclude that the assignment of pupils to each of these three grades reflects a wise school policy? Why, or why not? The effects of concentrating almost all the girls in one class, almost all the boys in another, and most of the children from minority groups in the same class need to be considered. Would it be better to divide classes completely by sex because boys tend to mature more slowly than girls? Some educators think so. Are some teachers more effective in working with boys than girls or vice versa? If so, should such teachers be given pupils with whom they can work most successfully?

Does a preponderance of one sex in a class affect the life style in that classroom? One may surmise, for example, that the predominance of working- and middle-class girls in Catherine Jordan's class contributed to the docility, stress on neatness, and attention to detail found in that group, and that the preponderance of boys in Martha Cope's class was a factor in the group's enthusiasm for scientific experiments and mechanical gadgets. Since our society encourages certain interests in boys and other interests in girls, finding these "sex-linked" concerns demonstrated in a class made up primarily of one sex is not surprising even if the teacher does not encourage such concerns.

Another consideration is whether placing pupils who differ in ethnic or cultural origins in one of the third grades is a desirable practice. On the one hand, the dominant social group may learn to accept minority group members by associating with them. On the other, pupils from the minority groups may gain security by being in the same classroom with others from their group.

The descriptions state that even under an authoritarian teacher, the pupils usually set the classroom purposes. The best example, of course, is Miss Jordan's class in which members demonstrated in their actions their acceptance of the teacher's judgment of worthy purposes. After all, pupils do not have to *spur* each other into competitive memorization of poetry, just because their teacher encourages it.

Are actions related to class purposes even when these purposes are not stated? This question is a thorny one for teachers and parents alike because so often both groups take the attitude with children, "Do as I say, not necessarily what I do." Actually what one *does* is more nearly indicative of his purposes as well as his values than what he says. Even though Miss Anton probably never explained to her pupils that they should learn to be restrained in their exercise of freedom and certainly the pupils would not articulate such a purpose, both her actions and those of the pupils indicated acceptance of this objective. Unfor-

TABLE 8. Three Classes Compared in Respect to Eleven Factors

Factor	Miss Jordan's Class	Miss Anton's Class	Miss Cope's Class
Location	Near office and front entrance	Near playground, a kindergarten, and Miss Cope's room	Near playground, a kindergarten, and Miss Anton's room
Composition	25 G, 15 B, homogeneous social origins	21 G, 19 B, including 2 Negroes, 2 Span-Ams, 1 Italian	9 G, 31 B, including 7 Negroes, 1 Span-Am, 4 Indians, 2 English
Purposes	Detailed excellence, neatness, memorization, speed, accuracy, competition, group solidarity through insularity	Search for relationships, using what is learned, experimenting with alternatives, competition between groups of changing membership, fairness	Freedom to inquire and experiment, learning by experimenting
Functions	Pupils check for accuracy, strive to be neat, compete through memorization, speed, tackling difficult work. Little interaction with other groups.	Pupils try out new ideas, new uses of things, but respond quickly to restraint; use books and materials freely but carefully.	Pupils experiment in science, art, music, etc. Written language used as a recording skill, show keen interest, explode into physical activity on playground
Values	Teacher approval, success in competitive achievement, order and accuracy, use of parliamentary rules, fairness	Freedom and security, excitement of exploring alternatives, fairness	Enjoyment of group's increasing ability to find answers

TABLE **8.** *(Continued)*

Factor	Miss Jordan's Class	Miss Anton's Class	Miss Cope's Class
Structure	Formal Authoritarian teacher	Authoritarian teacher modified by democratic ethics, pupils free within limits	Appears disorganized, girls operate as matriarchy; teacher permissive, gives attention to individuals
Kinship	Group cohesive against outsiders, compete among themselves as individuals and cliques	Group relationships open and friendly	Cooperative, transitory groups, except for the girls
Associations	Gossipy relation with office staff and parents visiting school	Protective attitude toward kindergarten, sharing with Miss Cope's class	Exchanges with high school art and science classes, sharing with Miss Anton's class
Change	Opposed by teacher	Teacher and class experiment with new ideas within limits	Teacher tolerates almost any change children want to make
Continuity	Regular schedule	Schedule subject to modification	Only regulation is school bell, whatever period of time is needed for projects is allowed
Equipment	Kept in place, minimum use	Valued for use, conserved	Extra equipment brought by pupils, crowded but available

tunately not all unstated purposes are as educationally desirable as this one.

What values a group shares are difficult to determine. In these case studies, values were determined by carefully observing the behavior of pupils and teachers and assuming that the values they cherish are reflected in their actions.

Other factors influencing school culture that may be of greater importance than is immediately apparent are structure, change, continuity, and equipment. Probably most pupils, but not all, find greater security and satisfaction in a structured than in an unstructured classroom. They prefer to have a definite time for certain activities, a definite place for equipment, and a routine that is not changed too drastically or too often. They expect the teacher to exert the authority of his position when necessary and to tell them what he expects of them. But the security of certainty, untempered by flexibility and wise changes that encourage pupil initiative, creativeness, and original thinking, leads to boredom and does not truly educate.

Miss Anton's teaching methods seem to be best designed to provide both the security and the freedom that pupils need. The inexperienced teacher, however, will find that deferring judgment on other teachers' effectiveness is a wise policy. Who is to say that an emphasis on accuracy, neatness, and excellence or on learning through experimentation is harmful to students? Among "good teachers," there are few "bad buys" and "good buys." Most pupils probably benefit by a year's exposure to any "good teacher," irrespective of what he chooses to stress.

SUMMARY

It is important for teachers to realize that many influences, including their own personalities and perceptions of their role as teachers, shape the subculture of the classroom. The importance of this subculture in determining the conditions in which the teaching-learning process takes place, what will be learned, and how individuals within the group will conduct themselves, can hardly be overestimated.

The illustrations provided in this chapter have demonstrated some of the complexities of studying the culture of a single classroom. The examples did not, however, present the concepts of status and role of pupils nor the facets of the informal pupil relationships with one another that are equally as important as the formal structure of a class-

room to understanding the behavior of a class's subculture. Nevertheless, the factors of cultural analysis applied in this chapter provide a
framework upon which studies at any grade level may be made.

IMPORTANT CONCEPTS

Subculture. A subdivision of a larger culture area that is marked by a special
set of cultural traits as well as by means of diffusing and perpetuating
these traits. See pp. 305 ff.

15. SECONDARY SCHOOL CULTURE

. . . in American culture, . . . every child must be a social engineer, able to use his 'appeal' and his skill at social maneuvering to construct a personal community for himself.

—JULES HENRY[1]

In the preceding chapter, the teacher's influence upon the social climate of elementary school culture was examined. In this chapter the role that students play in setting the social climate of the high school is discussed. Such an arbitrary division of teacher and pupil influence should not be interpreted to mean that pupils have no influence upon elementary school culture or that teachers have no influence upon secondary school culture. In view of the developmental needs of older students compared to those of younger students, the social climate in the high school is, however, influenced to a greater extent by students vis-à-vis teachers than is that of the elementary school.

[1] Jules Henry, *Culture Against Man,* Random House, 1963, p. 147.

The method of analysis used in this chapter will also differ from that in the preceding chapter. At the outset, the following premises about secondary school culture will be offered:

That a primary need of an adolescent is self-identity.

That a teen-age subculture exists.

That the content of that subculture is learned by its members.

That within a particular subculture, individuals have different roles and statuses.

That the high school student activity program is associated with the statuses that students attain.

That high school students may have several reference groups.

That high school students are influenced by "significant others."

That a high school student's "self-concept" is significant in determining the decisions he makes.

Each of these premises and relevant supporting data will be elaborated upon in the discussion that follows.

EGO IDENTITY: A PRIMARY NEED

Several years ago Erik Erikson enhanced understanding of the adolescent by inventing the concept of ego identity.[2] He pointed out that the search for identity, for finding one's place in society, and attaining a unity of personality are critical commitments of an adolescent. Throughout childhood, a youth has formulated and reformulated identities, but in adolescence he must effect a synthesis of earlier identifications with his own special qualifications and relate them to his social environment. Attaining ego identity, according to Erikson, reaches a crisis in adolescence. To establish a secure individuality an adolescent must uncover the nature of his own uniqueness as well as the meaning of his group relationships. For many young people, this search is accompanied by extreme levels of anxiety.[3]

Not only do adolescents vary with respect to the level of anxiety with which they face the problem of "Who am I?," but also they differ with respect to when and how they resolve the crisis. Sometimes a young person, seeming to be eager to settle quickly, bases his decisions on impulse. In other instances, a youth may seem to be afraid to grow up and choose to ignore serious commitments. For most young people, adolescence is a period when they may, however, assume various roles without definitely choosing any of them.

[2] Erik H. Erikson, "The Problem of Ego Identity," *Journal of American Psychoanalytic Association, 4* (1956), 56–121.

[3] Erik H. Erikson, "Youth: Fidelity and Diversity," in *Youth: Change and Challenge, Daedalus, 91* (Winter, 1962), 16–17.

The choices open to young people vary. The highly intelligent boy has many more choices than the boy of average intelligence. Boys tend to build their identities around an occupational choice, but a girl's identity is usually much more diffused because her commitment is likely to be dependent upon who and what her husband will be. The social-class status of an adolescent is also a factor in the identity crisis. It excludes some teenagers from the social activities of others. At a time when a youth is appraising his own attributes by many different criteria, to be excluded because of his social-class origin is devastating to his ego.

Being able to participate in teen-age culture is part of the status game for, as we shall see, it costs money, but all having money are able to participate irrespective of social-class origin. Learning teen-age culture is a necessary part of the effort to find one's place in peer society that is significant for identity formation. To be "cool" is important to peer-group acceptance, and a youth learns to be cool by keeping up with the elements of the teen-age subculture. Whether or not this society of a particular age group has the attributes of a subculture is, however, debatable.

THE TEEN-AGE SUBCULTURE

In one sense, a teen-age subculture exists, for as defined by Linton, "A society is an organized group of individuals. A culture is an organized group of learned responses characteristic of a particular society."[4] Teen-agers do have a group of learned responses characteristic of their age-group. In another sense, however, teen-agers cannot be said to constitute a subculture because their culture is restricted to an age group and is not systematically transmitted from generation to generation. Moreover, much of the value system of teen-agers is shared with parents, teachers, and other adults and is not unique to teen-age subculture.

Nevertheless, the pattern of learned responses characteristic of American teen-agers that is shared by almost all adolescents we shall call a subculture. Jessie Bernard attributes the development of such a subculture to an affluent society.[5] A more nearly equal distribution of income has made the conditions of adolescence similar for young Americans from all classes except the very poor, and the mass media have popularized elements of teen-age culture. Many working-class

---

[4] Ralph Linton, *Tree of Culture*, Knopf, 1955, p. 29.
[5] Jessie Bernard, "Teen-Age Culture: An Overview," in American Academy of Political and Social Science, *The Annals*, 338 (November, 1961), 1–12.

youth, however, leave the teen-age subculture by marrying and dropping out of school earlier than do middle-class young people who prolong their schooling. Nevertheless, in the younger teen-age culture, tastes and standards of the boys and girls of the lower socioeconomic levels are influential.

Recently teen-age subculture has extended downward to younger age groups and tends to disappear with graduation from high school. This change in the age level of participants may be a result of increased urbanization that encourages precociousness and it may also be a result of children's maturing physically at an earlier age than they used to. The early maturation of young people, especially girls, is manifested in some girls beginning to menstruate as early as age 8 and in boys and girls beginning to date as early as age 10 or 11. "Going steady" and even marriage between a boy and a girl in their middle teens is not uncommon. Wattenberg estimates that about 10 percent of the girls are physically mature at age 11, 50 percent by age 13, and 90 percent by age 15; while among boys, 10 percent are physically mature at age 13, 50 percent by age 15, and 99 percent by age 17.[6] Among older adolescents and young adults in the college, teen-age culture has all but vanished except perhaps among the fraternities.

Wherever it occurs, teen-age culture includes distinctive patterns of dress, speech, musical taste, humor, and entertainment. Adolescents enjoy talking their own language and wearing clothes that make them appear different from older people. One suspects that part of their admiration of their star musician or actor of the moment is derived from the disparagement of the star by adults. Much of their humor is a disparagement of adult society. In this way they seem to assert their "belongingness" to a peer society and their rebellion against adults.

The amount of advertising beamed at teen-agers indicates that merchants are keenly aware that they represent a new market of consequence. By catering to their tastes, interests, and whims, merchants sold them about 12 billion dollars worth of goods in 1966. (The amount spent on elementary and secondary education in 1966 was 20 billion dollars.)

Teen-age magazines, which have multiplied rapidly in the past 10 to 15 years, have attracted hundreds of thousands of readers. The contents of these magazines, which often include the word *teen* in their titles, have a strong confessional aspect. The subscribers write letters to the editors asking for, and giving advice about, boy-girl relation-

---

[6] William W. Wattenberg, "Youth Education: A Psychophysical Perspective," in Raymond H. Muessig, ed., *Youth Education: Problems/Perspectives/Promises,* Association for Supervision and Curriculum Development, NEA, 1968, p. 47.

ships, how to be popular, how to overcome shyness, and how to solve other personal problems. The contents also reflect the teen-agers' admiration for pop singers and musicians and stars of films and television. The magazines along with television and films also serve as purveyors of teen-age culture and spread its fads and fashions throughout the land.

The mass media tend to give the impression that teen-agers value popularity, "good personalities," material possessions, especially automobiles, and fun above all else. As a matter of fact, in 1967 the Purdue Opinion Panel found the need to be popular and to conform to peer group demands pervasive among representative high school students. Being overweight or underweight or having acne is a heavy burden for the victim. An overweight California girl, after mentioning that her brother calls her "fatty" or "glut," concluded "Many times I have thought seriously of committing suicide."[7]

A comparison of Purdue poll results in 1953 and 1966 showed, however, that whereas in 1953 most students considered social skills the most important value of education, in 1966 students ranked discipline and responsibility first and academic skills a close second. In 1967 adolescents studied more than students did in 1948, and three-fourths of them agreed that earning good grades is "extremely important" or "very important." Thus they seemed to be more serious about their school work than was the generation before them.[8]

One cannot assume that the content of teen-age culture is the same everywhere. The rural and small city teen-ager and his peers are much more traditional in attitudes than are urban teen-agers in metropolitan areas. Not all teen-agers are in revolt against adult values. Most of them, in fact, reflect rather than resist parental influences. Quarrels between teen-agers and their parents are usually about their status as children or young adults, about their privileges, not their values. One should also recognize that the content of teen-age culture is in constant flux. Especially in recent years, rituals, language, fads and fashions, and even certain values and attitudes have changed so rapidly that young people only 5 to 10 years apart in age have difficulty in understanding one another.

Although the content of teen-age culture represents learnings that a youth must acquire to be accepted in peer society, it is less directly related to the development of his ego identity than to his status in peer groups and the roles he plays. Both his statuses and roles are closely related to school success.

[7] Thomas R. Leidy and Allan R. Starry, "The American Adolescent—A Bewildering Amalgam," *NEA Journal, 56* (October, 1967), 8–11.
[8] *Ibid.*

THE IMPACT OF STUDENT ACTIVITIES
UPON HIGH SCHOOL LIFE

Adolescents, like adults, have many statuses and roles. *Status* refers to one's position in a group, and *role* to the behavior associated with a particular status. A teen-ager may be a son, a brother, a steady boy friend, a buddy, a part-time employee, a student, a football player, a class president, and a leading character in a school play. In each of these statuses, he plays a different role. How he plays the role is determined to a considerable extent by the manner in which others expect him to play it. Such role expectations become, in fact, a part of his self-concept.

The roles that a teen-ager plays in the social setting of the school are of great importance to him. School is the place where he meets his friends. Whether or not he "rates" in school may determine whether he graduates from high school, goes to college, or drops out of school. All of the social life of teen-agers does not, of course, take place within the school. In fact, extraclass activities more nearly approximate the kind of learning found in intimate peer groups than do class activities. For this reason, Gordon, Mallery, Coleman, and others have studied adolescent status systems in terms of participation in student activities.

In high school, student activities, also called the cocurriculum, are usually distinguished from formal classwork. Students are voluntary participants in organized sports, clubs, literary and dramatic groups that generally meet after school hours. Presumably students rather than teacher-advisers assume the leadership roles and choose the activities that engage the group. Educational leaders state objectives for such groups in global terms, yet they seldom seriously consider the significance of student activities in the social life of the school.

Many teachers also do not realize that participation in student activities is related to academic as well as to occupational success. Recent studies reveal that athletes make slightly better grades than nonathletes. Boys from working-class homes make better grades by comparison with working-class nonathletes than do boys from middle-class homes in comparison with middle-class nonathletes.[9] Athletes are also more likely to go to college and considerably more likely to graduate from college than nonathletes.[10] Conversely, those who quit

[9] Walter E. Schafer and J. Michael Amer, "Participation in High School Athletics and Academic Achievement," Paper presented to World Congress of Sports and Physical Education, Madrid, Spain, September, 1966.

[10] Richard A. Rehberg and Walter E. Schafer, "The Effect of Participation in High School Athletics and Academic Achievement," Paper presented at the International Seminar on Leisure Time and Recreation, Havana, Cuba, 1966.

school and those who are delinquents are usually not members of student organizations.[11] Other investigators find a relationship between students' achievements in activities and their later success in business[12] and in careers as aviation cadets.[13]

Several studies show that academic records and activity records are relatively independent measures of talent. One investigator found as high a correlation between a scale that evaluated a student's activity record and college grade-point-averages as between the College Entrance Examination Board's verbal test scores and college grade-point-averages.[14] Such studies suggest that student activities are important in the lives of students but do not explain why activities attain such significance. One hypothesis is that a student activity serves as a laboratory of human relations in which students learn useful, and sometimes, harmful social skills. Another hypothesis is that the social behavior of students is functionally related to the general social status they attain in the activity program. Several sociometric studies show that students who are popular with their peers are better behaved and come closer to working up to their potential abilities than those who are not liked by others.[15] Young people in activity programs appear to be more popular with their peers than are nonparticipants.

Although the research findings cited above do not reveal why teenagers who take part in activities make better grades and become relatively successful businessmen, the explanation seems to lie chiefly in the contribution of participation to identity formation. Hauser found that high school activists are more likely than the uninvolved to be integrated into school life and to hold high self-concepts.[16] Presumably the leaders who hold status roles benefit more than those who hold follower roles. Irrespective of role, a participant is likely to see himself as a member of the in-group in school social life. Such affiliation is important to his finding meaning in group relationships.

In some schools the meaning a participant finds may be unwholesome rather than healthy. For example, Gordon found in one high

[11] James W. Bell, "School Dropouts and School Activities," *School Activities*, 35 (September, 1964), 58; and Walter E. Schafer and Kenneth Polk, *Delinquency and the Schools, Report to the President's Commission on Law Enforcement and the Administration of Justice*, 1967.

[12] John A. Finger, Jr., "Academic Motivation and Youth-Culture Involvement," *School Review*, 74 (Summer, 1966), 177–195.

[13] John D. Krumboltz *et al.*, "Predicting Leadership Ratings from High School Activities," *Journal of Educational Psychology*, 50 (June, 1959), 105–110.

[14] Daniel W. Behring, "Activities and Academic Achievement," *Personnel and Guidance Journal*, 44 (March, 1966), 734–737.

[15] Richard A. Schmuck and others, "Interpersonal Relations and Mental Health in the Classroom," *Mental Hygiene*, 47 (April, 1963), 289–299.

[16] Gary Stuart Hauser, *Student Adaptation to High School Academics and Athletics*, Master's thesis, University of Oregon, 1965.

school that "the system of student organizations performed the function of differentiating students into a prestige hierarchy." Students, he said, competed vigorously for the prestigious roles. Girls seeking a place on the Queen's Court resorted to gossip, fierce rivalry, and insincere gestures of friendliness in order to win.[17]

Conversely, Mallery found that in City High an "intangible spirit" prevailed. An activity director found opportunities for shy, neglected as well as talented youngsters to contribute.[18] In many schools, unfortunately, no such roles are provided for such teen-agers with the result that *those who need activities most participate the least.*

Coleman suggests that teachers and principals unwittingly influence the school's status system by their use of rewards. High rewards for athletes and cheerleaders encourage a school-oriented, but not an academically-oriented, adolescent culture, he claims. High rewards for scholarship usually mean high rewards to a few pupils from "better families." High rewards for "all-around students" result in good but not superior academic accomplishment by athletes. Coleman believes that rewards for many different kinds of intellectual and social activities that bring glory to the school as well as to the individual participant would be a wholesome influence in the adolescent status system.[19]

The roles that a young person chooses to play, however, are related to the standards of a particular group by which he judges himself. Such a group is called a reference group. A student is not necessarily a member of the group he chooses as a reference group, yet his interpretation of their standards influences his behavior. Clearly parents, teachers, and other adults as well as their age-mates are reference groups for teen-agers.

Activists and hippies in colleges may also serve as reference groups for some high school students. The result is an increasing volume of student criticism in high schools of teachers' methods, school regulations, and curriculums. Some high school students are defying regulations about dress and haircuts, voicing disillusionment with middle-class values, and taking "trips."

ACTIVITISTS, HIPPIES, AND OTHER REFERENCE GROUPS

College activists and hippies influence high school students in subtle ways. Most college activists are middle or upper-middle-class whites

[17] C. Wayne Gordon, *The Social System of the High School: A Study in the Sociology of Adolescence,* Free Press, 1957, pp. 67–76.

[18] David Mallery, *High School Students Speak Out,* Harper & Row, 1962, pp. 132–133.

[19] James B. Coleman, *The Adolescent Society,* Free Press, 1961, pp. 320–322.

who grew up in the suburbs. They propagandize their commitments among suburban high school student leaders. In June 1968 a national conference of Students for a Democratic Society agreed that the S.D.S. should increase its activity in the high school. Without such deliberate intent, hippies attract teen-agers to their colonies. An examination of the values of these models for adolescents is therefore appropriate.

Clark Kerr, the ex-president of the University of California, says that college activists "are like the rest of us—only more so." They are a "little quicker and go a little bit farther." Kerr points out that in the twenties Joe College was simply having a better time than the rest of the people who were also having a good time, the G.I. student after World War II worked harder than most other hard-working Americans, and in the fifties the student generation was uncommitted and apathetic when the tone of the country was "we're fed up with troubles." Nowadays, some students, like the rest of us—only more so, are concerned with problems of war and annihilation, poverty and discrimination, the role of the individual in mass society and in the multiversity, and education that is relevant.[20]

Flacks' study of student activists supports Kerr's assumptions to the extent that he found such students are like their own parents—only more so. Most activists, he reports, come from highly educated, middle and upper-middle class families. Their fathers and frequently their mothers are professionals, political liberals, humanists, and often Jewish. They are usually deeply concerned with individual development and self-expression, the social welfare of others, intellectualism, aesthetics, and emotional release. They are likely to reject imposed standards of behavior, to believe traditional morality is hypocritical, and to accept situational ethics. Such parents tend to be permissive in child-rearing practices; they are likely to encourage their children to make their own decisions even if they violate parental standards of morality.

Activist students are likely to depart from parental standards in one respect. They disagree with the importance their parents attach to career and material values. Consequently, their parents cannot understand their rejection of creature comfort and their sometimes flagrant disregard of standards of dress and grooming.

Although the parents of such students have predisposed them to activism, the extent of their involvement in state and campus politics is determined by other factors. The colleges they attend, their friends and teachers, the organizations they join, and various personal experi-

[20] Mary Harrington Hall, "Clark Kerr," *Psychology Today, 1* (October, 1967), 27–28.

ences are influential factors. As activism spreads, it does, in fact, elicit the support of other students who may come from very conservative homes. Their commitment is dependent entirely upon these other factors.[21]

Involving students in politics has long been a declared goal of civic education. Why then do many teachers and professors view activists with alarm? Such a question is not easy to answer. Perhaps adults never really wanted students to assume responsibility. Or perhaps it is the elements of disrespect for experience, unwillingness to communicate and work within established organizations for making changes, intense emotionalism, demands for freedom without responsibility, and unreasoned rejection of cultural values that alienate many teachers and professors from activists. Then, too, the Student Power movement has often been associated with hippies.

The hippie subculture is simply the latest expression of bohemianism. The bohemian view is that a child's potentialities are crushed by society and current educational methods, that every individual's purpose in life is to express himself and his goal is to live for the moment, and that laws that curtail full enjoyment should be abolished. Bohemians also stress the equality of women, a paganistic concern for the human body, and a romantic love of the exotic. The "new morality" of hippies is then, Bennett Berger concludes, nothing new, although it is probably winning more converts than earlier movements. As Berger points out, the age group likely to be attracted is very large, the mass media inadvertently advertise the hippie "morality," and many hippie activities, such as obscene language and premarital sexual experiences, seem to be gradually becoming legitimated in films and poetry.[22]

Hippies, like activists—in fact, the two groups overlap in college— are generally from middle and upper-middle class backgrounds. They too are expressing their dislike of violence, aversion to bureaucratic regimentation, rejection of hypocrisy, and sentimental sympathy for the disadvantaged. (Disadvantaged Negro youth, by the way, who have not experienced the plenty the hippies reject, make fun of these strange creatures in hippie colonies who beg on city streets.)

Campus hippies differ from city hippies in that they do not want to "drop out" completely; they just want to "turn on" or "tune in." Two groups of campus hippies also differ from one another. Although they dress alike, one group is made up of political activists who spearhead

[21] Richard Flacks, "Student Activists: Result, Not Revolt," *Psychology Today, 1* (October, 1967), 18–23, 61.
[22] Bennett M. Berger, "Hippie Morality—More Old Than New," *Trans-action, 5* (December, 1967), 19–23, 26–27.

various protest movements and recruit followers among bright young freshmen, usually good students but not athletes or student leaders in high school. The politicals do not use drugs. The second group is made up of individuals who take "trips" and subscribe to the hedonistic "hang-loose ethic." Only the most deviant of them, however, are likely to drop out of college and join hippie colonies.[23]

Notwithstanding the filth, disease, obscenities, drug indulgence, sexual promiscuities and perversions said to be common in the hippie subculture, particularly in cities, many young people—not only the glue-sniffing, pot-smoking, trip-taking youngsters—are attracted to it. Perhaps more than the thrill of new adventures attracts them. Hippies are experimenting, Davis found, with alternatives to materialism by demonstrating that they can live on little. They are rejecting passive spectatorship in the arts by creating whatever they like. The product does not have to meet anybody's standards; it is "beautiful" because it is "authentic"—you made it. Hippies are replacing the future-orientation of middle-class America and its deferments of present pleasures for future rewards with a present orientation, a living intensively for the moment. Such social experimenting may be the hippie message that appeals to the younger generation who are more keenly attuned to new values than are older generations.[24]

Whether the life style of hippies or even activists will last is, of course, questionable. Irrespective of what form youth culture takes, adolescents and young adults will, however, be very likely to revise social values and practices in accommodating to an increasingly automated, urbanized life style that promises greater leisure for all. As they do so, parents, teachers, and others who are close to young people will need to be responsible models of maturity, personal integrity, and wisdom. The "hang-loose" ethic excuses irresponsibility as freedom; it denies that the accumulated wisdom and scholarship of the ages are helpful supplements to personal experience; it undermines respect for law without which our society cannot survive. Taking a critical look at one's cultural values is useful if it does not breed a cynicism of the "Stop the World—I Want to Get Off" variety, but most young people need the guidance of older and wiser heads when they criticize. After all, the young are neither faced with exercising adult responsibility nor are they yet fully aware that somebody has "to keep the store" in any social group. When they act responsibly and share the necessary labor

[23] Geoffrey Simmon and Grafton Trout, "Hippies in College—From Teeny-boppers to Drug Freaks," *Trans-action,* 5 (December, 1967), 27–30, 32.
[24] Fred Davis, "Why All of Us May Be Hippies Someday," *Trans-action,* 5 (December, 1967), 18–23, 61.

required in any organization, they are able to make desirable changes.

The question then is to what extent are hippies the reference group of many high school students? Although no evidence can be cited to answer such a question quantitatively, common sense tells us the influence is negligible. Goodman, Friedenburg, Henry, and other critics charge, in fact, that high schools make students into middle-class conformists.[25] They deplore the stress on conformity and urge that high school teachers encourage individualism. The connotation of the word *conformity* is bad and that of the word *individualism* is good. Conformity is compliance with established and traditional ways of behaving and thinking; individualism assumes that all values, rights, and duties originate in and should be expressed by individuals. Presumably the conformist is manipulated by society whereas the individualist is a free agent. The educator knows that such dichotomies are misleading. Man is dependent upon his culture; he cannot exist apart from it. As a consequence, conformity is not all bad nor is unbridled individualism all good. The serious problem among high school adolescents, Metzger suggests, is the identity crisis. This crisis is augmented by the freedom of choice adolescents enjoy, the ambiguities of the roles they play, and the multiplicity of possible reference groups.[26]

Age-mate groups and peer groups a few years older than themselves are not the only reference groups of teen-agers. Parents, teachers, and other adults are often very influential in the lives of boys and girls. In most instances, however, perhaps they are important as "significant others," rather than as "reference groups." The difference between these two concepts is slight: a "significant other" refers to an individual, a "reference group" to a group.

"SIGNIFICANT OTHERS" AND THE SELF-CONCEPT

An individual's self-concept or self-image is learned through interaction with others. As a matter of fact, everybody has many self-concepts, that is, a composite of many self-concepts that vary with circumstances. He may see himself as an interesting conversationalist, a poor mechanic, a clever manipulator of others, a clumsy athlete, an average reader, a thoughtful husband. In part he perceives his talents in various ways because he has experienced success, mediocre achieve-

[25] Paul Goodman, *Growing Up Absurd*, Victor Gollancz, Ltd., 1961; Edgar Z. Friedenberg, *Coming of Age in America—Growth and Acquiescence*, Random House, 1965; Henry, *op. cit.*

[26] Walter P. Metzger, "On Youth and Conformity," in Robert Morrison MacIver, ed., *Dilemmas of Youth: In America Today*, Harper & Row, 1961, pp. 77–86.

ment, or failure in different undertakings. Moreover, his perception of success in a given area is influenced by his interpretation of others' opinions of his capabilities. The opinions of "significant others," those whose evaluations he prizes, will affect his own self-image more than will the opinions of people who are not important to him.

A "significant other" does not necessarily hold this status with respect to all of an individual's self-concepts. Presumably parents are important to a child in developing his conception of his capabilities for academic work and for a particular vocational objective. Teachers' and counselors' opinions may also be important to a child's academic self-concept. Although peer groups probably have relatively little influence in these areas, since "Sputnik" the upsurge of interest in achieving good grades in high school has undoubtedly permeated high school peer groups. Peer groups generally are very influential with respect to a child's self-concept of his ability to mingle socially, to influence others, and to be an interesting conversationalist.

A student's academic self-concept is significant to his performance in school work because he tends to behave in ways that others expect him to behave. If "significant others" believe that he cannot do good school work, he will not. A student may achieve at a lower level than he thinks he can, but he is very unlikely to achieve at a higher level than he thinks he can. He is, of course, more likely to achieve if all "significant others" agree that he has the ability to learn and if he has internalized within himself these expectations of others. Since such internalization of others' expectations is usually achieved rather early in life, the attitudes of parents and teachers toward students in the elementary school may be more effective than those of the parents and teachers of older students. The expectations of "significant others" are important, however, at all levels because self-concepts do change over the years.

The expectations of "significant others" are important to young people of all ability levels. The following comment by an unknown writer pleads for recognition of "average" students:

> Our daughter graduated in the middle of her high school class. Her College Entrance Examination Board test scores were around 500. Although she's so sparkly and lively that I'm sure she never was faceless to her teachers, she was an average student in our suburban school; she received little praise, little stimulation. How I wish that she'd had counselors or teachers like [the author of an article accompanying the writer's plea], who would have seen beyond her averageness, recognized her talents, and helped her capitalize on them!
>
> "Talents? With all those C's?" I can almost hear her teachers. And the counselor said to her, "You were lucky to be accepted at college,

and I hope you'll be able to stay in. Those big colleges fail a great many freshmen."

"I'll probably flunk out, Mother," my daughter sighed. "I'm just not smart."

I wish her counselor had reminded her that her beautiful singing voice had helped the altos in the chorus be heard—though she didn't have a solo part—in *The King and I* and that her way of telling or writing a story made her experiences come alive for others. I wish the counselor had pointed out that her talent for friendship might prove more valuable than the ability to work quadratic equations and that the persistence she showed by trying out four times (unsuccessfully) for the swimming team and by foregoing snacks while she lost 30 pounds might compensate somewhat for not being a "quick study."

My daughter might now be meeting her new challenges with enthusiasm rather than dread, if her counselor had been a . . .[27]

Not much is known about the relative influence of teachers and parents on a student's self-concept. Obviously such influence differs according to differences among teachers and parents as well as among students. Nevertheless, a reasonable assumption is that in general parents have more influence than teachers. If such an assumption is valid, consideration of the influence of the student's self-concept on his learning ability should be given a prominent place on Parent Teacher Association programs and in parent-teacher conferences. Little is achieved, however, by simply *telling* a student he is capable of learning. A parent's attitude must reflect his respect for his child's abilities and his expectation that the child will do well in school. He should guard against such remarks as "Girls can't learn mathematics," or "Boys never learn to spell—they don't need to anyway. They always have secretaries." A parent should praise a child's successes, encourage him when his performance is not up to expectations, and help him to develop good study habits.

Perhaps neither teachers nor parents realize the many subtle ways in which they convey to a student their low opinions of his abilities. A student does not need to be told in words in order for him to realize that he is thought to be stupid. When a teacher ignores a student, never addressing his remarks to him or asking him a hard question, the student knows what the instructor thinks of his ability. When the teacher never comments "That's a good idea," or writes on his paper, "Your work is improving" or "You can do better than this," the student knows how his ability is judged. When the teacher accepts an inferior piece of work, he is telling the student without words, "You know and

[27] Anon., *NEA Journal,* 57 (January, 1968), 8.

I know that your work is poor. But I know you can't do any better so I'll accept it." When such an attitude prevails, the student's performance will always be poor.

Thinking that he is able to learn a body of knowledge goes a long way toward helping a student to learn it. Sometimes a student's thinking he can learn does not assure success because his skills, previous information, or level of ability are unequal to the task. Nevertheless, since most students learn fairly well the common elements of their own culture, they should also be able to learn more in school than many of them do. In short, their attitudes toward learning and their emotional blocks to learning—not their capacity for learning—are likely to be the chief obstacles to learning. It is in this respect rather than in the interest and time that they spend upon learning teen-age culture and participating in student activities that the academic work of teen-agers is impaired.

When Coleman studied the adolescent subculture, he concluded that age-peers dominated the teen-ager and that as a result his academic work suffered.[28] He ignored the fact that the most popular boys and girls in most of the school cliques were college-bound. From evidence cited earlier, a reasonable conclusion is that the boys and girls whose academic work suffers most are not those who are active in the school's social life but those who are inactive. Nonparticipants, rather than participants, are likely to drop out of school and make low grades. A reasonable hypothesis is that unless an adolescent attains self-identity, finds an answer to "Who am I?" which he usually must do in part through close contact with his age-mates, he is not likely to do well in school. If administrators and teachers fully recognized the influence of the social climate of the school on learning, they would redouble their efforts to promote teen-age activities that would include all boys and girls in an accepting climate of opinion in terms of peers, teachers, and administrators.

IMPORTANT CONCEPTS

Ego identity. See pp. 332 ff.
Reference group. See p. 338.
Role. The behavior associated with a particular status. See pp. 336 ff.
Self-concept. See pp. 342 ff.
"Significant others." See pp. 343 ff.
Status. One's position in a group. See p. 336.

[28] Coleman, *op. cit.*, p. 9.

16. THE TEACHER'S SUBCULTURE

Teaching can be anything you want it to be. It can be a dull routine of hammering dull material into dull little heads. Or it can be a part of the most exciting effort on earth.

—FRANCIS KEPPEL[1]

In this chapter some of the many roles that a teacher may play in the school are discussed. Whether teaching meets the attributes of a profession will also be considered as well as the relationship of professionalism to the rising militancy of teachers.

For some time old roles of the teacher have been undergoing change, and new roles emerging. How do these changing roles influence the teachers' subculture? How do they influence teachers' human relationships within the school?

[1] Francis Keppel, "Biggest Venture," in D. Louise Sharp, ed., *Why Teach?* Holt, Rinehart and Winston, 1957, p. 122.

TEACHER ROLES IN THE SCHOOLS

In school a teacher's life has seldom been monotonous because he has so many different roles to play. Tomorrow's school may require of teachers even greater flexibility and creativeness in order to adjust to new and to some extent very different roles. Let us examine first the primary roles of teachers as they now exist. Then we shall discuss changes in these roles that seem to be in the offing.

For many years the main roles of a teacher have been as a director of learning, a disciplinarian, a judge, a counselor, a model for the young, and a sponsor of student activities.

A DIRECTOR OF LEARNING. The traditional role of the teacher, and still his most important one, is that of instructor. In order that he may be effective in this position, the teacher is endowed with institutionalized authority. He is the leader because he is the school's representative. He has designated responsibilities and powers, and his patterns of behavior are to a considerable extent predetermined. Not the least among these expected behaviors is that he remain somewhat aloof from his charges. Prestige depends in part upon idealization and is usually an illusion based on the partial perception of a personality. Even a teacher who is exceptionally gifted in personal leadership knows that keeping his social distance is effective in the maintenance of leadership.

As an instructor, the teacher is expected to know his subject and how to teach it. It is presumed that he knows how to plan for effective learning. He and others in the profession select information and skills from the accumulated lore of society that are judged important and appropriate learnings for pupils at a particular grade level. He then seeks to kindle his pupils' interests in mastering skills that will enable them to acquire knowledge. In this endeavor he may use various methods designed to elicit pupil involvement, ranging from the contagion of his own enthusiasm to the utilization of group dynamics. He tries to assure pupil success in mastery of learning through his organization of content, his explanations and demonstrations, and his guidance in group or class discussions. Ideally he provides a favorable climate for learning by his techniques of classroom management.

A DISCIPLINARIAN. To carry out his work, a teacher must maintain order in his classroom. As an institutionalized leader he is legally empowered to establish reasonable rules of conduct and to mete out reasonable punishments to children who break these rules. The teacher stands in *loco parentis* to the child and temporarily takes over much of the authority of the parent. In most states he is also personally liable for harm that befalls a child who is injured as a result of his negligence.

In modern educational practice, the teacher's role as a disciplinarian is somewhat easier and at the same time more difficult than it used to be. The role is easier in that learners are no longer expected to remain silently immobile throughout the day. Modern techniques give pupils a share in making rules and divert hostilities inherent in subordination into constructive channels, thus relieving the teacher of some of the tensions that were inevitable under highly authoritarian methods of discipline. Notwithstanding these changes, the problems of discipline today may be more difficult than they once were for the inexperienced, the inconsistent, and the authoritarian teacher. Today schools exert less institutionalized authority, depend more upon personal leadership, and permit pupils greater independence in most classrooms than in former years.

A JUDGE. In his role as judge, the teacher determines the grades that pupils receive. Most teachers wish they did not have to perform this difficult task, yet many of them fear that pupils will not study if grades are eliminated. The conscientious teacher wants to be fair. Therefore he must grade every paper, utilize every scrap of evidence, evaluate and reevaluate before assigning grades. Even then he knows that his criteria may be open to question. What behaviors should be rewarded? Effort? Neatness? Punctuality? Original thinking? Memorization? Honesty? Class participation? Attendance? Obedience? Leadership? Achievement? And what is achievement? Finally, he is always concerned that he may have rewarded a student who cheated.

Probably no phase of teaching is more important to pupil-teacher, parent-teacher, and teacher-teacher relationships than awarding grades. The execution of no other job is so likely to elicit complaints of unfairness. Since grades are considered so seriously by others, the teacher cannot take his responsibilities lightly. It is very easy to say that one does not believe in awarding grades (and there are many objections to the practice), but such an attitude does not absolve a teacher from the responsibility of awarding grades fairly in schools that require them. Except in the primary grades, most schools issue report cards upon which some sort of objective evaluation of pupil achievement is required. Occasionally a maverick teacher tries to defeat the system by awarding all A's. Such a practice may temporarily make him popular with pupils, but when the word gets out, as it will in time, the pupils feel less respect for the instructor and find less pleasure in the A, and the teacher's colleagues feel that he has not played the game fairly.

In this country the teacher is the judge of his own product. Some of the hostilities aroused by the grading system might be averted if this were not true. In some countries systems have been developed that temper the teacher's role as a judge. In Denmark, for instance, beginning in what we call the junior high school, pupils are examined orally at the end of the year by the classroom teacher as well as by another teacher from a different school. The evaluation is very careful and thorough, and the effectiveness of the teacher as well as the performance of the pupil is judged. In such cases the pupil and teacher become allies in their attempts to impress the external examiner favorably.

A COUNSELOR. In recent years much stress has been laid upon the importance of the teacher's role as a counselor. It should be apparent that most teachers are limited in their effectiveness as personal advisor and confidant. This role is, in fact, in contradiction to his role as a judge and as a disciplinarian. When he is sought out by a child as a counselor, his first duty is to be aware of his own limitations. His teaching credential does not entitle him to become a practicing psychologist, and he may do more harm than good if he tries to act as one. Prospective teachers and teachers in service learn psychological principles to help them establish better conditions for learning, aid them in conferences with students and parents, and teach them to recognize children who need professional assistance. Although such assumptions about the teacher's role as a counselor are commonly held, almost everyone knows at least one great teacher who was, in fact, an excellent counselor. Often he used homespun methods of counseling that reflected his understanding of and respect for his student and his own integrity.

Since a student may discuss many different kinds of problems with a teacher, the teacher's role as a counselor varies. Sometimes he is asked only for information. At other times a student uses the teacher as a confidant. In such instances, the teacher is ethically bound to respect the confidences. When these confidences involve illicit, immoral, or questionable practices, knowing about them may be very disturbing to a teacher. The teacher is torn between responsibilities to the school, society, and parents and loyalty to the informer. When such a situation arises, the teacher can only rely on his own good judgment. Often a pupil simply wants to talk with an adult about his problems, and in this event the teacher's wisest response is just to listen. Amateur counselors, especially teachers who talk too much, underestimate the therapeutic value that a young person derives from simply telling his troubles to an adult whom he trusts. In analyzing his difficulties, he thinks through his own solutions. Since the goal of all teaching and counseling is to develop self-reliant individuals who can solve their own problems, the teacher who merely listens may contribute more than he can in any other way.

A MODEL FOR THE YOUNG. Parental and community expectations of teachers in this role are not so demanding as they were 20 or 30 years ago. Nevertheless even today parents may expect teachers to exemplify moral standards higher than their own. Admittedly teachers have less influence upon the attitudes, beliefs, and values of young people than do parents, but they have more influence, especially upon young children, than do other adults outside the family. It is difficult to evaluate the extent of their influence. Perhaps the most valid statement must be qualified with "weasel" words: *Some* teachers have *some* influence on the attitudes and values of *some* children.

A SPONSOR OF STUDENT ACTIVITIES. At the junior and senior high school levels, teachers serve as advisers of student activities. Individual teachers differ in their interest in, and perhaps in their aptitudes for, these duties. In a sense the responsibilities are more like those of a recreation leader than of a classroom instructor. Many teachers feel that they learn to know pupils better and develop closer affectional ties with them in cocurricular activities than they do in the more formal classroom situation.

These teacher roles are expected to change in several ways. Each of the teacher's roles may be greatly influenced by "systems engineering," sometimes called "systems." Systems engineering is the process of looking at the overall operation of an organization to determine if it is accomplishing its goals. Systems engineers study what people in various roles really do and how well they succeed in attaining their objectives. With respect to the teacher's roles, then, systems engineering would require that a teacher's objectives be expressed in terms of expected changes in student behaviors and evaluated in terms of whether such changes occurred. Likewise student goals and objectives would be clarified and evaluated. No longer would a teacher be the judge of his own product or relatively autonomous in directing learning in the classroom and in student activities. Even in counseling situations he would be aware of objectives expressed in behavioral terms and judge his success in these terms. On the other hand, systems engineering would help to eliminate dull teaching and to make it the "most exciting effort on earth," and also provide many teachers with an expertise they do not now possess.

Another innovation likely to change the teacher's role is the increasing use of audio-visual aids, computers, and programmed instruction. Since machines can relieve teachers of much burdensome detail and drill, teachers will be free to fully develop uniquely human capacities—the affective as well as the cognitive. The teacher's role regarding students must change if developing students' creativeness, esthetic appreciations, interpersonal skills, and independence of thought become primary goals.

The teacher's role will also change if new "social technologies" are widely adopted. Increasingly teachers are enrolling in "sensitivity-training groups," "T-groups," or "human-relations groups." Carl Rogers of the Western Behavioral Science Institute says that intensive group experience will "create a climate conducive to personal growth in which innovation is not frightening, in which the creative capacities of administrators, teachers, and students are nourished and expressed rather than stifled."[2]

Another new teaching invention is the simulation exercise or "educational game." Although such games may not represent a better method

[2] Quoted in Richard E. Farson, "Emotional Barriers to Education," *Psychology Today*, 1 (October, 1967), 35.

of teaching subject matter, they do alter teacher-student relationships. In a game situation, students become the content specialists, judges, disciplinarians, and record keepers. The games encourage students to engage in intensive inquiry, decision-making processes, and intimate communication. Farson believes that such innovations will make learning "fun, joyful, deeply involving."[3] They will also change the role of the teacher from that of a task-master to that of a guide, participant, and leader.

Other innovations, such as flexible scheduling, team teaching, and the ungraded classroom, as well as such new methods as the "inquiry" or "discovery" method, programmed learning, and interaction analysis are also modifying the role of the teacher. Teachers as well as adolescents are increasingly questioning the use of competitive grades. Since the role of the teacher as a judge is the chief handicap to developing many of the new roles, such questioning is a healthful development. Helping students to master the skills needed for lifelong learning and encouraging them to be sensitive to the needs of others, creative, and independent in thinking are more appropriate goals than imparting a body of knowledge in an era when knowledge itself is being rapidly expanded. Competence will be required of teachers in such a flexible, stimulating environment. Hence a teacher will need to acquire greater skills and knowledge than many teachers today possess.

The greater the teacher's expertise, the more likely he is, however, to be universally accorded the professional status to which he aspires. Just what does professionalism entail?

THE TEACHER AS A MEMBER OF A PROFESSION

A profession is generally defined as a vocation requiring special knowledge of a department of learning or science. In this discussion more specific attributes of a profession are delineated as a basis for judging teaching as a profession and for describing the teacher's role as a professional person.

Ernest Greenwood's article on professionalism, summarized and paraphrased here, will serve as the basis for an evaluation of teaching as a profession.[4] In using polar concepts of professionalism and non-

---

[3] *Ibid.*

[4] Ernest Greenwood, "Attributes of a Profession," *Social Work*, 2 (July, 1957), 45–55 *passim;* also in Sigmund Nosow and William H. Form, eds., *Man, Work, and Society*, Basic Books, 1962, pp. 206–218.

professionalism as Greenwood does, one must think in terms of a continuum rather than of discrete entities. That is, some occupations are more nearly professional than others, the range being from the most highly professional occupations to those that have little or no relationship to a profession. Hence the occupations of lawyers, professors, ministers, and physicians contrast sharply in degree of professionalism with those of migratory workers, garbage collectors, and scrubwomen; other vocations fall somewhere in between these extremes.

Greenwood isolates the following five characteristics attributed to professions:

Systematic Body of Theory

The difference between a profession and nonprofession does not necessarily lie in the element of skill; a diamond-cutter, for example, has more manual dexterity and infallible expertness than a professor. The crucial distinction is that professional skills "flow from and are supported by a fund of knowledge that has been organized into an internally consistent system, called a *body of theory*." Theory is the "groundwork for practice" in a profession. Since the practices of a profession are based on an acquisition of theory, "preparation for a profession must be an intellectual as well as a practical experience." Professional preparation is therefore more abstract and academic, includes more intellectual content, and requires more formal education than does apprentice training.

Because theory is essential to the development of practice in a profession, much activity within the profession is devoted to "theory construction via systematic research." Professionals test their theories by applying the scientific method to problems of the profession. Their attitude is characterized by rationality: They question existing theories and new conceptualizations. Much of the activity of professional associations involves theoretical considerations. The emphasis upon theory among professional people creates "an intellectually stimulating milieu" that is in marked contrast to the occupational environment of a nonprofessional worker.

In every profession some individuals devote their efforts to expanding knowledge through theoretical research and others put into practice the theory and research findings. Not only is there a division of labor between the theory-oriented and the practice-oriented groups, but also the developing body of theory creates cleavages within the profession by promoting specialties.

Does teaching have a body of theory? There can be little doubt that it does—unsystematized perhaps and sometimes contradictory. The psychological, philosophical, and social foundations of education usually provide the theoretical bases for methodology and research. Experimentalist philosophy, based largely on the theories of John Dewey, and theories of child development have been very influential in American schools, especially in elementary schools. Other theories of recent origin are being tested. For example, Flanders and others hypothesize that a dimension Flanders calls "indirectness" in teacher behavior leads to increased achievement on the part of students. The so-called "discovery method" is predicated on the same theory. Bruner, B. O. Smith, Ausubel, Gage, Hickey, and Newton theorize similarly with respect to the "cognitive structure" or organization of materials to be learned.[5] New theories of learning are expected to emerge out of biological research now in process.

Many teachers, almost totally unaware of the theoretical assumptions that they make in their daily work, are indifferent to the relationship between theory and practice and are prone to accept current theory as absolute truth. As undergraduates and perhaps as graduate students, they may jeer at professors who discuss theory and not practices and procedures. Professors of education are partly to blame for these attitudes. The professor who knows full well the benefits and limitations of theory is pressed by students for absolutes, for clean-cut, how-to-do-it recipes. If he hedges, the students brand him as incompetent. Finally under pressure what he started to expound as theory sounds like dictum. Any competent professor of education can and should make applications of theory, but if students graduate with only cookbook recipes about how to teach, they have been cheated. If they do not understand the theory and research behind practice, they do not know *why* they teach as they do. Furthermore, they cannot explain an educational program to the public nor develop new and creative approaches to teaching.

Let us take a simple illustration. Methods of helping children learn to read have changed because the theory changed. Traditionally children were taught the alphabet first, then short words and syllables, followed by longer words, and finally sentences. To early theorists this approach seemed logical. Later theorists began to think in terms of perception. Do we recognize a person because we have added together his various features, body structure, coloring, and the like, or do we recognize him at a glance when we see him or even when we see only

[5] Nathaniel L. Gage, "Can Science Contribute to the Art of Teaching," *Phi Delta Kappan,* 49 (March, 1966), 399–403.

part of him? Just as we may recognize a person without remembering the color of his eyes, we can recognize a word, a phrase, or a sentence without recalling whether a specific word had an "i" or an "e" in it. A radical change in the method of teaching reading developed from such concepts followed by experimentation. The result is that one widely accepted method of teaching reading today requires that children be taught to read whole phrases and sentences before they discover the alphabet and syllabication. This explanation is, of course, an over-simplification of reading theories, but it illustrates how a change in theoretical assumptions can set off a chain of new developments.

As theories are tested and elaborated and as new and sometimes better theories emerge, better methods of teaching are initiated. Unfortunately many practicing teachers fail to keep up with current theory and research. It is said to take 20 years for proved experimental results to trickle down to the level of common practice. Not all teachers, of course, should be judged by the shortcomings of some teachers. Certainly many professional-minded teachers are well acquainted with recent research, cognizant of theoretical assumptions, active in professional associations and in-service training programs where new research findings are discussed. Nevertheless, teachers probably would not fare well in comparison with some other professionals in their attitudes toward theory. The conclusion might be drawn that although teaching skills are derived from a body of theory, not all members of the teaching profession are fully conversant with the theories.

Professional Authority

The professional educated in the systematized theory of his discipline possesses a body of knowledge that the layman does not have. This knowledge gives the professional an authority in his field. Unlike the customer in a store who decides for himself what he needs, the client of a professional believes that the professional knows what he needs. Because the professional has a "monopoly of judgment," he is constrained by the professional-client relationship to restrict his authority. He cannot use the professional relationship in which his client is dependent upon him to satisfy his own need to manipulate others, to live vicariously, or as a sexual outlet. Extraprofessional relations between client and professional tend to impair professional authority and lessen the professional's effectiveness, as many a doctor has reason to know.

Does the lay public accord teachers a "monopoly of judgment"? Is he considered an authority? The criticisms of the teaching of reading clearly indicate that many people believe that they know how to teach children to read better than teachers do. Similar criticisms of teaching methods and of the knowledge of high school teachers suggest that many people, especially those in the middle class, do not consider the teacher an authority in his field. A factor that weakens the teacher's "monopoly of judgment" is the educator's view that "the schools belong to the people." Educational leadership has tried to draw a line between the public's authority and the teacher's sphere of expertness by pointing out that the community should decide the general policy in respect to what should be taught and the teacher should be responsible for details of content and methodology. But at the local community level the line has not always been held.

Although a teacher is not granted a complete monopoly of expertness, he has considerable discretion, through selection of materials for study, in the content of classwork. State departments of education provide guidelines. The NEA code of ethics warns him to "discuss controversial issues from an objective point of view, thereby keeping his class free from partisan opinions." The publications of professional organizations keep him posted on current issues. The teacher's subculture forbids his introducing discussions of sexual behavior except under certain conditions and prohibits his use of obscenity, profanity, and vulgarity. The teaching norms warn a teacher against extraprofessional relationships with pupils that may weaken his effectiveness as a teacher. The neophyte who becomes an equal and intimate of his pupils soon learns the error of his ways. He loses his equalitarian status among teachers and becomes a competitor or a love object rather than a guide to young people.

Sanction of the Community

The members of each profession try to induce society to recognize their authority by giving them certain powers and privileges. Professional organizations seek to control the admission of persons to the profession, the accrediting of training centers, and the licensing of individuals. Among the privileges members of a profession want is that of "privileged communication," the legal right to keep confidences between professional and client confidential. They want to be judged on technical matters by their colleagues, not by laymen. Such powers and privileges are not easily gained because many people resist strongly the profession's claim to authority. Members of the profession have to persuade lay people that they will benefit by giving them such privileges.

Specifically the profession seeks to prove: that the performance of the occupational skill requires specialized education; that those who possess this education, in contrast to those who do not, deliver a superior service; and that the human need being served is of sufficient social importance to justify the superior performance.[6]

To what extent do teachers have "the sanction of the community?" Teachers as a professional group have little control over who becomes a teacher. Unlike medical professionals who are accused of deliberately limiting the number of applicants to medical schools, teachers cannot prevent almost anybody who can earn a college degree from becoming a teacher. Although a few are eliminated by selection processes in professional schools, many persons who major in liberal arts and take the minimum number of hours in education are never evaluated formally by anyone except a critic teacher, and then only by one person using limited criteria. If they can pass the courses, they get a state credential. In 1946 the NEA created the National Commission on Teacher Education and Professional Standards, and in 1952 several agencies cooperated in founding the National Council for Accreditation of Teacher Education. Both of these agencies are working to raise the level of professional education of teachers.

In recent years many persons have entered teaching on emergency credentials at the recommendations of school superintendents and with the approval of the state departments of education. Some teachers on emergency credentials have had little formal college training in either liberal arts or professional education. The teacher shortage seemed to justify emergency credentials, but somehow the "emergency," with little abatement, has lasted for over two decades. The question might be raised as to whether lowering or raising standards is the better way to encourage qualified persons to enter teaching. The number of unqualified teachers who are employed in American schools is undoubtedly a factor in the folk belief that "anybody can teach school."

Martin Mayer, a professional writer who has observed hundreds of teachers, in *The Schools* says that teaching, like journalism, can never become a profession as long as a "gifted amateur" can do the work as well as a professionally educated person. By this criterion few professionals exist. A few years ago a clever impersonator posed as a physician, performed surgery, and served under the surveillance of physicians as a medical doctor in the armed forces. Another posed successfully as a college dean after falsely claiming that he had a doc-

[6] Greenwood in Nosow and Form, *op. cit.*, p. 212.

torate. It is still possible for a gifted and persistent person to read law on his own and pass a state bar examination, and much legal work is done by accountants, law clerks, and auditors who do not hold law degrees. The knowledge of subject matter or the theories upon which teaching skills are based can be learned without formal instruction. To deny that a gifted person can learn without the benefit of formal education would be to deny the very purpose of formal education, but rules are made to cover the usual and not the unusual cases. Clearly the majority of persons benefit from the education required of teachers. Exceptions can then be made for persons who offer equivalences for specific requirements.

Teacher-education programs differ somewhat, however, from state to state because the requirements for a credential are determined in different ways in different states. The power to specify the requirements is divided among legislatures, boards of education, teacher-training institutions, state departments of education, and superintendents of public instruction. The hodgepodge of programs that developed contribute to the layman's belief that there are no theories a person should understand or specific skills that he should acquire before he begins to teach.

Regulative Code of Ethics

Since a professional's monopoly can be abused by malpractice that might cause the community to revoke power and privileges, the profession as a whole adopts a regulative code to compel members to behave ethically. Such a code is in part formal and in part informal. In it the profession pledges itself to social welfare. It specifies that a member of a profession must provide services to anyone who requests them, irrespective of the applicant's income, religion, politics, race, and other such factors. Whether he likes or dislikes the applicant is irrelevant. He must give the best service of which he is capable, even at the sacrifice of personal convenience.

The code further requires that the professional's behavior in relationships with his professional associates shall be "cooperative, equalitarian, and supportive." He shares technical knowledge. He does not compete blatantly for clients. He regards his colleagues as equals and grants professional recognition to those whose performance in practice or whose contributions to theoretical research are superior to his own. He supports his fellow professionals by his words and actions in the presence of those who are not members of the profession.

The code is enforced by pressures upon individual members to exert self-discipline. Through consultation and referral, colleagues become mutually interdependent. When a professional behaves in an unseemly manner, he is excluded from this sytem of reciprocity. For serious offenses the professional association may censure a member or even bar him from further membership in the association. To be disbarred from the association can be a stigma that may prevent a member from pursuing the profession.

Do public school teachers subscribe to a Code of Ethics? The NEA Code is presumably accepted by NEA members. Over half of the state education associations use the same code or a similar one. This code sets out the obligations of teachers toward pupils, parents, the community, and the school administration.

Among other provisions, it states that the teacher's first obligation is that he "deal justly and impartially with students regardless of their physical, mental, emotional, political, economic, social, racial, or religious characteristics." He is admonished to maintain "a professional level of service." He should "speak constructively of other teachers" and deal with them as he himself wishes to be treated. The provisions spell out ethical conduct for a teacher in respect to securing and honoring contracts, his behavior in a community, and his obligation to respect the basic responsibility of parents for their children.

A professional code is effective to the extent that members of a profession understand and accept the code's principles and abide by them. The severest punishment that can be meted out to one who breaks such a code is the revoking of his membership in the professional association. Expulsion of a member from the NEA is, however, relatively meaningless since almost half of the nation's teachers do not belong to this association. Until the day when teachers must belong to a professional association as a condition of employment, an association's rebuke cannot effectively discipline offenders.

The Professional Culture

All occupations operate through a system of formal and informal groupings. The formal professional groupings are the institutions (universities, hospitals, law offices, public schools and the like) within which professionals give service to clients, the educational and research centers of the profession, and the professional associations. The informal professional groupings consist of cliques of colleagues formed around specialities, professional affiliations, place of work, personal attraction, and perhaps family, religious, and ethnic backgrounds. As a result, a professional culture develops that is quite different from the nonprofessional culture. Each profession also develops its own subcultures or variants of the professional culture.

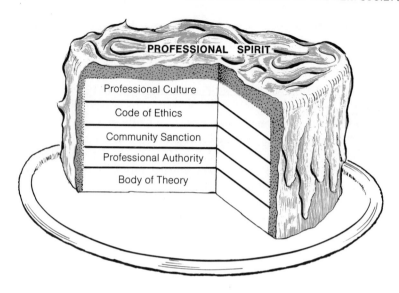

PROFESSIONAL SPIRIT

Professional Culture

Code of Ethics

Community Sanction

Professional Authority

Body of Theory

The content of professional culture is its values, norms, and symbols. The most fundamental of its beliefs is the social value that each subculture attributes to its own contributions to the general welfare. The members of a profession believe that they are far more knowledgeable in their sphere of expertness than are any outsiders. Nevertheless, within the subculture the professional's theory and technical knowledge are often challenged. Subcultural norms are the standards of behavior in social relationships. There are approved modi operandi for obtaining appointments, making referrals, and holding consultations. There are proper ways of relating to clients, peers, superiors, and subordinates. Greenwood defines the symbols of a profession as its "meaning-laden items," such as its distinctive dress, its history and folklore, its heroes and its villains; and its stereotypes of its own members, of its clients, and of laymen.

The professional thinks of his occupation as a career, a calling. His work is not "a means to an end; it is an end itself." He considers his service valuable, and performs it primarily for psychic satisfaction rather than for monetary gain. He is absorbed in his work, both on and off the job. His work is his life. The novice in a profession is not a part of it simply because he has learned its theory and mastered technical skill. He must also accept the subcultural values, norms, and symbols of the subculture. One of the purposes of a professional school is to screen out those who might be deviants. If a neophyte cannot acquit himself acceptably in relationships with clients, laymen, and colleagues, he will be judged unfit, irrespective of his academic qualifications.

A teaching subculture is a reality in the nation and in every community. The most significant element of this subculture is the general belief among teachers that they are serving mankind in an important way. Their chief concern is for the children they teach, and much of their "shop talk," sometimes ridiculed by outsiders, is about their pupils. Most teachers are willing to work overtime at night and on week ends if they believe the welfare of their pupils is thereby advanced. In 1915 Abraham Flexner analyzed a profession as basically practical, organized internally, altruistic, and intellectual, based on great knowledge and having techniques that can be taught and learned. After a careful analysis of these criteria, he almost tossed them away by declaring that:

> what matters most is professional spirit. . . . The unselfish devotion of those who have chosen to give themselves to making the world a fitter place to live in can fill social work [or teaching] with the professional spirit and thus to some extent lift it above all the distinctions which I have been at such pains to make.[7]

Most people, like Flexner, believed that a profession is distinguished by its moral behavior and its concern for other human beings.

The teacher's subculture has other distinctive characteristics. Although in many respects teachers are less confident of the expertness of some of their colleagues, less knowledgeable of theory, and therefore less intelligently critical of technical knowledge than might be expected of professionals, they are usually as cooperative and supportive of one another as are any other professionals. They use a specialized vocabulary in discussing school problems, develop patterns of behavior (such as addressing each other as "Miss" or "Mister" in the presence of pupils) deemed appropriate to the institutionalized setting, and maintain standards of dress. Teachers are sometimes hypercorrect in their patterns of speech. One of the unfortunate occupational hazards of teaching, which is perhaps less apparent today than in earlier years, is a habit of speaking with authority even on subjects in which the teacher is not an expert. Another characteristic common among elementary school teachers is a tendency to talk to adults as if they were children. Such practices contribute to the stereotype that a

---

[7] Abraham Flexner, "Is Social Work a Profession?" *Proceedings of the National Conference of Charities and Correction*, Hildmann, 1915, pp. 576–590.

teacher is a didactic person. On her first airplane trip, Miss Dove, the teacher-heroine of novel and film, sat close to the pilot to instruct him in celestial navigation!

The Discrepancy Between Reality and the Ideal

The preceding discussion may convey the impression that teaching does not really meet the criteria for a profession. When other limitations are considered, such as the number of girls who use teaching as a stepping-stone to marriage, the fact that teachers are public servants, and the number of diverse groups including school adminstrators that are bunched together as members of the teaching profession, the complexities involved in determining professional status of teachers are compounded. Clearly college and university professors have less ambiguous claims to the status than do public school teachers because they are more knowledgeable of theory, more highly educated in esoteric and difficult bodies of knowledge, and more likely to be accepted as experts in their fields. They have more but not complete control over admission to the profession, training of applicants, and evaluation of performance of colleagues, but they too are institutionalized employees who are imperfectly organized internally and subject to social pressures.

Significant to any discussion of professionalism is an acceptance of the view that professional status is actually an honorific symbol of prestige.[8] No group ever completely attains its professional goals or measures up to the ideal attributes of a profession. The medical profession is perhaps the most powerful of all career groups in such matters as controlling admittance to the profession, but it falls short in many respects. It does not have a monopoly of the knowedge of medicine, for much of the knowledge is known and created by scientists who are not doctors of medicine. The profession shares its social function of healing the sick with osteopaths, chiropractors, Christian Science practitioners, and others. Some physicians apparently place making money above service, and their numbers may be growing because medical students today, according to interest and value tests, are much like businessmen in their attitudes. Laymen do make judgments about doctors and demonstrate their lack of faith in the medical expert by shopping around for a "good" doctor. As in all professions, there are unethical practitioners. Even doctors who are usually ethical may be

[8] See Howard S. Becker, "The Nature of a Profession," in National Society for the Study of Education, 61st Yearbook, part 2, *Education for the Professions*, University of Chicago Press, 1962, pp. 33–46.

influenced by what the client wants, prescribing new drugs upon demand, for instance. Many physicians are also employees of institutions in which they are subject to the same bureaucratic pressures as professors and teachers.[9]

If the ideal of complete professionalism is unobtainable, why should an occupational group ever strive toward a professional goal? Becker says, "Symbols are useful things. They help people and groups organize their lives and embody conceptions of what is good and worthwhile. They enhance the possibility of purposeful collective action. They make more likely the realization of ideals held by large segments of society."[10] He suggests, however, that a symbol with so many dysfunctional elements, such as the monopoly of a sphere of knowledge and failure of clients to accept professional judgment, may need revision. He believes the symbol should fit the realities of the present-day world.

If the symbol of professionalism is to be useful to teachers, it must evoke at least five significant responses. These are great concern and effort on the part of teachers to keep abreast of elaborations of theory and research, participation in professional associations, high standards of competence, wholehearted acceptance of a code of ethics, and a sense of moral responsibility. Only in the last response, which fortunately is of great significance, do teachers compare well with people in other professions. Martin Mayer concludes that teachers are "good people," but he also thinks that most teachers believe themselves to be better teachers than they are in fact. Although Mayer's credentials as a critic might be questioned, his words should give us pause.

With the exception of his participation in national and state professional associations, the test of a teacher as a professional person is his behavior in his own school and community. Is he ethical in his relationships with pupils, colleagues, parents, the administration, and the lay public? Does he know and abide by the ground rules of his profession? Is he interested in improving his competence as a teacher? Does he honestly give the *best* service of which he is capable? Is he fair and unbiased in the classroom? Does he keep the confidences of his students? Is he respected for his skill as a teacher and for his integrity? These are criteria by which a teacher is judged as a professional.

Recent growth in membership of the American Federation of Teachers (AFT), an affiliate of the CIO–AFL, which encourages militancy and espouses teacher strikes under certain circumstances, has led to

[9] See Becker, *op. cit.*, pp. 41–45, for a summary and analysis of research on the medical profession.

[10] Becker, *op. cit.*, p. 45.

charges that this organization is unprofessional. If such is the case, does the lack of professionalism lie in AFT's failure to abide by the ground rules? Should they be changed? These questions will be considered in the discussion that follows.

TEACHER POWER

Nowadays many groups are staking out claims to "power": Black Power, Student Power, Teacher Power. All of these groups feel that they do not have or have not exerted enough "power." What is power? Power is a pejorative word in the sense that it usually implies force or control of others. Let us define it with respect to teachers' demands as "influence." In what spheres have teachers lacked influence in the past? In what spheres are many teachers now bidding for power?

Teachers have traditionally had a great deal of autonomy within their classrooms, but they have generally had little influence with respect to the formulation of school policies. As the agent of the state, the school board is the legal governing body responsible for school policies. The board employs the superintendent and other administrative officers who are responsible for carrying out the board's policy. Thus legally teachers are not responsible for policy-making.

The school board, representing residents of a school district, presumably assures the dominance of lay people and the community in the control of schools. The members of the board, who are considered state officials, hold a position of public trust. In the majority of states they are paid very little or given no compensation for their services. As a consequence, in very few states would a person offer his candidacy for the board because of the pecuniary rewards involved. Members of the board are sometimes appointed, but usually they are elected in a nonpartisan election. No matter how they are chosen, the majority of members are generally business and professional men, except in rural areas where many of them are farmers. Their incomes and educational levels tend to be higher than the average in their communities.

When board members are appointed, persons of influence in the community are usually selected. When members of the board are elected, any well-organized minority can easily elect its candidates. In school-board elections often no more than 4 or 5 percent of the electorate vote; a 25 percent vote would be considered heavy. The result is that the community's power structure often dictates the choice of school-board members.

A study of Springdale in upper New York State disclosed that four of the school-board members were farmers because of an informal political agreement made in 1937 when the school was consolidated. The fifth member, the village representative, was selected by the board itself and the town's "invisible government"—notably by two members of the power group, a feedstore-owner long interested in school affairs, and the school's legal counselor.[11] Keith Goldhammer found in Valley City that the school board was to a considerable extent a self-perpetuating group representing the power clique.[12] Since both of these studies were made in small towns, the power group was more directly interested in the school board than would probably have been the case if the power structure of cities had been studied.

Does the dominance of the school board by a special-interest group pervert the school's program? Researchers in Springdale claim it does. The school board there, dominated by farmers, had an uneasy alliance with the town's business interests in its support of low taxes, in protecting town property from possible vandalism by school children, and in making school purchases locally. Beyond that the interests of farmers were catered to by the board. Preference in hiring teachers was given to applicants who had rural or small-town backgrounds. Emphasis in the school curriculum was placed on home economics and agricultural training. Almost half of the boys graduated had followed a course in agriculture, yet only a fifth of them became farmers. The college-preparatory course barely met the minimum state requirements. One recent innovation was a business course, a response to demands of the town's businessmen.

A survey of superintendents' opinions in Massachusetts found that the Catholic members of boards of education were judged to be less strongly motivated than the non-Catholic members by ideals of civic duty and more interested in representing a special-interest group and in furthering their own political careers.[13] The situation in Massachusetts is, of course, complicated by the number of parochial schools in that state rather than by intrinsic religious differences in attitudes toward civic duty. In an increasing number of communities more and more persons, irrespective of religious affiliations, are using school boards as stepping-stones to political careers.

In spite of spotty evidence here and there, studies of school-board

---

[11] Arthur J. Vidich and Joseph Bensman, *Small Town in Mass Society: Class, Power and Religion in a Rural Community,* Princeton University Press, 1958, chap. 7.

[12] Keith Goldhammer, "Community Power Structure and School Board Membership," *American School Board Journal, 130* (March, 1955), 23–25.

[13] Neal Gross, Ward S. Mason, and Alexander W. McEachern, *Explorations in Role Analysis: Studies of the School Superintendency Role,* Wiley, 1958, p. 199.

activities covering several states usually conclude that the general welfare of all children is of greater concern to school-board members than are the special interests of a socioeconomic group. Researchers also conclude that well-to-do, well-educated board members are more liberal in their attitudes toward educational problems than are persons of humble status.[14] Despite such conclusions, the conservative tenor of the typical school board in regard to educational expenditures has undoubtedly hamstrung many schools that needed facilities, additional professional staff, and curriculum revisions. The plight of schools in underprivileged areas of big cities has been described. Sexton suggests that the first step in improving "education for lower-income children would be to elect board members who are aggressively interested in the problems of underprivileged groups." In the history of Big City, a midwestern metropolis, only one Irish-Catholic, one Jew, and one Negro have ever served on the school board, Sexton says, yet these minority groups, together with Italo-Americans and Polish-Americans, constitute a majority of the city's population. Probably labor unions are best equipped to sponsor a school-board member from the ranks of the lower classes, but in most communities they have not done so.[15]

Although the composition of the school board may indeed influence the decisions made, few of the decisions relating to the school's day by day operations are made by the board. Such decisions are usually made by the school administrators. A school superintendent, with the aid of a few favorites, may make all decisions that the school board permits the school to make or he may allow teachers and principals to share in making decisions.

Many teachers show little interest in having a share in decision-making. From results of a study of teacher attitudes toward their role in decision-making in a town and two small cities, researchers concluded, "teachers do not aspire toward a powerful role in decision-making in most educational questions, or, for that matter, in other spheres of community life." They found "no evidence that most teachers are dissatisfied with their present limited roles as participants or decision-makers."[16] Zeigler, studying high school teachers, found

[14] Hal C. Teal, *Attitudes of Selected School Board Members Concerning Problems Facing Public Education,* doctoral thesis, University of Pittsburgh, *Dissertation Abstracts,* no. 12, 1956, 16:2375; and Richard E. Whalen, Jr., *Effectiveness of Elected and Appointed School Board Members,* unpublished doctoral thesis, Indiana University, 1953.

[15] Patricia Cayo Sexton, *Education and Income: Inequalities of Opportunity in Our Public Schools,* Viking, 1961, pp. 234–237.

[16] Robert B. Carson, Keith Goldhammer, and Roland J. Pellegrin, *Teacher Participation in the Community: Role Expectations and Behavior,* Eugene, Ore. Center for the Advanced Study of Educational Administration, 1967, pp. 52, 55.

their political role limited and their political orientation generally conservative.[17] Anderson and Parker also found that teachers make few suggestions for improving educational practices. Only 13 percent of the teachers said that they had taken part in planning an innovation that had been instituted.[18]

Leaders of teachers' organizations have, however, been powerful at the state level of decision-making. After studying how and by whom decisions about schools are made in three states, researchers found that leaders of the Missouri State Teachers Association and the Illinois Education Association worked closely with responsible lay leaders, prominent legislators, and the governor in setting educational policies. In Michigan, public-school interest groups were, like the governor and the legislators, in conflict over educational policies. In all three states, affiliates of the NEA articulated the policy. In Missouri and Illinois the public-school lobby, having easy access to decision-makers, practiced "consensus politics." In other words, the educational leaders made the best deal they could. In Missouri they gave up tenure and minimum-salary laws to appease the School Boards Association. The Michigan Education Association, however, placed emphasis on teacher welfare largely because of American Federation of Teachers (AFT) competition for teacher loyalties. As a result the MEA antagonized the school boards and superintendents' organizations.[19] Thus Michigan educational politics seem to exemplify an emerging trend, demonstrated in several states, of teacher militancy and conflict over educational policy.

Teacher Militancy—Pro and Con

For a long time liberal educational leaders have urged teachers to become active in decision making at both the school and community level. They reason that teachers have an expertise about educational matters that makes them potentially valuable contributors. They reject the role of second-class citizen for a teacher, explaining that teachers cannot teach students how to function as effective citizens if they themselves do not know how from first-hand experience.

[17] Harmon Zeigler, *The Political Life of American Teachers*, Prentice-Hall, 1967, p. 142.
[18] Theodore R. Anderson and James H. Parker, *The Participation of Teachers in School and Professional Affairs*, Iowa Urban Community Reserve Center and the Iowa Center for Research in School Administration, State University of Iowa, 1964, pp. 8–10.
[19] Nicholas A. Masters, Robert H. Salisbury, and Thomas H. Eliot, *State Politics and the Public Schools*, Knopf, 1964, pp. 262–275.

In the past, however, teachers have tended to accept the view that crucial decisions about schools should be made by lay people. Teach-- ers believed they should be nonpartisan. They were not active in poli- tics, nor did they reward legislators who voted for educational policies the teachers approved.

The studies cited earlier show that many teachers are still very con- servative in their political outlook. None of these studies was, however, made in a large metropolis, and probably the findings should not be generalized. The relative strength and rapid growth of AFT member- ships in big cities suggests that teachers in large urban centers are more militant than those in smaller cities. It is also commonly assumed that although all school systems are bureaucratic, big-city systems are more bureaucratic than those in smaller places. It is further assumed that feelings of powerlessness among teachers are associated with in- creased bureaucracy.

In testing the relationships between feelings of powerlessness among teachers and bureaucratic organizations, Moeller and Charters found unexpected results. Teachers in the more highly bureaucratic school systems had a significantly higher sense of power, particularly when engaged in committee work, than those in the less bureaucratic systems. These researchers concluded that bureaucracy is not necessar- ily associated with size of school district, repressive authority, or posi- tions of responsibility in the hands of teachers. They speculated that teachers who work in highly bureaucratic school systems had a sense of power when they were hired. In other words, a sense of power is a personal trait.[20]

Whatever the source of a sense of power, which is presumably related to militancy in some way, the evidence of growing militancy is clear. Teacher strikes have been making headlines, NEA sanctions are being implemented, collective bargaining negotiations are increasing rapidly, and the professionalization movement is gaining momentum. Much credit or blame, depending on one's point of view, can be taken by leaders of AFT affiliates. AFT competition has forced the NEA into a more aggressive stance than it took in former years.

NEA sanctions that, in effect, blacklist a school district for teachers considering jobs there, would, if enforceable, damage a community more seriously than a strike; yet lay people and many teachers are much more opposed to strikes than to sanctions. There is no doubt, however, that in general the AFT is a more radical organization than

[20] Gerald H. Moeller and W. W. Charters, "Relation of Bureaucratization to Sense of Power Among Teachers," *Administrative Science Quarterly*, 10 (March, 1966), 444–465.

the NEA. In 1961 the NEA took a belated stand for desegregated schools; the AFT, with Negroes constituting one-fifth of its membership, declared against segregated schools before the Supreme Court decision of 1954. Despite the recent rapid growth of AFT, the NEA is a much larger organization. Its strength is in the South and in rural and small-town areas; AFT strength is concentrated along the Eastern Seaboard and in big cities. NEA leaders usually have ready access to community and state decision-makers, whereas AFT leaders usually do not.

AFT militancy tends to alienate decision-makers and to violate the ground rules of the teachers' subculture (but not those of liberal educational leaders) with respect to political activism. AFT's association with labor is also an affront to those who view education as a profession. As a matter of fact, only a thin line separates a professional organization from a labor union. Both associations seek to improve working conditions and to obtain various benefits for members by using similar tactics. Recently in Belgium, physicians went on strike. The differences between the NEA and AFT are, therefore, probably differences in degree rather than in kind.

To promote the best interests of students and teachers, it is, in fact, desirable that the two groups reconcile their differences and merge. In a pluralistic society composed of many competing special-interest groups, teachers need to present a united front. The AFT, lacking ready access to decison-makers, cannot be so politically effective as the NEA. NEA affiliates, on the other hand, must adopt a strong position with regard to student and teacher welfare. When more than 100 children are bitten by rats in Baltimore's school buildings in a single year and teachers in some areas must purchase their own teaching materials, a unified, militant organization is the only means that can be used to effect change.

IMPORTANT CONCEPTS

Consensus politics. Political action by mutual agreement of political leaders as to what legislation will be submitted and supported.

Flexible scheduling. Class scheduling that is free to exploit a learning situation without regard for predetermined time limits.

Inquiry or "discovery" method. A method by which a student is motivated to see or learn for himself.

Institutionalized authority. Authority that is assigned to an individual because of his particular position in a bureaucracy, such as the school.

Interaction analysis. An analysis of the reciprocal action or effect of persons within a group like a class.

Loco Parentis. A Latin phrase meaning "in the place of a parent."

Norm. Any socially acceptable standard or mode of behavior. See p. 360.

Polar concepts. Contrastive constructs used by social scientists as an aid to clarifying related patterns and trends.

Professionalism. See pp. 352 ff.

Simulation exercise. An artificial exercise that approximates a real situation.

Systems engineering. See p. 351.

Team teaching. A method of teaching whereby students in a given course are taught by several teachers, each of whom may sometimes teach the whole group and sometimes part of it.

V. EPILOGUE

17. THE FUNCTION OF SCHOOLS IN A CHANGING SOCIETY

If he is indeed wise [the teacher] does not bid you enter the house of his wisdom, but rather leads you to the threshold of your own mind.
—KAHLIL GIBRAN[1]

The purpose of this final chapter is to knit the threads of evidence presented in earlier chapters into a meaningful whole by answering two questions: What should be the major function of schools in our changing society? Why should schools have such a major function? Answers to these questions form an interpretation with which the reader may disagree. No one can foresee what course American education should take nor persuade others what values and educational objectives they ought to cherish. This chapter is intended to be provocative rather than informative. Whatever its merits or limitations, the reader may well ponder the problems presented.

THE RELATIONSHIP BETWEEN AIMS AND FUNCTIONS

The word *function,* in one of its many senses, implies activity with reference to accomplishing an end for which a person exists or a thing or institution has been designed. The word connotes that the specified action or activity is proper or appropriate to the agent. When one speaks of the functions of an institution such as the school, he is talking about what the school does. He may believe that teaching children to read is a function of the school but that teaching children to dance is not a proper function—is not something the school ought to do.

Determining the objectives of schools has been a task at which many persons busy themselves. Politicians, editors, clergymen, scholars, philosophers, parents, and others tell educators what schools should do. Periodically educators and representatives of the community prepare statements that set forth the objectives of education, of the elementary school or the secondary school, or of one of the curricular fields. These lists of objectives clarify to some extent what the school intends to do, its aims, its purposes. It cannot be assumed that some stated objectives are not questionable or that they encompass all possible aims or purposes of the schools. Some critics disagree with stated objectives on both counts. Differences of opinion in respect to what American

1 Kahlil Gibran, *The Prophet,* Knopf, 1955, p. 56.

schools should do increase the complexity of problems that administrators and teachers face. Translated into objectives within a local school, these differences also contribute to the variety of functions found within the school.

In a sociological context, function means "the type or types of action of which a structure is distinctively capable." As seen by a sociologist, one of the functions of religion is to help people accept death. In short, whether or not religionists assert as an objective of religion that it should help individuals accept the inevitability of death, certain activities of religion achieve this result for some people.

Defining a function as action of which an institution is distinctively capable may lead one to speculate upon the extension of functions undertaken by modern schools. Is the school accepting responsibilities that it is not distinctively capable of carrying out? Is the school neglecting objectives that could be translated into activities that the school is distinctively capable of undertaking?

Functions rather than objectives, a sociologist might suggest, describe how a school actually operates. Discrepancies between the stated objectives and what actually takes place in a school are readily apparent. Formally stated objectives like those adopted by representatives to the White House Conference of 1955 are not necessarily put into practice in the classroom. (See p. 285.) In Miss Jordan's class, described in Chapter 14, we saw little evidence that "intellectual curiosity" was encouraged; in Miss Cope's class we found little "appreciation for our democratic heritage" if we interpret "appreciation" more broadly than experimenting; in Miss Anton's class we read nothing about how the children learned ethical behavior "based on a sense of moral and spiritual values." Furthermore, listed objectives do not imply that schools should indiscriminately transmit all American values to the young. Only selected values—the democratic beliefs, the ethics, and the aesthetic appreciations accepted in our culture—are specified as objectives of schools. Nowhere in the stated objectives would one find an admonition that schools should inculcate materialism, ethnocentrism, social snobbery, or a fun morality; yet some schools do tolerate and inadvertently pass along these values to children. It is said that teachers in schools in the underprivileged areas of big cities are more permissive than other teachers in their attitudes toward illegal and, from a middle-class point of view, immoral activities. We must conclude therefore that not all stated objectives are carried out in schools and that not all functions in schools are the products of stated objectives.

COVERT AIMS AND FUNCTIONS

Early in the book the truism that schools mirror the society of which they are a part was stated. Throughout the text studies have been cited that bear out the conclusion that societal values are indeed reflected, albeit unheralded by formal acceptance, within the school. Tacit values of persons who believe in the "American way of life," the businessman's society, various special interests, messages of the mass media, philosophical theories, urban life styles, middle-class ethics, and bigoted assumptions about minority groups and foreigners influence what happens in schools. Teen-agers also contribute their value systems. Some of these values permeate the schools because they are widely accepted by teachers and pupils; others are implanted deliberately by persons who seek to identify their interests with those of the school. Many teachers and students do not seriously question the worth of values nor the validity of attitudes. Nevertheless, all these values and attitudes trigger action and produce activities in schools.

The school, for example, through its grading system and other systems of rewards, teaches children to be competitive. It perpetuates the social structure of the community in its selective function by steering middle-class children and gifted potential malcontents of the lower classes into college. It allows special-interest groups to propagandize their values. Since these activities are not subsumed under the stated objectives of schools, they are either unintended ends or they are functions that derive from covert aims. Because the school is assigned to do many things and because it also does other things that are not specified as formal objectives, teachers and others may become confused. Is there, in fact, anything that a school might do that is more important than many of its other activities? Is there an overriding goal or value that should prevail in the school?

Educators' Responsibilities for School Functions

The assumptions that a school reflects the society and its value-orientation and that a school belongs to the people provide teachers with an easy out when they are asked to face squarely the question of what functions exist in their schools. A laissez-faire attitude on the part of school personnel toward what the school does is a forfeiture of professional status by those who claim such status. In a pluralistic society, teachers cannot shirk their responsibility to operate as an organized group supporting certain values and certain school functions required of them by the nature of their work.

Their task is not easy. The multiple sources of values in a pluralistic society are complicated by the speed of cultural change. It has been said that today change is so rapid that persons separated by seven to eight years may be as far apart in their thinking and behavior as generations once were. Changes in social needs require modifications of school programs; for instance, adequate education for creative use of leisure is becoming imperative. Value-systems are changing rapidly. It is becoming increasingly difficult to decide what values the schools should maintain and what aims and functions are appropriate to schools.

Teachers have not been designated by society to become arbiters of values or of school policies. Neither are they second-class citizens who have no voice in social matters. On the contrary, they hold unique positions in respect to formal education. Teaching is their business; the education of the young is their major concern. To educate means to develop the special and general abilities of mind and body. It is reasonable to assume that all activities in which schools may be involved are contributory to this end for which schools were originally designed. A fundamental aim is to equip children with the basic skills and knowledge needed for intellectual development, but the mind can be developed in many directions through different kinds of experiences. What directions education chooses to take depends upon the values held by people in a society and particularly by those in charge of educating the young.

Parents and teachers can indoctrinate young people with totalitarian values. They can teach children to be obedient and obsequious, to be "other-directed" conformists, to be status seekers, to be anti-intellectual. They can close off compartments of the mind: they can teach the ideal and not the real, forbid the study of controversial issues, encourage dilettantism instead of scholarship. Those parents and teachers who subscribe to another set of values can present evidence that will encourage the young to value a free society, to become responsible, self-directing, and self-controlled individuals, to dare to be different when lack of conformity is desirable, to contribute to the general welfare, to be rational in decision-making. They can educate children to face real-life problems with open minds and with confidence that problems can be solved with knowledge, understanding, goodwill, and reason.

Such parents and teachers are transmitting their own values to children. The first group is inculcating values that are not useful to a democratic society; the second group is inculcating values that are more nearly in line with the highest values of a democratic society. They have chosen what, in the writer's judgment, is the wisest course that can be followed in the education of the young. What they value most are human dignity and freedom of the mind in its search for truth.

In a static society elders may transmit to the young their beliefs, and attitudes along with their skills and knowledge. No harm would result because all of these parts of the society's intellectual system would be useful to young people when they become adults. Even in a slowly changing society individuals would find most of the old mental patterns useful. In a rapidly changing society, however, many beliefs and attitudes that children acquire are outmoded when they grow up. The publicized business creed extols the virtues of a system of free enterprise that no longer exists, if it ever did. The kind of nationalism that patriotic groups urge schools to perpetuate hardly seems useful in our nation today. Puritan attitudes toward work, thrift, and play seem out of place in modern America. The perpetuation of such beliefs may be harmful in that they will handicap the young, when they become adults, in finding solutions to new problems.

Many traditional values and attitudes are, of course, still serviceable. A belief in the dignity of man, in freedom, in the use of reason, in cooperative endeavor and a feeling of concern for others are essential to the survival of a free society. In a search for the most important function that schools might undertake, we arrive at the conclusion that freeing children's minds to seek for truth is the activity that will best prepare them to face the problems in a changing society.

FREEING THE MIND:
THE MAJOR FUNCTION OF SCHOOLS

Freeing the mind to seek truth is a function that derives from accepting freedom of the mind as the highest value that public education should maintain. Selecting this value as particularly appropriate to schools is arbitrary. Some persons may choose ethical behavior, mental health, marketable skills, political democracy, or some other good. The choice of freedom of the mind can be justified on the following grounds. Education can be achieved only when the mind is free to explore wherever it will. Americans regard freedom from arbitrary restraints as a value of top priority, and freedom cannot exist without freedom of the mind. Freedom of the mind passes the basic test of a value of high priority, which means that it makes a maximum contribution to the survival of the society that accepts it. Finally, freedom of the mind (like freedom of the press) is a concept that can be readily translated into operational terms.

Just as the American press insists upon its right to publish "all the news that's fit to print" and is militant in its commitment to freedom of the press, American schools should insist upon their right to seek for truth wherever it may be found, and they should strongly resist inroads upon their freedom to do so. If American teachers believed in freedom of inquiry, books would not be taken from library shelves to pacify those who would censor them; oaths that test political belief and regulations that restrict the political rights of teachers would be fought by a united profession; administrative and school board decrees that curtail freedom of inquiry for either teachers or students would be protested; and the subjection of children to the biased points of view of special-interest groups would be carefully scrutinized. Controversial issues would be presented in the classroom, textbook study of problems would soon prove to be inadequate, critical thinking would be encouraged, and the atmosphere of the school would become exploratory, creative, and inventive. Teacher education, like all other subjects, would improve because freedom of inquiry implies a constant, creative search for better answers. The assumption made here is that a single value elevated above other values so as to become an ingredient of all aims to which schools aspire would revolutionize what schools and teachers do.

Brameld makes a strong case for freedom as a transcultural goal.[2] He believes that persons should choose between "eclectic aimlessness," "relativism," and "irresponsible neutrality" on the one hand, and a "normative commitment to the purpose of transcultural freedom" on the other. He states that a "man is free when he is able to consider and select that goal which among alternative goals is most desirable to him, to implement his choice by appropriate practice, and finally to have the satisfactions inherent in its achievement."[3] He would apply his concept to classroom discipline, administrative policies, teaching techniques, and curriculum construction. He suggests this principle to follow in the study of curriculum: "Does an established course of study demonstrably add to man's capacity to control nature and himself so that the quantity and quality of freedom are augmented further? If so, then let it remain. If not, then eliminate it and replace it with one that does."[4]

[2] Theodore Brameld, *Cultural Foundations of Education: An Interdisciplinary Exploration,* Harper & Row, 1957, chaps. 11 and 12.
[3] *Ibid.,* p. 230.
[4] *Ibid.,* p. 247.

Few would disagree with the selection of freeing men from arbitrary restraints as a transcultural goal. Specifying freedom in schools as the freedom of teachers and students to seek truth has three justifications. First, it is the kind of freedom that the school is distinctively capable of undertaking. No other institution in our society is so admirably suited as the school for considering issues dispassionately and objectively in relatively small groups. No other institution claims that its job is primarily to teach young people to think. No other institution deliberately provides the tools for thinking and sets a formal stage for practice in thinking under adult leadership. That some teachers and administrators fail to encourage independent, disciplined thinking is an indication of their personal inadequacies, not proof that the school is distinctively incapable of undertaking this task.

Second, freedom of the mind can become a rallying point for teachers and students, just as a free press has become the battle cry of newspapers; it can also be easily expanded when once grasped as a goal by a united profession. It can become a yardstick for measuring the adequacy of a library, a laboratory, and a resource center. It can encourage expansion of the curriculum so that all categories of knowledge appropriate to the pupils' level of maturity can be investigated. It can justify the provision of guidance services on the grounds that pupils handicapped by emotional problems and extreme anxieties are not truly free to think. It can change the "climate" of the school from threatening to nonthreatening as teachers and students work together with mutual respect at their task of finding better answers.

Finally, freedom of the mind is readily translated into purposes, techniques, and action. The teacher's purposes become clearly those of providing students with techniques for identifying and defining problems, finding and evaluating evidence, anticipating the consequences of decisions made from available alternatives, and of stimulaing students to think creatively, rationally, and reflectively. When the teacher's techniques reflect such purposes, students will do more than listening and memorizing. Then the school can bring its function (in the sense of what the school really accomplishes) in line with the objectives to which educators and parents subscribe.

IMPORTANT CONCEPTS

Covert function. Results or consequences not openly planned for by participants in a social system, such as the school.
Function. See pp. 373–375.
Objective. See p. 373.

SELECTED
READINGS

CHAPTER 1

BRAMELD, THEODORE, and STANLEY ELAM, eds., *Values in American Education, the Report of a Symposium,* Phi Delta Kappa, 1964. Papers by Gail Kennedy, Ronald Lippett, Hermann J. Muller, Morris E. Opler, and Theodore Brameld, followed by discussions.

GREENSTEIN, FRED J., "New Light on Changing American Values: A Forgotten Body of Survey Data," *Social Forces,* 42 (May, 1964), 441–456. Demonstrates that values have not changed as much as many people think they have.

HANDLIN, OSCAR, *The American People in the Twentieth Century,* Harvard University Press, 1954. Analysis of American values in this century by a well-known historian.

KIMBALL, SOLON T., and JAMES E. McCLELLAN, JR., *Education and the New America,* Random House, 1962. Offers many insights into the relationships between school and society.

MYRDAL, GUNNAR, *An American Dilemma,* Harper & Row, 1944. A classic work that has much relevance today.

WILLIAMS, ROBIN M., JR., *American Society: A Sociological Interpretation,* 2nd ed., Knopf, 1960. A reputable source of information on American institutions.

CHAPTER 2

CALLAHAN, RAYMOND E., *Education and the Cult of Efficiency: A Study of the Social Forces That Have Shaped the Administration of Public Schools,* University of Chicago Press, 1962. Examines, in historical perspective, the influences of the business ideology upon school administrators.

CURTI, MERLE, *The Social Ideas of American Educators: Reissue with a New Chapter on the Last Twenty-Five Years,* Pageant Books, 1959. Points to the influences of businessmen on education.

HEILBRONER, ROBERT L., *The Making of Economic Society,* Prentice-Hall, 1962. Economics for laymen by an economist.

HENRY, JULES, *Culture Against Man,* Random House, 1963, chaps. 2 and 3. Contains a bitter indictment of the business community.

KIMBALL, SOLON T., and JAMES E. McCLELLAN, JR., *Education and the New America,* Knopf, 1966, chap. 9. Points out the relationship of education and corporate society.

McCLELLAND, DAVID C., *The Roots of Consciousness,* Van Nostrand, 1964, chaps. 2 and 3. Presents psychological evidence that the achievement motive is allied to the entrepreneurial spirit.

RIPPA, S. ALEXANDER, *Education in a Free Society: An American History,* McKay, 1967, chap. 10. Discusses the impact of organized business upon education from the depression to the mid-1960s.

TAYLOR, OVERTON HUME, "The Free Enterprise Ideology and American Ideals and Institutions," *Daedalus,* 92 (Summer, 1963), 415–432. Presents a qualified defense of free enterprise.

CHAPTER 3

CICOUREL, AARON V., and JOHN I. KITSUSE, *The Educational Decision-Makers,* Bobbs-Merrill, 1963. Suggests that differences in treatment of students from different social classes is a built-in feature of counseling.

DAVIS, ALLISON, *Social-Class Influences upon Learning,* Harvard University Press, 1948. An early critique of mental testing and an insightful view of the disadvantaged child.

HAVIGHURST, ROBERT J., and BERNICE L. NEUGARTEN, *Society and Education,* 3rd ed., Allyn and Bacon, 1967. A thorough review of studies relating to the influence of social class upon education.

HOLLINGSHEAD, AUGUST B., *Elmtown's Youth,* Wiley, 1949. The earliest study of the influence of social class in a high school.

KAHL, JOSEPH A., *The American Class Structure,* Holt, Rinehart and Winston, 1957. A scholarly work on social class in the United States.

SEXTON, PATRICIA CAYO, *Education and Income,* Viking, 1961. A study of the effects of socioeconomic differences upon the schools of a large city.

CHAPTER 4

Belok, Michael, *et al.*, *Approaches to Values in Education*, Wm. C. Brown, 1966, chap. 6. A clear discussion of current disputes about the nature of democracy followed by an uncritical view of the school's role in fostering democracy.

Dewey, John, *Democracy and Education*, Macmillan, 1961. A significant work by a philosopher who viewed democracy as a "way of life" in which the school should provide experiences.

England, J. Merton, "The Democratic Faith in American Schoolbooks, 1783–1860," *American Quarterly*, 15 (Summer, 1963), 191–199. An analysis of democratic themes in early textbooks.

Muessig, Raymond H., "Youth Education: A Social-Philosophical Perspective," ASCD 1968 Yearbook, *Youth Education, Problems/Perspectives/Promises*, Association for Supervision and Curriculum Development, NEA, 1968, pp. 22–45. Relates democratic social philosophy to practices in secondary schools.

Steinberg, Ira S., *Educational Myths and Realities: Philosophical Essays on Education, Politics, and the Science of Behavior*, Addison-Wesley, 1968. Discusses democratic "myths" and the adoption of realistic perspectives in teaching citizens to be democratic.

CHAPTER 5

Brickman, William W., and Stanley Lehrer, *Religion, Government and Education*, Society for the Advancement of Education, 1961. A defense of aid to parochial and private schools.

Glock, Charles Y., and Rodney Stark, *Religion and Society in Tension*, Rand McNally, 1966. Covers a wide range of interesting and topical subjects, some of which, such as the relationship between science and religion, are pertinent to education.

Herberg, Will, *Protestant, Catholic, Jew*, Doubleday, 1955, 1960. Suggests that in this century traditional American religious distinctions have become eroded and that the major faiths are united in their veneration for the American way of life.

Lenski, Gerhard, *The Religious Factor*, Doubleday, 1961. A study of religion in the social and political lives of residents of Detroit. Claims the influence of religion is as great as that of social class.

Loder, James E., *Religion and the Public Schools*, The Association Press, 1965. A relatively up-to-date analysis.

Mills, C. Wright, *The Power Elite*, Oxford University Press, 1956. Speculative analysis of American elites.

Parsons, Malcolm B., *Perspectives in the Study of Politics*, Rand McNally, 1968. Attempts to provide the intellectual context of modern political science.

ROSE, ARNOLD, *The Power Structure*, Oxford University Press, 1967. Discusses the role of various groups in the United States that exert political pressure.

CHAPTER 6

BOULDING, KENNETH E., *The Meaning of the Twentieth Century*, Harper & Row, 1964. A thoughtful interpretation by a well-known economist.

CAFFREY, JOHN, and CHARLES J. MOSMANN, *Computers on Campus*, American Council on Education, 1967. A readable discussion of problems and uses.

CORWIN, RONALD G., *A Sociology of Education*, Appleton-Century-Crofts, 1965, chap. 2. A good discussion of bureaucracy.

DEGRAZIA, SEBASTIAN, *Of Time, Work, and Leisure*, Twentieth Century Fund, 1962. Overview giving historical background, current status, statistics based on 1960 census. Excellent bibliography and notes.

Developing Humane Capacities, ASCD 1970 Yearbook, Association for Supervision and Curriculum Development, NEA, 1970. Technological and human revolutions, the "knowledge explosion," and their implications for education. Papers by several well-known academicians and educationists.

GREEN, THOMAS F., *Work, Leisure and the American Schools*, Random House, 1968. Attempts to place work and leisure in perspective and to suggest implications for education.

KAIMANN, RICHARD A., and ROBERT W. MARKER, *Educational Data Processing*, Houghton Mifflin, 1967. Good source of information.

MARCH, JAMES G., ed., *Handbook of Organizations*, Rand McNally, 1965. An exhaustive treatment of bureaucracy and organizational problems.

MICHAEL, DONALD N., *The Next Generation*, Random House, 1965. A stimulating essay on the social effects of automation.

NOSOW, SIGMUND, and WILLIAM H. FORM, eds., *Man, Work and Society*, Basic Books, 1962. Well-selected articles.

ROSENBERG, JERRY M., *Automation, Manpower, and Education*, Random House, 1966. Implications for education of automation that include socio-psychological considerations. Government training programs. Labor-industry.

SCHULER, HERBERT, *et al.*, *Teacher Education and the New Media*, American Association of Colleges for Teacher Education, 1967. Cites research demonstrating results of new media.

SMIGEL, ERWIN O., ed., *Work and Leisure*, College and University Press, 1963. A good selection of articles.

Technology in Education, by the staff of *Education USA*, National School Public Relations Association, 1967. Reports recent technological developments.

CHAPTER 7

FERRY, W. H., and HARRY S. ASHMORE, *Mass Communications*, Fund for the Republic, 1966. A provocative discussion of the role of newspapers and television in a free society.

McLUHAN, MARSHALL, *Understanding Media*, McGraw-Hill, 1964, and *The Medium Is the Massage*, Random House, 1967. A provocative view of mass media.

MARCONNIT, GEORGE D., "State Legislatures and the School Curriculum," *Phi Delta Kappan, 49* (January, 1968), 269–272.

ORWELL, GEORGE, *1984*, Harcourt, Brace & World, 1949. Portrays a mass society as one in which people are completely manipulated by propagandists using the mass media.

ROSE, ARNOLD, *The Power Structure*, Oxford University Press, 1967. See page 386 for annotation.

SCHRAMM, WILBUR, JACK LYLE, and EDWIN B. PARKER, *Television in the Lives of Our Children*, Stanford University Press, 1961. One of the few studies of the effects of television viewing upon children's academic performance.

TOMLINSON, RALPH, *Population Dynamics, Causes and Consequences of World Demographic Change*, Random House, 1965.

CHAPTER 8

CAHILL, ROBERT S., and STEPHEN P. HENCLEY, eds., *The Politics of Education in the Local Community*, Interstate Printers and Publishers, 1964. A collection of symposium papers.

EPSTEIN, BENJAMIN R. and ARNOLD FORSTER, *The Radical Right*, Random House, 1966. Discusses the growth of right-wing groups, their financial backing, and purposes.

GROSS, NEAL, *Who Runs Our Schools?* Wiley, 1958. A study of pressures upon Massachusetts school boards and superintendents.

IVERSEN, ROBERT W., *The Communists and the Schools*, Harcourt, Brace & World, 1959. A historical study of the impact of communist activities in American schools and colleges.

KIMBROUGH, RALPH B., *Political Power and Educational Decision-Making*, Rand McNally, 1964. Examines literature dealing with decision-making in communities.

MASTERS, NICHOLAS A., ROBERT H. SALISBURY, and THOMAS H. ELIOT, *State Politics and the Public School*, Knopf, 1964. A study of the process of educational decision-making at the state level in Missouri, Illinois, and Michigan.

RAYWID, MARY ANNE, *The Ax-Grinders: Critics of Our Public Schools*, Macmillan, 1963. A study of extremist critics and their methods.

Rose, Arnold, *The Power Structure*, New York, Oxford University Press, 1967. Takes exception to the Mills-Hunter thesis that an elite dominates decision-making.

CHAPTER 9

Burgess, Ernest W., Harvey J. Locke, and Mary Margaret Thomas, *The Family*, 3rd ed., American Book, 1963. A revision of a standard work on the American family.
Frazier, E. Franklin, *The Negro Family in the United States*, University of Chicago Press, 1939. A classic study of the Negro family.
Goode, William J., *The Family*, Prentice-Hall, 1964. A summary of research studies, many of which are printed in full in Goode, William J., *Readings in the Family and Society*, Prentice-Hall, 1964.
Kephart, William, *Family, Society, and the Individual*, rev. ed., Houghton Mifflin, 1965. Covers historical background and recent research on the family.
McKinley, Donald Gilbert, *Social Class and Family Life*, Macmillan, 1964, chaps. 6–8. Reports empirical findings and theorizes on the impact of family status and values on academic aspirations and choice of occupational roles.
Nye, F. Ivan, and Lois Wladis Hoffman, *Working Mothers*, Rand McNally, 1963. Good coverage of research up to the date of publication.
Rainwater, Lee, "Crucible of Identity: The Negro Lower-Class Family," in Parsons, Talcott, and Kenneth B. Clark, eds., *The Negro American*, Houghton Mifflin, 1966.
U. S. Department of Labor, *The Negro Family: The Case for National Action*, U.S. Government Printing Office, 1966. The controversial Moynihan report.

CHAPTER 10

Bowman, Mary Jean, and W. Warren Haynes, *Resources and Peoples* and *People in East Kentucky: Problems and Potentials of a Lagging Economy*, Johns Hopkins Press, 1963. Describes rural poverty.
Copp, James H., ed., *Our Changing Rural Society: Perspectives and Trends*, Iowa State University Press, 1964. Discusses changing social, occupational, family, power-structure, and community patterns in rural America.
Caudill, Harry, *Night Comes in the Cumberland*, Little, Brown, 1963. One of the most readable books about Appalachia.
Ford, Paul, *et al.*, *Remote High Schools: The Realities*, Portland, Oregon, Northwest Regional Laboratory, 1967. The daily activities and student-

teacher relationships in three small high schools compared with activities and relationships in two large urban high schools.

For an excellent example of changing characteristics of residents in a small, isolated Missouri community, see James West, *Plainville, USA*, Columbia University Press, 1945; and Art Gallaher, Jr., *Plainville, Fifteen Years Later*, Columbia University Press, 1961.

CHAPTER 11

General

COLEMAN, JAMES S., *et al.*, *Equality of Educational Opportunity*, U.S. Government Printing Office, 1966. A mass of statistics and a brief summary comparing the school environment, pupil achievement and motivation, and teachers of minority-group pupils with those of dominant-group pupils.

CONANT, JAMES B., *Slums and Suburbs: A Commentary on Schools in Metropolitan Areas*, McGraw-Hill, 1961. Influential in calling attention to schools in slums, chiefly because it was written by a very influential man.

DOBRINER, WILLIAM M., *Class in Suburbia*, Prentice-Hall, 1963. Includes examples of suburban schools.

EDWARDS, T. BENTLEY, and FREDERICK M. WIRT, *School Desegregation in the North: The Challenge and the Experience*, Chandler, 1967. An account of desegregation experiences in California and New York followed by "Some Lessons for Policymakers."

GOLDSTEIN, BERNARD, *Low Income Youth in Urban Areas: A Critical Review of the Literature*, Holt, Rinehart and Winston, 1967. A valuable source.

HARRINGTON, MICHAEL, *The Other America, Poverty in the United States*, Macmillan, 1962. A widely read work credited with being instrumental in bringing about the "War on Poverty."

MILLER, HERMAN P., *Rich Man, Poor Man*, Crowell, 1964. Contains statistics on income distribution in the United States.

PARSONS, TALCOTT, and KENNETH B. CLARK, eds., *The Negro American*, Houghton Mifflin, 1966. An excellent collection of scholarly articles.

PETTIGREW, THOMAS F., *Profile of the American Negro*, Van Nostrand, 1964. A good reference for status and trends.

RAUBINGER, FREDERICK M., and HAROLD G. ROWE, *The Individual and Education: Some Contemporary Issues*, Macmillan, 1968. Well-selected articles dealing with threats to individuality and academic pressures on students.

WEINBERG, MEYER, *Integrated Education: A Reader*, Free Press, 1968. Selected articles from *Integrated Education* magazine.

The Disadvantaged

Among the most useful of many recent books about the disadvantaged are the following:

Bereiter, Carl and Siegfried Engelman, *Teaching Disadvantaged Children in the Pre-School*, Prentice-Hall, 1966.

Goldstein, Bernard, *Low Income Youth in Urban Areas, A Critical Review of the Literature*, Holt, Rinehart and Winston, 1967.

Keach, Everett T., Jr., Robert Fulton, and William E. Gardner, eds., *Education and Social Crisis*, Wiley, 1967.

Linton, Thomas E., and Jack L. Nelson, eds., *Patterns of Power, Social Foundations of Education*, Pitman, 1968, parts 2 and 4.

Miller, Harry L., ed., *Education for the Disadvantaged, Current Issues and Research*, Free Press, 1967.

Miller, Harry L., and Marjorie B. Smiley, eds., *Education in the Metropolis*, Free Press, 1967.

Passow, A. Harry, Miriam Goldberg, and Abraham J. Tannenbaum, eds., *Education of the Disadvantaged*, Holt, Rinehart and Winston, 1967.

Roberts, Joan I., ed., *School Children in the Urban Slum, Readings in Social Science Research*, Free Press, 1967.

Schreiber, Daniel, ed., *Profile of the School Dropout*, Vintage Books, 1967.

Smiley, Marjorie B., and Harry L. Miller, eds., *Policy Issues in Urban Education*, Free Press, 1968.

Webster, Staten W., ed., *The Disadvantaged Learner*, Chandler, 1966.

CHAPTER 12

Coleman, James S., *et al.*, *Equality of Educational Opportunity*, U.S. Government Printing Office, 1966. For annotation, see p. 389.

Coles, Robert, *Children of Crisis, a Study of Courage and Fear*, Little, Brown, 1967. The psychological impact of race—white and colored—on people's lives.

Katz, Irwin, *Conflict and Harmony in an Adolescent Inter-racial Group*, New York University, 1955. An early study of the effects of racial in'egration.

Madsen, William, *The Mexican-Americans of South Texas*, Holt, Rinehart and Winston, 1964. A good example of an ethnography that devotes scant attention to schools, yet has many implications for education.

Rose, Arnold M., and Caroline B. Rose, eds., *Minority Problems*, Harper & Row, 1965. Includes readings relating to the nature of minority problems, minority adjustments, and proposed solutions.

Simpson, George E., and J. Milton Yinger, *Racial and Cultural Minorities*, Harper & Row, 1965. A scholarly treatise.

Other useful studies of different ethnic groups are:

Lewis, Oscar, *La Vida: A Puerto Rican Family in the Culture of Poverty—San Juan and New York*, Random House, 1966.

WAX, MURRAY, ROSALIE WAX, and ROBERT V. DUMONT, JR., *Formal Education in an American Indian Community*, An SSSP Monograph, Supplement to *Social Problems*, Spring, 1964. A study of the Sioux.

WOLCOTT, HARRY F., *A Kwakiutl Village and School*, Holt, Rinehart and Winston, 1967. An analysis of problems of teaching in an Indian school.

CHAPTER 13

BIDDLE, WILLIAM W., with LOUREIDE J. BIDDLE, *The Community Development Process: The Rediscovery of Local Initiative*, Holt, Rinehart and Winston, 1965. Attempts to bridge the gap between theory and practice. Useful suggestions for educators.

CLINARD, MARSHALL B., *Slums and Community Development: Experiments in Self Help*, Free Press, 1966. Describes planned social change in slums.

CREMIN, LAWRENCE A., *The Transformation of the School*, Vintage Books, 1961. Develops the thesis that the spread of progressive education paralleled the development of the political progressive movement.

FISCHER, JOHN H., *The School Park*, Public Information Office, Teachers College, Columbia University, 1967. Support for the school park by the president of Columbia University's Teachers College.

LAUTER, PAUL, "The Short, Happy Life of the Adams-Morgan Community School Project," *Harvard Educational Review*, 38 (Spring, 1968), 235–262. Identifies a number of important considerations for such projects.

National Society for the Study of Education, Fifty-Second Yearbook, part 2, Nelson B. Henry, ed., *The Community School*, University of Chicago Press, 1953. Discusses philosophy, practices, and problems of the Community School.

OLSEN, EDWARD G., *et al.*, *School and Community*, Prentice-Hall, 1954. A how-to-do-it book based on the philosophy of the Community School.

U.S. Commission on Civil Rights, *Education Parks: Appraisal of Plans to Improve Educational Quality and Desegregate Schools*, Clearinghouse Publication No. 9, U.S. Government Printing Office, 1967. A series of articles by well-known authors. Annotated bibliography of additional articles.

U.S. Commission on Civil Rights, *Racial Isolation in the Public Schools*, Vol. 1, U.S. Government Printing Office, 1967, pp. 167–183, "Education Parks." Includes the same articles as the publication listed above.

CHAPTER 14

DUBOIS, CORA, "The Dominant Value Profile of American Culture," *American Anthropologist*, 57 (December, 1955), 1232–1239. Provides guidelines for cultural analysis.

HENRY, JULES, *Culture Against Man,* Random House, 1963, chap. 8. Includes an observer's record of what happened in a classroom.

JACKSON, PHILIP W., *Life in Classrooms,* Holt, Rinehart and Winston, 1968. Based almost exclusively on what happens in elementary school classrooms. Describes a "hidden curriculum."

ROSENTHAL, ROBERT, and LENORE JACOBSON, *Pygmalion in the Classroom: Teacher Expectations and Pupils' Intellectual Development,* Holt, Rinehart and Winston, 1968. Reviews research relating to the "self-fulfilling prophecy" among mice and men. Reports an experiment, the design of which may be criticized, in which significant relationships between teacher expectations and pupils' scores on mental tests were found.

SMITH, LOUIS M., and WILLIAM GEOFFREY, *The Complexities of an Urban Classroom,* Holt, Rinehart and Winston, 1968. An intensive analysis of of a single elementary school classroom based on an educational psychologist's observations and other data.

SPINDLER, GEORGE D., *Education and Culture—Anthropological Approaches,* Holt, Rinehart and Winston, 1963, part 2. Contains several articles relating to the culture of elementary schools.

TABA, HILDA, *School Culture,* American Council on Education, 1955. One of the early studies of school culture which includes a chapter on the elementary school.

CHAPTER 15

COLEMAN, JAMES B., *The Adolescent Society,* Free Press, 1961. A controversial study of the social life of ten high schools.

FRIEDENBERG, EDGAR Z., *Coming of Age in America,* New York, Random House, 1965. An ingenious and controversial study of adolescent reactions to hypothetical situations.

GRAHAM, GRACE, "Student Activities—Elementary and Secondary," *Encyclopedia of Educational Research, 1970,* American Educational Research Association. A review of the research in the field of student activities.

HENRY, JULES, *Culture Against Man,* Random House, 1963, chaps. 6 and 7. Attempts to explain why adolescents behave the way they do. Describes the social life of one high school.

JOURARD, SYDNEY, *The Transparent Self,* Van Nostrand, 1964. Argues that the only way to know one's self is to openly and honestly reveal one's self to others.

KENISTON, KENNETH, *The Uncommitted: Alienated Youth in American Society,* Dell, 1965. A psychological study of twelve alienated, twelve nonalienated, and twelve other Harvard undergraduates who are not extreme either way; explores the roots of alienation.

KVARACEUS, WILLIAM C., *Anxious Youth: Dynamics of Delinquency,* Merrill, 1966. Stresses early identification and prediction of delinquency and the role of the school.

SHERIF, MUZAFER, and CAROLYN W. SHERIF, *Problems of Youth: Transition to Adulthood in the Changing World,* Aldine, 1965. A group of provocative essays, most of which were based on papers given at a Social Psychology Symposium.

TURNER, RALPH, *The Social Context of Ambition,* Chandler, 1964. A study of 10,000 Los Angeles high school students which reveals "prestige-identification" to be a more important factor than class consciousness in upward mobility.

VON HOFFMAN, NICHOLAS, *We Are the People Our Parents Warned Us Against,* Quadrangle, 1968. Interprets the Haight-Ashbury hippie community as the product of drugs and a youth culture disillusioned with an adult society that does not need young people. Journalistic style.

Youth Education, Problems/Perspectives/Promises, Association for Supervision and Curriculum Development, NEA, Yearbook, 1968. Includes chapters on youth problems, perspectives, and education.

CHAPTER 16

BURRUP, PERCY E., *The Teacher and the Public School System.* 2nd ed., Harper & Row, 1966, parts 3, 4, and 6. Deals with the teacher's role in school, community, and professional organizations.

CARSON, ROBERT B., KEITH GOLDHAMMER, and ROLAND J. PELLEGRIN, *Teacher Participation in the Community: Role Expectations and Behavior,* Center for the Advanced Study of Educational Administration, University of Oregon, 1967. A study of teachers' social participation in the community as viewed by teachers and as viewed by others.

DAHL, ROBERT A., *Who Governs? Democracy and Power in an American City,* Yale University Press, 1961. Answers questions such as who has political power, and how is it acquired and used, in a middle-sized New England city.

FOSKETT, JOHN M., *The Normative World of the Elementary School Teacher,* Center for the Advanced Study of Educational Administration, University of Oregon, 1967. A study of how teachers and citizens view the position of the teacher.

LIEBERMAN, MYRON, *Education as a Profession,* Prentice-Hall, 1956. An excellent overview of teaching as a profession.

LIEBERMAN, MYRON, *The Future of Public Education,* University of Chicago Press, 1960. A provocative book about teaching as a profession.

MASTERS, NICHOLAS A., ROBERT H. SALISBURY, and THOMAS H. ELIOT, *State Politics and the Public Schools,* Knopf, 1964. See p. 387 for annotation.

STINNETT, T. M., *Turmoil in Teaching,* Macmillan, 1968. Expresses the point of view of an NEA supporter in its conflict with teacher unions in the 1960s.

WALLER, WILLARD, *The Sociology of Teaching,* Wiley, 1932. A classic study of value in terms of its method of analysis, although outdated in specific information.

ZEIGLER, HARMON, *The Political Life of American Teachers,* Prentice-Hall, 1967. A study of male and female high school teachers' political values and their political activities in the classroom, in teachers' associations, and in the community.

ZEIGLER, HARMON, *The Political World of the High School Teacher,* Center for the Advanced Study of Educational Administration, University of Oregon, 1966. Another version of the study listed above which contains the statistical data upon which the author bases his generalizations.

CHAPTER 17

BRUNER, JEROME S., *The Process of Education,* Vintage Books, 1963.

BRUNER, JEROME S., JACQUELINE J. GOODNOW, and GEORGE A. AUSTIN, *A Study of Thinking,* Wiley, 1958, 1962. This and the work listed above have important implications for teaching students how to think.

Educational Policies Commission, *The Central Purpose of American Education,* National Education Association, 1961. States that critical thinking is the central purpose.

HULLFISH, H. GORDON, and PHILIP G. SMITH, *Reflective Thinking: The Method of Education,* Dodd, Mead, 1961. Includes an analysis of thinking and suggests tools of thinking and methods of teaching.

INDEXES

INDEX OF NAMES

This Index includes the names of well-known persons and authors of selected studies and discussions summarized in the text. The chief criterion for including a contributor's name was that students might want to reread his saying or stand on issues, or to find a full text of his research study or discussion. The Index does not include the names of authors cited only in the Bibliography or, in the case of contributions by more than one author, any but the first listed.

INDEX OF SUBJECTS

69 70 71   7 6 5 4 3 2 1